FROM BONDAGE TO FREEDOM

from BONDAGE

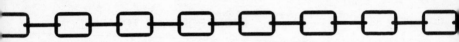

GOD'S VARIED VOICES

Narrative

Prophecy

Gospel

Epistle

THE COVENANT LIFE CURRICULUM
published by THE CLC PRESS
Richmond, Virginia

to FREEDOM

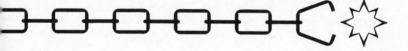

THE COVENANT LIFE CURRICULUM

the authorized curriculum
of the following denominations

ASSOCIATE REFORMED PRESBYTERIAN CHURCH

CUMBERLAND PRESBYTERIAN CHURCH

MORAVIAN CHURCH IN AMERICA

PRESBYTERIAN CHURCH IN THE UNITED STATES

REFORMED CHURCH IN AMERICA

affiliated denomination

THE EVANGELICAL COVENANT CHURCH OF AMERICA

THE COVENANT LIFE CURRICULUM starts with the fact of revelation. It is based on the conviction that God has made himself known to man in Jesus Christ. It has its roots in the Presbyterian and Reformed tradition with strong emphasis on the centrality of Jesus Christ as the source of the life of the church. It offers the Bible, the Church, and the Christian Life as three areas of study through which the living Lord may continue to confront men today. It is made available to the church in the hope that God will bless it, and in the prayer that through it the faith of our fathers will come alive in the life of each succeeding generation.

Illustrations on pages 16, 17, 40 and 41 are reproduced with the permission of Charles Scribner's Sons from EVERYDAY LIFE IN OLD TESTAMENT TIMES, pages 48-49 and 133, by E. W. Heaton, illustrated from drawings by Marjorie Quennell. Copyright © 1956 Charles Scribner's Sons.

Unless otherwise noted, Scripture quotations are from the *Revised Standard Version of the Bible,* copyrighted 1946 and 1952 by the Division of Christian Education of the National Council of Churches, and used by permission.

Other acknowledgments for copyrighted material are to be found on pages 442–445 which are hereby made a part of this copyright page.

PREFACE
to year IV

FROM BONDAGE TO FREEDOM—from bondage in Egypt, Babylon, Jerusalem or Galatia, to freedom—such is the story this volume tells.

But this is not really the study of a theme. The title actually grows out of a series of Bible studies of Exodus, Isaiah 40—66, John, and Galatians. Readers find themselves joining the Israelites as they flee slavery in Egypt, and the Babylonian captives as they prepare to cross the desert in what the prophet pictures as a "second Exodus"; they hear Paul call the Galatian converts back from legalism to the freedom that Jesus Christ offers to his own disciples: " . . . you will know the truth and the truth will make you free" (John 8:32). The title is the inescapable theme of three studies and quite appropriate to a study of John.

This unity in subject matter does not preclude a diversity in approach to Bible study. To some extent this was deliberately "built in." Four areas of study were chosen for this volume to echo "God's varied voices in Narrative, Prophecy, Gospel, and Epistle." Through this study of different types of biblical material adults will be given a broader base on which to do subsequent Bible study on their own. James Sprunt approaches Exodus as a drama. Robert H. Bullock studies the text of Isaiah 40—66 in detail, often paragraph by paragraph. Vernon H. Kooy leads us into certain themes that John develops in his Gospel. Bernard J. Mulder starts with Galatians and moves out to set forth theological insights. Which is the right way to study the Bible? Each is. Each seeks to help adults hear God speak, each tells us of God's love and his work of redemption, each would lead us from bondage to freedom in Christ Jesus.

The writers differ also in their approach to critical problems. There is not space to go into much detail about the authorship of Exodus, Isaiah 40—66, or John, or about the North versus the South Galatian theories of the destination of the epistle. Sprunt is aware of the problems that scholars face in dealing with the authorship of Exodus, but he prefers to concentrate on the positive message of the book; Bullock gratefully accepts the findings of contemporary scholars concerning the date and authorship of Isaiah 40—66; Kooy refers to the theories of the authorship of the Fourth Gospel and comes out for the traditional view that the information in the Gospel was furnished by John the Apostle; Mulder rejects the traditional North Galatian theory in favor of a view that seems to be finding increasing acceptance among scholars today. But each man is primarily concerned to confront the student with God speaking through his written Word, whoever wrote it originally, at whatever time.

Thus these writers are consistent with the basic principles of the Covenant Life Curriculum: They reflect the varied views toward biblical criticism that have been found historically among scholars and are found in the contemporary church; they are motivated by the concern that evangelical Christians have always had, that God's people hear the Holy Spirit speaking in the Scriptures.

The position of the Covenant Life Curriculum on this latter point is carefully defined on page 9 of Foundation Paper I:

> Because the Bible is recognized as both witness to and instrument of God's revelation of himself to man, the church must take care to keep the Bible an open book, continually putting itself in position to listen and to listen again to the story it tells. This suggests that the church's educational program should contain classes organized for study of the Bible itself, so that adults and young people alike may read for themselves and thus open themselves to the movement of the Spirit of God. It is not enough to know about the Bible or to receive secondhand accounts of what it says. Individuals and groups of persons should be taught how to study the Bible so that they may come to it directly, in the faith that in this book God

speaks and that in reading it they may be taken hold of by the free word of God.

As for the matter of critical issues, this volume also is in accord with basic positions set forth at the beginning of the development of the CLC in Foundation Paper I:

> While we must insist that those who interpret scripture shall be in harmony with its basic presuppositions, we must also recognize the inevitable contradiction involved in the concept of the word of God in the speech of man. In the written word we have "treasure in earthen vessels." This figure of speech was employed by Paul to describe his understanding of himself as the bearer of the good news of Jesus Christ (2 Corinthians 4:7). But it applies also to any attempt to witness in human language to the revelation of God. If we had in the church a written document preserved in the original manuscript and coming directly from the hand of our Lord, we would still have to interpret it in terms of the meaning of the words, the structure of the sentences, etc. The documents which are preserved in our Bible are human writings. We have every responsibility to try to understand the way in which they were written. We do not need to fear the critical approach to scripture if it is the approach of those who stand reverently within the believing community of those who acknowledge Jesus as Lord. As Paul said, 'We have this treasure in earthen vessels, that the exceeding greatness of the power may be of God and not from ourselves' (2 Corinthians 4:7 A.S.V.). The understanding of the Bible as treasure in earthen vessels leaves the way open for the critical approach to scripture by those who accept the basic biblical assumption that God has spoken to man in Jesus Christ.

With gratitude for the results of scholarship and with a fresh appreciation for the unity of the Scriptures in proclaiming redemption, the editorial committee puts into your hand this tool to aid *you* on *your* pilgrimage from bondage to freedom.

EXODUS: A Drama of Redemption

CONTENTS

ISAIAH 40—66: The Freedom of Servanthood

JOHN: The Way to Life

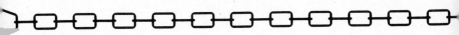

GALATIANS: The Life of Freedom

EXODUS

A DRAMA OF REDEMPTION

James Sprunt

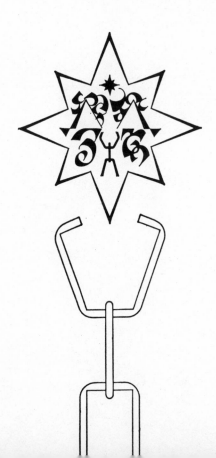

THE BOOK OF EXODUS

The Setting of the Stage

When you acquire a new book, especially one long desired, how do you treat it? Do you plunge into the reading of it at the first opportunity? Or do you examine it lovingly from all sides, noting its size and format, reading all of the material on its jacket, following with interest the author's preface, and, finally, scanning the table of contents to discover what courses are offered in the feast to follow? Surely some such gradual approach as this makes the actual reading of the volume a more delectable process.

Let us adopt this plan in our study of Exodus. When you take into your hands the book of Exodus, you are looking upon one of the most exciting books in the world. You may find some confirmation of this in glancing over some comments of other readers which we may imaginatively picture as the publisher's blurbs on the jacket:

> Exodus is undoubtedly the most significant book dealing with the birth of a nation that has ever been compiled.[1]

> . . . in some obvious respects, it is the most fundamentally important Book ever given to mankind. And the study of it is essential to a real and scholarly acquaintance with the history of man.[2]

> It is well-nigh impossible to overestimate the religious value of the book of Exodus. Nowhere else save in the Christian revelation is there to be found so sublime a conception of the nature of God, or a loftier and purer idea of morality as springing out of man's relationship to Him.[3]

Do these estimates not whet your desire to master this book for yourself?

The first requirement in mastering Exodus is to read it and reread it. [Some study suggestions and questions are *italicized* in each chapter. Your understanding of Exodus and your experience in the study group will be enriched if you carry out these suggestions or answer the questions through your personal study of the Bible.] The forty chapters can be covered in about one and a half to two hours; and if you will take the time to read it through at a sitting, you will find it a memorable experience. Plan also to read and reread the sections as they are successively studied. Reading books about the Bible is never an adequate substitute for the reading of the book itself. And never for a moment think that you are already sufficiently well acquainted with the message of this story. The Holy Spirit continually brings new light to bear on the old Book when we endeavor to make it ours under his guidance and illumination.

But what else do you think we might find upon this imagined jacket of Exodus, besides the comments of prior readers?

Its title? Yes. Its author? Yes. An indication of the main point of the story? Very probably. Its publisher? Ordinarily, yes. Let us then continue to look over this imaginary jacket before we settle down to a study of the book itself.

The "Publisher"

Let us dispose of the last item first. It is easily done, for Exodus has no publisher who has the exclusive right to it. It was, of course, originally "published" by its inclusion in the Hebrew Scriptures and thus later incorporated in the Divine Library of the Christian church, which we call the Bible. It was originally written in Hebrew, but since that is "worse than Greek" to most of us, we do well to acquire as many English translations of it as we can. The Revised Standard Version (R.S.V.) and the American Standard Version (A.S.V.) will be most helpful. Since Exodus is an integral part of the whole message of God to man, and a most important part, the study of it should throw us back to what precedes it and forward to the books that follow it, right on through to the New Testament and its fuller revelation of God's gift of life through Jesus Christ.

As one modern writer puts it, "The concepts of one biblical book have their complements in others. Every great scriptural truth is trunkline: it connects with tributaries in the unity of the whole."[4]

The Title

The title of our book in many English Bibles is simply Exodus, though it may be found often in fuller form "The Second Book of Moses Commonly Called EXODUS." In the Hebrew Scriptures, in accordance with the custom of naming books with their opening words, the book is simply called *w*e*eleh sh*e*moth,* "and these are the names," abbreviated to *sh*e*moth,* "names." It was first given our familiar title in the Septuagint, the Greek version of the Old Testament which was in widespread use in the days of the early church. "Exodus" is a Greek word taken over into English with only a slight modification by Latin; it refers to that event of primary importance in the life of Israel which dominates the book, the departure from Egypt. This name, however, as we shall see, is far from adequate to cover its varied and significant contents.

The Author

The dust jackets of most new books will include the author's name, with possibly a picture of him and a brief biographical note. This, the publisher hopes, will give the prospective reader renewed interest in the purchase of the book and will establish confidence in its trustworthiness.

In the case of our book, Exodus, we must here face up to our first real difficulty.

The book itself is anonymous. The title in some English editions, "The Second Book of Moses Commonly Called EXODUS," is not an original part of the authentic text.

It should be said, however, that from pre-Christian times, it was practically universally held that Moses was the author not only of Exodus but also of the other four books of the Pentateuch, which were commonly called "The Five Books of Moses." Sometimes they were just familiarly referred to as "Moses," as in our Lord's usage in Luke 24:27. This noncritical belief was by and large unchallenged until approximately two hundred years ago. In the last two centuries,

A Nomadic Clan entering Egypt in the age of

however, the question of the authorship of the Pentateuch has been the subject of intense debate and has produced a prolific literature.

It does not seem wise to the author to provide or to induce a discussion here on the relative merits of the opposing views of authorship—see the Preface, pp. 5–7. The student will find a brief but comprehensive treatment of this problem in Arnold B. Rhodes' student's book, *The Mighty Acts of God,* pages 90–96.

It may be helpful to quote the late Edward Mack, Professor of Hebrew and Old Testament Interpretation at Union Theological Seminary, Richmond, Virginia. With regard to the involvement of the student with the divergent questions of technical interpretation, he would say:

> . . . You need not hasten to accept the latest critical view of the Old Testament. The end is not yet. There are doubtless many other *final* views yet to come. Be prudent; wait and take advantage of a wide range of choice. Meanwhile use with confidence the great book already committed to your trust.[5]

Joseph Gettys has much the same thought in this apt illustration:

> . . . Suppose a birthday cake is brought into a group honoring some member of it. Before the cake is cut, the more scientific in the group may insist that the cake should first be taken to the laboratory to discover its component parts. Exact analysis of the kind and amount of flour, the probable fields where the wheat was grown and the mill where the wheat was ground into flour, with approximate date of the same; the amount and kind of sugar, the refining process, and the field where the cane was

the Patriarchs (*From a contemporary painting*)

grown; the amount and kind of flavoring, and the ingredients that made it up; the ingredients that went into the icing, and the sources from which they came—all these may be right and proper upon occasion. But it would hardly be right and proper to do that when this particular cake was made and baked to be eaten and enjoyed.[6]

Our paramount need and opportunity is to feed upon the Word of God itself and to hear God speak to our own souls through his living message to men.

The Place of Exodus in Scripture

What are the chapters of this book about? Where does it fit into the Divine Library? What relation does it have to other books? What are the main lines of its story? These and similar questions would probably be discussed in condensed form on our hypothetical jacket of Exodus.

That Exodus occupies a strategic place in the Bible is obvious. It rests upon Genesis and grows out of it. It is vitally connected both with the unfolding of God's plan of redemption of sinful men and with the reconciliation of man and God made necessary by man's rejection of God's authority in Eden.

If there was ever a book that ended on the note, "to be continued," it is Genesis. With the covenant family as guests in the land of Goshen, with the covenant promises in their hearts but no prospect of fulfillment, with their father dead and their brother and benefactor gone, Genesis ends, "and they embalmed him, and he was put in a coffin in Egypt." Exodus (in the Hebrew) even starts with a word of continuity, "And."

The covenant family in the subsequent generations of its sojourn and servitude in Egypt becomes a great multitude. Their slavery produces some of the architectural glories of their vain overlords, the reigning Pharaohs, and also motivates their quest for freedom. God raises up a leader, prepared in every way for the specific task he has for him to accomplish. Then Moses is commissioned and empowered to act. He demonstrates the power of the sovereign God of the universe before the intransigent ruler on the throne of Egypt. The aggregation of slaves is led forth and by God's power delivered from vengeful pursuit. They are tested on their weary pilgrimage to Sinai, and then at the foot of the mountain that glowed with the Presence they are welded into a new nation under God as they gladly respond to the offer of the covenant of grace. They accept its regulations and provide its house of worship, which is to symbolize the constant presence of their God and King.

This in bold strokes is the story of Exodus.

The echoes of the message of this book reverberate through the pages of the Word. The Old Testament is replete with references to its focal event. The New Testament unveils the fuller glory of its ultimate meaning in the coming of the Redeemer, "the Lamb of God, slain from the foundation of the world." We would be impoverished indeed in our knowledge of God's plan of redemption had we no book called Exodus.

The Table of Contents

Let us now turn to the "Table of Contents" of the volume we are examining. It is always an interesting quest in getting acquainted with a new book to see how an author intends to develop it, and to discover what is in store for us as readers. Let me suggest an outline that will enable us not only to trace the progress of it but also to remember it.

Let us adopt some such theme as "The Emergence and Establishment of the Covenant Nation" as the central thought of Exodus. Would you agree that this book is preeminently the book of the covenant? If so, then the section dealing directly with its institution should be a pivotal one. This would be chapters 19—24 [where no book is named, the scriptural reference is to Exodus], where the people hear it proclaimed and promise their acceptance. Until this time, they were being prepared for the covenant. After this time they were beginning to carry out the provisions of it. Hence we might label these three sections: The Preparation for the Covenant, chapters 1—18; The Covenant, chapters 19—24; The Privileges of the Covenant, chapters 25—40. We might prefer to designate these three sections by the three words: Deliverance, Decision, Dedication. In line with the theme suggested, an even simpler division would be Emergence, chapters 1—18, and Establishment, chapters 19—40.

Having drawn these main lines of cleavage, it is not difficult to break the sections down into five smaller segments of thought. These concepts might be, Preparation, chapters 1—4; Demonstration, chapters 5—10; Realization, chapters 11—18; Confrontation, chapters 19—24; and Consecration, chapters 25—40. From this point, it is easy to list the subject matter under these thought divisions.

The days of Preparation we see in the long bondage of the people (chapter 1), and in training of the leader, Moses (chapters 2—4). The Demonstration would be that of God's sovereign power over Pharaoh in the account of the ten plagues (5—10). The Realization is the actual departure of the people and their deliverance through the sea (11—15:21), and the wilderness trek southeastward to Sinai (15:22—18). In the Confrontation we see the covenant being proposed, proclaimed, and accepted (19—24). The Consecration would embrace the giving of directions for building the Tabernacle (25—31), the apostasy of the golden calf worship and its cure (32—34), and the construction of the Tabernacle as directed (35—40). These divisions might serve as convenient pegs upon which to hang our recollections of the contents of this book.

EXODUS IN ESSENCE

The Emergence and Establishment of the Covenant Nation

Chapters	1	2–4	5–10	11–15:21	15:22–18	19–24	25–31	32–34	35–40
	Emergence					Establishment			
	Deliverance					Dedication			
	Preparation for the Covenant					Privileges of the Covenant			
	Preparation		Demonstration	Realization		The Covenant	Consecration		
	Bondage	Moses	Plagues	Departure	Wilderness	Confrontation / Covenant (Commandments)	Directed	Tabernacle Rejected	Erected
	People prepared	Leader prepared	Plea / Plagues / Pharaoh's heart / Passover / Permission	Directed / Danger / Delivered	Tested for dependence	The People prepared, the Covenant proclaimed, the People promise	Purpose / Program / Pattern	Golden Calf / Restoration	Fulfillment

BONDAGE

Preparation by Bondage

Are you ready, after looking at the "jacket" this long, to go ahead into the study of this significant book? Let's get at it!

Though we may own books about Exodus and may borrow still others, there is no substitute for the biblical text itself. It must be said at the outset that all we can really know about the momentous and influential events related in this book is to be found in the pages of these forty chapters. This book is the one source of information for us and for all the scholars who have written the multitude of volumes about it. To the present time, there have been discovered no records on the monuments or in the papyri of Egypt that mention the Exodus of the Hebrews or confirm any of the accounts in Genesis and Exodus of their residence in Egypt. Many interesting facts have been turned up by archaeologists that illustrate the times and give us a better understanding of the background of our story. But the majestic pyramids which were there a thousand years before the children of Jacob arrived, the great temples and rock-hewn tombs of the Pharaohs, the inscriptions and documents, are all silent as to that event which burned itself so indelibly into the memory of God's people. While we may regret this, we need not be too surprised by it. As the distinguished archaeologist and former director of the British Museum, Sir Frederic Kenyon, explains it:

> ... The Egyptians were not historically minded, as the Assyrians were. There are no such chronicle texts as are found in the foundation cylinders of the Assyrian kings, and only exceptionally are there records of campaigns. Autocrats in their self-laudatory inscriptions, of which there are examples enough, do not generally refer to the less pleasing incidents of their

reign. Consequently the fact that no reference to the Exodus
has been found in Egyptian records proves nothing either way
with regard to its historicity.

So far as the Egyptian monuments are concerned, the most
that can be said is that the scenes depicted on the walls of the
tombs show us the surroundings among which the Israelites
lived in Egypt.[1]

So while we may and should lay hold of the many splendid books
available for what helps we can get for a better understanding of the
land and the times, we have in our Bibles all the facts that any others
have. It remains for us to master the facts and to understand, if we
can, their bearing upon us in our day and time.

And now to your Bible! *Read the first chapter of Exodus, not just
once or twice, but as many times as you can, letting it soak into your
mind. The first quest of Bible study is, What? What is here? What
are the facts? Then we may rightly ask, Why? Why is it so stated?
What does it mean? How is this related to me?*

The very first verse will throw us right back into Genesis which
precedes it. Its first word in the Hebrew is one which is commonly
translated "and." So before we can go forward we have to go backward. The first five verses summarize the descent of the Jacob clan
into Egypt. In Genesis 46 we find the full account of their coming.
That it was a sizeable household we can guess from the seventy who
are named, for to these must be added the wives and daughters, the
servants and shepherds who came with them. It was no small company that Joseph received and, with the Pharaoh's consent, established in the land of Goshen. This section of Egypt is not mentioned by this name outside the biblical record, but it seems to have
been the fertile valley in the delta of Lower Egypt now known as the
Wadi Tumilat, and now, as then, one of the richest areas in the land.

But this in turn forces us to go back a little further into the story
of Israel. Why was it necessary for the Jacob clan to come down into
Egypt? What was God's purpose in it? Joseph's statement to his
brothers in Genesis 50:20 gives us the heart of the answer. Not always is it possible to look back over the course of our lives and see as
clearly as he did the hand of God in the differing and difficult expe-

riences of the years. But to him, the pattern was plain. ". . . to bring about that many people should be kept alive, as they are today" included preserving physical life from death by famine and spiritual life from moral contamination and death in the evil environment of Canaan (the sordid story in Genesis 34 gives a hint of this evil).

How could they be located as a family in a place where they might increase and grow strong, unmolested by foes? There could not have been a better haven for such a purpose than the land of Goshen in Egypt. But how were they to get it? They couldn't pay for it. They couldn't take it by force. They had to be given it. And so they were! The whole of the remarkable story of Joseph is the unfolding of God's plan for the fulfilling of his purpose, summarized in Joseph's words to his brothers. Compare his statement with Paul's magnificent declaration in Romans 8:28. Do you have the faith and discernment to believe that Romans 8:28 still holds good, no matter what may befall you in the changing circumstances of life?

And so Joseph died, and all his generation. But though that is the ending of Genesis, it is not the end of the story. It is but the beginning of Exodus. They embalmed Joseph's body as the body of any high official of Egypt would be prepared for burial. And it was placed in a coffin. But note! The coffin was not entombed. There was no burial —not for a very long time. Joseph's express command was that his body should be carried back to Palestine when the Israelites left Egypt for the Land of the Promise. And so it was done. The books of Exodus, Numbers, and Joshua tell the story of the longest and slowest funeral cortege in history (see Joshua 24:32). But though his unburied coffin in Egypt should have served his descendants as a continual reminder of the hope of the covenant and of the fact that Egypt was not their home, in the generations that followed Joseph's death the flame of trust in the covenant promises flickered very low.

The Prosperous Years, 1:7

Verse seven is worth a long look, for it covers between two hundred and three hundred years.

No one knows with accuracy when the family of Jacob began their residence in Goshen. The best reasoned guess is that they came in the days when the Hyksos ruled Egypt. Around 1700 B.C. Egypt was invaded and conquered by these Asiatic Semites, sometimes called the "Shepherd Kings." Aided by a new military weapon, the horse drawn chariot, they defeated the Egyptians and set up a dynasty lasting a century and a half, until they were overthrown by a resurgence of native power, as the 18th Dynasty was being set up. These foreign rulers, though hated and despised by the Egyptians, built a formidable empire in the lower delta with their capital at Avaris. The seminomadic Hyksos rulers would naturally have given the Jacob clan a welcome, and it is thought that it was under one of these kings that Joseph rose to power as prime minister.

Egypt proved to be a true haven for the children of Jacob, Israel. It was the garden spot of the area. As W. W. Moore of Union Theological Seminary used to say, "You had but to tickle it with a hoe, and it would laugh a harvest." The land was lush and the Israelites increased, grew sleek, and prospered. Read again verse seven, and note the repeated emphasis of those prosperous years: "were fruitful," "increased greatly" (the Hebrew has "swarmed"), "multiplied," "grew exceeding strong," "the land was filled with them" (that is, the land of Goshen). The author makes his point! For a long time these guests in Egypt prospered beyond their fondest dreams. They had a "chicken in every pot and two cars in every garage!" But, as so often happens in prosperity, they almost forgot the covenant of their fathers. So they had to pass through the valley of trial before they set their faces to the Promised Land.

However, in all these years God was working one of his purposes out. *What was his promise in the covenant with Abraham? Look up Genesis 12:2, 13:16, and 17:2. How literally in these years was God keeping his promise! What outstanding attribute of God is revealed in this?*

But there was a second promise in that Abrahamic covenant. What was it? Read Genesis 12:7, 13:15, 15:18–21. But why should these comfortable sons of Israel in Egypt leave their featherbed in Goshen for the barren land of the Canaanites? Why relinquish present blessing for an uncertain future? The God of the covenant would nonetheless bring it to pass.

The Tide Turns, 1:8–10

"Now there arose a new king over Egypt, who did not know

Joseph." And the tide turned; there would be a dreadful ebb before it would come flowing back in beneficial power.

It would have saved a vast amount of speculation and study and the writing of many books if the author of this eighth verse had simply named that Pharaoh! His intent was not to give a history of Egypt but an account of God's hand in the history of his covenant people. Just which Pharaoh it was is secondary, but much time and effort have gone into the endeavor to synchronize at this point the histories of Egypt and Israel. It is an intriguing study. Older scholars were inclined to make this new king either Ahmose I, the first Pharaoh of the revolutionary new 18th Dynasty, or the most prominent ruler in the dynasty, Thutmose III. The majority of Bible students now regard the Pharaoh of the oppression as either Rameses II, the greatest king of the 19th Dynasty, or his father, Seti I.

While there is uncertainty as to which Pharaoh is meant, modern archaeology has made clear the grandeur of the empire which Moses and his God were to challenge. Rameses II, for example, was fond of having his own likeness carved in stone monuments sixty feet high, weighing eighty tons. (Some of these at Abu Simbel are, at this writing, being moved at the cost of some thirty-six million dollars to higher ground to preserve them from the rising waters of Lake Nasser being impounded by the Aswân High Dam.) His armies were the terror not only of North Africa but of Asia Minor. And often at the base of the giant statues of the vain king one may still see the carved figures of the half-naked slaves who built Pharaoh's vast temples. Scholars identify some of these as Semites, the racial group which includes the Hebrews.

Whoever the Pharaoh, conditions became radically different for the people of Israel. They were now the object of concern and distrust to the government. What about these foreigners who had battened on the best of the land and were burgeoning in a veritable population explosion? Were they loyal to the crown or potential allies of Egypt's enemies? Was it wise to allow these aliens to prosper immediately behind the frontier defenses of the land? Thus the children of Jacob became suspect, and when suspicions and accusations flow freely, persecution is apt to follow. But how would you have felt about these Hebrews if you had been a patriotic Egyptian?

The Valley of Sweat and Tears, 1:11-22

The Pharaoh acted! He launched a policy of anti-Semitism, the first instance of that baleful spirit that has been such a blot upon the history of the Western world from that day to this. He determined to strengthen his military security by sharply curtailing and controlling these alien folk, and to use them for economic gain by forcing them into slavery and hard labor. How modern this seems! We need but to mention the Third Reich and Siberia to bring it up-to-date.

What were the stages by which Pharaoh executed this evil design?

What was his first step? See verses 11-14. Men who completely lose their freedom are apt to lose their spirit also. Toilworn bodies do not encourage scheming minds. Broken slaves were robbed of power. Hence they were afflicted with burdensome tasks. They served in the slave-labor battalions of the greatest builder among the Pharaohs. Life became expendable, and individuals had no rights. They built cities and temples and storehouses. Shepherds and tradesmen became brickmakers and toilers, "their lives bitter with hard service." Paintings on the walls of tombs unearthed in Egypt show such slaves, clad in loincloths, laboring under their whip-bearing overseers. But though they were reduced to slavery, they still multiplied. And harsher and more hateful became the labor-bosses of Pharaoh. These were dark and cruel days and human life was cheap.

What was Pharaoh's second step? See verses 15-21. His policy of deliberate destruction sought help from the midwives, the obstetricians of the day. But they disobeyed him and got away with it. Their consciences were true to a higher authority and they were rewarded for it.

What was his third step? Read verse 22. Perhaps Pharaoh sought to justify his inhuman policy by making it a sacrifice of propitiation to the river god of the Nile. But God has a way of making even the wrath of man contribute to his plan. It was from the river Nile itself that a baby boy was drawn up to become the mighty deliverer of the Israelites.

Why was all this suffering allowed to come to the chosen people? Where was God, the covenant-keeping God of Abraham, Isaac, and Jacob? Was he asleep during these long years of grievous servitude? Was Pharaoh greater than God? Why? Why? Why? Do you ever echo that resentful cry?

It is not always possible for us to find the answer to this question in our own more bitter experiences in life. Neither could the slaves in Egypt. At the moment faith must believe where it cannot see. But with the passing of time we often judge more accurately. Read Deuteronomy 32:11. Moses' illustration is an apt one. The fledgling nation had to be pushed out of its nest by persecution. The lines of William Cowper's hymn are true:

> God moves in a mysterious way
> His wonders to perform;
> He plants his footsteps in the sea,
> And rides upon the storm.

It is sometimes a part of God's plan that his people are allowed to suffer. It was only thus that the Israelites would be moved to carry out God's covenant objectives. It was altogether too easy for Jacob's folk in those lush years in Egypt. They'd had it so good for so long that they felt no yearning for the Land of Promise. They already "had it made." But Egypt was not destined to be their home. Palestine was. And to Palestine they must go. Thus did God stir them up and out of their self-sufficiency and ease, and through bondage and persecution he kindled the longing for freedom, and for a deliverer, and for the Promised Land, their home. Thus the stage was set for the drama of redemption.

PREPARATION

God's Instrument Prepared and Commissioned

As the curtain rises upon Act One of this great drama of redemption, there enters the towering figure of Moses, the man whom God prepared to be the father of his country, the mighty liberator of his people. From every conceivable viewpoint we must agree that the estimate in 11:3 is true: ". . . the man Moses was very great." Prince of Egypt, victorious general, popular hero, sacrificial patriot, patient shepherd, triumphant champion, inspiring deliverer, wise administrator, accurate guide, faithful intermediary, authoritative lawgiver, dedicated servant of God —this man stands out among all the actors on the stage of Holy Writ as the supreme shaper of history, and the greatest spiritual leader prior to our Lord Jesus Christ.

The times were out-of-joint. They required such a one as Moses. The children of Israel were no longer guests in Egypt, but slaves. The covenant with Abraham, Isaac, and Jacob was a far-away, almost forgotten episode. Faith was faltering and hope seemed lost. It was time to act—and only God could act. The mighty act of deliverance must begin. As always, when God acts he prepares a man to be the instrument of his purpose. Such was Moses to be.

It is not surprising then that the Scriptures accord him so much space in the record of God's dealing with mankind. He is the central human figure in the books of Exodus, Leviticus, Numbers, and Deuteronomy, which together form one seventh of the Bible, an amount of space equal to two-thirds of the New Testament.

Yet few men ever came into the world with less promise of usefulness. He was actually born a fugitive, under the sentence of death. But God's power is demonstrated in this book to be far superior to the edict of earth's most powerful monarch. In a singular way God makes the very wrath of man contribute to the ongoing of his purpose.

The Birth of Moses, 2:1–2

Let us try imaginatively to reconstruct the scene. It opens upon the delta of the Nile, where the pitiless Egyptian sun all day had baked the brick-fields of the *bene-ysrael* (literally, sons of Israel; pronounced be-ne-is'-rä-āl). As the scowling Egyptian slave driver coiled his long lash at the close of the day, a man of Israel stood slowly erect, straightening his aching back. Amram had toiled all the long day at his task of furnishing water from the river for the clay-mixers. Though his body was covered with the scars from that same lash, his spirit was as yet unconquered. But now he had almost given up hope.

He and his wife Jochebed faced the future with dismay, for they were to have another child any day now. The Pharaoh's cruel edict had just been made known. Every male child of the Hebrews was to be cast into the river. This would not affect the other two children, a son Aaron and a daughter Miriam, who were old enough to expect to grow up to be the slaves their parents were. But this new one—what if it were a boy?

With a troubled and anxious heart Amram made his painful way back to the rude mud shack they called home—to be greeted by his young daughter's excited but muted cry, "O father, I'm so glad you've come! The baby's here—it's a boy!" "O God of our father Abraham," breathed Amram, "You have sent us a son—what *shall* we do?"

It is easy to picture the scene, but can you enter into the feeling of this family? Gratitude and love, distress and joy, anxiety and hope, concern, uncertainty, fear, and faith all formed a turmoil of emotion in that godly home (that it was a godly home we must believe, though all the homes of the Hebrew slaves were not). But God has a way of bringing peace and order out of chaos, of enabling a father's faith and a mother's ingenuity and love to win out.

For three months the secret is kept from the police of Pharaoh.

Amram and his neighbors nightly maintain their watch for the Egyptian patrols, and the mother and daughter do their best to keep the infant concealed by day. But the baby is a strong and healthy child, and his voice becomes increasingly lusty and insistent. They cannot hope to keep him hidden from the spies of the king. What to do? Thank God for a woman's wit and for parents' devoted faith in a sovereign and loving God!

The Preparation of Moses, 2:3–22

The word that best describes the movement of chapters 2—4 is *Preparation*. In them God prepares the man destined to be the deliverer of his people from bondage. It was a long process, beginning before his birth, and, according to the Scriptures, covering some eighty years (see Exod. 7:7; Acts 7:23, 30). Let it not be thought, therefore, that the years of our preparation for our life work are wasted years and so must be shortened; that our education must be the least we can get by with; that college days must be compressed; that getting a job now and making money is everything. When we are tempted to think along these lines, remember Moses!

Moses' preparation was in three phases: in the home of his slave parents; in the court of Pharaoh; and in the wilderness of Midian and Sinai.

(1) Getting to the Court of Pharaoh, 2:3–10. It was necessary in God's plan for this future leader of his people to be trained in the wisdom and skill of the state with whose all-powerful ruler he was later to contend. How was this Hebrew slave-baby, born under the sentence of death, to achieve such an education? The answer is that "God moves in a mysterious way, His wonders to perform."

Take your notebook now and list, as you discover them, the steps which led to his placement in the court, steps which would include his basic training in his own home.

First there was the nature of his home itself. It was pitifully poor in material equipment, but richly furnished with the spiritual. For his was a godly home; his parents were folk of faith and courage. How do we know that? Look up Hebrews 11:23. It has been often said that if a child wants the best start in life he should be careful in the selection of his parents and his grandparents. There was nothing wrong with Moses' heritage; see 6: 16–20. Were all the homes of the *bene-ysrael* in Egypt godly homes, do you think? Read Joshua 24:14 and Ezekiel 20:5–9 to find out.

Second, what about his physical heritage? Read Exodus 2:2, Acts 7:20, and Hebrews 11:23. Do you think this was just the pardonable expression of his parents' doting pride, or really an unusual endowment of God?

Third, what was the response of his parents to this perilous situation? What characteristics of theirs produced such a response?

Fourth, was the mother's plan a hurried and haphazard one, or the result of long and careful observation and deduction?

Fifth, what was Moses' own act that played its decisive part in this exciting drama? Upon what fragile hinges God's providential plans sometimes hang! Can you recall any other such apparently insignificant biblical events which have formed vital links in the chain of God's plan? Read Genesis 40:5–7, Ruth 2:3, Nehemiah 2:2. Can you think of others?

Sixth, do you not think that God prepared the princess of Egypt as carefully as he prepared the other actors in this scene? Does not God prepare supporting actors as well as the ones who take the main parts? Does he not work in the world as well as in the church? A bust in the Cairo Museum shows a princess of this general period. She wears her hair in elaborate curls. Her lipstick and eye shadow are in a carefully planned style. Her ornaments are gold and ivory. To such a lady Moses was given.

Seventh, what if a young girl's courage had failed in carrying out the cleverly laid stratagem? Do you think the princess suspected the truth? Why?

Eighth, how does God reward abundantly the courage and faith and ingenuity of Moses' family? To have been paid for doing what she most desired of all things to do must have caused the heart of Jochebed to overflow with praise.

Ninth, how long a period of training do you think Moses had in his own home, or under his parents, before he took up his life in the palace as "the son of Pharaoh's daughter"?

What could Moses have learned in these decisive and forma-tive years of training under his godly parents? List these truths as important steps in his education.

(2) His Training in the Court, 2:11–15. Having wrought this amazing change in his economic and social status, what training did God provide for his chosen instrument in Pharaoh's house-hold which would stand him in good stead later on?

That his foster mother, the princess, lavished her love upon him we may safely assume. Josephus, the first century Jewish his-torian, states that the princess was married but childless and found the greater joy in Moses because of her yearning for children. She gave him a name which is both Egyptian and Hebrew. It is found as a part of the names of some of the Pharaohs, and as a separate name in Egyptian records. It is also a form of the Hebrew word *mashah*, to draw out. The name is related thus both to his new family and to his rescue from the Nile.

There is no record of the years of growth and training in the Egyptian court. One must read between the lines, assisted by the references in Stephen's defense in Acts 7:21–22. There we read a summary into which we may imaginatively put much more: "Pharaoh's daughter adopted him and brought him up for her own son. And Moses was instructed in all the wisdom of the Egyptians, and he was mighty in his words and deeds." He re-ceived the complete education of a prince of Egypt, in the most cultured land in his world. That this included the arts (embrac-ing also the magic arts), science, theology, philosophy, law, and military science is virtually certain. His mightiness in word and work indicates something of the authority and prowess he at-tained. These were great days for the slave-baby who now had been lifted to the pinnacle of prestige and power.

Before Moses there loomed the possibility of a place of honor and leadership in Egypt greater even than that of Joseph, the prime minister of other days. But then occurred an event that changed the course of his life: he visited the Israelites. How much he knew then of his relationship to them is not clear here. Possibly just his sense of justice, mercy, and fair play led to his impetuous slaying of the Egyptian and his remonstrance with the quarreling Hebrews; but the light shed on this event by the New Testament in Hebrews 11:24–26 would indicate that this was a definite decision to take his place beside his enslaved brethren. A fascinating re-creation of the story of Moses is Arthur E. Southon's *On Eagles Wings* (McGraw-Hill, 1954), which gives a graphic description of his soul struggle.

Was the impulsive slaying of the Egyptian taskmaster the cause or the occasion for his break with the royal family? Do you defend this act, or condemn it? Do you think that he was in those days trying to claim and assert his leadership of his own people? How was his new allegiance to them received by the slaves of the bene-ysrael? Read also Stephen's illuminating comment on that in Acts 7:23–29.

At any rate, this impetuous act brought to a screeching halt his days as an Egyptian prince.

(3) His Training in the Wilderness, 2:15c–22. God rewarded Moses in his exile by sending him on into a new phase of his education. Though he had been well trained for a portion of his specific life, he needed more, a postgraduate course of a different character.

What were some of the virtues which Moses had acquired in his training in Egypt? What were some of his faults that needed correction? The change of the scene of his training was drastic, even appalling. *What could the deserts of Midian and Sinai contribute to the preparation of this man that the universities and the court of Egypt could not supply?*

His fugitive steps led him over into the Sinai Peninsula and across its rocky and barren wastes until he came to a camp of nomadic Midianites. Here, in an experience curiously reminiscent of Jacob's experience at the well at Paddan-aram (see Gen. 29), he found that his innate courtly chivalry and his concern for the mistreated paid off. The daughters of Reuel, whom he championed, mistook him naturally enough for an Egyptian. But their father was not minded to let such a one go unrewarded and un-enlisted. "Girls, don't let a man like that get away!" he cried. "Invite him to spend the night." Moses gratefully accepted, and stayed that night, and the next, and on and on. In fact this hospitable home became his home. There he fell in love with Reuel's vivacious daughter Zipporah (her name means "little bird") and married her. Thus he settled down to the new life of a shepherd of Midian.

Do you think this exile was a hard blow for Moses to take? Did he keenly feel the injustice of his having to flee the land he'd served so well and the slave-people he had befriended? Is there some evidence of his bitterness of spirit in the naming of his first-born son (see 2:22)? When his second son was born, we find him more reconciled and adjusted (see 18:4).

So we see Moses in this new school of God. Under a burning sun he tended the flocks of sheep and goats, moving them from pasture to pasture, and oasis to oasis. By night he camped with his charges under the starry skies or maintained his family life at home. What was this doing for his preparation? How was his character refined by his occupation as a shepherd and by his home life?

Surely one of the most precious contributions of those years was his growth in the perception and understanding of God. After his years of identification with all things man-made, he now was surrounded by all things God-made. How often must he have pondered the kind of thoughts expressed later by another shepherd of Israel in Psalm 8:3–4. Moses had time to learn the secrets of nature, to become versed in the wonders of the wilderness, to look up—and as a result to think God's thoughts after him.

There was another source of information and instruction—Reuel, his father-in-law. *Reuel* means "friend of God." He was also called Jethro, "excellency," which may have been his official title as the chief priest of his tribe. It must be remembered that these Midianites were also children of Abraham through Keturah (see Gen. 25:2). The knowledge of the God of Abraham may well have been treasured and transmitted by them. Jethro was the priest of Midian, and it is possible that through him Moses came to a more mature knowledge of the God of his fathers, as he was instructed in truth which he had had no way of learning at Pharaoh's court.

Not only was Moses trained in the knowledge of God in his desert years, but his whole attitude toward others was changed. Compared with his impetuous and imperious manner revealed in 2:11–15, note his calm assurance and reliance upon God in 14: 10–14, his patient dealing with a rebellious people in 15:23–25 and elsewhere, and his identification of himself with their suffering in 32:31–32. How do you account for this new character? Where did it come from?

Such was Moses' education in the wilderness and the fruit of it. Dwight L. Moody, the noted evangelist, is credited with this discerning and memorable summary of Moses' life: "In the first forty years, in Egypt, Moses learned to be a Somebody. In the second forty years, in the wilderness, Moses learned to be a Nobody. In the third forty years, he learned what God can do with a Somebody who is willing to be a Nobody."

The Call and Commissioning of Moses, 2:23—4:21

What was the purpose of this lengthy, varied preparation and education of Moses? Can we not say, in the light of later New Testament revelation, that God was equipping one to be his people's savior (and a preview of the Savior of the world)? According to Exodus 7:7, it was when Moses was eighty that he was confronted by God and called to the task for which he had been so well prepared. For him life began at eighty!

(1) The Place of the Call. As Moses shepherded his flock one day at the base of Sinai, his attention was arrested by the sight of a thorn bush afire upon the sharply rising slope of the mountain. As he drew nearer he was astonished beyond measure to see that this bush that burned was not being consumed by the flame. The flickering flames leaped up, but the branches were not harmed. Then somehow through his bewilderment and awe at such a sight he was made aware of the voice of God bidding him to re-

alize that he was standing on holy ground—in the presence of the Most High, the God of the covenant.

His dialogue with God at the burning bush was the pivotal event of Moses' life. Life was never again the same for him. The God of his fathers was thenceforth to him an ever-present, enabling, propelling, personal reality.

God confronts men today with an experience akin to this. The place is unpredictable. Samuel met him in the quiet of a night's rest; Isaiah in his worship in the Temple; Saul on the Damascus Road. John Newton was confronted by God in a dreadful storm on the Atlantic; John Wesley in a quiet little prayer meeting in Aldersgate Street in London; Starr Daily in a prison cell. The place is varied, but the result the same—an overpowering realization of a Presence, and a call that thenceforth changes all of life and service.

Do Christians have this experience today? Ought this to be the experience only of those destined to great leadership, or should it—in one way or another—be that of every Christian? Have you ever had any such confrontation? Does one always need a spectacular demonstration to convince him of the reality of God's call to special service or is the persuasion of the "still small voice" effective today? Are we open to God's call? Do we have eyes to see, ears to hear, hearts and minds to receive the message?

(2) The Fact of the Call. How God actually spoke to Moses we do not know, but of his conviction that God had spoken there can be no doubt. Moses had doubtless often asked God to hear and heed the plight of his people in Egypt. And now God calls *him* to go and answer his own prayer; to be God's instrument in bringing it to pass. This was not what Moses had prayed for! But, after all, what is a valid call?

William Carey, "the father of modern missions," said that his call consisted of an open Bible in his hand and a map of the world before him on his wall. David Livingstone protested that he'd had no special call save an overwhelming sense of his duty. Robert E. Speer used to say that a call is the realization of an existing need and the feeling that you are the one to fill that need. These concepts have much in common. Are these elements found today in God's calling us into less glamorous forms of service as well as to major endeavors? Are we called to be farmers and merchants, to be workers on an assembly line, to be filing clerks and typists, nurses and homemakers? Would it make any difference in our lives if we felt this sense of mission and commission?

(3) The Response to the Call. Did Moses immediately respond with the words that Isaiah was to use: "Here am I, send me!"? (Read again Isa. 6:1–8.) No, Moses does not give us an example of the ideal response to God's call, but he clearly illustrates a typical human response. He was understandably reluctant. He knew more than anyone else what a tremendous task it would be to effect the liberation of his people. He had tried it already and had failed. He felt totally insufficient. So he began to make excuses.

Study his replies. List them in the words of our own reactions to God's challenges today. They remind us of our modern excuses for nonperformance of duty. Pastors and church school superintendents have heard them all many, many times. *How would you rephrase them in the common language of our time? Consider these verses—3:11, 3:13, 4:1, 4:10, 4:13. What was God's answer to each excuse? Why was he stirred to anger at last by Moses' attempt to get out of this assignment? What was Moses' subsequent penalty and loss? What credentials did God give him for the task that lay ahead?*

(4) The Acceptance of the Call. Finally Moses gave in to God's will and began his obedient service of forty years as the leader of his people. Thereafter he was never to relinquish the task to which he had been so clearly called. "Moses went . . . ," and he kept going through thick and thin.

He went first to his father-in-law Jethro and won his approval of this hazardous adventure. His wife too was apparently willing to share it. The all-important trip began. The donkeys were saddled. Zipporah and the two lads, Gershom and Eliezer, were placed aboard one, while another bore the meager family belongings. Moses, with the wonder-working rod in his hand, strode ahead as guide and protector. Thus, as Winston Churchill described this event in his own inimitable words, ". . . through the dust-clouds and blazing sunlight the smallest, most potent and most glorious of all the rescue forces of history starts upon its expedition."[1]

There follows the strange episode at a camping place on the way. Moses seems for a time to have been in dire danger because of his neglect of the Abrahamic rite of circumcision for his child. Though this was remedied by Zipporah, he apparently sends her and the boys back home to Jethro (look up 18:2–6).

Aaron is met and his consent is won to share in the great adventure. The elders of the *bene-ysrael* are gathered in a secret meeting; Moses presents his credentials, the elders accept them, and in anticipation of the coming deliverance of the people they gratefully worship God. Thus the time is at hand to attack the entrenched power of the Pharaoh in the name of the Lord God of Israel. The leader is prepared and commissioned to his task, and as the curtain falls on Act One the first rumblings of the battle of the gods can almost be heard.

DEMONSTRATION

The Sovereign of the Universe Versus the Sovereign of Egypt

Act One of this drama was featured by success: success in the preservation of a baby's life, success in his preparation as a man for his vastly important mission, and success in the initial stages of that mission. Act Two starts on the note of failure. "Afterward Moses and Aaron went to Pharaoh"—and ingloriously failed in the request, "Let my people go!" But this was only the opening skirmish of the tremendous battle that was to follow.

The Opposing Forces

Let us pause here to take a look at these antagonists, Pharaoh and Moses.

On the one hand there is a man who is known only by his title. Just which Pharaoh he was is not clear. One must make up his own mind, from a study of the conflicting evidence given by biblical Egyptologists, as to whether Amenhotep II of the 18th Dynasty, Rameses II of the 19th Dynasty, or the latter's son Merneptah was the Pharaoh of the Exodus.

The Bible rightly gives him the title Pharaoh. *Pharaoh* comes to us, by way of the Hebrew and Greek texts of the Old Testament, from the Egyptian word *per-o,* which originally meant "the Great House." In the Old Kingdom (c. 2700–2200 B.C.), it was the custom to call the palace of the ruler the Great House, a custom which we parallel today in our use of the term White House. In time the residence became the word used as a respectful and brief designation for the ruler himself, as we often do for our president.

It is difficult to exaggerate the wealth and power of the Pharaohs. Even a relatively weak one, Tutankhamen ("King Tut"),

was buried in a solid gold coffin guarded by gilded lions and surrounded with treasures which are featured in museums more than 3,000 years later.

Whichever Pharaoh this one was, he was the absolute monarch of the greatest kingdom of the day, with unlimited power and authority. Nor was that all. Through changing dynasties and passing centuries the Egyptians clung to their belief not only in the divine right of rulers but in their actual deity. The Pharaohs themselves accepted this unique distinction. A direct result of this belief, held by ruler and people, can be easily seen in the indignant refusal of Pharaoh to acknowledge any order from the Hebrews' Yahweh, or indeed to give countenance to any demonstration of Hebrew loyalty to a rival god.

As his opponent we have the stalwart figure of Moses, accompanied by his brother-spokesman, Aaron. Humanly speaking, there was no comparison. Moses was in effect a nobody. If one cared to look up the record, it would be found that he was a returned political exile and a discredited champion of his slave kindred who had been in political exile. True, he had once been a court favorite and a popular idol, but that was years ago. Now tanned by the desert sun and in the rough garb of a shepherd, he was a commanding figure with no status, no authority. How dared he approach the deity who sat upon the golden throne, the ruler who wore the Double Crown of Upper and Lower Egypt!

That it did take immense courage on his part we must certainly grant, and there is only one explanation for it. Moses stood for another. He was the representative of the Sovereign God of the universe. He brought an order from the true God to this pretender god.

Captives making Bricks
(*From an Egyptian tomb painting of the fifteenth century* B.C.)

It was in his name that Moses dared to throw down the gauntlet, to challenge to mortal combat the mighty ruler of Egypt. And the whole of the drama that follows is the revelation of the conflict between Yahweh, the God of heaven and earth, and Pharaoh, the supposed god, and the other gods of the polytheistic religion of Egypt.

The Probing Skirmish, 5:1–21

The opening round of the battle is occasioned by the reasonable request of Moses to Pharaoh, "Thus saith the Lord, the God of Israel, let my people go that they may hold a feast to me in the wilderness!" But immediately comes back the scornful reply, "Who is the Lord, that I should heed his voice and let Israel go? I do not know the Lord, and moreover I will not let Israel go."

But Moses and Aaron stick to their guns. They renew their request, softened this time in its tone. This too is peremptorily refused. And Pharaoh tauntingly commands that they go to work in the brick-fields along with the rest of the slaves of the *bene-ysrael*. Furthermore, the order is issued to the taskmasters to cut off the straw supply and make these impudent slaves gather their own stubble. But they were to keep the brick output at the same level. This cruel directive was carried out, and the appeal made by the angry and agonized elders of Israel was futile. One can only imagine the bitter resentment which found an outlet against Moses and Aaron as the elders came upon them in their despairing retreat from the royal presence. "Where are your pretty promises now? You have only made us a stench to Pharaoh, and we are worse off now than we were before you came and hoodwinked us!"

The Retreat for Reinforcement, 5:22—6:9

What would you do at such a time as that? All your hopes have been blasted, your schemes gone awry, your efforts for others have been met with scornful rejection, your good name apparently ruined—what would you do? Would you give up in disgust at those you'd tried to help? Would you just cuss and quit? Go home and take it out on your wife and children? Renounce the whole enterprise as a case of stupid misjudgment? Morosely slink away and drown your frustration and resentment with alcohol?

How much better to take the way that Moses took! He went back to the God who started it all and laid it all before him. This writer has in the margin of his Bible here a quotation from G. Campbell Morgan, "Happy is the man who, when he cannot understand the Divine dealing, and indeed, doubts it, has yet faith enough in God to tell him all his doubt." It is a true word, and Moses demonstrated it. He pours it all out before God. He casts his burden on the Lord and finds that God will indeed sustain him. He is reinforced, rearmed, and renewed for the conflict to come. He is assured of the knowledge that Paul was later to express in Romans 8:31, "... If God is for us, who is against us?"

What was the substance of God's reassurance? Read 6:1. How was this backed up? Underline the personal pronoun "I," with its following verb, in 6:2–8. What does this visible emphasis bring home to you? Compare this passage with a similar one in Joshua 24:1–13.

How do you reconcile the statement in 6:2–3 with Genesis 12:7, 15:18, 22:14, 26:24–25, and 28:13? What two reasons lay back of God's promise to help (see 6:5)?

Moses' New Marching Orders, 6:10–13

Moses had been disheartened and deflated. His own people had turned against him again, blaming him for their added suffering. And who could blame them? How then could he ever hope to win out over Pharaoh? Yet all was not lost. Some good had come out of this seeming failure. The battle line was now clearly drawn: it was to be a showdown between Pharaoh and Yahweh, and God was going to demonstrate his power over this stubborn man. Moses too was learning the fickleness and ingratitude of his own people which would be shown more markedly in years to come. And the *bene-ysrael* were by added hardship being further weaned from their home in Egypt and prepared for their God-given deliverance. So Moses was ordered to carry on regardless, and to take the fight to Pharaoh.

A Genealogical Interlude—The Credentials of the Commanders, 6:14–27

What do you make of this apparently abrupt interlude right at the very moment of the renewal of hostilities? Why turn aside to dry genealogical tables?

This is a Hebrew book, remember. And this was a touch to delight the Hebrew heart. To the Jews genealogy was never dry. It was informative and authoritative. And here in the narrative of the beginning of God's battle with the royal god of Egypt this section is inserted to give the background and authority of the Hebrew leaders. It reveals the credentials of commanders whom the Israelites could accept and trust. It is no complete genealogy, but rather a summary showing who Moses and Aaron were. (In such a record, the word *sons* might also mean "grandsons" or "descendants.") You slaves, you can trust these two! They're genuine blue bloods of the tribe of Levi! These are the Moses and Aaron who have been commissioned to carry God's battle to Pharaoh.

The Campaign Begins, 7:8–13

"So Moses and Aaron went to Pharaoh . . ." Pharaoh too had to be convinced of their credentials, and not by genealogical lists, but by visible evidences that they were the authentic messengers of the God they professed to represent. Attended by his coterie of court magicians, he gave Moses and Aaron audience (2 Tim. 3:8 gives us the names of two of the principal magicians who led the contest with Moses).

"Show me a sign—a wonder—that I may know you are what you say you are," he commanded. And Aaron cast down Moses' rod, and it became a serpent on the palace pavement. "Phooey!"

cried Pharaoh, in effect, "That's nothing! My magicians can do that." And forthwith they did. The art of sleight-of-hand or magic was highly developed in the Egypt of that day and is still commonly practiced there. Egyptian magicians today can paralyze a cobra by putting pressure on a nerve in its neck so that it becomes rigid. At a distance it can be mistaken for a cane. When cast on the ground the resulting jolt brings recovery, and it crawls away.[1]

The fact that Aaron's rod swallowed up the snakes that the magicians had "produced" should have been an effective testimony of his superiority and validity. It only served to make Pharaoh stubborn and disbelieving—"his heart was hardened."

Perhaps we might well take up our pencils and notebooks right here and make an independent study of a problem that has puzzled many Bible readers, "the hardening of Pharaoh's heart." Throughout chapters 4 and 7—11 the expression is found again and again. *List the references where it is stated that God hardened Pharaoh's heart. List those which reveal that Pharaoh hardened his own heart. List those which simply state that his heart was hardened.* Three Hebrew words are used in these chapters to describe respectively a process of making strong, a process of holding fast, and a state of being severe, obstinate, heavy, or weighty. These all appear to be different ways of stating the same fact, that Pharaoh was stubborn, intransigent, and obstinate in the face of all the signs and wonders he received.

Was this God's fault or his own? How does this tie in with your concept of God's sovereignty and man's free agency? Can it be said that God is responsible for the flaming suicides of the Buddhist fanatics in South Vietnam, who, as these notes are being written, are taking this drastic means to declare their opposition to the status quo? God has created the "natural" laws by which certain materials when ignited will burn with severe intensity. But can God be said to be responsible for these people being burned to death? He has also created the psychological laws by which a perception leads to thought, a thought into resolve, a resolve into action, actions into patterns, patterns into habits, and habits into character. Who's to blame? The Hebrew mind jumped over second and third causes and attributed all that happened to the direct action of God. How do we view it? Where does our own responsibility come in, in making decisions for ourselves, our families, our church, our world? Read the treatment of this subject in Arnold B. Rhodes' student's book, *The Mighty Acts of God,* pages 75–77.

The Fight Is On! 7:14—11:10

There follows that dramatic conflict between the sovereign God, the Yahweh of the Hebrews, and the sovereign of Egypt, regarded as a god by himself and his people. We refer to it as the ten plagues. We do well to note certain facts about these celebrated signs or strokes or judgments which befell the Egyptians and ever after left their impress upon the people of Israel.

(1) The *purpose* of the plagues. Why were they inflicted upon the Egyptians—just to obtain the freedom of the Hebrew slaves? Why then did Yahweh not reveal his almighty power by one fell stroke and bring about the deliverance of his people? Fortunately, we are not left in doubt as to the answer to this. Read 9:15–16 and 10:1–2. The primary purpose of these visitations was to reveal the name and character and sovereignty of Yahweh to Pharaoh and the Egyptians, to the Hebrews themselves, and, through this event in history, to the whole world. There were also the secondary purposes: to make possible the escape of the Children of Israel from bondage (read 3:20, 6:1, 11:1); and to bring a rightful judgment upon the Egyptians for their cruelty and oppression (see 3:9, 6:6, 7:4).

The plagues are God's answer to Pharaoh's scornful, taunting challenge, "Who is the Lord, that I should hearken to his voice?" *Examine the following references carefully, making note of the purpose indicated in each: 7:5, 7:17, 8:10, 8:22, 9:14, 9:29, 11:7.* See also God's purpose that the Hebrews themselves become aware of the answer to Pharaoh's challenge, in 6:7 and 10:1–2, "Who is the Lord?" God would demonstrate to them all beyond a shadow of doubt that he is the God supreme over all.

He would also reveal conclusively, unmistakably, and overwhelmingly his superiority not only over the so called god on the throne, but also over all the gods in the pantheon of Egypt. The

Egyptians were a religious people, with a vast and influential priesthood and many gods. Each of the plagues was directed against one or more of their gods, and the cumulative impact of this testimony that Yahweh alone is God was devastating.

The first plague was an impressive victory over the Nile god, Hapi. For their famous river was personified and deified, and was hailed in their ritual as the ". . . giver of life to all men, bringer of joy, creator and nourisher of the whole land." [2]

In the second plague, of frogs, the frog-headed goddess Heka, whose cult was one of the oldest in Egypt, was made an object of loathing.

The third plague—whether of lice, sand flies, fleas, gnats, or mosquitoes—was apparently aimed at the worship of the earth god, Geb.

The fourth—which the Hebrew simply describes as "swarms," possibly of beetles of an unusually destructive sort—was an overthrow of Khopri, the beetle-headed god, whose image is found in profusion in Egypt in sculpture, painting, and engraving, on monuments and in tombs, and as amulets.

The fifth, the cattle pestilence ("cattle" being a general term to include the species mentioned in 9:3) in which all die except those previously housed, was in opposition to the celebrated bull-god Apis, the cow-headed goddess Hathor, and the animal worship of the Egyptians.

The sixth, boils, was possibly in defiance of the war-goddess, Neith; the seventh, hail, apparently against the air gods, Isis, Nut, Shu, and others; the eighth, locusts, in opposition to certain insect gods, of which there were a number. The ninth, darkness, was a bold demonstration of Yahweh's power over the sun-god, Amon-Ra, regarded as the king of the Egyptian pantheon, in whose honor and for whose worship the magnificent and awesome Temple of Karnak was even then being erected. The tenth, the death of the first-born, was a direct refutation of the sovereignty of the human-headed god Ptah, worshiped as the giver and sustainer of life.

Thus these all with ascending emphasis demonstrated Yahweh's absolute superiority and fulfilled his announced intent to execute judgments against all the gods of Egypt (see 12:12). *Why was Yahweh so eager to show his own people as well as the Egyptians his unique place as the true God? Think that through.*

(2) The *nature* of the plagues. To oversimplify, they were both natural and supernatural. It is clear that they were all based upon and closely related to natural phenomena with which the Egyptians were familiar. But that they were supernaturally directed is plainly seen in the fact that they appeared and disappeared at the command of Moses; that they were of such extraordinary violence; that they were sometimes, as foretold, of only a limited application; and that they came in rapid and cumulative succession. So one simply cannot explain away the plagues as natural calamities which were skillfully given a particular interpretation by Moses and thus turned to his desired end. To relinquish their supernatural element is to lose their message. It was God working in, through and above natural phenomena, not the quick thinking of Moses that made them the effective instruments of his purpose as signs and judgments.

(3) The *method* of presenting the plagues. They were orderly, rhythmic, and climactic. There were nine of these great demonstrations, leading up to and preparing for the awful, climactic judgment of the death of the first-born. These nine are described in three triads or in groups of three. Put some time on the study of these groups.

What was the character of the warning common to the first one of each triad? to the second? to the third?

What was the extent of the application of the first series of three? Of the second? Of the third?

What was the nature of the plagues in each group of three?

What was the attitude of the magicians who had been striving so desperately to match these demonstrations of God's power with the sleight-of-hand magic of their own at the end of the first group? the second? (In the third they are out of the picture completely.)

What have you discovered as to the time schedule of these

signs? Look up 7:25; 9:31–32; 12:2, 6, 15. These are the only direct references to actual times involved, though 5:11–12 does suggest indirectly the passing of time. Most scholars compute the length of time taken up in the plagues to be ten months to a year. Consider the cumulative effect of these awesome events extended over so long a period!

(4) The *result* of these great strokes. What did they do for the Hebrews in Goshen? What was their effect on the Egyptians? Read 8:19; 9:11, 20; 10:7; 11:3, 8. What was their effect upon Pharaoh, whose haughty refusal to hear the command of Yahweh brought them down upon his land? Read carefully 7:22–23; 8:8, 15, 19, 25, 28, 32; 9:7, 12, 27–28, 34–35; 10:8, 10–11, 16, 20, 24, 27–28; 11:10. Had no progress been made?

Pharaoh Offers to Compromise

Consider now the compromises which Pharaoh offered to Moses and Aaron. They are found in 8:25, 8:28, 10:10–11, and 10:24. Do you follow the subtle cunning that lay behind these adroit bargains that he sought to make? What were the answers that Moses gave to each? *How applicable are these compromises in their appeal to the Christian today in his pilgrimage toward the City of God? How would you express them in today's language?* Spend some time on this, as the question of compromise is of vital importance to our faithfulness in our Christian witness in our time. Only as we respond to the blandishments of the Evil One today as Moses did to Pharaoh will we be able to go forward in obedience and courage to the fulfillment of our destiny as the children of God.

REALIZATION

The Act of Grace,
Passing Over and Passing Through

The drama of Exodus drives swiftly on now to the amazing event of the passage through the sea and the transition of the *bene-ysrael* from bondage to freedom. Packed into the small compass of these chapters is the terrible final stroke that fell upon Egypt, the dramatic story of the preservation and liberation of the Hebrews, the beginning of their trek toward freedom, the astonishing deliverance by God, and the destruction of their enemies. The events of this section have left their permanent impression upon the followers of Judaism and Christianity and are memorialized in ritual, song, and story.

The Parenthetical Promise, 11:1–3

The eleventh chapter begins with a parenthesis. The account of Moses' stormy interview with Pharaoh is interrupted for this statement of a promise and a provision for future need. What is the promise? See verse 1. What is the provision? See verses 2–3 (for the later use of this provision, see 35:21–22).

But there was something the people had to do to obtain this wealth for future need. And here is where many Bible readers are disturbed—by the word *borrow* in the K.J.V. How could it have been right for God's people to borrow with no thought or intent of return or repayment? This is one of the very unfortunate mistranslations in the old version. The word should be "ask," not "borrow," as all modern versions reveal. There is nothing of dishonesty or trickery suggested here. They asked of their former masters what would be at best only partial payment for their long years of cruel servitude, and the Egyptians were only too glad to give them what they asked and to be rid of them, for they had come to fear and dread them (see also 12:35–36). This word is found in several other places in the Old Testament where it is consistently translated "ask" in the K.J.V. For samples of these, see Judges 5:25, 1 Kings 3:11 (five times in one verse!) and 2 Kings 2:10.

This brief statement closes with a reference to the great prestige of Moses among the Egyptians. Thus had the popular idol of other days made his successful comeback.

The Tenth Plague Announced, 11:4–10

With verse 4 the controversy of Moses and Pharaoh is resumed. The tenth and final catastrophe is announced in explicit terms and its result forecast. Moses then departs from the court indignant at the stubborn folly of the king.

Two Epoch-Making Events—Passover and Exodus

The twelfth chapter is a highwater mark of the book. It relates the actual Exodus—the going out—from which the book takes its name. It tells of the final judgment that broke the resistance of the king and made the event possible. It describes the act of faith that preserved the homes of the Israelites from loss and sorrow. It provides for their deliverance to be memorialized through all the succeeding generations.

The Exodus is the most important single fact in Jewish history. It is commemorated in every devout Jewish home today through the observance of the Passover, the festival which marks the beginning of their ecclesiastical year. The month Abib (meaning "the opening ear" of grain), corresponding to the close of March and the beginning of April, became the first month of the sacred year. (After the Exile it was called by the Babylonian name, Nisan. See Neh. 2:1, Esther 3:7.) This chapter tells of the establishment of the Passover, which points us forward to Christ and the supreme act of grace upon the cross. It therefore merits our best study.

The Passover Instituted, 12:1–28, 43–51

The Passover was of divine origin. It is held by some biblical students that the Israelites simply took over an ancient shepherd's festival held in the spring of the year and gave it new meaning and purpose; but there is no evidence for this assumption in the Scripture text. Its importance in the life of the people is attested by its preservation through the years; this was the act of faith which under God made their emancipation possible.

The chapter begins with the directions given by Yahweh to Moses and Aaron for the observance of this ritual by families on the night when the blow would fall and the destroying angel would pass through the land of Egypt (1–13). Then follow the words regarding its perpetuation as a memorial in the future (14–20). These instructions are transmitted to the people through the elders and accepted and obeyed (21–28). Let us think through what lies behind these directives.

What does the term Passover *mean? See 12:12–13, 23, 27. Upon whom was God's judgment to fall? Do you think the Egyptians merited this judgment, and why? Did they have sufficient evidence of God's power? sufficient time through God's mercy to repent? sufficient warning of what was to come if they did not?*

Was God's judgment also to fall on the Israelites who did not take the way of faith that he provided? Do you think all did? Later events in the life of Israel reveal that the whole community was seldom of the same mind and response. This was probably true here.

It is not clear how long a time elapsed between Moses' warning to Pharaoh and instructions to his own people, and the falling of the blow. One can imagine something of the suspense and fear that gripped the land in view of its previous calamities, so explicitly foretold and so exactly carried out. While the Egyptians awaited this new terror with anguish the Hebrews who believed fulfilled with faithful care the details of Moses' instructions.

And what were those instructions? As we read the details, we who are Christians bring to mind the amazing manner in which our Lord Jesus Christ fulfills in himself the provisions of the Passover, and how our appropriation of Christ as our Savior fulfills our Christian observance of this age-old ritual. Nor is this surprising, for Paul tells us plainly in 1 Corinthians 5:7b, "For Christ, our paschal [Passover] lamb, has been sacrificed."

As you consider the directives for the observance of the Pass-

over listed below, you may find it profitable to examine the suggested New Testament references. Although they do not refer directly to the Old Testament ritual of the Passover, they throw the light of Christian teaching upon the similarity of our salvation from the bondage of sin.

THE JEWISH PASSOVER	THE CHRISTIAN REDEMPTION
It was a way of escape from God's judgment on sin. 12:12–13, 23, 27	See John 5:24 Romans 6:23
The lamb must be without blemish, the best possible. 12:5	See 1 Peter 1:18–19
The lamb must be tested four days for impurities. 12:3–6	See Hebrews 4:15
The lamb had to be slain. 12:6; Leviticus 17:11	See Luke 24:26 Hebrews 2:9; 9:22 Revelation 13:8
The lamb was to have no bone broken. 12:46	See John 19:36
The lamb's blood was the vehicle of their salvation. 12:13	See 1 Peter 1:18–19 1 John 1:7
The blood must be applied by the individual family. 12:7, 13	See John 3:36 Acts 16:31 Romans 10:9–10
There was to be no safety except behind the blood marked portal to those who would accept and follow this way. 12:27	See Acts 4:12
Although safe, they must feed on the lamb. 12:8	See John 6:53, 56
They must eat as pilgrims dressed for the journey. 12:11	See 1 Peter 2:11
The Passover was to be a memorial to God's people forever. 12:14, 42; 13:3	See 1 Corinthians 11:23–26

Such a comparison as this should lead us to a better understanding of the Lord's Supper as the Christian memorial of the Christ who is our Passover.

Verses 14–20 and 43–49 are apparently instructions supplementary to the original directives concerning the Passover and form the basis of the Feast of Unleavened Bread, which was kept by the Jews along with the Passover throughout biblical times and since. The modern observance of these feasts has undergone modifications and changes. There is no sacrifice now involved, but anticipation is expressed of the day when it will be resumed in Jerusalem. Further details of the present-day Jewish observance will be found in the teacher's text.

The Final Blow Falls—The Tenth Plague, 12:29–30

On the midnight when the *bene-ysrael* were gathered in their homes by families eating the paschal lamb, the blow fell that proved to be the knockout. The account simply states that Yahweh smote all the firstborn of man and beast. How, we do not know, and it is idle to speculate. Not a house was spared where there was a first-born.

The Immediate Result—Dismissal and Departure, 12:31–36

From all the stricken land rose the awful cry of desolation, terror, and grief. It was an outcry that moved Pharaoh, himself bereaved, to do something and do it at once. His chariot was dispatched in furious haste for Moses and Aaron, and when they appeared he peremptorily commanded them to take their slave people and their goods and be gone. Then in the abjectness of his surrender he asked a blessing from his conquerors. The Egyptians too everywhere urged the Hebrews to leave and plied them with treasure and whatever they asked, if only they would go away.

The Going Forth, 12:37–42

Then came the Exodus that marked the beginning of their long and arduous journey to freedom and the setting up of a new nation under God.

This was no mob, no panic-stricken rabble, no straggling mass of refugees with their luggage and cattle, struggling to get away from the wrath of the ruler and the vengeful fury of the people. It was an orderly withdrawal. We can read between the lines and assume that Moses, trained as a successful general in the armies of Egypt, had made preparations for this day of days. Doubtless he had his staff officers and deputy commanders and other leaders appointed. He had a plan of mobilization and an order of march.

Even granting this, as we must, it seems to us an utter impossibility for him without our familiar modern means of communication to have directed effectively so vast a company as is described in 12:37–38. There we read that the fighting men of Israel numbered 600,000. Multiplying this by four or five for an average family for each soldier would run the total to two and a half to three million. To this should be added an indeterminate number of adherents—a rabble of fugitive slaves, defecting Egyptians, and others of miscellaneous origin. And flocks of sheep and goats and herds of livestock accompanied them. This startlingly enormous and unwieldy company presents a real problem to those who would take the account at its face value, and a little arithmetic makes it still more difficult to understand. This number of fighting men alone, marching in columns of five at an ordinary pace without pause, would require more than twenty-four hours to pass a given point. How much longer would this whole multitude require? Such a vast company would form a line of march of 350 miles or more in extent, and, as John Bright points out, "such a host even if marching in close order (as it did not) would more than have extended from Egypt to Sinai and back!" [1]

Biblical historians compute the population of Israel during the monarchy's heyday in after years to be no more than this. And when we compare this large figure with the fact of their panic at the pursuit of the chariot force of Pharaoh, the plain statement of their crossing the sea during a part of one night, and the intimation in Exodus 23:29–30 that there were not enough Hebrews to occupy all of the land of Canaan at one time but that it would have to be done gradually as they grew in size, then we realize that something must be wrong with the translation or interpretation of this number.

There are many reactions to this problem, from incredulous rejection, to plausible explanation, to complete silence. One solution, first proposed by the eminent Egyptologist W. M. Flinders Petrie, is that the word *elef,* (translated here "thousand") also meant "family," "clan," or "tribal subunit." This is, in fact, the translation of this word in the R.S.V. in such places as Numbers 1:16 and Judges 6:15. He estimates that nine could be counted as an *elef,* a "tent group." Whether this or a larger number is regarded as the subunit of a tribe, such an interpretation drastically

lowers the total figure from 600,000 fighting men to 5400 men, if
the size of the *elef* can be considered to be nine. It must be admitted, however, that the problem of numbers in the early history
of Israel is a puzzling one.

The Instructions Concerning the First-Born and the Reemphasis on the Passover, 12:43—13:16

At the outset of their march toward freedom, the author of
Exodus pauses to emphasize again the necessity for the proper orientation of the people to God. All Israel was to be in a special
way holy unto the Lord (see 19:5–6). To represent this fact the
first-born of man were to be consecrated as priests, while those of
animals were appointed for sacrifice; first-born animals that were
unclean and so unfit for sacrifice were to be redeemed at a price or
destroyed. Later on the whole tribe of Levi were consecrated as
priests in lieu of the first-born of all the Israelites, though there was
a price levied for this redemption (see Num. 8:16). When did
Mary and Joseph fulfill this ritual for the infant Jesus? (See Luke
2:22–24.)

Verse 9 is especially interesting to us for the origin of the Jewish custom of wearing "phylacteries." Many Jews, taking this injunction literally instead of figuratively, to this day bind to their
left arms and foreheads at stated hours of prayer small boxes con-
taining parchment inscriptions of four passages—these two here
and 13:1–10, 11–16, and Deuteronomy 6:4–9 and 11:13–21. For
our Lord's comment on this, see Matthew 23:5.

The Freedom March, 12:37, 13:17—14:2

With joyous abandon the clans gathered in the early morning
of the day of Egypt's sorrow and Pharaoh's order of expulsion.
Starting out from Rameses (the same as Avaris-Tanis), and gaining new units as they went, they covered the thirty miles to Succoth, which seemingly was the mustering place in Goshen, the
Wadi Tumilat. To this rendezvous the slaves came pouring in,
with their goods and chattels, whatever could be carried, and we
can but faintly imagine some of the excitement and joy and confusion of that first taste of freedom.

"And now where?" By what route would they go on to the

Land of Promise? "The nearest way is by the coast road. It's only 150 miles or so to Canaan. Come on, let's go!" But there God took over.

Why did he prohibit the short route? Why the alternate?

Off they go—in regular military formation, not by any means a congolmerate rabble. Moses was too smart for that! And think of the problem of disciplining and training newly freed slaves. Moses was indeed a magnificent leader!

And in the excitement of the departure they did not forget the coffin of their hero, Joseph.

The Way to the Sea, 14:2–9

The route of the Hebrews toward what turned out to be their final escape through the sea is not clearly and easily discerned. Because of this there has been a sharp difference of opinion among biblical scholars as to the exact path the Hebrews followed. One sketch map will show "the probable route" one way and another sketch will suggest another.

The best solution to this puzzle, in the writer's opinion, is found in Jack Finegan's *Let My People Go,* chapter 6. This scholar presents a convincing case based upon detailed study of the latest archaeological information relative to places and the ancient topography of the region. His conclusions show the Hebrews traveling from Succoth, in the Wadi Tumilat, eastward to Etham, a border fortress between Lake Timseh (the Crocodile Lake) and the Bitter Lakes to the south. There they are turned back either by the refusal of the Egyptian garrison to allow them to take this well-known route eastward across the wilderness of Shur toward Canaan, or by God's special commandment, or both.

Thence, led by their beacon of smoke that glowed at night, they went south with the Bitter Lakes on their left and a converging mountain range, Jebel Jenefeh, on their right, to Migdol, which was apparently another Egyptian tower or fort at the south end of the Bitter Lakes. These lakes were then probably united with an arm of the Gulf of Suez, a stretch of water of some ten or twelve miles which was comparatively shallow called in Hebrew *yam suph,* "Sea of Reeds." (The "Red Sea" in Exod. 15:4, 22 is a translation of

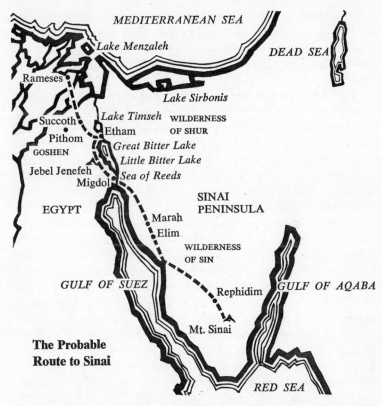

MEDITERRANEAN SEA

DEAD SEA

Lake Menzaleh

Rameses

Lake Sirbonis

Succoth

Lake Timseh WILDERNESS

Etham OF SHUR

Pithom

Great Bitter Lake

GOSHEN

Little Bitter Lake

Jebel Jenefeh

Sea of Reeds

Migdol

SINAI
PENINSULA

EGYPT

Marah

Elim

WILDERNESS
OF SIN

GULF OF SUEZ

Rephidim GULF OF AQABA

Mt. Sinai

**The Probable
Route to Sinai**

RED SEA

the Greek Septuagint which found its way into other references
to it in Scripture. The original Hebrew reads "Sea of Reeds.")[2]
Here the *bene-ysrael* were hemmed in between the mountain and
the sea, and Pharaoh would indeed think " 'They are entangled
in the land; the wilderness has shut them in' " (14:3). Hence,
having changed his mind about letting these profitable slaves go,
he dispatches his fast chariot corps in pursuit of them with every
expectation of their easy capture and return.

The Passage Through the Sea, 14:10–31

We now come to the event made famous in song and story, the
mighty redemptive act of God in the physical deliverance of his

people. *What was God's purpose in this spectacular event? Who led the Hebrews into this trap?* See 14:1–2. *Who sent the Egyptians in pursuit?* See 14:3–4a. *To what end?* See 14:4b–5, 18. This was but the climax of God's reply to Pharaoh's disdainful question in 5:2.

The appearance of the dust cloud of the approaching chariots in their rear threw the Hebrews into panic. Were they justified in their fear? Hadn't they had sufficient evidence of God's preserving power in the long year of the plagues? But does panic ever take time to consider the facts? Isn't that what makes it panic? In contrast Moses stands, as did Jackson's brigade at the First Battle of Manassas, "like a stone wall." And Israel rallied behind his calm and trustful leadership.

Egyptian carvings still in existence show two-wheeled war chariots of that day. Each carries a driver and a fighting man, armed with bow, spear, and shield, and each is drawn by two horses. Pictured, too are the foot soldiers, with their six-foot lances and leather-covered shields, marching in columns of four. The runaway slaves had reason to fear. Such armies had conquered an empire. But the antidote to fear is faith.

God sometimes delivers his own through the act of an intermediary or the arrival of rescue forces in the nick of time. This miraculous rescue was all of God. Read the following references and on a separate piece of paper jot down the steps in his act of grace and redemption: verses 19–20, 21–22, 23–25, 26–27b, 27c–28, 30–31.

That the demonstration was complete and convincing we see in the reaction of the Egyptians (14:25) and that of the Israelites (14:31). *What does this have to say to us of the sovereign power of God? of his grace to those who walk in his way? of our assurance in time of peril?*

The Song of Triumph, 15:1–21

One can only partially imagine the scene of wild exultation that took place on the farther shore next morning! When that awful, violent night was over (see Ps. 77:15–20), with their enemies destroyed by the returning waters and its expanse now a barrier between them and any further pursuit, fear and cowardice were succeeded by overwhelming relief and unrestrained joy. Then, led by Moses, and to the timbrel accompaniment of Miriam and the women, the host of Israel sang their *Te Deum* of victory.

Note, as you read again this ancient song, how it ascribes their present and future redemption wholly to the overlordship of Yahweh, and how it applies this mighty revelation of God's power to the individual. Not until we, who are the recipients of God's saving love and power today, can say with them, "The Lord is *my* strength and *my* song; he has become *my* salvation" (Ps. 118:14, italics added), will we have appropriated to ourselves the message of this age-old story of God's redemptive act.

What is the bearing of this event upon our time? Does it not have a message of hope and instruction to all who long for freedom and to all who struggle for it, and to all who have any relation to the newly-freed peoples and the infant nations of our day?

The world has never seen anything comparable to the emergence of the new nations in this era. *What is our Christian mission to them today? What should be the Christian's attitude toward the Negro's struggle for freedom in our land? Are we to be on the side of those who, like Pharaoh and his taskmasters of Egypt, would subjugate and suppress with club and whip, tear gas, and police dog, or do we stand with those who in the name of the God of grace champion the cause of human dignity and freedom?* We may well make the prayer for ourselves and our so-called Christian land:

> Set our feet on lofty places;
> Gird our lives that they may be
> Armored with all Christ-like graces
> In the fight to set men free.
> Grant us wisdom, grant us courage,
> That we fail not man nor Thee![3]

PRESERVATION

The Tests of Faith
on the Pilgrimage

Israel could not stand and sing for long on that farther shore! There was an arduous march ahead and much to do. But in new courage and assurance they turned their faces toward the wilderness and its unknown perils. With the heady tonic of freedom coursing through their blood and putting a new vigor to their stride, they set out for the south and Sinai.

One can imagine that the pace soon began to slacken. The sun beat pitilessly down. The wind blew long waves of stinging sand. The going was hard, and the wilderness hemmed them in, the line of march lengthened. The calls for water were heard more and more frequently, but there was but little for man or beast.

The third day was the worst. Women and children fainted by the way. The column slowed to a snail's pace. A few miles were painfully covered. Then a cry of cheer went up in the vanguard and rippled its way down the strung-out company, "Water ahead!" The cattle smelled it and began to low, and the whole line surged forward toward the vegetation that marked the water hole. One can but imagine their consternation and despair when, flinging themselves down to slake their thirst, they found the water too bitter to drink.

With cries of bewilderment and rage they turned upon Moses: "We can't drink this bitter stuff! What have you done to us?" And Moses, apparently the only one with sufficient faith even after their miraculous rescue at the sea, turned to the true source of help. "And he cried to the LORD." And God reminded him of something he'd doubtless learned before in his shepherd days (for it is known even today by the Bedouin of the wilderness) that there is a certain thorn tree which if cast into the bitter waters makes them palatable.

What was the immediate result of this evidence of God's care? See 15:25b–26. This leads us to the basic question: Why were they brought into this barren wilderness at all? See 15:25b, 16:4. What was the Lord proposing to "prove" or test? See 14:31. They had been wonderfully established in their faith at the sea. Now God was going to test it for genuineness and strengthen it by exercise. Could this then be a prior necessity for the covenant that was to come? Their faith had grown dim in the generations of slavery in Egypt; now it had to be developed and reinforced before they could be ready for the climactic experience at Sinai. As M. R. Turnbull expressed it, "The wilderness was the gymnasium in which Israel's spiritual muscle might grow strong." [1]

What does this have to say to us when we find the going tough in our Christian experience? See Peter's answer in 1 Peter 1:6–7.

The Tests on the Wilderness Road, 15:22—17:16

This section of the Exodus story is the account then of how God tested and proved the quality of his people's faith by taking them on this journey through a barren area to the covenantal experience at Sinai. These tests were not capricious and arbitrary acts. They were designed to produce the kind of true faith upon which the nation could rightly be established under God. Let us look at them and discover this ultimate purpose of God. *Pause now and list the occasions on which the* bene-ysrael *came face to face with certain crises on their wilderness journey to Sinai in chapters 15: 22—17. What was the test involved in each? the response of the people to this test? the provision God made for their need?* Have you found them to be four as I did? Let us consider them.

(1) Marah, 15:22–26. What was involved in this trial of faith at Marah? What was the response of the people? Did their faith fail this first test? What provision did God make? What was the lesson to be learned from it? What was the "statute"—or "ordinance"—that God proclaimed, and that the people were to heed?

From Marah the people journeyed only a short march to Elim

—now known as the Wadi Gharandel—with its delightful oasis and its abundant water supply. Here they encamped a month or more in pleasant surroundings. Then on again, to the shore of the Red Sea (Num. 33:10), and to the Wilderness of Sin, an inhospitable, dreary, desolate tract, the modern El Markha.

(2) The Wilderness of Sin, 16:1–36. What was the problem here? What was the response of Israel's faith? Was their complaint and rebellion against Moses or really against Yahweh? What provision did God make for their need?

The substance which was furnished supernaturally by God was new to them all. As they saw this strange white matter everywhere on the morning after Moses' announcement, they looked at it with questioning wonder: "What is it?" (in the Hebrew, *man hu*). On every side they were asking, *man hu? man hu?* And the name stuck; "manna" it became, and for forty years it was their staple article of diet. Ingenious explanations are found for it today on naturalistic grounds (discussed somewhat fully in the teacher's book), but they are inadequate to account for what was evidently a sustained, sufficient, available supply.

The gift of meat was not repeated regularly. God caused the spring migration of enormous numbers of quail to provide them with flesh which they could use both fresh and sun-dried. Read Psalms 78:17–29 and 105:40. (Cf. Num. 11:31–32.)

What were the instructions given for the gathering of the manna? An omer was the equivalent of 3.36 quarts, or roughly 7 pints. In what way do the instructions remind you of a petition in the Lord's Prayer? What do you deduce from these directions regarding the place of the Sabbath prior to the giving of the law at Sinai? *What was the first and obvious lesson Yahweh intended to convey to his people in this remarkable supply of manna?*

(3) Thirst at Rephidim, 17:1–7. These marchers face another test at Rephidim. Here again it is thirst. The exact location of Rephidim is uncertain, but it was presumably a spot known previously by Moses as a good watering place. This time they are again grievously disappointed. At Marah the water was unpalatable. Here there is no water at all. The springs had dried, and the

oasis is parched. Their terrible thirst is unrelieved. That they expected better things makes this trial the more difficult when their hopes are shattered.

How did they take it? To what lengths were they apparently willing to go in their resentment against Moses? What did Moses do? What was Yahweh's counsel?

(4) Warfare at Rephidim, 17:8–16. In this neighborhood of Rephidim they faced another crisis in the sudden attack of the Amalekites. This fierce nomadic tribe roved the Sinai Peninsula. The Deuteronomic comment on this incident reveals that they had been harassing Israel from the rear, falling upon the stragglers in the long line of the march; see Deuteronomy 25:17–19.

The people braced themselves for an all-out onslaught. What was Moses' surprising strategy? Moses' uplifted arms on the mountainside are usually regarded as a symbol of intercessory prayer. What relation did this bear to the clash of arms in the valley, as Joshua's warriors closed with the men of Amalek? *What was the crowning act of the encounter, and how did it show their recognition of the true source of their strength?*

A Look at the Hebrews and Ourselves

As you look back over this march of Israel from the sea to Sinai, what could you list as the benefits to the Hebrews from it? What was the primary lesson they had learned in each one of these critical tests of faith? How were they better prepared for the covenant to be made at Sinai than they had been while in Egypt? God had taken the Hebrews out of Egypt—to what extent had he taken Egypt out of the Hebrews?

It is one thing to meditate on the Israelites. It is another, and more personally profitable, to meditate upon ourselves in the light of what we have read here. These months of wilderness preparation of the *bene-ysrael* have long been looked upon as an analogy to the Christian's pilgrimage through life. That which happened to the Hebrews as a group happens to us as individual Christians. *What, then does this experience of theirs have to say to us?* Think through such questions as the following, and come up with your own answers.

(1) Is it possible for us to sustain always the "spiritual glow" with which we started out upon the Christian life? Does it sometimes seem easier to go back to the "flesh pots," the old way of life we once had?

(2) What means does God use to make bitter experiences sweet? Do you find any suggestion in 15:25 of Calvary's "tree"? Have the "statute and ordinance" of Marah ever been revoked? Does this mean that obedient Christians are spared sicknesses?

(3) Is it wrong for Christians "at Elim" (15:27) to rejoice that "the lines have fallen unto us in pleasant places"?

(4) What does the manna have to say to us regarding our day by day dependence upon God? Is this thought still applicable? Do we rightly pray, "Give us this day our daily bread"? Who should be included in "us"? How does the gift of the quails underscore the promise of Philippians 4:19? Which word in that verse would you underline?

(5) Do we, like the Israelites at Rephidim, tend to forget past mercies that should lead to trust and rebel against God when times are rough? Why so?

(6) Is it right to fight against the onslaught of evil? Is there any place for the Christian to be neutral in the conflict of God with the gods of this world? Are you now dodging such a struggle?

(7) How may we hope to conquer in our daily warfare with the enemies of God? by our strength alone? by prayer alone? It was said of "Stonewall" Jackson that "he prayed as if everything depended upon God and fought as if everything depended upon Jackson." Is that a proper strategy for our Christian warfare?

(8) In these episodes, and throughout Exodus, Israel is pictured in God's eyes not as a cluster of individuals, but as one people, a unity. Moses shared this sense of oneness—see 32:30–32. What light does this Old Testament concept throw on the nature of the New Testament church?

The New Testament Usage of This Wilderness Journey

Two incidents in this section are used in the New Testament for definite Christian teaching—the gifts of manna and of water from the rock at Rephidim.

Our Lord made use of the account of the supplying with

manna to interpret his own ministry after the feeding of the five
thousand. *Read through this teaching in John 6:22–59, and note
pp. 282–283 in the third section of this text.*

The Apostle Paul, inspired by the Holy Spirit, lays hold of the
account of Israel's sustenance at Rephidim and declares "the rock
was Christ." What does he mean by this? What does he mean by
"the rock that followed them"? See 1 Corinthians 10:4.

Jethro's Wise Counsel, 18:1–27

We are anticipating a bit when we come to Jethro's visit to
Moses in chapter 18, for as the fifth verse indicates he came to
the camp of Israel after their arrival at Sinai. Yet because of its
place in the record, we consider it here.

We see the picture of a happy family reunion in the opening
paragraph. Moses relates to Jethro the saga of their escape from
Egypt and the trials of the journey so compellingly that Jethro is
moved to express his reverence and respect for Yahweh and his
grace. Then in his capacity as a priest of God he offers a sacrifice
of thanksgiving in the presence of the elders of Israel. To refresh
your mind about Jethro, look back at what we learned of him in
2:18–20, 3:1, and 4:18.

Jethro also made a real contribution to the welfare of Moses
and his people. Observing how Moses was everburdened with his
duties of serving as a judge, he made some practical and helpful
suggestions. What were they? Do you agree that they were wise
ones? Moses evidently did, and he shows his own largeness of
heart in his willingness to accept constructive criticism, a trait
which all too few of us have. Moses gives evidence too of his being
a wise administrator. He not only is ready to accept sound advice
and act upon it, but is willing to distribute responsibility and to let
the people choose their own lesser leaders (see Deut. 1:13). Note
the splendid qualifications laid down in verse 21 for the judges who
were to be elected.

What New Testament ideals for church officers do you find
which seem to reinforce and adopt the qualifications for these
early judges of Israel? See 1 Timothy 3:1–7, Titus 1:5–9, and Acts
6:3. According to the pattern laid down in 18:21, would *you*
qualify for a place of leadership among your people?

REVELATION

The Offer of Grace
in the Covenant at Sinai

At last the weary marchers reach their first real destination. At last the promise of Yahweh to Moses at the burning bush is fulfilled, and the delivered slaves are able to worship God at that same mountain where their leader had received his divine commission. Read Exodus 3:12.

It has taken them two months to make the toilsome journey of one hundred and fifty miles from Egypt to Sinai, for they had stopped often, sometimes for long halts. But here they were, and here they would remain for eleven months (see Num. 10:11–12). And these eleven months were to be of the utmost importance to them, for in this time a company of ex-slaves and their adherents would be welded into a nation under God, a theocracy, and launched upon their supreme mission in life as God's Chosen People. It is of particular value to us in our study of this book that we should master this section of it.

The Dramatic Setting

The "Wilderness of Sinai," the site of their prolonged encampment, is generally identified with the modern plain of Er-Rahah, which, together with its adjacent wadies (ravines through which a stream flows in the rainy season), is a suitable and ample camping ground for the host of Israel. Approximately two miles long by a half mile wide, it is surrounded by precipitous mountain ranges of black and yellow granite. Mt. Sinai itself is a great mountain mass two miles long, running northwest to southeast above the plain. Of the two peaks at either end, Jebel Musa, altitude 7,363 feet, is the traditional Sinai. It is at the base of this that one may find today in the Wadi ed-Deir the impressive fortress-like monastery of St. Catherine, founded A.D. 527. The whole area has been described as one of the most awe-inspiring regions on earth; as such it forms a perfect backdrop for the stupendous happenings which took place there in the history of God's people.

The Importance of the Event

This section of Exodus, 19—24, has been regarded by many as the pivotal point of the whole book. Reference to the suggested outline on pages 18–19 reveals the strategic nature of it. Whenever the book is divided into three parts, this section forms the central portion of it, the hinge upon which the whole book turns. All that precedes this section is preparatory to it; all that follows proceeds from it. It is the covenant section. In it we see the covenant proposed, 19:1–8; the covenant prepared, 19:9–25; the covenant proclaimed, 20—23; and the covenant accepted, 24. It is this covenant made between God and the people that forms the basis of the Old Testament relationship between God and man. It is this covenant which, when fulfilled in Christ, became changed into the new covenant, which is the basis of the Christian gospel of the New Testament. Thus these two main divisions of the Scriptures could more properly be referred to as the Old Covenant and the New Covenant. It is this covenant which is the background of our understanding of the Covenant Life Curriculum.

What Is This Covenant?

There is much in the Bible about covenants. Essentially a covenant is a pact or agreement between two parties which implies mutual understanding and obligations. Today we refer to such ordinarily as a contract.

There are two types of covenants mentioned in the Bible. The familiar one we might call bilateral. It is an agreement made between equals, such as between Isaac and Abimelech (Gen. 26: 31), between Jacob and Laban (Gen. 31:44–54), between David and Jonathan (1 Sam. 18:3), or between Asa and Benhadad (1 Kings 15:19). Then there is what might be called the unilateral or royal covenant, such as that between King David and the northern tribes (2 Sam. 5:3), which is offered by the greater to the lesser and is expressive of kingly rule and rightful authority. The covenant at Sinai is of this latter type. God alone initiated it and he alone stipulated the terms to which the people would be asked to agree.

This covenant, furthermore, was an act of God's free grace. It was an expression of his unmerited favor to a people who had done nothing to deserve it. God had made promises to the patriarchs conditioned upon their faith, and they had accepted by faith. The heart of God's covenant with Abraham was that through him and his seed the world would be blessed, though there were two other promises, that he would have a son and numerous seed, and that he would be given a land. "And he [Abraham] believed the LORD; and he reckoned it to him as righteousness" (Gen. 15:6). He died with only one phase of that covenant promise fulfilled; he had a son Isaac.

This covenant of grace with Abraham had been renewed through Isaac and Jacob, and now, in an altered form, it is being extended to the many children of Jacob, the ex-slaves of Egypt. God offers them the opportunity of entering this new covenant, an agreement which springs only from his love as it has been revealed by his deliverance and preservation of them from Egypt to Sinai. This is the mighty act of God's election in the Old Testament. Of the peoples on earth, all of whom rightly were Yahweh's own (see 19:5), he chose the Israelites to be his special people, and now he offers to them this royal covenant upon condition of their willingness to accept it and obey its provisions. Read Deuteronomy 7:6–15; this is the clearest possible statement of the undeserved election of the *bene-ysrael* by the sheer love and grace of God.

Here the covenant faith of Israel stands in utter contrast to the religion of Egypt and to all human efforts to win God's favor. Paintings on Egyptian tombs repeatedly boast the good deeds of those buried there, done in the hope of meriting reward in a future life. The covenant under Moses was exactly the reverse. It was God who won man, reaching down to rescue the unworthy, and the scene of God's action was the very real world of the present, not just some remote future.

The Covenant Proposed, 19:1-8

When the people had arrived at this spacious and awe-inspiring camping place and had set up their tents in the plain before the mountain, Moses was called up to hear the proposal of God's covenant (19:1-6).

God made it abundantly clear that the basis of his proffered covenant lay only in his grace toward them. They had done nothing to deserve his favor. It was all of God. He based his claim only on the fact that he had brought them forth from their bondage and had borne them along as though on eagles' wings to this hallowed place. It was God who had saved them from their misery as slaves; they could never have merited their rescue. But as an expression of their gratitude for all that God had done, he would expect them to be his people and keep this covenant. *And what would be the result for them, the party of the second part? There are three provisions in verses 5-6. List them for yourself, now. What did you discover that God would do, provided they would obey his terms? Let us take them up one by one.*

(1) ". . . you shall be my own possession among all peoples; for all the earth is mine" . . . (verse 5). What a wonderful assurance of the prestige and place of this new nation! From all people on earth to be singled out and chosen! There could be no greater distinction. How better could he have described Israel's close and unique position with God? The closeness of that relationship is the closeness of husband and wife. He would be the husband of Israel, and she would be his faithful wife. It was this figure of speech which the prophets later laid hold upon to denounce their country's unfaithfulness in going after other gods. But this election—this marriage—was not just a privilege, it carried real responsibility.

(2) ". . . and you shall be to me a kingdom of priests . . ." (verse 6a). They would inherit the priests' responsibility. And what was that? To serve as the mediator between God and men, to transmit the knowledge and blessing of God to others, to be the

instruments of service for God in the world. This was the reason
for their being God's own, to be the means of passing on to others
the knowledge of God's mercy and love. And the Jews have been
that, have they not? *Taking Jesus' word to the woman of Sychar
as a starter (see John 4:22), how many of the spiritual blessings
that we now enjoy can you list as having come to us from the Jews?
Take time to do this.*

The full reach of this covenant blessing was not attained in
Old Testament days; Peter applies the fulfillment of it to the Christian church in 1 Peter 2:9–10. Through our faithfulness today in
witnessing, the world-wide blessing promised in the covenant with
Abraham will be more completely realized, and we will success-
fully fulfill our priestly function of being the channels of God's
universal blessing to all men for whom Christ died.

(3) ". . . you shall be . . . a holy nation" (verse 6*b*). This is
the third provision of the covenant promise. Israel was selected to
be a people set apart, separated, consecrated to God; in a unique
sense to be the depository of God's Word, the vehicle of his plan
of salvation, the people from whom the Savior would come to bless
the world. It would necessitate Israel's being separated from the
practices of a pagan world and nurtured through generation after
generation in the faith of God, so that they might preserve the
faith and produce the literature that would blossom into the
kerygma, the proclamation of the good news of the Messiah, the
Savior of the world. That they did not steadfastly do this, but became contaminated by their pagan neighbors, ingrown, self-
righteous, and unworthy, is a matter of record; and their function
as the people to proclaim the blessing has passed on to the Christian church.

Such were the provisions of the covenant which Moses was instructed to offer to the people. But before they were ready to hear
and act upon it, the way had to be prepared.

The People Prepared, 19:9–25

Read these verses over and over again until you can visualize
the scene. Yahweh did not spring this covenant upon them un-

expectedly. The way was well-prepared. Day after day the freedom marchers had trudged through those wild and tumbled mountains; under huge cliffs, over rugged passes, through rocky defiles they had made their slow and painful way; and all the while the feeling grew that they were being led farther and farther into this strange, forbidding area for some great purpose. And now as they camped in the plain Er-Raha and beheld the majestic mass of Sinai rising up before them, they realized that surely here they would have some new and wonderful experience. Nor were they long kept in doubt. Moses, their commander, was summoned up into the mountain, to return with God's amazing offer of grace.

Then the specific instructions were given to ready them to hear the voice of Yahweh upon the mountain. They were to have three days of intensive preparation. Their clothes were to be scrubbed, and they themselves were to be ceremonially pure (see verse 15). The mountain was made off-limits, not even to be touched by man or beast. On the third day they were to draw near to the boundary lines and watch and wait, look and listen. With what trepidation and expectancy must they have prepared for God's revelation!

Finally the day came, and the great mountain was covered with smoke; fire flashed upon its summit; the mighty mass of it quaked; thunders rolled; and then the sound of the trumpet was heard announcing the Divine Presence. Once again Moses went up at the behest of God. They saw no form of God himself, no likeness of man or animal or bird, such as they had so often associated with the gods of Egypt. They saw no one; they only heard the voice. The people were overwhelmed with it all, and in trembling awe they withdrew from the Presence as far as they could. Read Deuteronomy 5:22–27 for another description of this climactic event.

What was the meaning of this graphic scene? Was it simply to make a grand display of God's power? Why all these fearsome and spectacular accompaniments of God's revelation? Did they have a deeper meaning?

Was it not to impress upon them the tremendous truth of God's unutterable, unapproachable holiness, and their own exceeding sinfulness and unworthiness to have any fellowship with God? How better could Yahweh have taught them this fundamental lesson? Surely we do need it reaffirmed in our sophisticated, blasé age. We have so largely lost our sense of awe at anything; a true reverence for Almighty God himself has been eclipsed on the one hand by the glib and saccharine familiarity with the Divine Being expressed by certain pious groups and individuals, and on the other hand vitiated by the disgusting flippancy of the poems and records of certain beatniks of our time.

The Covenant Proclaimed, 20:1—23:33

Chapters 20—23 contain the actual terms of the Book of the Covenant. These covenant laws are divided into the greater law, the Ten Commandments of chapter 20, and the lesser law, the ordinances of chapters 21—23.

The twentieth chapter is in some respects the greatest chapter in the Old Testament. One can hardly overemphasize the importance and relevance of the Ten Commandments to our day. Therefore we will take them as the subject of our next chapter of this study guide and omit any discussion of them here.

While the Ten Commandments comprise the highest moral code of ancient times, the many ordinances which follow them form a civil law code based upon the moral and spiritual principles of the greater law. Naturally they applied chiefly to a people devoted to agriculture and animal husbandry. Although the Israelites were not yet settled to this way of life, they soon would be, and these ordinances were to guide them then. Differing from the Decalogue, they are not all timeless and universal. In fact The Westminster Confession of Faith (XXI:IV) teaches that these judicial laws ". . . expired together with the state of that people, not obliging any other, now, further than the general equity thereof may require."

There are codes of law that precede these that are found in the Book of the Covenant. Notable among such are the Sumerian Code of Ur (about 2050 B.C.), the Akkadian Code of Eshnunna (the nineteenth century, B.C.), the Sumerian Code of Isin, and the Code of Hammurabi of Babylon (both around 1700 B.C.). By and large, though there are some close similarities, the ordinances of Moses

mark an advance over the codes of other nations of that and preceding eras. Even so, there are some laws that seem to us to be
very severe, and others that seem quite trivial, not to say inex-
plicable.

They were designed not to change the existing framework of
society, but to better life within it. Though there were laws to protect slaves, for instance, there was no opposition to slavery as
such. There were laws safeguarding the rights of persons, as in
21:1–32, and the rights of property, as in 21:33—22:15; miscellaneous rules about the daily life of the people; the stipulation of
the three annual feasts; and a word of encouragement about their
secure future in the land of promise, 23:23–33. Some of these we
find to be interesting and helpful, others retain no lasting value
with the passing of time and the changing nature of life.

The Covenant Accepted, 24:1–18

A covenant to be valid must be ratified. It must be participated
in by both parties. It must be accepted by those to whom it is offered if it is to be binding. God's part in this Sinaitic covenant has
been seen in his promises extended as an act of grace, in 19:5–6.
The code of law by which his people were to live in faithful response to his promises is revealed in the greater and lesser law of
chapters 20—23. These were written in a book prepared by
Moses. The people then formally accepted the covenant, promised
their full obedience to God's words, ceremonially demonstrating
their sincere intent to keep this covenant. After this the traditional
fellowship feast was held by their representatives, the elders, in
the presence of God.

Consider now the steps in this process, 24:1–8.

(1) The Declaration of Acceptance, 24:1–3. ". . . and all the
people answered with one voice, and said, 'All the words which
the LORD has spoken we will do' " (verse 3). Thus they were committed as a people to the obedience which the covenant required.

(2) The Sacrifice, 24:4–5. The promise was followed by the
sacrifice. The altar symbolized the presence of Yahweh and the

twelve pillars represented the twelve tribes of Israel, the two parties to the covenant. Then the young men offered the burnt offering and peace offering, as there was no priesthood as yet. Why was a sacrifice necessary as the first phase of this ceremony? Read Hebrews 9:22 for the answer. The shedding of blood signifies the putting away of sin. If the people were to enter into this intimate fellowship with God sin must be put away, atoned for. This particular offering has been termed by Edersheim "the most important in the whole history of Israel. By this one sacrifice, never renewed, Israel was formally set apart as the people of God; and it lay at the foundation of all the sacrificial worship which followed." [1]

(3) The Interchange of Blood, 24:6–8. The blood was caught in two basins, and Moses sprinkled the contents of one of them upon the altar. Thus God's part was solemnized. Then, turning to the people, Moses read the words of the Book of the Covenant. They in turn with one voice promised obedience thereto. Then Moses took the remaining half of the blood and sprinkled it upon the people, signifying their act of assent. The solemn declaration then was made of the completion of the covenant.

Walter W. Moore, the distinguished former president of Union Seminary in Virginia, used to say that this eighth verse is the climax of the book of Exodus.

For this most solemn covenant God used the method then in vogue for the sealing of the most important contracts, the interchange of blood. A blood covenant, sealed by the intermingling of blood from the veins of the parties involved, was the most sacred and inviolable of all. One is reminded of the fact that many of our sturdy Scottish forefathers signed their names to their Solemn League and Covenant in Greyfriars Churchyard in blood from their own veins rather than in ink.

The Consequence of the Covenant, 24:9–11

When the covenant was thus "wrapped up," as we say, the first immediate consequence was full fellowship with a loving God. Then, right away, Moses and Aaron, with Nadab and Abihu (Aaron's sons, later to be appointed priests, and later still to die for disobedience), and seventy of the elders of Israel, all of whom represented the nation now set apart and consecrated to God, went up into the mount and partook of the sacrificial meal. This meant, of course, the fellowship of acceptance, and its joy was the consciousness of this wonderful fact. Note the contrast here with the situation in 19:12–13, 21–25. *In what sense, do you think, could it be said that "they saw the God of Israel"?*

The Fulfillment of All This in Christ

Before the group discussion of this section of Exodus, make a study yourself of how this climactic event in Israel's history at Sinai is carried forward and fulfilled in Jesus Christ. Fill in the comparisons indicated in the following New Testament passages:

(1) Hebrews 8:6–13 _____

_____

(2) Matthew 26:28, Hebrews 9:19–20, 12:24, 13:20 _____

_____

(3) Hebrews 12:18–24 _____

_____

Read Ephesians 1:4 and Romans 8:29 for a renewed understanding of what God expects of us now as his covenant people. *What progress are we making toward that goal? To what extent are we giving ourselves to the living of the covenant life with God today, so that he may increasingly work his will through us and transform us into the image of his Son?*

CONFRONTATION

The Guidance of Grace
in the Ten Rules for Living

If the covenant section is the heart of Exodus, the first seventeen verses of this twentieth chapter are the heart of the covenant. At every turn of the road we are confronted with the Ten Commandments. They are inevitable, inescapable. These few verses contain the greatest set of rules to guide man's living that can be found anywhere. The lesser laws which follow were but applications in detail of these primary laws.

The Purpose of the Commandments

They were set up as guideposts for the life of the Chosen People. Guideposts are very useful. They serve to orient us by revealing our present position, so keeping us from becoming lost. They also point the way we must walk to reach our destination.

God's purpose in the law was to reveal to his own the kind of life they were to live under the covenant. They were to be a holy people, as God was holy. The law was a revelation of God's own character; these were some of the marks of a holy life. That purpose continues to be applicable to us. These are God's rules for the living of a life that is commensurate with our Christian discipleship.

The purpose of the law in the old covenant was also to give his folk a mirror by which they might see themselves and their failings revealed—and thus sharpen their consciousness and understanding of sin, which is a violation of God's law or a failure to measure up to it. The law does this for us still, especially as it has been interpreted and clarified by the teachings of our Lord in the Sermon on the Mount. "This shall you do, or be," says the law to us; and my conscience tells me, "But I have failed to be or do this!" In its light we recognize our sin and our utter inability to live as we ought and want to do. (See Paul's clear description of the law's effect upon him in this way, in Rom. 7:7–25.)

A major function of the moral law was that it served as a preparation for the coming of the Lord Jesus Christ our Savior. Paul wrote, ". . . the law was our custodian [pedagogue] until Christ came, . . ." (Gal. 3:24; see pp. 392ff). The pedagogue was a servant who led a boy to school, and when the child was safely turned over to the schoolmaster the servant's responsibility ceased. The law was such, says Paul, to bring us to Christ our Master, that we might be justified by faith. It makes plain our need of a Savior and turns us over to him for our salvation through faith in him.

The Permanence of the Commandments

It is often stated that we are living in a different age, so that the Decalogue is no longer applicable to and has no authority over our lives. "We are not under law, but under grace," some say, smugly intimating, "We have nothing to do with the Ten Commandments; they are out-of-date and are only of historical interest to us now." This statement has a pious note and even smacks of the truth, but distorts the facts.

It is true that the basis of Israel's salvation in Old Testament times lay in faith evidenced by keeping the law. See, for instance, Christ's words in reply to the inquiry of the rich young ruler, Mark 10:17–19, and to the lawyer, Luke 10:25–28. Now, since the cross, our hope of eternal life lies in our faith in Jesus Christ who died for us on Calvary and rose again from the dead. See Acts 16:30–31, John 20:31, and 1 John 5:11–13.

But, as a matter of record, the Israelites were charged to keep the law as a result of God's grace which had already freed them from bondage. See Exodus 19:4–5, 20:2. Their salvation was all of grace, as is ours. They were to show their faith by the keeping of the covenant, a covenant summarized in the moral law (and when they failed they were to find forgiveness through their act of repentance in bringing the animal sacrifices which God's Word prescribed). In our age of grace under the New Covenant, we accept with gratitude and faith the salvation effected for us by the Lamb of

God, and we seek to live to his glory the life of discipleship. To this end the Holy Spirit enables us "more and more to live unto righteousness and die unto sin." An understanding of the purpose of the law reveals its permanence. For it still functions for us as it did for the people of Israel, to guide our faithful response.

Furthermore, we see its abiding value as an expression of the character of God. Times change, but God is the same yesterday, today, and forever. The God revealed most fully to us in Christ is also revealed in these rules for a holy life.

> A thing is either right or wrong ultimately because of the nature of God himself. Morals are not relative to what for the moment seems fashionable, or sophisticated, or what the latest theories of psychology propose, or what everybody else is doing. Goodness and integrity and purity are based on the character of the eternal Creator of the universe.[1]

The enduring nature of these commands is seen not only in the unchanging nature of God himself, but also in the fact that essentially man is the same through all the centuries. His environment and his possessions have changed, but they are only on the surface. Basically, human nature is the same as in the day when God thundered from Sinai. As long as human relationships are as they are and have been, these laws of God for man will be applicable and authoritative.

The Ten Commandments are not true and permanent just because they are in the Bible; they are in the Bible because they are true and permanent. They are built into the structure of our moral and spiritual life as surely as are the natural laws into that of the physical universe.

James Russell Lowell sums it up well in his lines:

> In vain we call old notions fudge
> And bend our conscience to our dealing.
> The Ten Commandments will not budge,
> And stealing will continue stealing.

The permanence of the Ten Commandments is seen also in the fact that the principle of every one of them is continued and reinforced in the New Testament, as rules for the living of the Christian life. *Take a sheet of paper now and write out an abbreviated list of the Commandments on one side, and opposite to them the New Testament application of each.* Here are some references to look up and classify. (Warning! Take care; they are not in the same order as the Commandments!) 1 John 3:15, Colossians 3:9, 1 John 5:21, 2 Timothy 2:22 or 1 Corinthians 6:9–10, Acts 14:15 and Matthew 6:33, Ephesians 4:28, Ephesians 6:1–3, Matthew 6:9 and James 5:12, Luke 12:15, Acts 20:7 and 1 Corinthians 16:2. You may want to find others that appeal to you more.

The Phrasing of the Commandments

Most of us have been familiar with the Commandments since our earliest youth. They were among the first portions of the Bible we memorized. How many of us can repeat them from memory now? If not, why not relearn them? If we cannot repeat them in their original form as found in this chapter, can we name them in their shorter form? They were long ago called "The Ten Words." Many believe that they were first written on the tables of stone in abbreviated form, then later amplified. Such a short form might be something like this:

    (1) No other gods before me.
    (2) No worship of images.
    (3) Keep my name inviolate.
    (4) Keep the Sabbath holy.
    (5) Honor your parents.
    (6) Do not kill.
    (7) Do not commit adultery.
    (8) Do not steal.
    (9) Do not bear false witness.
  (10) Do not covet.

If it helps you to put them into rhyme, try storing them in memory in this form:

    Above all else love God alone,
    Bow down to neither wood nor stone.
    God's name refuse to take in vain,
    The Sabbath rest with care maintain.

Respect your parents all your days;
Hold sacred human life always.
Be loyal to your chosen mate;
Steal nothing, neither small nor great.
Report, with truth, your neighbor's deeds;
And rid your mind of selfish greed.

Or, if you prefer, here is another such version:

Thou shalt have no other gods but me,
Before no idol bow the knee;
Take not the name of God in vain,
Nor dare the Sabbath day profane.
Give both thy parents honor due,
Take heed that thou no murder do.
Abstain from words and deeds unclean;
Nor steal, though thou be poor and mean.
Nor make a wilful lie, nor love it;
What is thy neighbor's dare not covet.

The Commandments were first written upon stone. Those tables have long since been lost. How much better that they be written on the tablets of our hearts and fulfilled in our daily life (cf. 2 Cor. 3:3).

The Divisions of the Commandments

The moral law was written first upon the two tables of stone by "the finger of God." This may mean either by supernatural power or by his authority. The expression is an idiom which points to a supernatural source; see Exodus 8:19, and cf. Luke 11:20 and Matthew 12:28. The tables were small enough to be carried by Moses down the long slope of Sinai. Just what was on them we have no way of knowing. On the walls of Jewish synagogues today they are summarized in very few Hebrew words.

Which of these commands were on one table and which on the other we do not know. The division most commonly adopted places the first four, with the "preface," on the first table, and the last six on the second. The first group are drawn from the relationship of God and man; the second are rooted in the relationships of man and man. Some place the fifth word in the first group, making five in

each. The Roman Catholic and Lutheran Churches combine the first
two commandments into one and divide the tenth into two. Our
Lord, with magnificent clarity of insight, summarized the ten into
two—love for God and love for other men—by quoting two verses
of the Old Testament, from Deuteronomy 6:5 and Leviticus 19:18
(see Matt. 22:34–40). He then gave a "new commandment" in
John 13:34–35.

The tables of the law were placed by the Hebrews in their most
sacred spot, within the Ark of the Covenant in the most holy place
of the Tabernacle and, later, of the Temple. With the destruction
of the Temple and the loss of the Ark, these priceless relics disappeared.

The Preface to the Commandments

The preface to a book is always important and it should never
be skipped in our desire to get on with what follows. It gives the
author's reason for writing, and his aim and hope in so doing.

The preface to these great rules for life is found in the simple
but profound statement, "I am the LORD your God, who brought
you out of the land of Egypt, out of the house of bondage." It is
simple, in that it is short, direct, and understandable. It is profound
in its implications. In the study of this preface as in that of all the
Ten Words, we should hold in memory the rule of the Westminster
Assembly of Divines of 1643, spelled out in the first chapter of The
Confession of Faith (I:VI), that they would incorporate nothing in
their Confession which could not be drawn directly from Scripture
or "by good and necessary consequence" be deduced therefrom.

The preface declares who God is and what he has done for his
own. This, as Calvin said, was "to prepare the souls of the people
for obedience."

There are two statements in this preface which bear upon all
that follows: First, God is, and is the sovereign, covenant-keeping
God of Israel; and second, God entered into the life of the people
he had chosen and wholly by his grace delivered them from
bondage.

What proof had the people of the first statement? Had they not
been fascinated witnesses of the mighty conflict between Yahweh
and Pharaoh, in which Yahweh had so clearly demonstrated his

authority over the once proud and disdainful ruler of Egypt? This God who had so triumphed is the Eternal, the everlasting One, who keeps covenant with his own.

Jewish expositors were later to make this the first commandment, requiring belief in the existence of God. (They maintained the Decalogue as ten by combining the first and second on our list.) But it would be better to say that this declaration is the basis of authority on which all others rest.

This living, covenant-keeping God is your Redeemer, your Deliverer! The *bene-ysrael* had just gained their freedom. They knew his providential care along the wilderness way. He had fully demonstrated his love and mercy and grace as well as his sovereign power. What more would they need as a motive for their obedience to the laws he now would reveal? Their obedience was to spring not from fear but from gratitude and love. This was to be fully brought out in Deuteronomy again and again. So it is with our Christian discipleship. See Romans 12:1, 2 Corinthians 5:14 and 1 John 4:19. God is! God loves! God saves! This is the gospel and precedes the law.

The Westminster Larger Catechism, in answering Question 101, "What is the preface to the ten commandments?" cites Exodus 20:2, and, in the language of the seventeenth century, adds, by way of explanation:

> Wherein God manifesteth his sovereignty as being Jehovah, the eternal, immutable, and almighty God; having his being in and of himself, and giving being to all his words and works; and that he is a God in covenant, as with Israel of old, so with all his people; who as he brought them out of their bondage in Egypt, so he delivered us from our spiritual thralldom; and that therefore, we are bound to take him for our God alone, and to keep all his commandments.

C. Ellis Nelson, in the language of the twentieth century, says this:

> The Ten Commandments are different because the first four commandments describe a God who is different from any other god mankind has ever known. Because God is alive, the

Ten Commandments have stayed alive. Because this God loves and works with every generation in a living stream of history, his commandments have shaped history. There is nothing in the history or religion of any ancient people like the first four commandments. The Ten Commandments are first of all about God and secondly about the moral principles he expects us to follow.[2]

Let us then consider these "Ten Words"—the Decalogue—one by one.

The First Commandment, 20:3

This first command prescribes the valid *object* of our worship—the one true God. He is named in the verse preceding, but for his existence no argument is made. Nowhere does the Bible argue the existence of God. It begins with the primary assumption of Genesis 1:1. Nor is this primarily a command to accept monotheism, the doctrine of the existence of one God only. It is rather a directive to observe monolatry, the practice of worshiping one God only, though others might be recognized as existing. The Israelites were acquainted with many gods in the pantheon of Egypt. Here is a clarion call to them to cling to but one God, Yahweh, as their one object of worship.

We may think that this does not therefore apply to us, for the polytheism of that ancient day has long since disappeared. But has it? Would you accept Luther's definition, "Whatever thy heart clings to and relies upon, that is properly thy god"? *Does this open the field to many gods whom we worship today? Write down now as many as you can think of that form the pantheon of Americans today.*

We no longer worship Isis, Moloch, and Baal, the gods of Egypt and Canaan, but they have their successors. We no longer worship as such Mars, the god of war, nor Venus, the goddess of love, nor Bacchus, the god of revelry, but what counterparts do we find so prevalently worshiped in American life today? What about our adoration of certain forms of food or drink? or recreation? or popularity? or making money?

Can we even substitute the Bible, or church, or "churchianity," or ritual for the true worship of God? Do you recall chapter 1 of *The Christian Life* by Waldo Beach?

As you search your own heart, what lesser god are *you* worshiping with your first loyalty and allegiance?

To what extent is this commandment the basis on which all the others rest? Read Deuteronomy 6:5, 13; 10:12, 20. What preeminence did Jesus give to it? See Matthew 22:34–38 and 6:33. Note what our Lord said, "all . . . all . . . all . . . !" How does your life measure up to that high ideal?

The Second Commandment, 20:4–6

The second commandment prescribes the *mode* of the worship of the one true God, that he is to be worshiped directly. This was of vast importance to the Hebrews at Sinai because they had just come from a land filled with images revered as representatives of deity. This word sets forth the spirituality of God and the spiritual nature of the worship which he requires. Our Lord made this truth plain to the woman of Sychar (see John 4:24). Both the Old and New Testaments are constantly opposed to idolatry. The prophets thundered against it. Isaiah poured scorn upon the futility of it. Be sure to read Isaiah 44:9–20. The closing plea of the First Letter of John to Christians is to refrain from idols (1 John 5:21).

The later Jews taught that verse 4 prohibited all cultivation of the imitative arts. Is that a justifiable conclusion? Does this bear on the fact that the Jewish race has not excelled in sculpture and painting? Is this the intent of the command, or is it rather that God must not be worshiped through any representative object?

What bearing then does this command have on the use of crucifixes, images of the saints, rosaries, etc.? Are we guiltless in this matter: is it proper to have a painting of Christ above the pulpit or communion table in the church before all the worshipers? How about on the wall of a child's bedroom? What about the wearing of crosses?

Does the idea of God being "a jealous God" in any sense offend you? Does it refer to Shakespeare's "green-eyed monster," or rather to earnest concern, vigilant and watchful care?

Is it unjust that children should be punished for the sins of parents? Is it not true that sin is contagious? Is it a fact of the human race? Is Shakespeare right in saying, "The evil that men do lives after them" (Julius Caesar, Act III, Line 79)? An old proverb states, "A man is an omnibus in which all his ancestors are seated." Can you think of illustrations of that? Is not the mercy and grace of God far more limitless than his punishment here? The effects of sin persist to the fourth generation, but a thousand generations inherit the good.

The Third Commandment, 20:7

The third commandment goes on to prescribe the *spirit* of our worship, that it be sincere. God's name is to be held in absolute reverence, and our words and conduct must reveal this.

The "name of God" is more than the appellation by which he is called. It includes all by which he reveals himself, every title, attribute, or action. If we would then be covenanters with God we are to use his name and all references to him in a manner true to his character. Any use of God's name which is contrary to or a denial of his character or being is a transgression of this command. Isaiah 48:1 presents an illustration of such an infringement, when men use God's name "not in truth nor right." It is not to be used trivially, for every little cause. The positive corollary of this third word is, as Joy Davidman suggests, "Thou shalt take the name of the Lord thy God in earnest!" [3]

Since the Hebrew word translated "guiltless" means "clean", we find that a test of a person's moral cleanliness is his attitude toward God's name and all it represents. Our Lord held up the ideal for which we pray, "Our Father . . . hallowed by Thy name . . . on earth as it is in heaven." How many of us are guilty of making that petition a mockery?

G. Campbell Morgan wrote that we break this command in three ways today—"by profanity, frivolity, and hypocrisy." [4] Is profanity a mark of intellect or shallowness, of fluency or paucity of vocabulary? Lord Byron once said of a man, "He knew not what to say, so he swore."

Do you tend to believe or disbelieve the person who habitually reinforces his assertions with the use of God's name? What did Jesus say about telling the simple truth? See Matthew 5:33–37. Do our Lord's words here, or the commandment, preclude the use of judicial oaths? What light do Matthew 26:63–64, Exodus 22:10–11, and Hebrews 6:16–17 throw on this question?

To "take" God's name means literally "to bear" or "to carry." How do we bear God's name in our Christian daily life? Is it only a matter of Sunday morning discipleship, denied when we get home or during the week? Is the old Hebrew injunction applicable to us, "Be ye clean, ye that bear the vessels of the Lord" (Isa. 52:11 K.J.V.)?

Morgan writes, "Prayer without practice is blasphemy; praise without adoration violates the third commandment." [5] Do you agree to that? Our Lord evidently did; see Matthew 7:21. Does it shock you then to realize that we professing Christians often do more violence to this law of God than does a thoughtless user of profanity?

The Fourth Commandment, 20:8–11

The fourth commandment prescribes the special *time* of worship—that it be kept inviolate. By a regularly recurring day of worship man is reminded that everyday is to be lived reverently in obedience to God. One day of each week is to be kept holy—separate, different—for the worship of God; the other half of the command is that we are to be diligently at work the remaining six days. These are interrelated. He who will not work is unfit to worship. He who will not worship is unfit to work. By reason of his kinship with the Almighty, man is to be a worker and a worshiper. The original Sabbath to the Hebrew was a day of gladness and delight, a holiday from daily work, and a fulfillment of his own spiritual nature. From it he went back to the turmoil and struggle of toil, remembering that, as Henry Van Dyke put it, "Honest toil is holy service, faithful work is praise and prayer."

This prescribed day commemorated God's own cessation from creation (Exod. 20:11) and his deliverance of his people from bondage (Deut. 5:15).

The change of the Christian Sabbath from the seventh day to the first day of the week dates from our Lord's resurrection on that day, and the immediate observance of it by the early church as their day of worship.

How many older folk who read these lines were brought up to experience a more meaningful use of the Christian Sabbath than they observe today? Why is it that *Christians* do not stand more firmly against the flood tide of Sabbath desecration that marks our time? How is Sunday to be a "holy" day?

The later Jews burdened themselves with some 1521 prohibitions—things they were *not* to do—on the Sabbath. The Puritans took after them in many of their ideals. *But what use did Jesus make of the day? Make a careful study of that, and list his Sabbath activities on one day as recorded in Luke 4:31–39. What positive suggestions do you find there for the Christian's use of Sunday?*

Are we to keep Sunday mornings holy, and care little that the rest of the day and the rest of the week is unholy? Do you have the "early service" type of Christianity? Or is our use of Sunday to help make our whole week holy? Is life to be segmented or wholly sacred to God?

The drift of our times is toward a secularized, pleasurized, paganized holiday on Sunday. What can *you* do to try to stop this drift? If a Christian makes no better use of Sunday than a non-Christian, what happens to our Christian witness? What happens to us?

As you consider your usage of the day, will you subject it to these tests?

(1) Does what I do on Sunday better fit me for the week that follows?

(2) Does it keep someone else from his day of rest?

(3) Does it contribute to my own spiritual development, and that of my family?

(4) Does it help someone else in need of me?

(5) Does it help or hurt my witness in the community?

(6) Does it fulfill my promise in the covenant I have made with God?

Read and ponder Isaiah 58:13–14.

The Fifth Commandment, 20:12

The fifth commandment requires children to give respect to parents, and, by implication, calls upon parents to be worthy of such honor. It has been called "the children's commandment," but it is applicable to all of life, not simply childhood, and it is directed to the parent as well as to the child. Children are to honor their parents by loving obedience, as parents are ordained to be God's representatives to the young. Adults are to honor their parents by respect and care. Parents, by inference here, are to be worthy of love, obedience, and care by their own faithfulness and devotion.

This has been called by Paul "the first commandment with promise" (Eph. 6:2). Its promise is long life. This is applicable to the individual and to the race.

This is the first commandment of the second table of the law—those commandments that relate to our duty to our fellowmen. This second section of the Decalogue deals with man-to-man relationships, the horizontal plane. But it is resultant from and dependent upon the perpendicular, man's relationship to God. Our God-ward allegiance colors and determines our man-ward responsibilities and actions. Our Lord summed them up in his incisive words, "You shall love the LORD . . . and your neighbor as yourself." The fifth commandment is the first of these because on the solidarity and sanctity of home life rests all our hope of a better society.

How did Jesus fulfill the provisions of this command? Consider his attitude toward Mary and Joseph in the few instances of record of our Lord's home life in Luke 2. What was the import of his words in Matthew 12:50? How did he show loving care for his mother at the end? See John 19:26–27.

Study the comprehensive descriptions of Christian home life and responsibilities in the New Testament; see Ephesians 5:22—6:4 and Colossians 3:18—4:1.

Is it ever justifiable to refuse to obey your parents? What is the implication in the words "in the Lord" in Ephesians 6:1?

Does our corporate social conscience revealed in Social Security laws, care for the aged, and other secular provisions for old people, relieve Christians of their individual response to this command? Do such governmental programs reflect an attempt as a nation to obey this commandment?

To what extent does this command include our respect for and obedience to rightful civil authority? Is all civil authority such that it can be obeyed " in the Lord"?

The Sixth Commandment, 20:13

With this commandment, concerning the sanctity of human life, the Decalogue becomes a series of terse prohibitions that forbid injury to our neighbor in deed—by depriving him of life, disrespecting his person, or taking his property; in word—by destroying his reputation; and in thought—by desiring what is his.

"You shall not kill" is regarded by many scholars to mean "You shall do no murder." Though there is a difference, either has wide implications. It is of special relevance to our day.

The homicide rate in this country is the highest of any civilized nation. More people are murdered in almost any large American city per year than in all England, Ireland, Scotland, and Wales. The frightful killing on our highways goes up year by year, and now accounts for almost as many deaths yearly as there were American soldiers killed in battle during all of World War I. Deaths from motor vehicle accidents in our country during only the last twenty years far exceed the total number of American battle deaths in all our wars, from the Revolution to Vietnam. Suicides are all too frequent. "Brush fire wars" go on and on. In one crisis after another the world trembles at the very real possibility of another general war, which could be a holocaust of international destruction. And, of course, there are other ways of killing not so obvious as these.

What is the Christian's response to this command? Is it simply to say blandly, "Well, that lets *me* out—I never killed anyone, nor do I intend to"?

What responsibility does the Christian have as a member of a society that produces a man who in cold blood assassinates our president? Or, for that matter, for the society that sends police dogs on praying Negroes, or creates conditions which prompt lawless Negroes to riot and destroy and kill officers of the law? What is it in this so-called Christian land that stimulates the high homicide rate we have?

How did our Lord strengthen, elevate, and sharpen this sixth commandment? Study Matthew 5:21–22, 38–39, 43–44; 15:19; 26:52; and John 18:36. Consider John's statement in 1 John 3:15, and Paul's in Ephesians 4:26 and Romans 12:19–21. *Is it ever right to be angry? Our Lord was, several times. But what is the dif-*

ference between his anger and what ours all too often is? What do you believe should be the Christian's conviction about capital punishment? What about war—is it ever justifiable? why or why not? Moses and his people seem never to have interpreted this command to apply to war or to capital punishment. In the light of Christ's teachings in the New Testament are we to take a different view? To what extent?

Is drunken driving or reckless driving a transgression of this command? Is the suicide of a sane person? What about killing ourselves by degrees through self-indulgence or lack of care?

What is the application of this command to euthanasia or "mercy killing"? What other areas does "reverence for human life" cover?

The Seventh Commandment, 20:14

The seventh commandment strikes directly at one of the paramount problems of our time, sexual immorality. It is a call for purity of life and for the upholding of the sanctity of the marriage relationship. As over against the sexual demoralization of our day this seventh word stands like a beacon warning of destruction. Surely The Westminster Shorter Catechism is correct in stating, "The seventh commandment requireth the preservation of our own and our neighbor's chastity, in heart, speech, and behavior. (It) . . . forbideth all unchaste thoughts, words, and actions." The Heidelberg Catechism (Question 108) is explicit about this when it states that the seventh commandment teaches us "that all unchastity is condemned by God, and that we should therefore detest it from the heart, and live chaste and disciplined lives, whether in holy wedlock or in single life." [6]

Here again our Lord Jesus penetrates to the causal root of the problem and lifts the prohibition of this command from the overt act to the lustful thought. Meditate on Matthew 5:27–32 and consider your own guilt; let that lead to confession and forgiveness. What was our Lord's attitude toward a caught-in-the-act transgressor? See John 8:2–11.

What should be the Christian's standard of moral purity in these days of general laxity, of sexual promiscuity among youth, college students, and married couples, of "the new morality," "freedom," *and "the pill"?* What can the Christian do toward overcoming this evil at its source: the flood of immoral movies and plays and of impure books and pornographic magazines that have become generally "acceptable," at least to the extent of being flaunted in public. Or are these the *source* of this evil? If they are not, what is?

If sexual unchastity is wrong, why is it wrong? If it should become the general practice of the land what would be the ultimate result in our society? How can a Christian keep clean today? How can the church measure up in this time of need in the education of its own young people for purity of life and the sanctity of marriage?

Is it true to say that America's place of leadership in the world is threatened today by our widespread violation of the seventh commandment? To what extent is the stability of our nation founded upon a firm and loyal home life?

What is the biblical view of marriage? Among other passages, look up Genesis 2:18–24, Ephesians 5:22–23, 31. The Mosaic law of divorce is found in Deuteronomy 24:1–4. How did Christ revise this law? See Matthew 19:3–9. What is your church's official position on marriage and divorce?

The Eighth Commandment, 20:15

The eighth commandment is couched in words that we all understand. "You shall not steal" means to us as it plainly did to the Hebrews of Moses' day, "You shall not take what belongs to the other fellow." In its positive form it declares, "Be honest!"

The Bible teaches as the first principle of Christian stewardship that all property ultimately belongs to God who created it. If we would be in right relationship to God this must be recognized. But man in relationship to man can claim to own property which is to be held inviolate by his neighbor. This is implicit in this commandment.

To steal is to take by stealth or force or cleverness that which rightly belongs to someone else. This can be done by positive acquisition or by withholding what lawfully is another's. This has many ramifications and the more we think about it the more we realize that old Diogenes was probably right and that a scrupulously honest man is hard to find.

We all recognize the violation of this command in armed robbery or purse snatching, or in appropriating property from stores or hotels or other people, which we try to camouflage sometimes as "souvenir hunting." We recognize what is "plain" stealing, but we are not so sure what to an enlightened conscience constitutes "fancy" stealing.

In certain other countries dishonesty is the norm; it is expected and guarded against. In America in past years honesty was the norm and dishonesty the unexpected, but we are fast reversing this. Aside from the realm of professional crime, we find dishonesty in every area of our life. Someone has computed, I know not how, that stealing in the United States costs over ten billion dollars per year. A sum that vast is beyond our comprehension. Our question is, do we contribute to that enormous loss ourselves?

Make a list of all the common, everyday forms of stealing. Let's start with cheating in school, on papers, tests, and exams; in business with false weights and measures, swindling, racketeering, and fraudulent advertising; in personal life, in failing to pay one's bills, picking up "souvenirs" here and there, and on and on.

Make another list of "fancy" stealing. Such things could be included as rigging contracts, bribing officials, padding expense accounts, cleverly evading income taxes, paying inadequate wages, rendering inadequate service, etc., etc.

What do you condemn at once? What do you condone? What, God forbid, do you participate in? Be honest with yourself!

How does this command apply to both capital and labor? James 5:1–6 may indeed apply to employers, but does not 2 Thessalonians 3:10–12 and Ephesians 6:5–8 apply to employees? A fair wage should receive fair work.

Is gambling a violation of this commandment? Does the fact that it may be the mutual agreement of two parties nullify the wrong involved? It was a bitter man who remarked that "the great American dream is getting something for nothing." Is not this the philosophy at the heart of stealing? Is it right for a Christian to match pennies or nickels and wrong for him to spend great sums on gambling devices? Can you name any real social benefits from gambling? What are some of the inevitable evils accompanying it?

What does the New Testament have to say about this? Study

Ephesians 4:28. It outlines the only three ways by which we can acquire property. What are they? The eighth commandment recognizes and approves two and condemns the third. The line is clearly drawn. Property which is not acquired by honest labor or gift is stolen property.

The New Testament goes further. We are not to be content as Christians with merely refraining from plain or fancy stealing; we must see that the property we have rightly acquired is used for the relief of the needs of others. See Philippians 2:4; Romans 12:8, 13; Galatians 6:2; Ephesians 4:28.

The Ninth Commandment, 20:16

The ninth commandment leaves the realm of deeds and passes into that of words. It recognizes that the power of words is incalculable.

> Boys flying kites haul in their white winged birds,
> But you cannot do that when you're flying words . . .
> Thoughts unexpressed may sometimes fall back dead;
> But God himself can't kill them when they're said.

It demands absolute sincerity of speech of all who would be in right relationship to God and man. It seeks to guard reputation against the sabotage of evil speech.

Originally this commandment applied directly to false testimony in a court of law—perjury. The violation of it as such was actually what sent our Lord Jesus Christ to his death. Yet in its wider application as a prohibition against lying and insincerity of speech, this directive is said to be the one which we break more often and worry about less than any other. "A lie," defined Augustine, "is a voluntary speaking of an untruth with an intention to deceive." It is a common failing ranging all the way from "white lies," joking lies, and social lies to malicious and malevolent lies. A lie does not have to be spoken or written. One can lie by a gesture or even by silence.

All right-thinking folk will condemn perjury. It may give a guilty criminal freedom from his just desserts, or it may bring an innocent man conviction, imprisonment, and even death. Slander is a raw violation of this commandment. It is a lie maliciously invented and communicated which may cause untold harm. Tale-bearing is the repeating of a story without effort to determine its veracity. Gossip may start as innocent chatter, but it often leads on to slander. Innuendo may be a truth so conveyed that it creates a false impression, such as the entry in the ship's log by a mate angry with his skipper: "The Captain is sober today!" The imputation of a false motive is another variety of this evil: "He knows which side his bread is buttered on!" A simple question may deliberately distort the truth; see Job 1:9. Flattery is another form, as in Psalm 55:21. Constant fault finding, judging without investigation, passing on half truths as though they were whole, are all infractions of this command, and all these transgressions do irreparable harm to another's good name. And, in the oft-quoted words of the Bard of Avon,

> He who filches from me my good name
> Robs me of that which not enriches him
> And makes me poor indeed.

What would you say of such generalities as "All Jews are out to make money," or "All teen-agers are reckless drivers"?

Are nations and people as well as individuals given to this sin? What of the deliberate attempts of the Russian and Red Chinese press and radio to create false impressions of America, and vice versa?

The New Testament has much to say to the Christian regarding this commandment. What does James tell us in the third chapter of his letter of the danger of loose speech? What insight does Paul express in Ephesians 4:15, 25, 32? Or Peter in 2 Peter 2:1–3? Or Jude in verses 14–16.

What does our Lord pointedly have to say to his disciples on this evil? See Matthew 7:1–5 and 12:34–37.

Do you think the following lines comprise the Christian's proper way of dealing with this question? Do they fulfill Paul's counsel to "speak the truth in love"?

> If you are tempted to reveal
> A tale someone to you has told
> About another, make it pass
> Before you speak, three gates of gold,

Three narrow gates: First, 'Is it true?'
Then 'Is it needful?' In your mind
Give truthful answer, and the next
Is last and narrowest, 'Is it kind?'
And if to reach your lips at last
It passes through these gateways three,
Then you may tell, nor ever fear
What the results of speech may be.

Martin Luther put a positive turn to the ninth commandment
when he said, "We should fear and love God that we may not de-
ceitfully deny, betray, nor defame our neighbor; but defend him,
speak well of him, and put the best construction on everything."
Love is the answer—1 Corinthians 13:7. In short, you shall love
your neighbor as yourself.

The Tenth Commandment, 20:17

This last commandment of the Decalogue is in a sense the summary and key of them all. If we could keep this one we would be
able to keep all, for the violation of this one lies at the heart of the
transgression of them all. It reaches into the realm of the mind. It
can be broken in secret. It is warning against sin in the inner life.

It is a command much misunderstood because the word "covet"
has two connotations. The word itself means to desire eagerly, "to
set the heart on," "to long for." There is nothing wrong with eager
desire in itself, provided it is directed toward the right things. The
psalmist certainly was expressing a laudatory desire when he sang,
"As the hart longs for flowing streams, so longs my soul for thee,
O God!" (42:1.) To covet the best fulfillment of one's life—a good
wife or husband, a happy home, a successful business, a worthy
career—is to desire lawfully, and it even lends power to our efforts
to attain. Paul put it, ". . . covet earnestly the best gifts" (1 Cor.
12:31, K.J.V.). Our Lord said, "Blessed are those who hunger and
thirst for righteousness, . . ." (Matt. 5:6). This is the right use of
coveting.

The prophet Habakkuk states, "Woe to him that coveteth an
evil covetousness . . ." (2:9, K.J.V.). That is different! It is this wrong

kind of eager desire that is prohibited in this tenth word. We are not to covet what we may not lawfully have—our neighbor's spouse, his home, his cook, his seniority, his cars, his customers (or his church members!), his status in the community, his social leadership, his affluence, his health, or *anything that is our neighbor's*. They are "verboten." They are off-limits. To desire them is wrong.

Covetousness of this kind not only is in itself sinful but leads to all manner of other evils. It lies at the basis of the violation of the whole law. *Review carefully the Ten Commandments in the light of this statement, and determine just how the wrong kind of covetousness causes the breaking of each one of them.* Take time for this, as it is a fruitful study. See if you can illustrate it from biblical or other incidents (such as David's coveting of his neighbor's wife, Bathsheba, leading him to violate one commandment after another).

When Hernando Cortez launched into the conquest of Mexico, he said to the Aztecs, "We have a disease of the heart that only gold can cure." What *is* the only cure for covetousness? History has proven that it is certainly not more gold.

To desire possessions is not in itself evil. But what is the peril that our Lord pointed out so clearly and illustrated so forcefully in Luke 12:13–34? What was his final conclusion as to the cure for covetousness and the proper orientation of life? See Luke 12:31.

We see this command transgressed right in the company of Christ's disciples, and again our Lord had to point the way to overcome it. What was it? See Matthew 20:20–28 and Mark 9:33–35.

The writers of the New Testament have much to say about evil desire. With what does Paul equate it? See Ephesians 5:5. What does James say of its effect on society? See James 5:1–6. What are Peter's plain words about this "evil eye"? See 2 Peter 2:14. How does John declare it to be the opposite of a holy life? See 1 John 2:17. Hebrews places covetousness and contentment in opposition in 13:5–6. How was Paul able to reach this goal of contentment? See Philippians 4:11–13.

What is the final answer, the ultimate solution, for the keeping of this law through the help of our Lord Jesus Christ? See John 13:34–35, 14:21 and Philippians 4:8, 11–13.

CONSECRATION

The Tabernacle,
the Symbol of the Presence

In "Jefferson's Bible" the Gospel of Matthew closes with the words "and he rolled a great stone to the door of the sepulchre and departed." In equally dolorous and inconclusive fashion some books on Exodus close with the giving of the law to the Israelites at Sinai. Thus a bit of space is saved, but at what loss! How hopeless would be the case of the covenant people, then and now, if the story ended there!

The law is a guide to God's will, but there is in it no indication of his sustaining presence. The law leaves us hopeless, exposed in our sin, unless it points to and urges us on to the One who alone can enable us to keep it, in whom we find refuge from its condemnation. It is the last act of the drama of Exodus that forms the keystone of the arch. It gives the final answer. It leads us on into the heart of God.

Furthermore, we see the importance of the Tabernacle in the sheer fact of the space accorded it. One third of Exodus, all of Leviticus, and most of Numbers is taken up with the Tabernacle, its priests, and its ritual.

Its importance is recognized in that it was "the most splendid portable structure ever made, not only as the first building erected by divine command for divine worship; but also and chiefly, as a primitive embodiment of the great truths of redemption."[1] Let us then not neglect it, or overlook it, as if it were merely of interest to an antiquarian or an architect.

Three words might be used to sum up this last third of Exodus— Direction, Rejection, Erection. Or we might adopt this terminology —Consecration commanded, Consecration desecrated, Consecration consummated. The first and last points are closely connected, being an order and its fulfillment. The second one represents an historical interlude which is of real significance to the other two.

The Direction for the Establishment of the Tabernacle and Its Ministry, 25:1—31:18.

Many of us are reasonably familiar with the Tabernacle of the covenant people, but any serious study of this section of Exodus is likely to produce some surprises. One is the amount of space given to detailed directions for its construction, so much that it may at first confuse us. Others are its small size, the richness of its material, and the unusual purpose for which it was erected. And, finally, we are surprised at its wealth of symbolism.

The Purpose of the Tabernacle

The purpose of this "Tent of Meeting" was to provide a place where God's presence would symbolically dwell among his people, and a place to which believers might come to worship through the mediation of their representatives, the priests; see 25:8, 22 and 29:42–46. God's presence prior to this had been visibly represented on the top of Sinai—apart, distant, unapproachable. Now in their newly established God-and-man relationship, when in gratitude and obedience the people had accepted his covenant based on his grace and mercy, Yahweh would dwell among his people to be worshiped and to make available to them forgiveness and guidance.

The Plan of the Tabernacle

The plan for the Tabernacle, its furnishings and its ministry, was entirely God-given; see 25:9, 40; 26:30; 27:8.

It was a comparatively small, portable, rectangular structure—smaller than most of our churches today. The dimensions were only 30 cubits by 10 cubits. Taking the usual standard for a cubit, 18 inches, that means 45 feet by 15 feet, and 15 feet high. Composed of a wooden framework covered over with cloth and skins, it was divided into two rooms. The first, the outer, was called the Holy Place and was 30 feet by 15 feet. The inner room, the Holy of Holies, separated from the first by a heavy veil, was a cube measuring 15

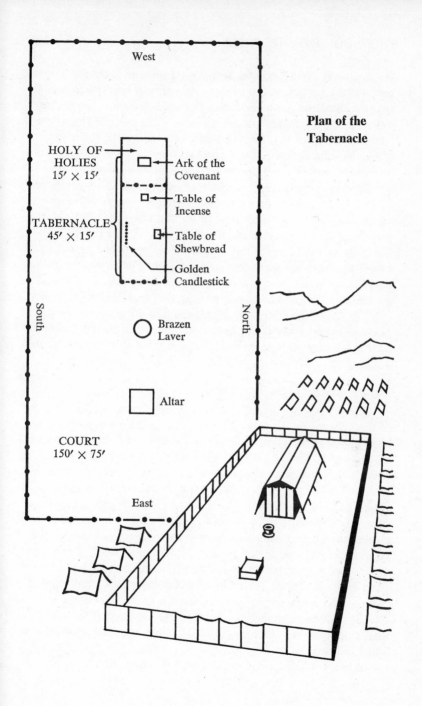

Plan of the Tabernacle

feet each way. While no specific mention is made of the form of the roof, the framework was to be covered over with four layers of material; the inner one was a horizontal cloth of fine linen, while the three outer ones, presumably stretched over a ridge pole making them a tent (see 26:7, R.S.V.), were of goats' hair (as are the Bedouin tents of today), ram skins dyed red, and seal skins or porpoise skins (not badgers, as in the K.J.V.), for protection from weathering.

This structure was set up within an open court 150 feet long and 75 feet wide, enclosed by a fence supported by pillars, with a gate, of curtains, at its eastern end only. Inside this court, between the gate and the Tabernacle, were the brazen altar, 7½ feet square by 4½ feet high, and the laver. Into this court worshipers and priests could come to offer their sacrifices. Into the Holy Place only the priests could go. Into the Holy of Holies only the high priest was allowed to go, and then only on one day of the year, the great Day of Atonement.

The whole structure was to be located in the center of the camp of Israel at every stopping place, with the tents of the various tribes distributed around it (see Num. 2). On the march the dismantled Tabernacle would be carried in the center of the procession.

The Furnishings of the Tabernacle

The plan also included the detailed description of the furniture of the Tabernacle. These articles are described from the inmost, and most important one, out. The *Ark of the Covenant,* the only piece in the Holy of Holies, was a small chest, 45 inches long, 27 inches wide, and 27 inches deep. It was made of acacia wood overlaid with gold within and without, with detachable staves overlaid with gold with which it could be carried. Upon it was the mercy seat, a flat slab of pure gold covering the top of the Ark, which was surmounted by two golden cherubim, facing one another with out-spread wings. Pagan religions of the time sometimes centered around idols enthroned between winged sphinxes. Not so here! The mercy seat between the cherubim was empty. No image could even begin to represent the true God. The Ark was to contain the tables of the law (Exod. 25:16, 31:18); later were added the book of the covenant (Deut. 31:24–26), a pot of manna (Exod. 16:33–34), and, still later, Aaron's rod which budded (Num. 17:10).

In the Holy Place, on the north side, was to be the *table of show-*

bread (or the "table of the presence"). On the south side was located the seven-branched *golden candlestick*. On the west side, before the veil of the Holy of Holies, there was to stand the small golden *altar of incense*. In the court were, as previously mentioned, the *altar of burnt offering,* and, between the altar and the tent, the large bowl of the *brazen laver* for the cleansing of the priests before their ministry in the Holy Place. There were also various implements to be used with these pieces.

There follows then, in the direction to Moses, the description of the garments of the priests, particularly the intricate and costly regalia of the high priest. The consecration ritual for Aaron and his sons as priests is outlined in chapter 29, followed by the instructions for the daily offerings.

The Provision for the Building of the Tabernacle

Perhaps your first reaction upon reading of plans specifying such costly materials is the same as that of many a church building committee in looking over drawings for a proposed new building: "How will it be paid for?" The answer is that this was all thought out beforehand and provided. The building plan was preceded by the call for a voluntary "every member canvass"; see 25:1–8. It was, in a sense, a "pre-budget canvass" (a canvass taken before the preparation of a budget; the call to give came before the specifications were outlined). It was emphatically to be a free will offering—no bingo, bazaars, barbecues or rummage sales; no lawn parties, teas, or cake walks; no box lunches, turkey-and-ham suppers, or raffles. They were to bring their material treasures, their abilities, and their dedicated labor.

Where would it all come from, wealth like this from a company of ex-slaves? There were some materials at hand, such as acacia wood, skins, and goats' hair. There were doubtless heirlooms kept from earlier and happier days, but, above all, there was the treasure brought out of Egypt with them, bestowed in profusion upon them by the people of a wealthy land, anxious to be rid of them; see 12:35–36. And they were to give of their skill—skill in weaving, skill in designing, skill in craftsmanship, skill in building. Bezalel and Oholiab were to be the chief overseers.

How does this compare with the stewardship program, methods and practice of your own church? How does your own stewardship of possessions look in the light of this response?

The Symbolism of the Tabernacle

The actual structure is of interest to us from a historical point of view. *But what was its meaning and message to them and to us?* What principles of worship do we see in this ritual and how are they related to our own Christian worship?

The Tabernacle, as Charles R. Erdman wrote,

> . . . furnished a permanent object lesson in divine worship. It spoke of the abiding presence of God, of His holiness and grace, of the way by which He could be approached, of the demand for purity, and consecration, and of the necessity for mediation and sacrifice and intercession. How far these were understood by the Israelites may be uncertain. For the Christian, however, there is a rather definite norm of interpretation: whatever is clearly indicated in the New Testament to have been symbolic and typical in the ancient ritual should be eagerly accepted and cherished, but one should ever be on his guard against allowing mere fancy or traditional analogies to translate supposed resemblances into religious dogmas. The interpretation of types requires great humility and restraint.[2]

If you would try a bit of firsthand study, and a not too easy one, take your paper and pen and write down the following. In one column to the left write the articles named.

The Tabernacle as a whole
The Court
The Altar of Burnt Offering
The Laver
The Table of Shewbread
The Candlestick
The Altar of Incense
The Veil
The Holy of Holies
The Ark of the Covenant
The Mercy Seat
The Priestly Garments
The Ephod
The Breastplate

*In the space to the right of your paper, write out in a word or two
what you think these symbolized in their original usage, and in their
New Testament fulfillment.*

Rejection—Consecration Desecrated, 32—34

This historical interlude coming here in chapters 32—34 is both
a surprise and a shock! But it has its definite place in the record, a
place of real significance, for it reveals most graphically the need
for the Tabernacle as a focal point of their worship and consecration.
It illustrates the fact that when men do not have the true God to
worship, they will make one of their own and worship him.

Does it seem incredible to you that they could have so soon forgotten and forsaken the leadership of Moses, that they would have
forgotten the dramatic manner in which the law had been given, that
the covenant promise would so tragically soon be broken? Or are you
aware of your own bent to forget and to disobey?

With Moses out of sight for so long upon the mountain top, they
betook themselves to Aaron with the primitive request for a visible
god to worship. And Aaron obliged. He was not of the stamp of his
younger brother. He made them a calf of gold (probably wood overlaid with gold) in the likeness of a god whom they knew well in Egypt,
Apis, the bull-god. This was pointed out as their deliverer, and then
they proceeded to worship it with licentious orgies (see 32:18–19,
25).

Upon Moses' descent from Sinai the sight and sounds which met
him from the camp filled him with righteous fury. He cast down the
tables of the law he had received in his summit meeting with Yahweh,
and their shattering was symbolic of the breaking of the covenant
by the people below. Demanding an explanation of Aaron, he received what must be the father of all fatuous and naive excuses! I
cast the gold into the fire, "and there came out this calf"!

Moses then destroyed the idol, and, having thrown its ashes into
the water course, he compelled the people to drink of the water it
polluted. With sterling courage and flashing eye he stood alone to call
for those who would stand with him for God. His own tribe responded. Then followed a bloody major operation by the Levites
whereby the cancer of idolatry was removed from the body of Israel,
at least for the time being.

The severest judgment to befall them was the withdrawal of God's presence. In an effort to reverse that disastrous sentence Moses twice intercedes for his apostate people, in the most memorable instances of Christ-like self-sacrifice that the Old Testament affords; see 32:11–14 and 32:30–34. In the first, he pleaded with Yahweh on the basis of God's redemption, God's glory, and God's covenant. In the second, he sought to make atonement for the sins of the people by offering himself, his life, his soul (". . . blot me, I pray thee, out of thy book . . .").

Such a spirit won from God reassurance of his presence, a rewriting of the tables of stone, a renewal of the broken covenant, a clearer revelation of God's glory to Moses, and the reflection of God's presence in the face of his friend and servant (see 33:12—34:35).

Was the sin of the people here a breaking of the first or second commandment—or both? Why was it considered an especially serious one? What light does this incident throw on the characters of the two brothers, Moses and Aaron? Does the human heart cry out for a God—do you agree with the famous prayer of Augustine, "O God, Thou hast made us for Thyself, and our hearts are restless until they find their rest in Thee"? We may scorn the idea of worshiping a golden calf, but what other gods do Americans actually worship? How is it possible for grateful allegiance to turn so swiftly into apostasy? Can "one man die for the people"? Even in the case of Christ's eternal sacrifice, what is necessary on our part? Exodus 34:29 gives us a wonderful illustration of unconscious spiritual growth; is there such a thing as unconscious spiritual decay?

The Erection of the Tabernacle— Consecration Consumated, 35:1—40:38

The last six chapters of Exodus tell the remarkable story of the complete fulfillment of the God-given directions by a now repentant and obedient people. Within the space of nine months after their arrival at Sinai, the Tabernacle stood completed, resplendent in its beauty and a constant witness to the presence of a covenant-keeping God in their midst.

Consider how many had labored for its completion! *Make a list of all the kinds of workmen that it required.* Rendering a holy service, with what joy did they see it rise! Our modern methods of construction deny us this personal participation.

Consider the vast outpouring of treasure that made it possible. A careful estimate made some years ago of the value of the gold and silver used in this remarkable structure reveals their gifts to have amounted to the sum of $1,250,000! At today's prices it would be worth a great deal more.

The result of the "every member" participation was spectacularly successful. They brought enough and more than enough, until they had to be stopped from giving. What joy this stewardship brought to the givers is only to be imagined. What it meant to Moses only a pastor can imagine. When we can reach this level of response our problems of church financing will be no more.

With care and thoroughness the work was done according to the pattern given on the mount. Again and again we read the refrain, ". . . as the LORD had commanded Moses."

The priests were consecrated to their task of ministering. The Tabernacle was consecrated to the worship of God. And then—in final consummation—the cloud of the Presence covered the tent and the glory of Yahweh filled the Tabernacle.

With all of its symbolic furniture this place would mark for them the means of access for an unholy people to a holy God, the expression of their daily dependence upon him, and the source of their forgiveness at the mercy seat. To us, in the light of the New Testament, we see in it the promise of the coming of the Savior who in his flesh would one day "tabernacle" among his own.

Thus the covenant people, by God's grace delivered from bondage, constituted a new nation; and, forgiven and renewed, they were prepared to worship their holy, merciful, covenant-keeping God. Thus the curtain falls upon this portion of the drama of God's Word.

The Fulfillment of the Drama

An epilogue is a section added at the end of a work to complete it, frequently by showing the plan and purpose of the whole.

Let us then, as we come to the close of this all too scanty study of one of the greatest books of the Divine Library, look back over it and see anew the main thrusts of this work for our time.

In reviewing this drama of redemption, give thought to such questions as these: What are its principal acts? What are its main contributions to the unfolding revelation of God's message to men? Pause here and write out your own conclusions.

Now will you consider these suggestions: In Exodus we see God. In Exodus we see a man. In Exodus we see a people. In Exodus we see the foreshadowing of the God-Man, who is the sufficient Savior for all people.

In Exodus We See God!

What is the primary purpose of Bible study? Is it not to gain a more adequate concept of God and enter into a more vital relationship with him? The Scriptures are our only sufficient source of revelation. Will Rogers used to say, "All I know is what I read in the papers." The Christian, while realizing that something of the knowledge of God can be gleaned from the universe around us and from the news of the current happenings of our day, must nevertheless affirm that the only really adequate knowledge we have of God is what we read in the Word. This is what the Scriptures principally teach: ". . . what man is to believe concerning God . . ." (we are not unaware of

the balance of that significant statement in The Shorter Catechism—
"and what duty God requires of man"—and this must also receive
our attention).

What are the main facets of truth about God that Exodus con-
tributes to our knowledge of him?

(1) It tells us that God is Faithful. Chapters 1—4 especially
reveal this fact. From the welter of their suffering in Egypt there
emerges the picture of Yahweh, who hears their cries, who remembers his covenant with the patriarchs, who preserves and prepares
Moses and finally calls and commissions him to be his instrument.
From the bush that burned and was not consumed God said, "I am
the God of your father, the God of Abraham, the God of Isaac, and
the God of Jacob," and, . . . "Say this to the people of Israel. 'I AM
has sent me to you.' " Was this revelation simply to give them a pride
of family lineage in the midst of their shame of bondage? Not at all!
It was to remind them of a relationship God had not forgotten. Yahweh is saying in effect, "Tell them they can count on me!" And they
could indeed. He carried out his promise until, settled in the Land of
Promise, Joshua could look back and declare, "Not one of all the
good promises which the Lord had made to the house of Israel had
failed; all came to pass" (Joshua 21:45). Our God is a faithful God!
What is our duty in relationship to this truth?

(2) It tells us that God is Sovereign. Chapters 5—15 of this
drama of redemption are concerned primarily with this fact. We see
God as sovereign over the forces of evil. All the crafty and wicked
measures designed to degrade and decimate the *bene-ysrael,* to destroy their spirit of resistance and their desire for freedom, were
made to boomerang upon their oppressors. The Hebrews grew in
number, their yearning for freedom was unquenched, and their
bodies became inured to hardness and conditioned for their difficult
journey and their rugged existence in the wilderness.

Yahweh is also revealed as sovereign over the forces of nature.
The plagues were conclusive demonstrations to Egyptians and Hebrews alike of God's supernatural power over the animate and in-
animate elements of land and water and air.

He was also shown to be sovereign over the forces of man. Pharaoh was the absolute ruler of the wealthiest, most cultured, most powerful nation of the world. But when God's servant stretched forth his arm in the name of Yahweh, the hand of Pharaoh was powerless to stay him, and his military might was unavailing to deter the Hebrew people from their march to freedom.

And God is here revealed to be sovereign over the forces of other gods. One by one the gods of Egypt were shown up and disastrously defeated in the mighty contest of the plagues. Small wonder that the Israelites standing upon the farther shore of the waters that had witnessed their victorious emancipation, were moved to sing, "Who is like thee, O LORD, among the gods?" "I will sing to the LORD, for he has triumphed gloriously . . ." *What is our duty in relationship to this truth?*

(3) Exodus tells us also that God is Provident. Chapters 16—18 cry aloud that the God mighty to deliver is also able and willing to provide for and to sustain his own. The journey from the sea to Sinai was to demonstrate again and again, even in the face of their lack of faith, that without Yahweh they were helpless but with him they could find grace and strength in time of need. Impotent apart from him; all sufficient with him! Thus, the hard way, they learned one of life's priceless lessons. *What is our duty in relationship to this truth?*

(4) Exodus also reveals that God is Holy. Chapters 19—24 emphasize this aspect. The days spent before Sinai, the summit which was clothed with fire and smoke and from which the voice of Yahweh was heard, were days of awesome revelation to the people of the unapproachable holiness of God. But the covenant which was offered there, with its law that granted guidance and its promise of his presence in their new role as a holy nation, enabled the people to see that they would find this holy God to be their God, not distant and demanding but among them to transform and to lead them. *What is our duty in relationship to this truth?*

(5) Exodus warns us that God is Just, but Merciful. Chapters

32—34, the interlude of the people's apostasy in their idolatry and worship of the golden calf, show that God is just in that he must always punish sin, but that he is merciful in forgiving the penitent. The new nation under God had so soon turned their backs on him and broken the covenant promise they had made. This sin had to be excised, and God in his justice did so. But he yielded to the importunate and self-sacrificing plea of Moses for the forgiveness of their sin, and then renewed his covenant and restored his favor. *What is our duty in relationship to this truth?*

(6) Exodus reveals that God is Accessible. Chapters 25—31 and 35—40 give us the account of the planning and construction of the Tabernacle. The primary purpose of this singular sanctuary was to show the people at all times that God was among them and that he was available to all believers who came in faith and in obedience to receive atonement for sin and guidance for the way ahead. The Tabernacle with its sacrificial system was erected and dedicated, to foreshadow in all its contents and ritual the coming One who would be Immanuel—God with us—the Savior of all who would come in faith to him. *What is our duty in relationship to this truth?*

In Exodus We See a Man!

The outstanding human character in this magnificent drama of redemption is the man Moses. And what a man! He surmounts all the figures of his day, and all the succeeding days of the Old Testament. He has more profoundly influenced the history of the world than any other mere man who ever lived. The words of 11:3, ". . . the man Moses was very great . . ." is a vast understatement. Yet the striking mark of greatness of Moses is seen in the fact which he himself sensed and voiced (in Deut. 18:15), that he was but the forerunner of a greater One. "The LORD your God will raise up for you a prophet like me from among you, from your brethren— him you shall heed—. . ." That greater One, who in the far years of God's plan came in the fullness of time, was Jesus Christ, as the New Testament makes plain. See Acts 3:22, 7:37, and compare John 1:21, 25.

Moses not only foretold this fact, but also in his own life foreshadowed the One who was to come. This we see in his relationship to self, to God, and to his fellows.

(1) In relationship to self, Moses was a man of humility. He would not shirk the leadership, but he was willing to take a back seat; read Numbers 12:3. True meekness is never a sign of weakness, but of strength. He dared to give up self that he might be a servant; see Hebrews 11:25. He was called "the servant of God," and few were more faithful in service.

(2) In relationship to God, he was obedient. He could say with Paul, "I was not disobedient to the heavenly vision." Scorning opposition from without, and jealousy and backbiting from within, he obeyed the great commission he received, and carried it out to the end. Hebrews 11:27 sums it up well.

(3) In relationship to others, he was mediator and intercessor. He spoke for God to the people and spoke for the people to God. He was willing to be included with the transgressors in their sin (34:9), and he was willing to be blotted out for their forgiveness (32:30–33).

Now will you think through the way in which Jesus Christ was the fulfillment of all that was best in Moses? What then is our duty in the light of this truth?

In Exodus We See a People!

This is the stirring drama of the birth of a nation. From the matrix of bondage they came, from the low estate of blood and sweat and tears. They had a noble ancestry but a detested present. Somehow the residuum of faith never failed. They clung to hope. Through the long years of bitter servitude they could still look up and cry out for help to the only source that could help. Beaten into the bloody mud of the Nile, they carried on, until the fullness of their time came, and God sent his man Moses to lead them out. Suspicious and fearful, they nevertheless followed him in his efforts to effect their escape. And when the contest was over they gathered up what goods they could carry and left the house of bondage.

Freed by divine power alone, they yet failed in faith often and complained of their lot. But, sustained by a merciful providence, they arrived at Sinai. Awed, they gazed upon the holy mount and gladly they vowed their obedience to the covenant God proposed. Then all too tragically soon they fell into apostasy and sin, which merited and received bitter and lasting punishment. Again, through their selfless intercessor, they were forgiven and restored to the presence of God. The way for them to approach a holy God and have communion with him was set forth, and with sacrificial enthusiasm they responded with their treasure and their labor. At the end of the story we see them rejoicing in the presence of God visibly among them.

Is this saga of ancient Israel an analogy of our Christian pilgrimage? How does it provide a foregleam of our individual journey toward the City of God?

In Exodus We See Our Redeemer!

This book is of inestimable historical value in our understanding of the origin of the theocratic nation: how they came to be rescued from bondage and set up as the Chosen People of God, and how they learned to express their worship and to follow the leadership of God. But its main value lies in its message of redemption— redemption from bondage, redemption from destruction, redemption from death by hunger and thirst, redemption from alienation from God, redemption from apostasy and failure. This process was all of God. In its story it foretells the redemption wrought out for us by God through Jesus Christ. In so many ways this book is a preview of what Christ has done for us.

Now will you please work out on this suggested outline the parallel between their redemption and ours, as seen in the fuller light of the New Testament. Study the references given and write out in a brief sentence the corresponding truth of the New Covenant.

ISRAEL	OURSELVES
THE NEED OF REDEMPTION	
They—	We—
In bondage to Pharaoh as slaves.	John 8:34
	Romans 6:16
REDEMPTION ALL OF GOD	
They—	We—
While they were helpless, God originated	Ephesians 2:1
and carried through his plan to save.	John 3:16
	Philippians 1:6
REDEMPTION THROUGH A PERSON	
They—	We—
Through Moses.	John 3:14–17
REDEMPTION IS BY BLOOD	
They—	We—
"When I see the blood, I will pass over you."	Peter 1:18–20
	Hebrews 9:22
REDEMPTION IS BY POWER	
They—	We—
By the sovereign power of God.	Romans 1:16
	1 Corinthians 1:18
REDEMPTION IS ALL OF GRACE	
They—	We—
Were ill-deserving slaves and sinners.	Ephesians 2:1–9
	Romans 3:23–24
THE BLESSINGS OF REDEMPTION	
They—	We—
1) Freedom from bondage.	1) John 8:36
2) Provision for daily need.	2) Philippians 4:19
3) Fellowship with God.	3) 1 John 1:3
4) The Land of Promise	4) Hebrews 9:15
	Revelation 14:13

Thus Exodus, the book of the redemption of Israel, becomes for us the forecast of the gospel of God's grace, that proclaims to sinners everywhere the good news of the redemption effected by Jesus Christ our Lord.

Do you know this Savior of mankind as your personal Savior today? In gratitude for his deliverance will you renew in your heart now your pledge to keep his covenant?

SUGGESTED REVIEW AND STUDY QUESTIONS

1. *What seem to you to be the three or four ideas in the book of Exodus which have the greatest meaning for our own day?*

2. *This commentary has outlined Exodus in seven "acts." Name as many of these as you can, and indicate what you regard as the most important event in each.*

3. *What events in the life of Moses best illustrate for you the providential plan and purpose of God?*

4. *Exodus is, in part, the story of God's repeated acts of sovereign grace and of repeated acts of rebellion on the part of God's people. List several examples of each.*

5. *Exodus provides essential background for understanding the New Testament. List what seem to you three or four of the most important ways the covenant in Exodus is like the new covenant and three or four of the most important differences.*

6. *In what ways, if any, has your own life tended to change as a result of this study of God's Word?*

ISAIAH 40–66

THE FREEDOM OF SERVANTHOOD

Robert H. Bullock

1

What Shall I Cry?

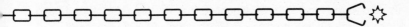

A DISPLACED PERSON SPEAKS

Do you know how it feels to be what they call a "displaced person," an outsider in the land? No, you couldn't possibly know. You have a home and a job. You are secure. Your name doesn't have a foreign sound to it. You don't speak with an accent. Your skin is the right color. You own real estate that your forefathers owned before you. You have a place in the life of this country. We are different. We are outsiders. We don't belong in these surroundings. Everyone needs to belong somewhere, and we are no different in that respect. It is true that I have never lived anywhere but right here, but that does not make this home to me by any means. You know, I have a home I've never seen. It isn't a big land, and the scenery is nothing to speak of. In almost every way it is a poor land compared to this lush country. My grandfather had only a modest vineyard on the side of a hill and devoted his life to keeping it alive. But, you see, it was a piece of land that really belonged to him in a country that belonged to his people, and that makes a difference!

The Displaced Person in Our Time

The *displaced person* is a familiar figure in our time. At the time of writing there are more than a million Arab refugees in the Middle East. A considerable proportion of them have been born in refugee camps and have never known any other life. A million or

117

more refugees from Red China have fled to Hong Kong and beyond, and there is an annual flow of more than 100,000 from behind the bamboo curtain. A quarter of a million Algerian refugees are in Morocco and Tunisia. For several years Cuban refugees have flocked to the United States whenever the way was open—and have come secretly when it was not. By the end of 1965, thousands had been reestablished in this country. Fleeing from poverty and destitution in their island home, the Puerto Ricans have poured into Latin ghettos of New York in great numbers for many years. All over the world, in India, Nepal, Uganda, Tanzania, Burundi, and the Congo, displaced persons constitute one of the major problems of our time.

But the persons uprooted by war and political persecution are not the only displaced persons today. In many countries, such as South Africa and the United States, minority races are a kind of displaced people. For generations they have lived in, but have not been a part of, the societies in the midst of which they have been set. How frequently this feeling is echoed in the plaintive lament of the Negro spiritual!

There is another sense in which vast numbers of modern Americans are displaced persons of a sort. The forces of transition which have so vastly altered the American manner of life have resulted in the uprooting and displacing of millions of American families. Many children today grow up with no really permanent home, no nearby relatives, and no loyalty to community traditions and ideals. They are sojourners rather than residents. Restless and rootless, they long for a homeland where they might really belong.

Israel, the Displaced Persons of the Sixth Century B.C.

Isaiah 40—66 was written specifically for the people of God when Israel was a displaced people in the land of Babylon in the sixth century B.C. The critical problem involving the division of the book of Isaiah at chapter 40 will be dealt with in a later chapter. Let it suffice to say at this point that the whole book would have been meaningless had it been written to Israel two centuries earlier, in the eighth century B.C. when the prophet Isaiah lived and worked. In Isaiah 40—66 the readers were not being threatened with the chastening of national disaster; they were enduring it. The Exile was not a possibility; it was a reality.

The Story of a Displaced People

Sometime around the beginning of the second millenium before Christ, that is, around 2000 B.C., a man and his family set out on a journey from Ur in ancient Chaldea. The westward movement of Abram, as he was first called, carried him initially to Haran in Syria, and later into the land of Canaan. From the moment he set out in response to the call of God this man was a displaced person with no settled home. He and his descendants for three generations lived as nomadic sojourners among people of another nation. But they lived in the hope of a land which the Lord promised Abraham under the terms of the covenant.

The patriarchal period ended with the migration of the family of Jacob, the grandson of Abraham, into Egypt. From all indications this family was a displaced people in that country. At the beginning of the period, during the reign of the Hyksos kings who were a kindred Semitic people, the descendants of Abraham fared well. The service rendered to Egypt by Joseph in a time of economic crisis was remembered and honored. But a successful revolution against the Hyksos dynasty brought a new line of kings to the throne of Egypt which was hostile instead of friendly to Israel. The descendants of Abraham, Isaac, and Jacob were reduced to abject slavery, and their misery was compounded by the murder of their male children to keep them from multiplying.

Shortly after the beginning of the thirteenth century B.C., God heard the cry of his oppressed and displaced people and raised up Moses, one of the great liberators of history. His life being spared by God in infancy, Moses was reared in the king's court with all of the privileges and educational advantages of a prince. But he never lost his sense of identification with his people. Though he was separated from them as an aristocrat is inevitably separated from the slave class, he could never forget that he, too, was a displaced person, sharing a common destiny with the oppressed people of God.

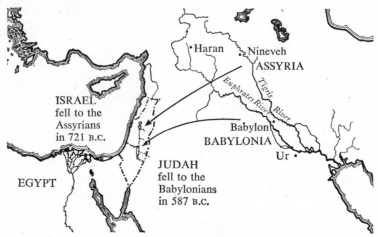

But, however much Moses may have identified with the Hebrews, his own people at that time felt little affection for him. Because of his rejection by them he fled to Midian where God further prepared him for the work he was later to accomplish. Many years later, at the burning bush, God disclosed to Moses that it was his destiny to lead Israel out of bondage.

In Egypt Moses was God's instrument in a great struggle with Pharaoh. The ten plagues were invoked and at long last Moses succeeded in gaining the king's permission for Israel to go into the desert to worship their God. Pharaoh's last-minute change of mind, that led him to pursue Israel in order to bring them back, ended in great tragedy for Egypt and a great victory for Israel. The waters opened to give passage to Israel but closed to drown the hosts of Pharaoh.

In the desert the displaced people of Israel found no new home. After the tests of faith in the early stages of the journey, they came at last to Mount Sinai where they camped for about a year. Here the Lord entered into covenant with his people, renewing the ancient promises made to Abraham, including the promise of a land for their national home. The establishment of the covenant as a climax to God's deliverance from slavery in Egypt became the most outstanding event in Israel's national memory. Centuries later, in captivity in Babylon, the Prophet of the Exile revived Israel's fading hopes by prophesying a second exodus in which God would once again deliver his people.

After their failure to trust God to give them the land and an abortive attempt to take it without divine assistance, Israel wandered for some forty years in the desert regions of the Sinai Peninsula. In these years the discipline of displacement prepared them for the next chapter in their national history, the conquest of Canaan.

A new generation of Israelites, strengthened by the stringencies of rugged life in the desert, went into Canaan under the leadership of Joshua. Three campaigns gave them a tenuous foothold in the land which had been promised to them, but for centuries they lived a precarious life in a land that had not been completely conquered.

Again and again they were victimized by the plundering and aggression of their neighbors. In each instance God raised up a "judge." The judges were primarily military leaders under whose command Israel was able to throw off the yoke of their oppressors for a time.

At last the time of fulfillment of the Lord's promise drew near with the rise of Samuel, the last of the judges. Under his leadership the kingdom was established. Under Saul, and later David and Solomon, the loose confederation of tribes which characterized the age of the judges was transformed into a brilliant oriental kingdom. This was the golden age to which Israel ever after looked back with wistful longing. But the monarchy was disrupted by an inevitable revolt against the excessive taxation and forced labor of Solomon's regime. Under the reign of Rehoboam, the son of Solomon, the monarchy was divided by revolution.

The two relatively weak kingdoms that resulted from the revolution were destined to be caught up in subsequent military crises in which the ancient world was involved. The expansionist policies of the Assyrian Empire brought an end to Israel, the kingdom to the north, in 721 B.C., but the Southern Kingdom, Judah, was spared in this particular crisis. Israel's tragedy was the result of her persistent sin, of which Amos and Hosea spoke.

It was during the Assyrian threat that the first Isaiah lived, who gave us chapters 1—39 of the prophetic book which bears his name. The leadership which he gave his nation in this time of trouble accounts in great degree for the fact that Judah did not then suffer the same fate as the Northern Kingdom. Isaiah's wise counsel to kings, together with the strength and conviction of his preaching and writing, helped save Judah from extinction during the Assyrian crisis.

But the spirit of rebellion against Israel's covenant-God was never completely extinguished. Religious revivals under Hezekiah and Josiah could only put off the inevitable time of retribution. In both instances the reform was enforced by governmental authority rather than by personal piety and conviction. The final day of reckoning came in 587 B.C. The Babylonians, then in ascendancy in the ancient world, made a breach in the walls of the beleaguered city of Jerusalem. The Temple was razed, the city sacked, and the walls torn down. Many of the survivors were carried into captivity, and only a small group of the humblest members of society were left to occupy the ruins. The king's eyes were put out and his sons were slaughtered. Humbled and tortured, the last descendant of David to rule in Judah was carried away in chains, the laughing-stock of common soldiers. Thus it was that the people of God, who began their national existence as a displaced people, once again were reduced to that condition.

A generation passed, and the displaced people of Israel fell into despair. Nowhere is the mood of Israel more poignantly expressed than in Psalm 137:1–3:

> By the waters of Babylon,
>   there we sat down and wept,
>   when we remembered Zion.
> On the willows there
>   we hung up our lyres.
> For there our captors
>   required of us songs,
> and our tormentors, mirth, saying,
>   "Sing us one of the songs of Zion!"

Paul Scherer writes thus of the spiritual agony and the mood of desperation that enveloped Israel in captivity.

"How shall we sing the Lord's song in a foreign land?"
It is a problem for all of us!
You remember how it was with them. Jerusalem, the burnished city of God, etched on their brain with fire, had been running with blood when they saw it last; its proud, fair women sitting in rags on heaps of offal; only a poor mound now where the Temple had been, jackals prowling over it. And some lumpish, drunken sot here in Chaldea would stagger along shouting at them in the evening to sing! The plaintive, odd-sounding music and the strange twist they gave the words would raise howls of laughter. The revelers could roar out the chorus, never mind the tune, and keep time to it with the rattle of their wine-cups. You yourself could have done nothing but choke, as you looked around at that flat landscape, with its innumerable canals and its willow trees, so unlike the hills of home and the glens and the rushing streams: this Babylon, where you were not much better than a slave. Sing! they would shout again . . . . And you could only shake your head, dry-eyed, at the thought of all the dead splendor of the past. There was no song that would not blaspheme and tear your heart out and drop lifeless from your lips like a solid thing! "How shall we sing the Lord's song in a foreign land?"[1]

The Christian as a Displaced Person

As you study the Prophet of the Exile in the weeks to come you will undoubtedly sense a spiritual kinship with the captive people of Israel, for we who are Christians are, in a sense, displaced people. Life itself is something of an exile from God and his perfect rule. We become weary of a world that worships false gods and approaches life with worldly sophistication. Discouraged by prevailing worldliness we may share the desperation of Israel in exile, and say, "How shall we sing the Lord's song in a strange land?"

The writer of the Epistle to the Hebrews was aware of this

dimension of Christian consciousness. This is seen in Hebrews 11:13–16.

> These all died in faith, not having received what was promised, but having seen it and greeted it from afar, and having acknowledged that they were strangers and exiles on the earth. For people who speak thus make it clear that they are seeking a homeland. If they had been thinking of that land from which they had gone out, they would have had opportunity to return. But as it is, they desire a better country, that is, a heavenly one. Therefore God is not ashamed to be called their God, for he has prepared for them a city.

Study these verses in the larger context of Hebrews 11:1–40. This passage is an excellent one for this introductory study since it recounts in a sketchy way the history of Israel. Examine this famous chapter on faith as if you were reading it for the first time. Give special attention to discovering the relation between 11:13–16 and the rest of the chapter. In your special study of this passage seek answers to the following questions:

(1) What was promised by God that was not received during the lifetimes of the heroes of faith? What is promised you that will probably never be received in this world?

(2) What had the heroes of faith seen and greeted from afar? What have you greeted from afar?

(3) In what sense are God's people in any age strangers and exiles on the earth? How about you?

(4) What is the homeland Christians seek? What is your true home?

(5) What is the city of God? Are you a citizen of it even now? [Some study suggestions and questions are *italicized* in each chapter. Your understanding of Isaiah and your experience in the study group will both be enriched if you carry out these suggestions or answer these questions through your personal study of the prophecy.]

The Christian can never really be *at home* in this world. For him, the city of man is a poor substitute for the city of God. The Christian is possessed by an incurable restlessness, a divine discontent. He is forever evaluating the world in terms of heavenly standards, and the world is forever falling short. In the heart of the Christian there is an unmeasurable longing which no earthly gratification can extinguish, a longing which will continue to agitate him so long as this world is his home, even though he is set in the midst of plenty and satisfaction. The world is too small for him, its rewards too meager, its achievements too limited. The Christian realizes that he was born to play out his role on a larger stage in a drama of which God himself is the playwright.

In short, he confesses that he is a stranger and exile on the earth who looks for a city whose builder and maker is God. He desires a better country than that in which he must in the providence of God live out his earthly existence. Through the prophetic vision of such a great religious genius as the Prophet of the Exile he gets a glimpse of that which he seeks, even though it be from afar. Never possessing in this life the object of his quest, he lives out the duration of his exile from that better and heavenly country which he has seen at a distance on the horizon of his earthly life. He is confident that God has prepared for men of faith in all generations a city that has foundations. In the ecstasy of his vision the Seer of Patmos caught sight of the city:

> Then I saw a new heaven and a new earth; for the first heaven and the first earth had passed away, and the sea was no more. And I saw the holy city, new Jerusalem, coming down out of heaven from God, prepared as a bride adorned for her husband; and I heard a great voice from the throne saying, "Behold, the dwelling of God is with men. He will dwell with them, and they shall be his people, and God himself will be with them."

> (Rev. 21:1–3)

2

A Panorama
of the Prophecy

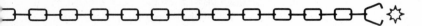

How does one best view a city? There are some who will maintain that one has not really seen a city until he has seen it from the window of an airplane. This viewpoint has its advantages. There are few more thrilling sights than the view one gets of a great metropolis as he flies over it at high altitude. From the vantage point of ten thousand feet one sees things that he could never see on the ground. The landmarks are seen in their relation to each other. The relative size and shape of the segments of the city that lie within the boundaries of the great arteries of traffic are obvious to the observer who is aloft as they could never be to the earthbound observer. Yet there are distinct advantages to viewing the city through the eyes of the motorist or pedestrian. Here one may detect the character of neighborhoods, the architectural flavor of the buildings, and the mood of the inhabitants. These things could never be known by the high-flying observer.

One needs the advantages of both viewpoints if he is really to *see* the city. And both viewpoints are needed if one is really to understand a piece of literature. On the one hand, a student needs the panoramic view that comes with a swift, one-sitting reading. This kind of reading saves us from getting lost amid the welter of detail that comes with a more detailed study. It is good to see the landmarks and major divisions in relation to each other and to the whole. On the other hand, one also needs the pedestrian view with its careful attention to details. In this study we shall employ both views and both methods of observation. The present chapter will strive to lead the reader through chapters 40—66 of Isaiah with a view to discovering the major sweep of ideas. This kind of study will supply the student with a frame of reference that will be helpful in the more detailed study which will follow in subsequent chapters.

It is important that you read chapters 40—66 for yourself. This text is not to be thought of as a substitute for a study of the Scriptures. If this chapter is to be helpful it must be regarded as a guide to your own study of these great discourses. *Do not pause to observe details in this reading. Read as swiftly as you can. Try to do it all in one sitting if possible.* An ordinary reader should be able to do this in an hour and a half. *Observe and mark in some way what you consider the landmark passages in these chapters. Look for major divisions of the material. At what points does the mood of the writer change? Where do you find shifts in emphasis?* Get a panoramic view as you "fly" over the book. There will be plenty of time later for a more detailed study.

The Date and Authorship of Isaiah 40—66

At this point it is necessary to deal with the question of the date and authorship of these chapters. Since the latter part of the eighteenth century there has been a growing belief among scholars that Isaiah 40—66 could not have been written by Isaiah, the son of Amoz, who lived in the eighth century B.C. and who wrote the first thirty-nine chapters of the prophecy. There are many reasons for holding this view.

When you make your survey reading of Isaiah 40—66 you will observe that chapters 40—55 seem to have been written to Israel in captivity in Babylon. Two references are made to Cyrus, the Persian conqueror of Babylon who lived in the sixth century B.C. (44:28 and 45:1). It will be remembered that Isaiah lived some two centuries earlier. Of course, God could have given the prophet the ability to foresee the future and to write for people who lived two hundred years later, but this would have been a unique situation, for no other prophet wrote in this manner. To be sure, the prophets were endowed with ability to scan the future, but their messages were consistently addressed to the people of their own day and not to generations yet unborn. Furthermore, the future when it was foreseen always illuminated the present. The comforting words of Isaiah 40 would have been highly inappropriate if spoken in the eighth century B.C., when Isaiah was pleading with Israel to repent lest the hand of God's punishment be laid upon them.

Chapters 56—66, on the other hand, seem to be addressed to a people who have been resettled in Palestine. The mood of these chapters is different from that of 40—55. [Where no book is named, the scriptural reference is to Isaiah.] The problems dealt with here are the problems that Israel faced during the time of the return from exile. What are we to make of all of this? There are two possibilities. Either the Prophet of the Exile returned with the exiles and wrote subsequently, or these chapters were written by one or more of his disciples. There is a persistence of the major motifs of chapters 40—55, such as the glorification of the God of Israel, the covenant of the peoples, the redemption of Israel, and (perhaps) the servant theme in a slightly different guise in 63:1–3. There are so many similarities that it cannot be certainly maintained that the last eleven chapters were written by some other or others than the Prophet of the Exile. However, there is enough difference in the mood and spirit, and certainly in the background, of these chapters to make this a distinct possibility.

How shall we consider the book of Isaiah as a whole? There is little doubt that chapters 1—39 were written by Isaiah, the great eighth-century prophet who lived and worked during the Assyrian crisis. Chapters 40—55 seemed to have been written for the comfort and encouragement of the exiles in Babylon. Perhaps these chapters were attached to chapters 1—39 to show clearly the other side of God's nature in his dealing with his people. While chapters 1—39 dwell upon the righteousness of God and the inevitability of his judgment, chapters 40—55 emphasize the love of God and his redemption of his people. Chapters 56—66 present the point of view of the Prophet of the Exile at a different time and in a different setting. When the fond hopes aroused by the preaching of the Prophet of the Exile are not literally fulfilled in the experience of the returning exiles, the prophet turns to an eschatological interpretation of God's redemptive acts: that is, while dealing with the vexing problems of the people of God who were in the process of making a new life for themselves in Palestine, he looks beyond the horizons of history to discover the ultimate fulfillment of Israel's hopes.

In fairness to all points of view it must be pointed out that there are some commentators who hold to the single authorship of Isaiah. The arguments for this position are well stated by Arnold B. Rhodes in his student's book, *The Mighty Acts of God,* pages 196–197, and need not be repeated here. Until fairly recent times this work was regarded as the product of one author, and it has been studied with profit by many generations of Bible students who never heard of "Second Isaiah," to say nothing of "Third Isaiah." You are urged to study this matter of date and authorship of Isaiah for yourself. The number of authors of the book is not of ultimate importance. What *is* important is the fact that God has gloriously revealed himself throughout the whole book from chapter one to chapter sixty-six. The same Holy Spirit inspired the writer or writers of the whole book. In the opinion of this writer Old Testament revelation reaches a high water mark in the book of Isaiah.

It is my own position that the book of Isaiah reflects a multiple authorship. This has never given me any particular difficulty. My reasons for holding this position are two-fold. First, the weight of scholarly opinion seems to uphold this viewpoint. Second, chapters 40—66 make a great deal more sense to me when interpreted as an exilic and postexilic document. As an interpreter of the Bible it is my responsibility to make sense of it, and to do so it is necessary for me to view chapters 40—66 as prophecy addressed to a people who lived later than the time of Isaiah, the son of Amoz. I have no quarrel with those who believe otherwise, and the reader need not agree with me as to the date and authorship of chapters 40—66 in order to study the book with understanding and spiritual profit.

A Reading Guide to Isaiah 40—48

As you read through these chapters remember that they were written to bring comfort and hope to a people caught in the grip of despair. Try to put yourself in the place of the captive Israelites. Remember that in a sense you too are a captive, and that these words of comfort, hope, and challenge are addressed to you as well as to captive Israel.

Pay particular attention to the prophet's view of God in contrast to the popular, pagan, polytheistic conception of deity. Here the Old Testament statement of the nature of God reaches its highest expression. Try to get the full flavor of the magnificent passages which deal with this topic.

The *servant theme* is of particular importance and interest. Mark the references to the *servant* as you come to them, and in each instance try to determine to whom the author is referring. Is the servant Israel, is it the servant of Israel, is it Israel serving Israel, or is it an individual? Be prepared to discuss your impressions of these important passages.

Mark all the verses in these chapters that are quoted in the New Testament; you can get help in doing this through marginal notes that appear in some Bibles or through a commentary. You will be surprised to discover how frequently the writers of the New Testament used quotations from these passages. .

Note the references to Cyrus. You will learn more about this outstanding historical figure in the detailed study of the following chapters in the text. Let it suffice to say here that it was Cyrus who toppled the Babylonian empire and issued the edict that permitted the return of the exiles to Palestine.

Now read Isaiah 40—48 before going any further with a study of the text. Nobody can do your homework for you, and nothing takes the place of your individual study of the Scriptures.

A Reading Guide to Isaiah 49—55

In reading these chapters you will notice many points of continuity with chapters 40—48. You will observe, however, that there are no references to Cyrus nor to the fall of Babylon. The prophet's interest seems to be focused not on the present circumstances looking toward the release of Israel, but rather on circumstances that are yet to be realized in the future.

While chapters 40—48 seem to be addressed to the whole nation of Israel, chapters 49—55 seem to appeal more to individual Israelites. What do you make of this shift of attention? Is it possible that different conditions prevailed when chapters 49—55 were written?

In chapters 49—55 you will find three dominant themes:

(1) *The servant theme.* Is there any progress in the development of the servant idea? How is the servant in chapters 49—55 different from the servant in chapters 40—48?

(2) *Addresses to Jerusalem.* What seems to be symbolized by the city of Jerusalem? Is the Jerusalem of these chapters a city that *is,* or a city that *is to be?*

(3) *Encouragements and admonitions addressed to individuals.* What are some of the specific messages to individuals in these passages? How do they apply to individuals in our own day?

Now read Isaiah 49—55 before reading any further in this text. Do not yield to the temptation to skip this part of your personal preparation.

A Reading Guide to Isaiah 56—66

If you have gone through chapters 40—55 carefully you will notice some rather profound differences as you read chapters 56—66. For one thing, the setting on the whole seems to be Palestinian rather than Babylonian. You will sense that the optimism of the earlier chapters is replaced by a more somber mood in chapters 56—66. You will probably draw the conclusion that these chapters were written under entirely different conditions. Could it be that these chapters were written after the return to Palestine? If this is true, were all of the expectations of chapters 40—55 realized in the return?

Notice the references to the law in chapters 56—66. Does there seem to be a more definite spirit of legalism than in the earlier chapters? Does this suggest a different approach to public and private morality? Notice the references to divine judgment. In the earlier chapters judgment seems to be a thing that has been completed (i.e., 40:1-2). How do you account for the fact that in chapters 56—66 judgment is a dark cloud on the horizon? How would you explain this change of mood?

Now read the passage as a unit, noting the suggestions of the paragraph above. Do not permit me to make up your mind for you on the questions raised. Read the material for yourself and form your own conclusions.

Important Ideas of Isaiah 40—66

Even the casual reading of Isaiah 40—66 suggested above has probably brought to your attention certain recurring themes. These ideas, which form the ideological patterns of the book, will be dealt with in much greater detail when they are encountered in the study of the text. They are suggested here in capsule form in order that the reader may view them in relation to each other.

(1) The absoluteness of God, as in 40:9–31. The author's view of God is perhaps his most characteristic theological idea. Fundamental to all else that is said about God is the assertion that he alone is God, and besides him there is no other. Monotheism was not a novel idea in Hebrew religious thought when this prophecy was written. It is implicit in Old Testament theology from the very beginning, but distortions of the doctrine and open deviations from it characterized the religious thought and life of Israel for centuries. Idolatry was the besetting sin of the people of God from the incident of the golden calf to the fall of Jerusalem. The advocacy of monotheism reached its highest and noblest expression in the oracles of the great Prophet of the Exile. Nowhere in the Bible is monotheism preached with greater vigor and eloquence, and nowhere is idolatry ridiculed with more cutting and convincing sarcasm.

In the thinking of the Prophet of the Exile the one God is a great God. One of the most outstanding masterpieces of all religious literature, Isaiah 40:12–26, gives eloquent testimony to the incomparable greatness of the God of Israel. The fault of Israel in exile was to think of their God in limited terms. The task of the Prophet of the Exile was to push back the horizons of Israel's thought about her God.

A part of God's greatness is to be seen in his creation of all things. To this the Prophet of the Exile refers again and again. The creative act reveals the Lord in all his glory and power. Because he is Creator, he alone is capable of sustaining his creation and making it the arena of his ultimate redemption of all things.

The one, great Creator God of whom the Prophet of the Exile

writes is the sovereign Lord of man and nature. He controls all the natural forces and causes them to serve his purpose. He reigns in human history, and even the rulers who do not know him unwittingly fulfill his purposes. Nothing in heaven or earth can thwart or alter his predetermined course.

Finally, the Prophet of the Exile emphasizes the peculiar relation of the Lord to Israel as her Redeemer. He is gracious to forgive and mighty to save his people. His redemption is both outward and historical, and inward and spiritual. His redemption is not limited or conditioned by the fact that Israel is weak and unworthy of redemption.

(2) The meaning of history, as in 43:14–28. The Prophet of the Exile sets forth a full-blown theology of history. For him all that transpires is in keeping with the divine will. While it is true that God is the moving force behind all history at all times, he also comes in a special way at particular times to act redemptively on behalf of his people. As the book opens, the Lord is about to visit his people anew in their distress, and to lead them forth in a new exodus. Again and again the prophet reminds Israel of the mighty acts of God in their past history to assure them of God's impending act on their behalf in the near future. The history in which Israel plays an important role moves inevitably toward the universal consummation of the redemptive purpose of the Lord of history.

(3) The divine vocation of servanthood, as in 42:1–4; 43:10–13; 44:1–5, 21–28; 52:13—53:12. The so-called servant passages of Isaiah embody some of the most important insights of the book, and, indeed, of the whole of biblical revelation. The problems involved in the interpretation of these passages cannot be dealt with here. The exploration of their meaning will be the major undertaking of several of the lessons in coming weeks. All that can be said at this point is that these passages set forth the astounding insight that Israel's role is to be that of servant, and a suffering servant at that. In the light of the New Testament revelation it becomes apparent that Israel's role of servanthood is in reality an imitation of the redemptive acts of a servant Lord. Thus both the

nature of God and the true destiny of the people of God are illuminated by the servant figure.

(4) The messianic mood, as in 56:1–8. The Prophet of the Exile gave a new dimension to the redemptive purpose of God and to Israel's role in the fulfillment of that purpose. God's purpose, far from being confined to a favored few, reaches out to embrace all mankind. Israel is merely the instrument of God for the ingathering of the nations. She is to be a "light to the nations," all of which are included in God's saving purpose. This idea which had been implicit in God's revelation in times past now becomes explicit. Israel's redemption is instrumental to the higher purpose of him who is the Savior of all men.

HOW TO USE THIS TEXT

It is not my purpose to write a commentary on Isaiah 40—66. Rather, it is my hope that the text may serve the student as a guide for his own study of the Scriptures. If they are needed, good commentaries may be secured, and several are listed in the teacher's book. But even commentaries cannot serve as a substitute for your own careful examination of the biblical text for yourself.

If you have not already done so, take the time now to devote an hour or so to reading Isaiah 40—66. Use the sections of this chapter which give study suggestions as preparation for the reading of each of the three larger sections of the book. Make up your mind now that you are going to pursue your own study in such a way that you will go to class not only to receive something from someone else, but also to share your own insights with others.

3

The Voice of Hope in a Time of Tragedy

A DISPLACED PERSON SPEAKS

Some of us do better in this country than others. You know how it is. Some people adjust more readily than other people, but there are a great many of us who have never put down our roots here and never will. The older people talk about how it used to be in the old country, but I get small comfort from thinking how things used to be. I have to live now, and my life is slipping away. When one is younger he becomes frustrated. He beats his fist on a wall until it bleeds. He vows he is going to change things. But things do not change, and soon he is approaching middle age, and still he is a stranger in a strange land.

Have I told you how things used to be with us? We have not always been as you see us now. We were a proud, independent people once. We had our place in the sun. We had our chance, but it looks as though we shall never have another. I still go through the motions of worshiping with the rest—but largely out of respect for the older ones, for to tell the truth my heart is not in it. If God cares about us, or if he exists at all, he would have done something for us before now, don't you think? The older people say that it is because of the sins of another generation that we are here. As a people, I guess we have had our day, but I missed it. I belong to a lost generation. Now and then some optimist gets up and talks about

135

our national destiny, but I can't respond with any enthusiasm. Let the old folks die with their dreams. They are all they have. What about me? Well, I could dream as a child, but you know what? I don't have any more dreams in me.

A Call for Comfort, 40:1–2

Israel in exile was beset by many problems and difficulties. While many Jews prospered in Babylon and through their ingenuity made some sort of place for themselves in an alien culture, nevertheless they were always aware of the fact that they were a people separate and apart—a peculiar people who could never really *belong* in Babylon. As they dwelt upon present circumstances a generation after their deportation from their homeland, they were overwhelmed by doubt and despair. What about God? Where was he while his people endured captivity? Was he comparable to the gods of the Babylonians, the conquerors? They felt themselves hopelessly doomed, forsaken and uncared for by the God to whom they had historically been related.

A half a century earlier the prophet Jeremiah (as Jesus later would do) had wept over Jerusalem while vainly calling "the people of God" to repentance. The task of the Prophet of the Exile was much different. It was his role to bring hope to a people who had surrendered themselves to self-pity, self-laceration, and despondency. This is the burden of the prophet's message in 40:1–2. Read these verses, noting the evidences of a changed attitude on the part of God toward his people and the expressions of his continued love.

He Is Coming! 40:3–5

The prophet makes a startling and dramatic announcement to the disheartened exiles in 40:3–5. The Lord God Almighty is coming! The God they thought had forgotten them has not forgotten after all. He has been standing in the wings waiting for the appropriate moment to make his appearance. He is coming as a conquering King. The cry goes out to prepare the way for his majestic appearing on the scene of history. The obstacles of wilderness, mountain, and rough place shall not impede his inevitable advent. The hitherto hidden Lord shall now be seen by all flesh. The authority for this amazing declaration is none other than God himself. "The mouth of the LORD hath spoken it."

The Christian church early identified this passage with the coming of Jesus Christ. The "voice in the wilderness" was none other than the voice of John the Baptizer preaching by the Jordan, "prepare the way of the LORD. Make his paths straight." The coming of the Lord was only partially and conditionally fulfilled in the historical experience of the exiles. When Christ appeared in history, God's chosen ones recognized and greeted him as the conquering King of Isaiah 40:3–5. The triumphant affirmation of the Christian faith is that the Lord has not forgotten his exiled people, but has come to deliver and restore them. The whole world has witnessed the Christ event. "All flesh" has seen it.

Proclaim His Eternal Word, 40:6–11

The mood of despair is persistent and does not give way readily to the message of hope. Read 40:6–7 and sense the temper of this disheartened reply to the announcement above. But the prophet will not tolerate a pessimistic outlook! True, we may live in a dying world, but the undying word of God must be proclaimed. "Stop mouthing gloom," he seems to say in 40:8–11. "Get up on the highest mountain top you can find and proclaim to the whole world the good news: Your God is coming!" On the one hand, he comes as a conquering King who rules with a mighty arm. But look at him again. He comes as a gentle Shepherd gathering the lambs in his arms and carrying them in his bosom, leading those that are with young. Here is a colossal giant with infinite strength whose mighty hands are capable of the tenderest and most delicate ministration. What a picture of God! What an expectation this announcement must have created! What a fulfillment the world beheld in Jesus Christ, who set out deliberately to fulfill this hope!

The Incomparable Greatness of God, 40:12–31

Few biblical pictures of God reach such lofty heights of expression as Isaiah 40:12–31. This is a passage that you should read aloud to savor its full flavor. Notice the figures of speech the prophet employs to drive home the conviction that our God is a *great* God. It may prove helpful also to read two modern expressions of the greatness of God. James Weldon Johnson, in *God's Trombones,* recalls a series of sermons by Negro preachers. The first, on creation, speaks to another people in another time of the greatness of God.

> And God stepped out on space,
> And he looked around and said:
> I'm lonely—
> I'll make me a world.
>
> And far as the eye of God could see
> Darkness covered everthing,
> Blacker than a hundred midnights
> Down in a cypress swamp.
> Then God smiled,
> And the light broke,
> And the darkness rolled up on one side,
> And the light stood shining on the other,
> And God said: That's good!
>
> Then God reached out and took the light in his hands,
> And God rolled the light around in his hands
> Until he made the sun;
> And he set that sun a-blazing in the heavens.
> And the light that was left from making the sun
> God gathered it up in a shining ball
> And flung it against the darkness,
> Spangling the night with the moon and stars.
> Then down between
> The darkness and the light
> He hurled the world;
> And God said: That's good!
>
> Then God himself stepped down—
> And the sun was on his right hand,
> And the moon was on his left;
> The stars were clustered about his head,
> And the earth was under his feet.

And God walked, and where he trod
His footsteps hollowed the valleys out
And bulged the mountains up.

Then he stopped and looked and saw
That the earth was hot and barren.
So God stepped over to the edge of the world
And he spat out the seven seas—
He batted his eyes, and the lightnings flashed—
He clapped his hands, and the thunders rolled—
And the waters above the earth came down,
The cooling waters came down. . . .[1]

Ernest Gordon in his *Through the Valley of the Kwai,* tells the story of "displaced" soldiers in a Japanese prison camp during World War II. He relates how these men who were at first reduced to an animal level by the sheer brutality of their captors were restored to manhood by the rediscovery of the greatness of God. They were able to endure their horrible experiences of suffering only because they found faith in such a God.

I recalled what Dostoevski had said in *The Possessed:*
"The one essential condition of human existence is that man should always be able to bow down before something infinitely great. If men are deprived of the infinitely great they will not go on living and will die of despair. The Infinite and the Eternal are as essential for man as the little planet on which he dwells."[2]

Many Christians suffer from a diminutive view of God. They look at him through the wrong end of the telescope with an inverted faith. They see him, but they see him small! How big is your God? Can you believe in a *great* God?

The Conqueror Comes, 41:1–7

Continuing his discourse on God's mighty acts in creation and history, the prophet reminds his hearers that the God of Israel is the God of all the nations, and that all history is but an unfolding of his divine purposes. The nations are bidden to listen in silence as he speaks words of judgment (41:1). Then the question is asked, "Who stirred up one from the east whom victory meets at every step?" The reference here and in the verses which follow (41:2–7) is to Cyrus.

Cyrus was one of the most fascinating figures ever to cross the stage of history. His remarkable career began in 558 B.C., when he succeeded to the throne of Anshan where he reigned as a vassal of the Medes. From that time on Cyrus, who was a Persian, went from victory to victory. He fought his way to supremacy in Persia. From this position of power he proceeded to extend his empire to the west into Asia Minor where he defeated Croesus of Lydia. In 539 B.C. the conquest of Babylonia was completed and he marched unopposed into the city of Babylon itself. The following year he issued the famous edict which permitted the Jews and other captive peoples to return to their homelands if they chose to do so.

At the time of the writing of this oracle the news of Cyrus' victories was spreading like wildfire through the eastern world. The Prophet of the Exile saw the victories of Cyrus as the outworking of a divine masterplan. It was the Lord, the God of Israel, who stirred up this "one from the east." The victories of Cyrus were really the Lord's victories, for in a sense Cyrus was his servant. "Who has performed and done this, calling the generations from the beginning? I, the LORD, the first, and with the last; I am He" (41:4).

The Servant Need Not Fear, 41:8–16

In Isaiah 41:8–16 we encounter the servant theme for the first time. This is a dominant note in chapters 40—48. The prophet returns to it again and again. Yet for all its prominence, the servant theme is somewhat confusing. The identity of the servant is by no means clear nor consistent. Acts 8:26–40 tells the story of Philip's encounter with the Ethiopian eunuch on the road to Gaza. The eunuch, who was reading one of the servant passages from Second Isaiah, asked the question, "About whom, pray, does the prophet say this, about himself or about some one else?" The eunuch was neither the first nor the last to inquire about the identity of the servant. In this passage (41:8–16), the servant is obviously the nation Israel. In other passages, as we shall see, the identity of the servant is not so obvious. At times the servant is the ideal Israel, at other times the instrument of Israel's redemption, at still other times an individual despised and rejected by Israel.

The call to be a servant is not one that men readily hear and obey. As Anthony T. Hanson points out,

> Some men can only hear God's call to service after they have been awakened by suffering. So it was with Francis of Assisi. He only began to think about serving God in any extraordinary way when his carefree career as a rich merchant's son was checked by two events in succession, an imprisonment and a serious illness. We may say the same thing about the people of Israel as a whole. Indeed, we can even trace the parallel in greater detail and say that Israel had to experience a serious illness and an imprisonment before it could awake to God's call to service. . . . It was only national suffering that could bring about the circumstances in which Israel's mission as the servant could be either understood or carried out.[3]

Being the servant of the Lord meant for Israel a life of humility and lowliness. "You worm Jacob" (41:14) was a title that Israel had to accept. But the role of servant carried with it the dignity of being *the servant of the Lord*. As such, Israel could expect the help and protection of God as she fulfilled her role. Read the passage (41:8–16), noting the repetition of the words, "Fear not."

Water in the Wilderness, 41:17–20

Between Babylon and Palestine there stretched out a vast and formidable desert. No doubt this desert was a symbol of all the many and varied obstacles that stood between Israel and the fulfillment of her hope of restoration to the homeland. In the lyrical interlude, 41:17–20, the prophet uses water, a scarce commodity in the desert, as a symbol of God's intention to care for his people in the face of all the obstacles to their aspirations. Read the passage, underscoring the references to water. The desert of desperation will be literally dripping with water and green with the vegetation that could not survive without the refreshing springs and pools which God will provide. The great thirst of God's people for dignity, freedom, and reconciliation is about to be assuaged by the cool streams of his life-giving grace.

The Ridicule of the Gods, 41:21–29

No doubt there were some in Israel who were impressed by the gods of Babylon and their worship. The prophet therefore makes a point of heaping ridicule upon the Babylonian deities. They are summoned in 41:21–29 to prophesy concerning the future. The ability to foretell the future is set forth as an indication of the power and reality of a deity. They are challenged to reveal the future, but they cannot do it. In 42:24 the prophet says in scorn, "Behold, you are nothing, and your work is nought; an abomination is he who chooses you."

The rise of Cyrus as a dominant figure on the world scene is set forth as a case in point. God has stirred up Cyrus, and he has come forth as the rising sun from the east. He has gone from victory to victory, but none of the Babylonian deities were able to predict what he has done or will do. But God has declared to Zion what he is doing through Cyrus. In 41:29 the conclusion of the matter is stated, "Behold, they [the gods of Babylon] are all a delusion; their works are nothing; their molten images are empty wind."

SOME THINGS TO THINK ABOUT

What does this message to ancient Israel in exile mean to you and to the church today? There is a sense in which the church today is living in a "Babylonian Captivity," to use the phrase that Martin Luther used in his day. *If this is true, what force or forces have brought the church into captivity?*

Do you find a mood of pessimism in the church today? If so, why? Does the message of Isaiah 40—41 sound a call to hope?

How do you like the designation "servant"? Do you think the church today is fulfilling the servant role? What would be involved if it did? Are you indeed a servant of the Lord?

Can the gods of contemporary culture serve man today? If not, why?

4

God's Handicapped Servant

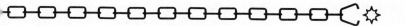

THE DISPLACED PERSON SPEAKS

Things began to change with us when the Poet started singing his songs. You never knew when he might appear. Maybe it would be in the field while we were working; maybe in the marketplace where the women were buying supplies; or maybe in the evenings when some of us sat by the river after the day's work was done. He seemed to make up the songs as he went along. The songs he sang were about us. He knew how we felt, and somehow after he sang we felt better about things. He had a way of saying things in his songs that gave us courage. People listened to him who wouldn't listen to the preachers. He made us all feel that something was brewing that would change things for us.

He said some strange things to us in his songs! He kept saying, for instance, that we were servants. Now that's not a very popular thing to say around here. Many of us work as servants in the big houses. We're a servant class for the most part, but we don't like to be reminded of it. But the Poet gave us a new interpretation of servanthood. He made us feel that there is something great and noble about being a servant—that is, if you are the Creator's servant. He said the Creator chose us centuries ago out of all the people in the world to serve him in a special way. Of course, he said we hadn't always been very good servants! One day he said we were so blind

143

we couldn't see daylight, and so deaf we couldn't hear thunder. He said the Creator had been trying to show us things and tell us things but because we were blind and deaf we just didn't grasp his message.

But he went on to say that the Creator had chosen us and was going to stick by his choice even though we are blind and deaf. He feels the Creator has his heart set on doing something great and important through us no matter what we've done or haven't done in the past. You know what? He makes me feel like I am somebody. After he sings his songs I stand a little taller, and I'm not ashamed to look anybody in the eye.

The Servant's Call and Mission, 42:1–9

The role of the servant is not coveted by many men in our generation. In one of his books, Paul Scherer describes one popular attitude prevailing in our society:

> . . . Listen to one of our current philosophies. "This world in which we live is not a milk and bun shop. It is a thieves' den in which the violent survive and the submissive succumb. In it two things predominate—you grab, or you are grabbed. Every kingdom or republic or empire has been built out of loot; and every kingdom, republic, and empire is ultimately lost to a looter. That you can knock me down and I can knock you down is the supreme fact of history. Grab or be grabbed. . . . And whatever your politics or morals may be, I, anyhow, prefer to be a grabber rather than a grabbee. Grab, grabbing, grabbed—in these three words is condensed ninety percent of world history, and in war the remaining ten percent doesn't count." That was not written by Goebbels or by Hitler; it was written by a general of one of the United Nations, and published in a Sunday pictorial as "a challenge that should be read by every man and woman"! If it is true, then there is no God. Then injustice is ultimate. Prejudice and arbitrariness, chance and brute force are at the bottom of things. Dives is up and Lazarus is down. . . .[1]

We live in a world where economic and military power are often
the ultimate factors by which men make their decisions. We live in
a time when it is every man and every nation for itself. Distorted
ideas of liberty often degenerate into libertinism. The vocation of
servanthood is more often avoided and escaped than sought and
embraced. The sixth century B.C. was no different from our own in
this respect. Yet it was to this vocation that Israel was called—not
to be served but to serve and give up her life.

Read Isaiah 42:1–9 with a view to discovering answers to the
following questions: *Who called Israel to servanthood? Why was
Israel called? What was Israel to accomplish through servanthood?
What was the spirit in which the ideal Israel was to accomplish her
mission? What assurance of success in the mission was given? What
relationship between Israel and the Gentile world was involved in
the fulfillment of the vocation of servanthood? How would God
equip Israel to accomplish her mission?* The answers to all these
questions are in this passage.

Israel was not called to greatness as the world measures it.
Jesus once said to his disciples, "You know that the rulers of the
Gentiles lord it over them, and their great men exercise authority
over them. It shall not be so among you; but whoever would be
great among you must be your servant, and whoever would be first
among you must be your slave; even as the Son of man came not to
be served, but to serve, and to give his life as a ransom for many"
(Matt. 20:25–28). Jesus was merely restating the divine criterion
of greatness. It has always been a strange and unnatural measuring
rod to the world, but it is the only valid one for the people of God.

Matthew 12:15–21 tells of the healing miracles of Jesus
wrought upon the multitudes of sick who sought him out. And
then, quoting our text, he says, "This was to fulfill what was spoken
by the prophet Isaiah: Behold, my servant whom I have chosen, my
beloved with whom my soul is well pleased. I will put my Spirit
upon him, and he shall proclaim justice to the Gentiles. He will not
wrangle or cry aloud, nor will any one hear his voice in the streets;
he will not break a bruised reed or quench a smoldering wick, till
he brings justice to victory; and in his name will the Gentiles hope."
In fulfilling the role of servant in his own life Jesus set before God's
people the perfect example of greatness in service.

Israel was called, and the church today is called, to that strange sort of greatness that manifests itself in humility, self-abasement, and self-giving. The people of God are not called to ease and plenty, nor to the blandishments and plaudits of a world that seeks reward in terms of being served rather than of serving. In his strange wisdom God calls his people to bring forth justice among all the nations of the world—strange wisdom because this justice is to be achieved not through worldly might, but rather through the invincible power of lowly service rendered in the name of God and through the Spirit of God.

The Servant Set to Singing, 42:10–13

The anticipated victory of God and his servants is celebrated in song. In the psalm the ancient Hebrew exile sang, "How shall we sing the LORD's song in a foreign land?" The old song of national pride has been silenced—drowned out by the thundering roar of the fall of Jerusalem which was still echoing in Israel's ears. But here in a strange land God puts a new song in the hearts of his people. The song of the servant is sung to the accompaniment of the music of desert, mountain, and sea, all of which proclaim the greatness of a God who is about to manifest himself in might to his enemies. Read the song of the servant in 42:10–13.

The Silence Only God Can Break, 42:14–17

The Prophet of the Exile was doubtless asked many times why the God of Israel had not spoken more consistently during long decades of captivity. The dismal years of the Exile were for the most part a time when God remained silent. The prophet explained that now the time of silence was over; the God who had held his peace during the time of chastening was about to cry out in a roar that would be heard throughout the created order. His voice would be like a fire that burns up the vegetation of the hills and dries up the waterways. His word would be like a brilliant light that turns the night into day, so that the dim-of-sight would no longer stumble and fall, but would find their way with ease. He will not forsake his own, but those who worship idols shall be utterly put to shame. Read 42:14–17.

God's "Handicapped" Servant, 42:18–25

It would seem that the Almighty would have become disillusioned about the Chosen People long before the Exile. Two hundred years before the writing of this prophecy Isaiah had written,

And he said, "Go, and say to this people:
'Hear and hear, but do not understand;
see and see, but do not perceive.'
Make the heart of this people fat,
    and their ears heavy,
    and shut their eyes;
lest they see with their eyes,
    and hear with their ears,
and understand with their hearts,
    and turn and be healed."
                                    (Isa. 6:9–10)

Two centuries later the tragic blindness and deafness of Israel still persisted. There is a striking difference between the portrayals of the ideal servant of the Lord in 42:1–4 and of the spiritually handicapped servant of 42:18–25. Read these two passages now to get the full force of the contrast. The wonder is that God could and would use Israel, who was still spiritually deaf and blind, to be his servant. The people of God who in past centuries had been insensitive and disobedient to God were still his chosen instrument of redemption.

The church, the New Israel, is often as blind and deaf as Israel of old. The wonder of God's redemptive purpose is that he can and does use such a handicapped servant to accomplish his will. Israel of old (and the church today) lived in a tension between the vision of the ideal servant of 42:1–4 and the reality of the actual servant's handicaps as set forth in 42:18–25. If God judges the church today as he did Israel of old, it is to restore her lost sensitivity to the vision and word of God.

The Preservation and Regathering of the Servant People, 43:1–7

The Lord's judgment upon his blind and deaf servant in

42:18–25 is contrasted with his mercy shown in 43:1–7. Israel has no cause to be afraid in the face of great events that are taking shape on the horizons of history, for the Lord has already redeemed her and will preserve her. Neither water nor fire can destroy her, for the Holy One of Israel is her Savior. Israel's freedom will be purchased at no less a cost than of such great nations of the world as Egypt and Ethiopia. Not only will Israel be preserved in the midst of danger, but she shall be regathered from all the nations of the world. Israel is not to be a lost and forgotten minority scattered throughout the world, but a people regathered and restored to all her former glory.

The regathering of Israel seems to have been confidently expected by the Prophet of the Exile. History proved this to be little more than a grandiose dream so far as the Jews of the Exile were concerned, for only a small proportion of those in Babylon ever actually returned, to say nothing of those who remained scattered among other nations of the ancient world. The Jews are to this day dispersed throughout the world. Either the regathering of Israel is a hope yet to be fulfilled, or there is fulfillment in some other way than that expected by the prophet. Most Christians prefer to believe the latter. The two thousand years of Christian missionary history is a record of God's gathering his people from among all the nations of the world. However, the effect of this prophecy upon Israel of the sixth century B.C. was important. It undoubtedly gave rise to a kind of pre-Christian "Zionism" that stirred a disheartened and discouraged people to hope and action.

The Witness of the Deaf and Blind, 43:8–13

In this passage an imaginary tribunal is called. All the nations are gathered before the Lord, and in the midst of the nations Israel is set as the witness of the Lord to testify to his truth. Israel is God's living testimony to a monotheistic conception of God.

> Before me no god was formed,
>> nor shall there be any after me.
> I, I am the LORD,
>> and besides me there is no savior.
>> (Isa. 43:10b–11)

Despite all her blindness and deafness the very fact of *Israel's* continuing existence was evidence of *God's* existence and work in the world. What about the church, the New Israel, in the world today? Do you feel that the same can be said of the present people of God? In what ways do you feel the church is bearing witness in spite of its "deafness" and "blindness"?

The New Exodus, 43:14–21

The greatest obstacle to the realization of the dream of a re-gathering of Israel was overcome with the overthrow of Babylon. In this passage the prophet specifically predicts the downfall of this great world power that had carried Israel into captivity (43:14). After accomplishing that end, the Lord will prepare a way in the sea and in the desert for the return of Israel. In the formidable desert, streams of water shall flow to give drink to the Chosen People of God as they make their journey home. This is a "new thing" which God is doing. It is unlike anything that he has done before. The blind servant is challenged to behold this "new thing" (42:19).

All of this must have come as heartwarming good news to those who had eyes to see and ears to hear. No doubt there were some who did see and hear and others who though they had ears did not hear and though they had eyes did not perceive. Why do you think some responded to the good news while others did not?

God's Unmerited Grace, 43:22–28

The prophet takes a realistic view of the actual Israel in exile in 43:22–28. Read this passage, noting the points at which Israel has failed. They have not called upon the Lord. They have been weary of their God. They have not offered sacrifices. They have burdened the Lord with their sins and iniquities. How can God use such a servant? Why has he not chosen a more responsive and obedient people?

The only satisfactory answer to these questions is to be found in the nature of God himself. On the one hand he is a God who can and does forgive sin (43:25). At the same time he is a God who judges his people (43:26–28). It is obvious that Israel does not deserve to be dealt with bountifully because of her persistent sin. But God comes in mercy to forgive and restore his erring people. In the particular circumstances under which the prophet wrote it was the mercy of God rather than his justice that needed emphasizing. Israel had known the fires of judgment; now she needed to experience the soothing balm of forgiveness. What does this passage tell you about the way God deals with his people today? Can you think of contemporary illustrations?

SOME THINGS TO THINK ABOUT

The servant theme obviously lies at the heart of the passages under consideration today. To get at the meaning of this lesson for twentieth-century Christians it is necessary to remember that the church of Jesus Christ is the New Israel. If the old Israel was called to be God's servant, the same is true of the New Israel. *What correspondence do you see between the mission of the servant in these chapters and the mission of the servant today? Is the servant people of God "establishing justice" in the world today?*

What assurance of success does the servant have today?

Is the servant today in any sense a handicapped servant, deaf and blind? If so, in what respects? What should the servant church do today in view of the discrepancy between the ideal servant and the actual servant?

5

Once Begotten, Not Forgotten

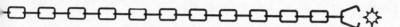

A DISPLACED PERSON SPEAKS

Do you know how it feels to think you're forgotten and forsaken by somebody you really depended on? Well, I know—or I thought I knew. Perhaps you have seen a child lost in a crowd. His father says, "You wait here, son, and I'll be back after while." So the child waits and waits, but the father doesn't return. After a while the child becomes frightened. What if his father has forgotten him? What if he isn't ever going to come back? There are crowds of people around, but there is not a familiar face. The people keep on passing by, but none of them stops to speak to the child. They see that he looks as though he's been forsaken, but they do not wish to get involved. By this time the child has tears in his eyes. He begins wandering around looking frantically at every face. There's just one face he wants to see, and he doesn't see it anywhere.

I think I know how that child feels, for that's the way many of us felt for a long time. We had the feeling that the Creator had gone off and left us in this strange place and had forgotten all about us. You can imagine how glad we were to hear that song the Poet sang about being "begotten, and therefore not forgotten." He said the Creator formed us in the womb of Egypt, and at the proper time we were born as a nation. He said that because the Creator formed us, he never really forgot about us at all. It was we who

151

forgot about him and went around looking for other gods we thought might do more for us. He said that our trouble was that we had been too keen on making our own gods. He said we have the whole thing backwards. We thought we had to "make us a god," when all the while it was God who made us. But the Poet says the Creator has forgiven us everything. He tells us he has swept away all our stupid mistakes as he chases the clouds out of the sky after a spring rain.

God's Gift to His Begotten, 44:1–5

In previous servant passages, the servant is *chosen*. In chapters 44—45 there is repeated reference to the fact that the servant is *begotten* by God.

> Thus says the LORD who made you,
> > who formed you from the womb
> > and will help you . . .
> > > (Isa. 44:2)

> This one will say, 'I am the LORD's,'
> > another will call himself by the name of Jacob.
> > > (Isa. 44:5)

> Remember these things, O Jacob,
> > and Israel, for you are my servant;
> I formed you, you are my servant;
> > O Israel, you will not be forgotten by me.
> > > (Isa. 44:21)

> Thus says the LORD, your Redeemer,
> > who formed you from the womb . . .
> > > (Isa. 44:24)

The Lord will bestow upon the servant whom he has begotten the gift of his Spirit. Read 44:1–5, noting the references to water, which in this instance is symbolic of the Spirit which God will pour out upon his people. The response to the gift is that God's people, instead of continuing to identify themselves with other gods, will openly and proudly confess that they are "the LORD's" (44:5). They will go further. They will offer their hand to be tattooed with the Lord's name, signifying his unquestioned and perpetual ownership. They will be proud rather than ashamed to bear the name Israel.

The reference to the Spirit brings to mind the experience of the church on the day of Pentecost recorded in Acts 2. You will find it interesting to read this chapter now in connection with Isaiah 44:1–5. Also compare John 1:33, "I myself did not know him; but he who sent me to baptize with water said to me, 'He on whom you see the Spirit descend and remain, this is he who baptizes with the Holy Spirit.' "

The gift of the Spirit was a normative (normal, customary, and expected) aspect of New Testament religious experience. This was considered a fulfillment of the promise of the outpouring of the Spirit in Isaiah and other Old Testament prophecies. From the divine standpoint the gift of the Spirit represents God's gift of life, light, and power. From the human standpoint it represents the beginning of a new relationship to God in which we accept the divine name and become his people.

The Only God and His Witness, 44:6–8

This passage contains another great affirmation of monotheistic faith. "I am the first and I am the last; besides me there is no god" (44:6b). He is the Incomparable One. He alone tells from of old the things that are happening. Israel is the living historical witness to the only God. She is charged to bear her witness without fear.

Israel's function as witness to the only God becomes in the New Testament the function of the New Israel, the church. Thus the risen Lord charges his disciples in Acts 1:8, "But you shall receive power when the Holy Spirit has come upon you; and you shall be my witnesses in Jerusalem and in all Judea and Samaria and to the end of the earth." In his defense before the Sanhedrin Peter said, "But you denied the Holy and Righteous One, and asked for a murderer to be granted to you, and killed the Author of life, whom God raised from the dead. To this we are witnesses" (Acts 3:14–15).

Later, before the same body, Peter affirmed, "And we are witnesses to these things, and so is the Holy Spirit whom God has given to those who obey him" (Acts 5:32). In the speech to Cornelius, Peter said, "And we are witnesses to all that he [Jesus Christ] did both in the country of the Jews and in Jerusalem" (Acts 10:39a). The people of God, whether under the Old Testament or the New Testament dispensation, by their existence, their word, and their work say to all men that there is but one God, who is Creator, Redeemer, and Lord.

In Ridicule of Idolatry, 44:9–20

No prophet of the Old Testament attacked idolatry with greater vigor and effectiveness than the Prophet of the Exile. In preceding ages Moses, Elijah, Amos, Hosea, Jeremiah, Isaiah, and others each in his own way denounced Israel's persistent sin of idolatry. The Prophet of the Exile merely laughed at the gods and idolatry. Ridicule is often a more devastating weapon than denunciation. Denunciation may tend to magnify the thing denounced. Ridicule, on the other hand, tends to minimize the importance of the thing scoffed at. Before going any further read Isaiah 44:9–20, preparing yourself for the prophet's sardonic humor. The absolute folly and futility of the whole theory of idol-making becomes apparent.

The making and worshiping of idols is a universal weakness of mankind. Paul went to the root of the matter when he wrote in Romans 1:21–23, "For although they knew God they did not honor him as God or give thanks to him, but they became futile in their thinking and their senseless minds were darkened. Claiming to be wise, they became fools, and exchanged the glory of the immortal God for images resembling mortal man or birds or animals or reptiles." The essense of idolatry is worshiping the creature rather than the Creator.

If this be a valid definition of idolatry, then modern America cannot disclaim guilt for this sin. In a materialistic and power-conscious culture we have set up our modern rivals to God in the form of wealth, power, prestige, and popularity, to say nothing of physical beauty and bodily pleasure. When any or all of these things (which fall within the category of the *created*) demand of us the allegiance that only the Creator deserves, we then become twentieth-century idolaters. All that the Prophet of the Exile says about the folly of idolatry applies as much to the present day idolater as it did to the idolater of the sixth century B.C.

Remember Who You Are, and Sing, 44:21-23

In this lyrical passage Israel is bidden to remember who she is —the servant of God whom he has begotten and all of whose sins he has forgiven. Israel had thought that she was forgotten by God. In fact, it was God who had been forgotten by Israel. Israel's memory of who she was was clouded by centuries of disobedience and lawlessness, but deep in the national unconscious the fact that she belonged to God was written indelibly on her soul. The Prophet of the Exile told the people of his day that they must *remember*. Her hope lay in remembering who she was and who God was.

The joyous fact of God's remembered love and present forgiveness of his people calls forth a song in which all nature joins. Read Isaiah 44:23 to get the full flavor of this joyous expression.

The biblical faith is essentially the *remembrance* of the people of God. The great creeds of the Old Testament, such as Deuteronomy 26:5-9, are the corporate remembrance of God's gracious acts with respect to Israel. The great creeds of the Christian church are the church's corporate remembrance of God's creative and redemptive acts through Jesus Christ. This passage challenges us who are God's people today to remember who we are and who God is and bids us sing for joy, for we are the begotten of God whom he in his redemptive love never forgets.

The God Who Acts and Speaks in History, 44:24-28

God's acts in history are seen in his redemption of Israel whom he formed in the womb, his creation of heaven and earth, his frustration of the diviners and the wise men of Babylonian culture, his confirmation of the word of his servants (the prophets), and his performance of the counsels of his messengers. God's word, which is but another aspect of his act, declares that Jerusalem shall be rebuilt and the foundations of the Temple laid.

This passage is in preparation for the remarkable passage concerning Cyrus in chapter 45. It presents a picture of God as the sovereign Ruler of history who makes even the pagan Cyrus serve his purposes. The Lord is not merely the God of Israel as Bel and Nebo were the gods of the Babylonians. Rather, he is the God who orders all things and who even at the moment of the writing of the prophecy was using people and events beyond the religious life of Israel to accomplish his will. If this view of God be true, then we may conclude that in our own time he still orders the lives of all men everywhere. Now, as in the days of the Prophet of the Exile, he can and does use persons and events *outside* the religious life of his people to work out his purposes in human society.

The Commission of Cyrus, 45:1–8

The most important aspect of this passage is the prominence it gives to the person and work of Cyrus as God's appointed instrument in the accomplishment of his redemptive purpose. In previous passages Cyrus has been viewed as a providential figure in God's world-embracing plan. In 44:28 he is even spoken of as "my shepherd." But in this passage the Persian conqueror is referred to as the Lord's "anointed." This word in the Greek of the Septuagint is *tō christō*. The Aramaic translation of the same word is *messiah*.

It is obvious that these are titles that were later given to Jesus of Nazareth by his disciples. We are not to suppose that Cyrus was a "Christ figure," though there is a tempting parallel between Cyrus' release of the Hebrew captives and our Lord's release of captives of of sin. Cyrus was not a worshiper of the God of Israel. "You do not know me," says the divine Speaker to him in 45:4. However, it is obvious that the title, "the anointed," does place Cyrus in an exalted position as regards the divine plan for the ordering of world events and the redemption of Israel. At this time read 45:1–8, noting what the Lord says in his address to Cyrus.

In 45:1–3 Cyrus' victories are foretold. He will subdue nations, disarm kings, and open gates that have been fast closed in defense against his forces. He shall plunder the riches of Babylon. By these things he shall know that the Lord is God. Not only will Cyrus know this, but also all the peoples of the world who witness his triumphs will know it. By Cyrus' victories all men should learn that the Lord is ruler of both nature and history.

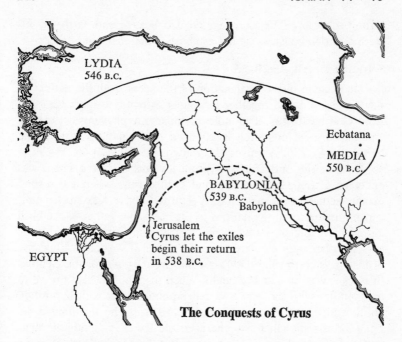

The Conquests of Cyrus

Don't Argue with God, 45:9–13

In these verses the prophet addresses his fellow Israelites who are shocked by what he has said about the pagan conqueror Cyrus. Read 45:9–13, noting the figures of speech and questions by means of which the divine Speaker rebuffs the *creatures* who presume to sit in judgment on the *Creator*. The same God who created the universe has stirred up Cyrus to set the exiles free and rebuild Jerusalem, "not for price or reward" but simply because God has so ordered it.

The Victories of God's Servant, Cyrus, 45:14–19

In this passage a contrast is drawn between what will happen to the wealthy nations of Africa as a result of Cyrus' victories and what will happen to Israel. The former will be spoiled and humbled by the conqueror and will acknowledge that God is with him. These idolatrous nations shall be put to shame and confusion. But not so with Israel! The people of God will be saved with an everlasting salvation. The Lord has created heaven and earth. By his truth and righteousness he has established not chaos but order.

Salvation for All, 45:20–25

Once again in the imagination of the prophet all the nations of the world are called together in a great assembly to hear what the Lord God has to say. The idol worshipers are challenged (45:20–21) and a great invitation is extended to the nations to turn and be saved (45:22). A universal turning is predicted in 45:23–24.

Both before and after this prophecy was delivered Israel was guilty of a tragic introversion and exclusivism. When the second exodus actually took place Israel returned not to take up her universal mission to all the nations of the earth, but rather to establish an exclusive society based upon the law. She turned inward upon herself rather than outward upon the world. It was in part because of his views concerning God's redemptive purpose for the Gentiles that Jesus was hounded to death. When the Apostle Paul turned to the Gentiles with the gospel of redemption he met with opposition and hostility on the part of Jewish Christians who maintained the rigid exclusivism which had characterized Israel's thinking throughout so many centuries of her history. But the prophetic word of the Prophet of the Exile remains as a constant reminder that the people of God are both a redeemed and a redeeming community, the chosen servant through which God will ultimately draw to himself all the nations of the world. The time of fulfillment of what God says, "To me every knee shall bow, every tongue shall swear" (45:23b), is not yet, but it shall be.

The people of God in any day stand in danger of the temptation to forget the world mission that God has entrusted to them. There is a danger even today that we think of the gospel as the "white man's religion" or "the religion of the western world." What are you doing, and what is your church doing about the world mission of the church?

SOME THINGS TO THINK ABOUT

Has God today forgotten his people, the church, when so many of them live under the oppression of dictators? If you were re-

quired to live under these conditions, what would you want to be assured of above all else?

How are we to evaluate spiritually men and movements that overshadow the history that is being made day by day in the world?

Do you think that the time will come when every knee shall bow and every tongue confess that Christ is Lord to the glory of God the Father? What conditions will have to be fulfilled on the part of God's people before this can happen?

6

God's Triumph over Tyranny

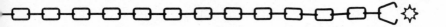

A DISPLACED PERSON SPEAKS

The Poet sings of serious matters, but he also has a sense of humor! You know how it is. One lives here and sees the gods these people worship, and he gets to wondering about it all. If his God is so great, why isn't the Poet rich—and free? They worship their gods and they have everything going their way. We worship our God— the invisible One—and we have nothing going our way. Yes, you get to wondering about it.

Some of our people began carrying around those little statues you see so often in this country. The Poet noticed it and began making up some songs about the gods. He made us laugh at those stupid little gods! He said, "What good to you is a god you have to carry around? You had better worship a God that can carry you around."

He can make you laugh, all right, but he can be very serious, too. He sang some songs about what's going to happen here before long. He says everything is going to change once that man from the east arrives. He said this country is like one of the fancy, painted women of Babylon. The time's coming when she's going to be stripped of her fine clothes and she will be naked and looking for a place to hide and for something to cover her up. She's going to be like a woman whose husband and children have been murdered.

160

All the gods and all the fortune-tellers in this country won't be of any help when the man from the east appears on the scene. He says it will be like a great fire that starts on one side of the country and burns all the way over to the other side, leaving everything in ashes. This will not be a nice, cozy little fire to sit by on a cold day. It is going to be a big, hot fire, and everybody in the country will be running for his life. The Poet says we've been poor servants, but that the Creator is going to do something with us. He says we will be protected when the fire begins. "Pack your belongings," he said, "You're going back home where you belong."

This lesson may be divided as follows: Chapter 46 deals with the coming humiliation of Babylon's gods, chapter 47 with the coming humiliation of Babylon, and chapter 48 with admonitions to escapees. Read the three chapters through before going any further, considering their contents under these three heads.

The Coming Humiliation of Babylon's Gods, 46:1–13

The Poet's gift for ironic humor is again evidenced in Isaiah 46:1–13. In this passage he draws a vivid contrast between Bel and Nebo (the two principal gods of the Babylonians) and the God of Israel.

Bel was the father of the gods in Babylonian mythology. He was later identified with Marduk and the two came to be regarded as one god. In the Babylonian story of creation it was Bel who created the universe. Nebo, on the other hand, was a lesser deity, the son of Bel-Marduk. It was the religious custom in Babylon to carry images of Bel and Nebo through the streets in a New Year's Day procession. The sight of this procession with the beasts of burden bending beneath the load of the heavy statues probably stimulated the writing of 46:1–2. The incongruity of gods who had to be carried about by men and beasts struck the prophet as being utterly ridiculous.

In contrast with the gods who must be borne by men, the prophet writes a noble statement about the God who "bears," "carries," and "saves" his worshipers. The contrast between the gods who must *be carried* and the God who *carries* suggests that there are some forms of religion that are borne like a heavy burden. Do you know of people who "carry" their religion? How about you? Is religion for you a *load* or a *lift?*

The religion that the Bible offers men is one that carries us, not one that we must bear as we would a burden. Psalm 55:22 calls upon us to lay upon the Lord the weight of care which we bear about with us: "Cast your burden on the LORD, and he will sustain you." Jesus issued his great invitation to burden-bearers thus, "Come to me, all who labor and are heavy laden, and I will give you rest" (Matt. 11:28). Peter, in his First Letter (5:7), admonishes his readers saying, "Cast all your anxieties on him [God], for he cares about you." The Prophet of the Exile called God's people to remember who had carried them throughout all the circumstances of their national history.

It is impossible to compare the Lord with other so-called gods. This is the message of Isaiah 46:5–7. Certainly he cannot be compared with gods who must be manufactured and carried about by human hands. Such gods cannot save anyone. Rather, in the time of crisis it is the idol that must be saved by him who worships it.

In 46:8–11 Israel is called upon to remember "the former things of old" as they think about the nature of deity. In all of Israel's history God has repeatedly foretold the outcome of events. He has been a God who has spoken through his prophets of things before they actually happened. God was said to be so speaking in the days of the writing of this prophecy, with special reference to Cyrus. It is the Lord who has called up "this bird of prey" from the east. God is telling of the coming deliverance and salvation of Israel before it actually takes place.

Now read chapter 46 for yourself. I personally find it helpful to read these great poetic passages aloud. No one should be permitted to usurp your right of private interpretation of Scripture. Read the passage and let it speak directly to you.

The Coming Humiliation of Babylon, 47:1–15

Babylon, no less than her gods, faced imminent humiliation. At the time that this prophecy was written, Babylon still seemed on the surface to be strong and vigorous. Her people were in all likelihood complacently unaware of the catastrophe which was soon to come. Like so many other great empires and nations since that time, Babylon felt secure behind her protective walls. There were doubtless those who said, "Things are not as bad as they seem. It can't happen here." But wealth, luxury, and the pursuit of pleasure had weakened the moral fiber of Babylon, and her downfall was nearer than she thought. She was quite unaware of her lack of ability and will to resist the fresh, vigorous military and political force that centered around the personality of Cyrus. Babylon was a ripe plum ready to fall, and she did not know it.

Chapter 47 is a "taunt song" thrown in the teeth of the mighty nation to which Israel was captive. In this passage Babylon is personified by a female figure, "the virgin daughter" (as yet unravished by the conqueror), "daughter of the Chaldeans" (47:1), and "mistress of kingdoms" (47:5). Reading this chapter one gets the picture of a gorgeously arrayed and highly perfumed lady of the harem. Suddenly she will be reduced to abject humiliation. She who is accustomed to sitting on a throne will be made to sit in the dirt. She whose delicate hands have never been devoted to hard work will be made to take her place as a slave-woman at the mill wheel. Her fine clothes will be stripped off, and she will stand naked before the mocking gaze of the world. She who has been a queen, "the mistress of kingdoms," will be driven from her position of security. In a terrible, shocking moment, she will be widowed and her children will be taken away. Evil, disaster, and ruin will soon overtake her. The soothsayers that have attended her will be unable to help or save her. A great conflagration will envelop her and destroy her.

Read chapter 47 now for yourself. Note the things in Babylonian culture that made divine retribution inevitable. Pay particular attention to 47:6, 8, 10, 13. Are any things suggested in these verses that might be characteristic of American life today?

Listen and Learn, 48:1–11

Chapters 46 and 47 contain a judgment on the gods of Babylon and upon Babylon as a nation. Chapter 48 is a judgment upon Israel, yet with a difference which shall be noted later. Israel can hardly gloat over the imminent humiliation of Babylon and her gods when she considers her own past failures and present tendency to err.

As wise men contemplate their past experience they ask themselves a question: What have I learned from my past experience that will help me make a present decision? Some people have the happy facility of making constructive use of the past as they contemplate action looking towards the future. However, this is a somewhat rare quality. Someone has cynically remarked, "The only thing we learn from history is that we do not learn from history." Chapter 48 would lead us to believe that Israel did not learn much from her past. This is evident in 48:1–11.

In 48:1–2 God's disappointment in his people is evident. Israel is called by the name Israel (Prince of God), and she piously swears by the name of the Lord and confesses the God of Israel, "but not in truth or right." She has the outward appearance of fidelity to the Lord, but something is missing. In the next two sections (48:3–6a and 48:6b–8) the Lord speaks of Israel's response to *the former things* and *the new things*. In neither case has she listened with spiritual and moral profit to what God has said. *The former things* spoken of in 48:3–6a refer to what was prophesied and later accomplished by God in the past. All that the prophets foretold, including the captivity, they would not listen to or believe; but these things came to pass nonetheless. The foretelling of these things by the prophets of God should keep Israel from imagining that some false god had accomplished them; that is, that Bel-Marduk brought Israel into captivity.

God will make another try with his people. He will declare to them *new things* that they have never heard before (46:6b–8). Israel is severely rebuked for her deafness, treachery, and rebellion. At this point it seems doubtful whether they will pay any more attention to the new things being revealed (the coming of Cyrus and the downfall of Babylon) than they did to the former things which God had revealed through the prophet.

From the above it is obvious that Israel deserved to be cut off and forsaken by her Lord. In spite of her unworthiness, however, Israel is still the object of God's gracious love. In 48:10–11 there is a lofty statement of God's grace (unmerited favor) in his present dealing with Israel.

These three paragraphs in 48:1–11 might just as well be addressed to the church today as to ancient Israel in Babylon. Explore this whole passage as if it were being addressed to your denomination and your congregation today.

A Renewed Call to Listen, 48:12–19

Isaiah 48:12 begins the second section of this chapter. Here the mood changes. Israel, who has failed so badly to hear in the past, is challenged anew to listen to what the Lord says today. Verses 12–13 identify the speaker as the Creator, the First and the Last. In verses 14–16 attention is directed once again to Cyrus, through whom the new thing is being accomplished. The nations are bidden to assemble to hear what the Lord has to say. As you read these verses note what God says about what he has done for Cyrus and what he proposes to do through him. Verses 17–19 contain a plea to Israel to remember who it is that teaches and leads her. There is a lament that in the past Israel has not harkened to her Lord and therefore has suffered the chastening fires of captivity.

Summons to Flee from Babylon, 48:20–22

Once again the mood changes. One cannot read 48:20–22 without being caught up in the joyous enthusiasm of the new passage. God has redeemed his people; now it is time to go. There will be water in the desert for the fleeing captives in the hour of their deliverance. There will be no peace for the wicked who are left behind.

In the first chapter of this text we observed that the Christian is a sort of "displaced person." This world, in which he is in some sense held captive, is one that has manners and mores, ideas and ideals, radically different from those dictated by his Christian commitment. The redeemed of God are not made for this world, but for another and a better world. So long as we live in this world we are strangers and pilgrims in an alien land. Read through the chapters of this lesson again with this perspective. When you encounter *Babylon* substitute our modern, godless, secular culture. When you come to *Israel* substitute the idea of the New Israel, the church. We must not read into texts meanings that are not there. But we must endeavor to find in the ancient word to Israel a contemporary word for us. Otherwise, Bible study is reduced to the level of literary study, and what comes to us from the Scriptures ceases to be the living word of God. You have not really studied the lesson until you have projected yourself into the text and explored its meaning for you today.

SOME THINGS TO THINK ABOUT

Here are some thought questions based on Isaiah 46—48 that may prove helpful as you get into the passage:

Why do men find it easier to worship things they can see rather than a God whom they cannot see? In what ways do modern men break the second commandment?

What experiences have you had that illustrate the folly and futility of putting your ultimate trust in anything less than God?

Has God acted in judgment against godless culture in our twentieth-century world?

Some modern prophets think that this country is riding for a fall. Do you think this is true? Why, or why not? Should judgment come to us, what form do you think it might take?

What is "secularism," and what are its chief values? What are some substitutes for true religion in a secular society?

Do you think that the church has learned valuable lessons from her own history? If so, what lessons has she learned? What lessons has she failed to learn?

What does fleeing from a godless, secular culture mean for the individual and the church today? Is it possible to live in the world without being of it?

7

Jerusalem

A DISPLACED PERSON SPEAKS

You asked about my people. I grew up an orphan and was cared for by relatives. My father died in the fall of the city, and my mother had her baby on the long trek which followed. Somehow I lived and they brought me on here, but they left her in a shallow grave somewhere along the way. But I have a mother nonetheless. The Poet made me see that. My mother is not a person. My mother is a far-off place that I've never seen, but a place I shall see one day before I die! It is a city that has been burned and ruined, but the builders are going to catch up with the burners. The Poet says so! That's good enough for me.

This city that is my mother has had her woes. Divorced by the Maker because of what she was, and stripped of her children as punishment, she has suffered much for her sins. But that is not the end of the story, sir. She's going to be a faithful wife and mother again—you can count on it. The Poet makes you proud of her in spite of what she has been. He says some of us must lead the others back to her. I don't feel like an orphan any more. I have a mother, and I am going to see her before I am through. And she will not be all bedraggled and shamed. She's going to be the most beautiful mother in the world, and the Creator will be her husband—just as he was before. But this time it is forever!

And in the Spirit he carried me away to a great, high mountain, and showed me the holy city Jerusalem coming down out of heaven from God, having the glory of God, its radiance like a most rare jewel, like a jasper, clear as crystal. It had a great, high wall, with twelve gates, and at the gates twelve angels, and on the gates the names of the twelve tribes of the sons of Israel were inscribed; . . . And the twelve gates were twelve pearls, each of the gates made of a single pearl, and the street of the city was pure gold, transparent as glass. And I saw no temple in the city, for its temple is the Lord God the Almighty and the Lamb. And the city has no need of sun or moon to shine upon it, for the glory of God is its light, and its lamp is the Lamb.

(Rev. 21:10–12, 21–23)

Three important ideas dominate Isaiah 49—50. First, the servant theme is given a new, individualistic treatment. In earlier servant passages the servant has been identified with Israel; now, the servant is called *to serve Israel*. Second, Jerusalem assumes a new importance as a symbol of the restoration of God's rightful rule over his people and of the establishment of the ideal community of the redeemed on earth. Third, the prophecy of the ingathering of the nations makes Jerusalem a symbol of the fulfillment of God's expanded redemptive purpose that includes all mankind in its scope.

The Servant Born and Hid for a While, 49:1–4

In Isaiah 49:1–4 the servant addresses the "coastlands," and the "peoples from afar," that is to say, the Gentile world. He speaks first of his birth, divinely ordered, and his naming by the One who has called him into being. Note the two figures of speech in 49:2. The servant's mouth is made like a *sharp sword* and a *polished arrow*. We are reminded of what is said about "the sword of the Spirit, which is the word of God" in Ephesians 6:17. The writer of Hebrews expressed a similar idea in speaking of the word which is "living and active, sharper than any two-edged sword" (Heb. 4:12). The writer of Revelation presents the striking picture of the Son of Man with a sharp two-edged sword issuing from his mouth (Rev. 1:16).

The mouth of the servant is a mouth through which God speaks. Israel is his spokesman, and his word conquers. After his birth, the servant was hidden for a while. Notice the repeated phrase, "he hid me," in 49:2. This is reminiscent of God's servant Moses, who in his childhood was hidden in order that he might be preserved to become in due season the mouthpiece of the Lord. Isaiah 49:4 is a statement of the servant's mingled doubt and faith as he faces his mission. Looking backward he sees his labor done in vain and his strength spent for naught. Yet he cannot escape the conviction that his right and recompense is with the Lord. He shall yet fulfill his mission.

The Mission of the Servant, 49:5–7

The ideal servant's mission is made clear in 49:5–6. The first aspect of the mission of the servant is in relation to the nation Israel. The ideal servant is not identified with Israel herself. This would seem to indicate that all Israel did not respond to the message of the Prophet of the Exile. The appeal here is to a spiritual elite within Israel who will become sensitive to the nation's mission and carry it out.

Note the ways in which the servant is to serve Jacob (Israel). The servant has been born "to bring Jacob back" to God. God has called the servant to "raise up the tribes of Jacob and to restore the preserved of Israel." The servant thus becomes not only the object of salvation but also the instrument through which it is accomplished. But the servant's mission is not confined to Israel. The prophet here, as elsewhere, reveals the universality of God's purpose of redemption.

> I will give you as a light to the nations,
> that my salvation may reach to the end of the earth.
> (Isa. 49:6b)

The *Nunc Dimittis,* which was sung in the early church and which is quoted in Luke 2:29, bespeaks the Christian conviction

that this universal purpose is fulfilled in the birth and ministry of
God's servant, Jesus Christ.

> "Lord, now lettest thou thy servant depart in peace,
> according to thy word:
> for mine eyes have seen thy salvation
> which thou hast prepared in the presence of all peoples,
> a light for revelation to the Gentiles,
> and for glory to thy people Israel."
>
> (Luke 2:29–32)

The servant's mission to the people of God and to the world
beyond the community of the redeemed is still the mission of the
church. This mission cannot be forgotten by the church without
imperiling her own life.

Verse 7 provides a glimpse of the *suffering* servant who is fully
disclosed in Isaiah 53. The very fact that Israel was "deeply despised, abhorred by the nations, the servant of rulers," amazingly
fitted her to fulfill the mission to which she was called. Before the
spectacle of Israel's humility in the fulfillment of her vocation of
servanthood kings and princes shall prostrate themselves. Because
God has chosen Israel as his servant, all earthly rulers shall ultimately recognize the sovereignty of servanthood. This constitutes a
startling reversal of the world's prescription for greatness and
power. The living fulfillment of this idea is seen ultimately in the
kingly Christ on a cross, who by his servanthood bids all earthly
powers fall at his feet in humble obedience.

The Return of the Servant to the Mother, 49:8–13

Notice the three parts into which this section falls. Verses 8–9a
refer to God's providential care of the servant in the *past*. Make a
list of the things the Lord has done for his people that supply evidence of his loving favor. The second part, 49:9b–12, holds forth
the promises of what God will do in the *future* for Israel. Here we
encounter the second exodus theme again. Just as Israel was called
forth out of Egypt in the time of Moses, even so will God now call
forth his people in a new exodus in which his providential care

will be no less evident than in Israel's past. The third part of the section in verse 49:13 is a call to rejoice in the *present* hope of Israel.

The covenant people of God today, like Israel of old, are a people with a history in which God has been an ever present reality. Like Israel, the church today cherishes an indominitable hope based on God's past record of faithfulness. For this reason the people of God in all ages, when they recognize their true condition, join in the song of the spheres that proclaims the faithfulness and goodness of God. Jerusalem the Golden is an ever present hope of the servant of God in any age.

The Consolation of the Mother, 49:14—50:3

In this passage Jerusalem is compared to the wife of the Lord and the mother of Israel. The opening words of the passage are a cry of desolation of the chastened woman. "But Zion [Jerusalem] said, 'The LORD has forsaken me, my LORD has forgotten me.' " Words of reassurance follow throughout the remainder of the passage. Before going any further with this text read Isaiah 49:14—50:3, listing every element of assurance that is given Zion. Foremost among these assurances is the promise of the return of the exiles after their release from captivity.

This passage manifests the unchanging love of God. In his justice he chastens, as in the case of Jerusalem. But in his love he never forgets or forsakes his people. The figure of the unfaithful wife forgiven and restored by the husband whom she has wronged is not new with the Poet of the Exile. Nowhere is the figure used more dramatically than in Hosea 1—2. These chapters from an earlier prophecy will throw light on the passage under consideration. In both passages the glory of the wife is not to be found in her own moral achievements but in the free grace bestowed upon her by a loving and forgiving husband. The latter glory of the restored and forgiven wife is greater than the former.

The exiles in Babylon must have received these words of the Prophet of the Exile with great joy. The memory of a Jerusalem in ruins was heart-rending and had a chastening influence. The prospect of a Jerusalem restored, forgiven, and glorified by the very

One who brought down upon her the purifying fires of humiliation inspired in them new hope and renewed dedication to God.

Jerusalem is more than a city which has had its ups and downs through the centuries. For both the Old Testament and New Testament people of God it stands as a symbol of that spiritual homeland which they seek.

> Jerusalem the golden,
> With milk and honey blest,
> Beneath thy contemplation
> Sink heart and voice oppressed.
> I know not, O I know not,
> What joys await us there;
> What radiancy of glory,
> What bliss beyond compare.[1]

Ernest Gordon in *Through the Valley of the Kwai* tells of the suffering of the prisoners in the Japanese concentration camps during World War II, and of their rediscovery of God through servanthood. For him and his fellow prisoners the idea of the *New Jerusalem* came to have fresh meaning.

> I was hobbling back to my shack after a rather late discussion session. Passing one of the huts, I stopped. I thought I heard the sound of men singing. They were singing—singing "Jerusalem the Golden." Someone was beating time on a piece of tin with a stick.
>
> The words of the grand old hymn seemed symbolic to me as I listened. Maybe Jerusalem, the Kingdom of God, is here after all, "with milk and honey blest." Maybe man "shall not live by bread alone" (or "rice alone," as we were literally doing). Maybe there is the milk and honey of the spirit that puts hope into a man's eyes and a song on his lips.
>
> They went on as I stood there, singing the hymn once more. The sound made the darkness seem friendly. In the difference between this joyful sound and the joyless stillness of months past was the difference between life and death.

This hymn had the sound of victory. To me it said, "Man need never be so defeated that he can do nothing. Weak, sick, broken in body, far from home, and alone in a strange land, he can sing! He can worship!"

The resurgence of life increased. It grew and leavened the whole camp, expressing itself in men's concern for their neighbors.[2]

The Suffering and Vindication of the Servant, 50:4–9

This passage gives another fleeting glimpse of the suffering servant who is to be fully and shockingly portrayed in 52:13—53:12. Though the word *servant* is not used in this passage, the speaker in these verses is obviously the same servant whose portrait has been developing on the prophet's canvas. Read the passage carefully, noting the following items:

(1) The use of the personal pronoun *I. Who is the speaker?*

(2) The repetition of the phrase, "those who are taught." *What is the implication for servants of God in any age?*

(3) The use of the words "tongue" and "ear" referring to the functions of speaking and listening. *What does this mean for the servant people of God?*

(4) The humiliation, rejection, and suffering of the servant. *Why this suffering? What may the servants of God expect in any age?*

The servant speaker identifies himself as one who has both the tongue and the ear of "those who are taught." This indicates two important aspects of servanthood, speaking and listening. The servant can speak with authority only when he listens to *the* Authority. This has important implications for the servant people of God today. The church can fall and has fallen into one or the other of two errors. Sometimes she has spoken without listening, and sometimes she has listened without speaking. In the first error she has forfeited her divinely appointed power and authority and has become another human voice among many others. In the second error she forsakes her prophetic role and forfeits her mission as the servant teacher. The true servant is one who is taught. "Morning by morning . . . he awakens my ear." But the true servant must also speak what he hears. He must have the "tongue of those who are taught." His mission is in relation to God and to the world, and the key to fulfillment is the divine word.

As his reward for listening and speaking the servant receives the rejection and abuse of the world (50:6). The servant today can expect no other treatment than that which was given to the Servant on the cross. The servant who listens and speaks is on trial before the world. But in the final analysis, no one can declare him guilty, for the great Judge of all men will help him and vindicate him. Those who condemn and accuse him will wear out and disappear, while he shall remain. How true this is of Christ and his accusers! How much this passage has to say to the church today concerning the way in which she listens, speaks, and bears her consequent trials!

An Appeal to Apostates, 50:10–11

Realist that he is, the Prophet of the Exile ends this passage with a ringing challenge to those in Israel who do not listen and do not speak, and who do not obey the voice of his servant. There is a contrast between the faithful who are addressed in verse 10 and the faithless who are addressed in verse 11. The faithful fear, obey, and trust. The faithless kindle their own fire for light, but their end shall be torment.

SOME THINGS TO THINK ABOUT

Among those who are outwardly the people of God in any day there are those who kindle their own fire, who set their own brands alight. Walking in the light of their own wisdom and "common sense" they often feel that *they* have the light while others do not, but in truth it is they rather than the faithful who walk in darkness; they shall miss the reward of those who walk in faith, trusting in the name of the Lord and relying upon God. *What does all of this say to you and your church?*

8

Tidings of Comfort and Joy

A DISPLACED PERSON SPEAKS

Do you know anything about how outsiders feel? You never cease to resent being looked down on by the majority. You see hate and rejection in most eyes you meet. You live in a place where you are isolated from all others except members of your own group. When others treat you as inferior you begin to think of yourself in the same way, but you try not to let it show. I remember that as a youth I secretly felt that I would give half my life to be a member of some race other than my own. I did not especially want to be someone else; I just did not want to be myself. The treatment I received in this country made me wish to forget who I was.

By his songs the Poet began to change this feeling which so many of us had. He keeps telling us to remember, not forget, who we are. As he says, we are "chips off a very old block," Abraham, and we have every reason to be proud of it. You may not know, sir, that Abraham and his wife were a single family, but from that one family all of us sprang. Like Abraham, we have the Eternal on our side, and there is no occasion to be afraid of men whose life is short and passing. Sir, I have learned to be proud of who I am. I belong to the Creator's people and I am the Creator's man. Yes, I know who I am, and I have a lot to live up to. With God's help I will.

The God of Abraham praise,
All praised be His name,
Who was, and is, and is to be,
For aye the same!
The one eternal God,
Ere aught that now appears;
The First, The Last: beyond all thought
His timeless years!

His spirit floweth free,
High surging where it will:
In prophet's word He spoke of old—
He speaketh still.
Established is His law,
And changeless it shall stand,
Deep writ upon the human heart,
On sea, or land.

He hath eternal life
Implanted in the soul;
His love shall be our strength and stay,
While ages roll.
Praise to the living God!
All praised be His name
Who was, and is, and is to be,
For aye the same! [1]

In Isaiah 51:1—52:12 there are two major divisions, each with its own sub-sections. The first section, 51:1–16, speaks comfortingly of the coming salvation of Israel, while the second speaks of the return of the Lord to Zion (Jerusalem) as a conquering King.

The first section starts with a three-fold repetition of the admonition to *harken* or *listen* (51:1–8). Each of these marks the beginning of a new strophe or stanza in the poem. These are followed by a prayer to "the arm of the Lord" (51:9–10), to which prayer comes a response (51:12–16). The second section may be divided into four subsections as follows: a call to Jerusalem to "sober up" from her drunkenness from having drunk deeply the cup of God's wrath (51:17–23), a call to Jerusalem to awaken from sleep and clothe herself in preparation for the coming King (52:1–6), a picture of the triumphant entry of the Lord into the city of Jerusalem (52:7–10), a summons to depart (52:11–12).

Before going any further with the study of this text, read this passage in its entirety, remembering the major divisions and subsections as outlined above. Mark the passages that you do not completely understand with a question mark. Mark other passages that speak to you in some particular way with an exclamation mark. Only after you have made your own study of the passage should you proceed to the study of the analysis below.

Look to the Rock, 51:1–3

This passage is addressed to a people "who seek deliverance," Israel in captivity. Being a minority race in a foreign land must have had a depressing effect upon the spirits of God's exiled people. They lived in the midst of a strange and alien culture. All about them were people who spoke a different language, worshiped different gods, and followed different folk ways. Israel was small and different. How often God's people in the Christian era have felt the same way as they have lived in the midst of godless cultures dominated by pagan ideals. So far as statistics go, Christianity is a major religion in the Western world today, but even here the really dedicated Christian must often be painfully aware of his minority status when all about him there is a way of life strange and alien to the Christian way.

In a sense this passage is addressed to the godly minority in every age. It is a call to the people of God to remember who they are.

> Hearken to me, you who pursue deliverance,
> you who seek the LORD;
> look to the rock from which you were hewn,
> and to the quarry from which you were digged.
> (Isa. 51:1)

The rock referred to here is Abraham. When he was a minority of one God called him, and from a single family sprang a whole race of men. Aside from the minority status of Abraham, attention is called to the quality of Abraham's life and faith. The prophet is saying to Israel, "Remember who you are!" To be quarried from the solid rock of Abraham is to share in the quality of his faith and the faith of all those who have followed his example.

William L. Sullivan makes application of this idea to one's membership in the Christian community.

> . . . When she [the church] takes him [the Christian] to her embrace, he ceases to be a casual atom of humanity; he becomes an heir of the ages, a citizen in the commonwealth of God; his name thenceforward is entered in the vastest brotherhood ever known on earth, and written through this august mediation in the book of life above. . . .[2]

Christians today, like Israel of old, are called upon to remember who they are. They stand in a great succession that goes back to Abraham. The heritage of faith becomes theirs to possess and to impart to subsequent generations when they place their faith in God.

Consider God's Universal Salvation, 51:4–6

As in the case of the first strophe of the poem, this passage is addressed to Israel, but it speaks of the universal application of God's purpose of salvation.

> My arms will rule the peoples;
> the coastlands wait for me,
>   and for my arm they hope.
>   (Isa. 51:5b)

It is especially important to note the nature of God's salvation in this passage. It is characterized by *law, justice,* and *deliverance.* The salvation spoken of here has a *here-and-now* quality. It is not a pie-in-the-sky sort of thing that we are sometimes prone to make of salvation. It is "of the earth, earthy." This salvation is based on moral law; it delivers persons from military and political captivity; it brings justice to oppressed and downtrodden peoples. This kind of salvation has a peculiar appeal for the world today. There are legions of oppressed people who do not get very excited about "going to heaven" but who are terribly concerned about economic and political emancipation and social justice. As this is written the cry is going up around the world, "Freedom now!"

The eternal quality of divine deliverance is described in 51:6. Heaven and earth may pass away, but the deliverance wrought by God shall stand. God's redemption begins here and now in this world, but it extends into eternity. The whole missionary movement of the church today needs to take a fresh look at the meaning of salvation as set forth in Scripture. While being concerned about the souls of men, we must also be concerned about taking measures to establish justice in the lands to which we send our missionaries. The social order as well as the individual is the objective of God's redemptive purpose.

Don't Fear Hatred, 51:7–8

This passage would seem to indicate that Israel in captivity was required to live with the sometimes smoldering, sometimes burning, hate of their oppressors. This passage is addressed "to the people in whose heart is my law." Those who hold the law of God in their hearts inevitably incur the reproaches of men. Jesus prepared his disciples for this when he said,

> Blessed are you when men revile you and persecute you and utter all kinds of evil against you falsely on my account. Rejoice and be glad, for your reward is great in heaven, for so men persecuted the prophets who were before you.
>
> (Matt. 5:11–12)

Paul recounted his own experience of the "reproaches of men" when he wrote,

> Five times I have received at the hands of the Jews the forty lashes less one. Three times I have been beaten with rods; once I was stoned. Three times I have been shipwrecked; a night and a day I have been adrift at sea; on frequent journeys, in danger from rivers, danger from robbers, danger from my own people, danger from Gentiles, danger in the city, dan-

ger in the wilderness, danger at sea, danger from false brethren; in toil and hardship, through many a sleepless night, in
hunger and thirst, often without food, in cold and exposure.
(2 Cor. 11:24–27)

In all their suffering at the hands of their enemies, the people
of God are to remember that their oppressors abide but for a moment, while God's deliverance is forever.

A Prayer for Divine Action, 51:9–11

This is a prayer addressed to "the arm of the Lord," the same
arm that had been employed in the creation of the universe and
in the deliverance of Israel from the Egyptian bondage. The reference of Rahab and the dragon suggests on the one hand the Babylonian myth of creation, but on the other hand it points to the
Lord's defeat of Egypt, for Rahab is also a symbol of Egypt. In
any case, this passage points to the fact that God is the Creator
and Lord of the universe, the Sovereign God who accomplishes his
will in all that comes to pass.

How often the people of God, wearied with injustice and oppression, have cried out to the Lord to step in and take a strong
hand in human affairs. Such a cry is natural in a world where so
often goodness seems to occupy the cross while evil occupies the
throne! This is a prayer of remembrance in which God's activity
in the universe is recalled in perspective. We do well to remember
that God has never forsaken his universe and his people since the
day of Creation. He will yet bring joy and singing to Zion.

The Divine Response, 51:12–16

These are words of comfort addressed to an oppressed people.
The recipients of the oracle are bidden to put away their fears of
men who live, die, and are forgotten like the grass. Unlike the men
of whom the oppressed are afraid, God is eternal and omnipotent.
In an earlier passage Israel was called upon to remember her heritage (51:1–3). Now she is called upon to remember her God, who
created the universe and will deliver the oppressed and captive people of God. God's special providence with respect to Israel may be
traced to the fact that he has committed to her the prophetic word.

Deliverance is due not to the fact that Israel is the object of divine favoritism, but rather to the fact that she has a divine vocation to speak the word that has been put in her mouth.

Sober Up! 51:17–23

These verses constitute the beginning of the second major section of this study. The prophet returns to the Jerusalem theme dealt with at length in the preceding chapter of this text. Here Jerusalem is pictured as a staggering, drunken woman. The intoxicant that has made her drunk is the wrath of God of which she has imbibed freely. But the time has come for her to sober up! The bowl of God's wrath from which she has drunk has been removed and has been given to Babylon. The time of divine chastening is over for Jerusalem; it is about to begin for Babylon. God may use a Babylon to punish the infidelities of his people, but he also is a just God who punishes the instrument of his wrath for her cruelties.

Wake Up! 52:1–6

Continuing the figure of Jerusalem as the woman who has staggered in drunkenness, Zion is now bidden to waken from her stupor and to dress herself properly to meet her Lord. "You have slept long enough in the gutter," the prophet seems to say. "Put aside the signs of the gutter. Put on your beautiful clothes which are befitting your station. Get up out of the dirt. Put off the bondage of your drunkenness and dress yourself appropriately for the freedom to which you are about to be restored."

Isaiah 52:3–6 is a great proclamation of the grace of God. Salvation is free. It is not something that can be earned by good behavior. Israel could not qualify on those grounds and neither can we. God's people were sold for nothing; they shall be redeemed for nothing. The prophet makes references to prior enslavements of Israel by Egypt and Assyria. As God delivered them from prior oppression, so now he will deliver them from the Babylonian oppression. God's name is despised by the pagans, but it shall be known and cherished by his own people. In the final words of this passage (51:6) the coming of the Lord himself is presaged. Israel will know that it is the Lord who speaks, for he will be present.

The King Comes, 52:7–12

This passage points to the answer to the prayer for the awakening of the arm of the Lord in 51:9. The Lord is coming! His advent is near! He will bring good tidings of peace! He will publish salvation! Already the watchmen (the prophets) have seen his coming from afar, even before the people in the city are aware of his approach, and they sing out for joy. The Lord's actual coming is so certain that it may be regarded as an accomplished fact. The whole world will behold his mighty act of redemption and shall see the salvation of the Lord when he comes.

SOME THINGS TO THINK ABOUT

The early Christian church cherished this bit of prophecy for obvious reasons. To them it was clearly and decisively fulfilled in the life and ministry of Jesus Christ. In Peter's sermon to the household of Cornelius he said, "You know the word which he sent to Israel, preaching good news of peace by Jesus Christ (he is the Lord of all), . . ." (Acts 10:36). In his letter to the Romans (10:14–15) Paul wrote, "But how are men to call upon him in whom they have not believed? And how are they to believe in him of whom they have never heard? And how are they to hear without a preacher? And how can men preach unless they are sent? As it is written, 'How beautiful are the feet of those who preach good news!' "

We are not to suppose that the Prophet of the Exile had distinct information about the coming of Jesus Christ. It was his task to announce the coming event, the divine advent. It was God's prerogative to fulfill this in his own time and in his own way. To Israel in exile this word of prophecy meant that God would not stand at some remote point to direct the deliverance of Israel. Rather he would himself enter the human scene. He would return to the forsaken city and take up his abode with her whom he had for a while forsaken. As Christians we have no alternative but to view this passage through New Testament eyes.

9

The Suffering Servant

A DISPLACED PERSON SPEAKS

Suffering has become a way of life for us. There are all kinds of suffering, you know, and we have experienced them all. There is the suffering of being despised and rejected. Sir, we are dirt under the feet of our conquerors. Once we were a proud people, holding up our heads among the nations of the world. As you see, we are now nobodies. We have suffered every indignity. We have been humiliated before the eyes of all men. There is also the physical suffering to which many of us have been subjected in this land. Many of us bear the scars of the whip and the rod. Many of our noblest people have made their graves among these wicked people, having died undeserved deaths at the hands of our masters. Our hearts are heavy with grief and sorrow. Our tears and our blood have watered the soil of this alien land.

Some of us have found it hard to understand the Maker's ways. If, as the Poet says, we are his very own people, why does he permit our suffering? Why does he not intervene to end our agony and punish our oppressors? Oh, we have sinned and our fathers before us sinned, but the Poet says we have received double for all our sins. Why then this continued suffering? Does the Maker neither know nor care what is happening to his people? These are the questions that we put to the Poet.

He gave us a strange and unexpected answer. He said that suffering is our national vocation. This is what the Maker has called us to do. Someone asked the Poet if suffering were not the penalty of sin. Do you know what he said? He said that this was true, and that because it was true the Maker has called us to bear the suffering due the unrighteous. It is the righteous servant's lot to suffer for others. The Poet made us see that the Maker, who made all men, is as concerned about the unrighteous man as he is about the righteous man, and that we must share this concern. This is what it means to be the Maker's righteous servant—to bear the burden of the sins of others.

Then the Poet said the strangest thing of all. He said that the cost of redemption was the suffering of the Maker himself. Our suffering, he says, is the mark of the Maker's men. We suffer as he does—for the sins of the whole world. With him we must embrace the tragedy of mankind, that we and all men may one day triumph over sin.

The Song of the Suffering Servant (Isaiah 52:13—53:12) is the high point of prophetic insight of Isaiah 40—66. It sets forth the astounding idea that the suffering of the righteous, deliberately and vicariously undertaken, may bring redemption to the unrighteous. Here, in the suffering of the lonely, humble figure of the Servant, Israel's role in the redemptive plan of God in history is revealed. The passage likewise furnishes the Christian church a blueprint for its life among men as it fulfills its mission to the world. The unique means of the salvation of the sinful, rebellious race of men is spelled out in terms of the humiliation and exaltation of the Servant.

But does the prophet merely personify Israel (and the church) in the person of the suffering Servant? There are some scholars, to be sure, who maintain that this is the case. However, most interpreters of this passage since the days of the early church have seen it as a prefiguration of the suffering Savior on his cross. Most Christian readers of the passage will share the view that has been dominant in the church throughout all its history.

The form of the poem is that of a dramatic dialogue between God and the peoples of the earth. It is divided into three well defined strophes as follows: the coming exaltation of the Servant, 52: 13–15, the career and death of the Servant, 53:1–9, and the success and destiny of the Servant, 53:10–12.

The Coming Exaltation of the Servant, 52:13–15

These verses form a prelude to the rest of the poem which follows in Isaiah 53. In this strophe the Lord proclaims the brilliant destiny that awaits his Servant. Though the Servant has been held in contempt, he will startle the whole world so that even kings will become reverent and humble in his presence. *How has this been historically fulfilled in Christ's humiliation and subsequent exaltation in history?* (From this chapter on, instead of having a closing section, "Some Things to Think About," the author has scattered such material throughout each chapter.)

The Career and Death of the Suffering Servant, 53:1–9

Chapter 53 begins with a complaint about the world's unbelief that has resulted in the misunderstanding and rejection of the Servant (53:1). Then follows an account of the Servant's career: his youth (53:2), his rejection by men and his consequent life of sorrow (53:3), his vicarious bearing of the sins of men (53:4–6), and his death, like that of a sacrificial lamb led to the slaughter (53: 7–9). *It will be an interesting exercise on your part if you will think of, and, better yet, write down, the events in the life of Jesus of Nazareth which bear out what the poem says concerning the suffering Servant.*

The Success and Destiny of the Servant, 53:10–12

The suffering and death of the Servant do not constitute a meaningless tragedy. A divine purpose is served by his humiliation and death. The Servant becomes the instrument for the establishment of true religion. His self-offering is the means by which he achieves an eternal status. Though he has been cut off from life without a normal progeny, he shall nevertheless see his seed, and in his hands the will of God shall prosper. He shall look back upon his sorrow with satisfaction and joy. Through the perfect righteousness of One, many shall be accounted righteous (the New Testament idea of justification by grace). The Servant shall be numbered among the great because he has borne the sin of transgressors. *How do New Testament interpretations of Christ's death coincide with the meaning of the suffering and death of the Servant as set forth herein?*

The New Testament Understanding of the Suffering Servant

It is safe to say that the church's basic understanding of the life, ministry, and death of Jesus Christ rests more on the foundation of the book of Isaiah, especially Isaiah 40—66, than upon any other book of the Old Testament. The Gospel of Mark opens with a quotation of Isaiah 40:3. The connection between the Old Testament prophecy and the Incarnation of Christ is echoed in the other Gospels. The Christmas songs from Luke indicate a prophetic understanding of the birth of Jesus. In connection with the baptism of our Lord, Isaiah 42:1 is quoted. Jesus viewed his ministry as a fulfillment of the servant role as set forth in Isaiah 61:1–2. Again and again there are clear echoes of the book of Isaiah throughout the Gospels. The connection between the Servant Lord and the Servant of the book of Isaiah is unmistakably reflected in Mark 10:45 where Jesus says, "For the Son of man also came not to be served but to serve, and to give his life as a ransom for many."

The early church found an answer to the scandal of the cross as they identified the crucified Savior with the Servant of Isaiah 52:13 —53:12. In Peter's first sermon, the death of Christ was interpreted as the crime of unjust men wrought upon the righteous Lord, a crime for which they would be held guilty by God. By the time of the preaching of the second recorded sermon Peter had gained a deeper insight into the meaning of Christ's death. ". . . the God of our fathers, glorfied his servant Jesus, whom you delivered up and denied in the presence of Pilate, when he had decided to release him" (Acts 3:13). The important thing to note is that the crucified

Lord is referred to as God's *Servant*. Philip, preaching to the Ethiopian eunuch on the road to Gaza, interpreted Isaiah 53, which the eunuch was reading, in terms of the death of Jesus Christ. Paul in the letter to the Philippians sees the Incarnation of Christ as the assumption of the servant role by Christ:

> Have this mind among yourselves, which you have in Christ Jesus, who, though he was in the form of God, did not count equality with God a thing to be grasped, but emptied himself, taking the form of a servant, being born in the likeness of men. And being found in human form he humbled himself and became obedient unto death, even death on a cross. Therefore God has highly exalted him and bestowed on him the name which is above every name, that at the name of Jesus every knee should bow, in heaven and on earth and under the earth, and every tongue confess that Jesus Christ is Lord, to the glory of God the Father.   (Phil. 2:5–11)

The Redemptive Suffering of God

Human sin produces guilt, which has a two-fold dimension. On the one hand, guilt is *subjective* or *felt guilt*. It is felt specifically because one has committed particular sinful acts, and it is felt generally (in the form of anxiety and alienation from God) because one has a sinful nature that is in rebellion against God. This kind of guilt is a fact of human consciousness, the degree depending upon the moral sensitivity of the individual.

But guilt has another dimension. It is not only subjective or felt guilt, it is also *objective* or *actual guilt*. It is not only a feeling; it is also a fact that must be dealt with in some objective way. Because of the hardness of the human heart men may not feel their guilt keenly, if at all. But the mere absence of feeling of guilt does not change the fact that sinners are guilty before God. Robert Clyde Johnson puts it this way:

> Jesus . . . *redirects* our guilt by revealing, to our utter chagrin, that it is first of all guilt *before God*. When we betray the trust of our employer, offend a friend, or inflict suffering

upon our family, we have of course sinned against our employer, our friend, or our family. This is serious enough. But Jesus forces us to recognize that there is something infinitely more serious: the fact that all sin is initially sin against our Creator. . . .

What can we do about *this* kind of guilt?

Nothing.

Nothing?

Exactly nothing.

We live in a do-it-yourself age, but here all "self-help techniques" are futile. We cannot solve this problem by taking up a hobby, or going to Florida, or buying a book, or adopting a cause, or thinking positive thoughts. Even psychiatric treatment finds its limits here. Much can be done for exaggerated or misplaced feelings of guilt or for an irrational "sense of guilt." But we can do precisely nothing, and there is precisely nothing that anyone can do for us to rid us of our guilt.

. . . *Unless God himself should do something.*[1]

In the death of the suffering Servant believing Christians discover for themselves that God *has* done something—something concrete, tangible, and historical—something that no one else could do. The spectacle of the suffering Servant discloses, on the one hand, the depth of man's sin. Here sin is stripped of all its deceptive and alluring enticements. It appears as it is: stark, ugly, outrageous, contemptible, and utterly damnable. At the same time, the spectacle of the suffering Servant also discloses the height of God's love, because of which he offered up his own Son for the sin of the whole world. The cross of Christ historically demonstrates that God is serious about our sin, but that he is equally serious about our redemption. The cross is not merely the brutal execution of a Galilean carpenter; it is also the ultimate disclosure of a divine love that fulfilled the moral condition of the forgiveness of human sin. Forgiveness is costly business. Forgiveness that costs nothing is merely tolerance of evil which is worse than evil itself. But a love that pays the infinitely costly price of forgiveness not only effects the remission of sin but also the restoration of the sinner to God.

The vicarious (substitutionary) suffering of Christ is a theological doctrine to be sure, but it is infinitely more. It is a fact, potential or actual, of human experience. We can only really know this doctrine as we know it in our experience; otherwise it is sterile dogma. Christ's suffering for men must become in my mind Christ's suffering for me. It is said that Martin Luther was once found on his knees in a chapel with a crucifix in his hands. Tears flowed down his cheeks as he sobbed over and over again, "Für mich! Für mich!" *For me* he bore my sins in his own body on the tree. What does Christ's death mean for you?

The way of the suffering Servant is also the way of the servants of the Servant. He took upon himself the burdens of mankind, and his followers in all ages since have been men and women who have taken upon themselves the burdens of others. Redemption is costly, and it is our privilege as servants of the Servant Lord to suffer with him for the redemption of the world.

> Therefore, since we are surrounded by so great a cloud of witnesses, let us also lay aside every weight, and sin which clings so closely, and let us run with perseverance the race that is set before us, looking to Jesus the pioneer and perfecter of our faith, who for the joy that was set before him endured the cross, despising the shame, and is seated at the right hand of the throne of God.   (Heb. 12:1–2)

G. A. Studdert-Kennedy was an English chaplain during World War I. He found the inspiration for many of his poems in the experiences that came to the common soldier during those terrible and tragic months in the mud of the trenches of France. In the poem, "The Sorrow of God" he captures in cockney English certain important facets of the meaning of God's suffering on behalf of us men in the crucifixion of Christ.

> . . . The Sorrows o' God mun be 'ard to bear
>   If 'E really 'as love in 'Is 'eart,
> And the 'ardest part i' the world to play
>   Mun surely be God's part. . . .
> I wonder if God can be sorrowin' still,

And 'as been all these years.
I wonder if that's what it really means,
    Not only that 'E once died,
Not only that 'E came once to the earth
    And wept and were crucified?
Not just that 'E suffered once for all
    To save us from our sins,
And then went up to 'Is throne on 'igh
    To wait till 'Is 'eaven begins.
But what if 'E came to earth to show,
    By the paths o' pain that 'E trod,
The blistering flame of eternal shame
    That burns in the heart o' God?
O God, if that's 'ow it really is,
    Why, bless ye, I understands,
And I feels for you wi' your thorn-crowned 'ead
    And your ever piercèd 'ands. . . .
The beacon light of the sorrow of God
    'As been shinin' down the years,
A flashin' its light through the darkest night
    Of our 'uman blood and tears.
There's a sight o' things what I thought was strange,
    As I'm just beginnin' to see:
'Inasmuch as ye did it to one of these
    Ye 'ave done it unto Me.'[2]

10

The God Who Keeps Covenant

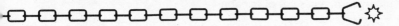

A DISPLACED PERSON SPEAKS

I have a friend named Aheb. A few years ago he fell in love with a girl. A beautiful girl she was—the kind that men turned around and stared at when she walked down the street. Aheb was about the happiest person in the world when she said yes. Well, she seemed to love Aheb as much as he loved her, and after a while they were married. When Aheb made his marriage vows he meant every word he said, but it seems the girl didn't. Wasn't long before Aheb's friends began dropping hints about what was going on behind his back. It seems that he tried not to see that she was being unfaithful to him. You see, he loved this girl more than anything in the world and wanted to believe the best about her. Of course, I think he must have known what was going on and hoped she would come to her senses and change her ways, but she didn't. Every day after Aheb went to work her "friends" would drop by, first one for a while, then another. You know how neighbors begin to talk, but it wasn't just gossip.

Aheb was always patient and kind, but when he came home one day and found out that what the neighbors had been saying was true, he got crying mad and ran her away. Nobody blamed him for it. Aheb took it all very hard. It almost broke his heart. You see he'd given her every chance in the world to change, but she was

191

headstrong and wanted to have her own way. He told me later that he talked to her time and time again. She would either say the neighbors were lying, or she would say that she was sorry and promise not to do it again. I guess there just had to be a breaking point somewhere. After all, Aheb had his honor to think about, so he finally turned her out of his home.

Well, she walked about the streets and took a lot of men's money. After a while she began to look pitiful and bedraggled. Aheb kept on watching her day after day in all her shame, his heart aching all the time. You see, he loved her still in spite of everything. Finally, he went up to her on the street one day and said, "Look, do you want to come home and be my wife again? If you do, just follow me home and no questions will be asked." He turned around and walked away, and she bowed her head and followed him. He treated her as though nothing had ever happened. She had learned her lesson, I guess. She and Aheb have a whole houseful of children now. Ever since that day she has been a real wife to him. He never mentions what went before. He seems happy just to have her there at home, loving him and taking care of the house and family.

Now the Poet says that the Maker is just like Aheb. He had to run us out of the house a generation ago. That's why we're here. But he says the Creator is going to take us back, just as Aheb took back his wayward wife after she had wronged him terribly. He says that the Creator has married our nation, and that he still loves his people.

The cement that binds chapters 54 and 55 together is the idea of the covenant. The idea of marriage, which dominates chapter 54, implies the covenant bond. After speaking of the everlastingness of the covenant with Noah the writer goes on to speak of the "covenant of peace" (54:10) which shall not be removed. In chapter 55 the prophet speaks of God's "everlasting covenant" with David. Chapter 54 may be designated, *the restoration of a broken covenant,* and chapter 55, *an invitation to renewal of covenant.* In chapter 54 Jerusalem is again personified as a woman who has been put away by her husband for her unfaithfulness, but who is now about to be restored her former place in the husband's home and affection. Chapter 55 is an urgent and beautifully stated invitation to Israel to return to her former covenant relation with her God. This chapter is one of the most appealing foretastes of the Christian gospel to be found anywhere in the Old Testament.

The Barren Has Given Birth, 54:1–3

In Hebrew culture barrenness was a reproach to a woman and fruitfulness a blessing. The Old Testament abounds in accounts of women who were apparently barren, but who, because of their faithfulness, were finally blessed with children. In Isaiah 54 Jerusalem is compared to a woman without children who will soon be blessed with a great multitude of offspring. Read 54:1–3, noting the two imperatives, "sing," and, "enlarge the place of your tent," each followed by a clause beginning with the word "for," denoting the reason for the imperative. The sense of the whole passage is that Jerusalem, the barren woman, should rejoice, for she is soon to be enlarged by the birth of many children. This is a poetic way of saying that God will vastly increase the number of Israelites. The new Jerusalem will far exceed the former.

The Wife Restored, 54:4–10

This is a theme already made familiar by Hosea, Jeremiah, and Ezekiel, and by the Prophet of the Exile himself in earlier passages. Jerusalem (Israel) is the unfaithful wife. The Lord is the husband. The divorce is the fall of Jerusalem and the Exile. The covenant is the marriage vow between the Lord and Israel. Here we observe the stark tragedy of a broken covenant between God and his people. Because God is righteous he has put the wife away. Because he is merciful and gracious he takes her back again. *Read the passage now, noting* that the shame and reproach of the divorced wife is about to be removed, 54:4; note also the call of the husband to the erring wife to return, 54:5–6; the wrath and mercy of the husband, 54:7–8; and the everlasting character of the covenant, like the covenant made with Noah, 54:9–10.

The Restored Wife Adorned, 54:11–17

The wife who has been afflicted (in exile) is about to be adorned as a bride. Read 54:11–12, noting the mention of precious stones denoting the beauty and costliness of the bride's attire. In 54: 13–17 a series of promises is made to the wife who is about to be restored: Her children will be instructed. Her sons will prosper. She shall be established in righteousness. She shall no longer fear oppression. She shall enjoy divine protection.

Invitation to Covenant, 55:1–5

This is one of the most appealing statements of God's call to men to be found anywhere in Scripture. The call of the Christian gospel to a spiritually hungry and thirsty race of men is clearly anticipated in this Old Testament passage. Read 55:1–2, noting some of the aspects of this call. Give special attention to:

(1) The nature of the appeal. As food and drink are necessary to man's physical life, so God is necessary to his spiritual life.

(2) The broadness of the appeal. The call is to "every one who thirsts." The call was directed primarily to Israel in exile, to be sure, but the universalism of the prophet expressed in many other passages would suggest that no one is excluded from the divine call.

(3) The opposite pull of other satisfactions. "Why do you spend your money for that which is not bread, and your labor for that which does not satisfy?" (55:2a.) The people to whom the prophet addressed himself in this passage were as human as we are. Like us, they were spending their resources for that which did not really satisfy. What the prophet offered Israel was the uncertainties of life in a country which they had never seen and which had lain in ruins for more than a generation. Even though it be in captivity, life in Babylon offered some security.

(4) The abounding grace of God. "Come, buy wine and milk without money and without price" (55:1b). Even if she wanted to do so, Israel could not pay for the satisfactions freely offered by

God. This is the meaning of grace—that God gives when we cannot possibly pay. No price is placed on divine mercy.

(5) The invitation to hear. "Hearken diligently to me, and eat what is good, and delight yourselves in fatness. Incline your ear, and come to me; hear that your soul may live" (55:2*b*–3*a*). The hearing spoken of here is the kind of hearing that evokes an obedient response.

(6) The promise of life as the essence of the divine gift. ". . . hear that your soul may live." The life spoken of here is not such as can be *quantitatively* measured; it must be *qualitatively* measured.

God's offer to his people is concluded by an everlasting covenant, "my steadfast, sure love for David" (55:3). This passage has been given several different interpretations. That which is most apt to appeal to Christians views this covenant as centering around a Messianic Figure of the line of David in whom God's promises to David and to Israel would one day be fulfilled. The coming Messianic Figure would bear his witness to the nations and rule the people of God. In him all that Israel should be would be fully summed up. His call to the nations (55:5) would be what we know as the Christian evangel. These very important verses deserve your most careful thought and study.

The Urgency of the Appeal, 55:6–9

This passage is an earnest call to repentance. It notes first of all that the moment of response to the call is *now*. There had not been such a moment previously; it was by no means certain that there would be another such moment subsequently. "Seek the LORD while he may be found, call upon him while he is near" (55:6).

The urgency of the moment in which the prophet wrote suggests two ways of thinking about time. On the one hand, there is clock time (*chronos* in the Greek) which can be exactly measured in minutes, hours, days, months, and years. But there is also another kind of time (*chairos* in the Greek) which is the right, appropriate, propitious, or only time. The first thinks of time quantitatively, the second qualitatively. In 55:6 the second kind of time is contemplated. The prophet's thought may be paraphrased thus: "Now is *the* time for your rapprochement, your reconciliation with God. This is a peculiar time in which God has drawn near in a unique way. It may be that this is one of those now-or-never moments. There may not be another opportunity. Grasp this one while you can. God can be found now, for he is near. Tomorrow it may be different. You may look for him in vain."

The key to this passage lies in two words, "ways" and "thoughts." Read the passage through, noting and underlining where these words are used with reference to men, and where they are used with reference to God. The wicked man is bidden to forsake his way, and the unrighteous man his thoughts. Here are two essential dimensions of a man's life, what he does and what he thinks, and both are determinative of what he is. It is not enough in personal repentance to forsake evil ways. One must also forsake evil thoughts. In the final analysis thought patterns determine action patterns. To really forsake the latter, one must utterly uproot the former. The need for radical change in the sinner's ways and thoughts is bound up with the character of God's ways and thoughts, which are utterly different from those of the sinner. If we are to have fellowship with God we must not only forsake our own sinful ways and thoughts, but must learn to think God's thoughts after him and walk where he walks. Great is the gulf between sinful man and the infinitely holy and righteous God, but somehow this gap is progressively bridged by repentance and the life of faith.

Urgent calls to repentance, especially the repentance of individuals, are seldom heard in the church today. Men often entertain the mistaken notion that God's grace is cheap, and that God does not require or expect radical transformation of life on the part of those who accept his call. *What does God expect of you? Does he expect you to forsake certain ways and thoughts in order that you may turn to him, that he may have mercy upon you? Are there things for which you are sorry, but about which you have done nothing? How do your ways and thoughts look alongside of God's ways and thoughts as revealed to you in Jesus Christ?* You may wish to discuss this with the class when you meet next time.

The Redemptive Word, 55:10–11

God's purpose of salvation is not only embodied in his word; it is likewise accomplished by his word. Read 55:10–11, noting the figure of speech that is used to describe the redemptive function of the divine word. What rain and snow are to the thirsting earth, God's word is to a spiritually thirsting race of men. As the rain does not return to heaven without accomplishing its purpose of watering the earth, so also God's word does not return to him without accomplishing its redemptive purpose.

The *word of God* is an important concept both in the Old Testament and in the New Testament. In the Old Testament it was a word that came primarily through Creation, through the words of the prophets, and through the law. In the New Testament it comes preeminently in Jesus Christ, who not only spoke but who *was* the Word become flesh. In him the word and act of God become one. All that God had to say to humanity, all that he may ever have to say, was said, is being said, and will be said through this same Jesus Christ. With Christian insight we become aware of the fact that the Word of God in Jesus Christ was no innovation. "In the beginning was the Word, and the Word was with God, and the Word was God. He was in the beginning with God; all things were made through him, and without him was not anything made that was made" (John 1:1–3). Or, as the writer of Hebrews puts it, "By faith we understand that the world was created by the word of God" (Heb. 11: 3a). Christians cannot read the important passage at the beginning of the Gospel of John without being deeply aware of the fact that God's Word "became flesh and dwelt among us, full of grace and truth; we have beheld his glory, glory as the only Son from the Father" (John 1:14).

When your class meets you may wish to discuss with fellow class-members the various ways in which God's word comes to his people today. *Do you think that most Christians are aware that God is trying to get through to them today?* You may also wish to ponder the purpose of the divine word and its infallible effectiveness, spoken of in 55:11.

Praise the Lord, 55:12–13

The joyful poetry of this passage is better read than interpreted. Note how all creation seems to join in the song of praise occasioned by the coming deliverance of Israel. Mountains and hills will join in the song, and trees shall clap their hands. What beautiful imaginative figures! Notice the disappearance of the thorn and the brier, bothersome vegetation that they are, and their replacement by the useful and beautiful cyprus and myrtle. The way of Israel has been hard, but she has great blessing in store for her today.

Ours should be a joyful faith. Have we not much to incline us to rejoicing? The biblical faith is a response to the good news of God's redemptive act in our behalf. Yet there is sometimes a marked absence of the joyful spirit among Christians. *How do you account for the fading joy of so many Christians today? Could it be because some of us have never really understood what God proposes to do for us through his grace?*

11

Laws and the Liberated

A DISPLACED PERSON SPEAKS

No, life here in the city is not what some of us anticipated. Just as the Poet said, we were liberated. The oppressors were defeated and a new ruler, the man from the east, took over the government. He was not a worshiper of the Lord, but he served the Lord's purpose nonetheless. There was great rejoicing when the decree went out by which we were freed, but when it came to actually pulling up stakes and making the long journey to this country, there were few who came. I suppose it was a matter of choosing between a known situation that was less than ideal and an unknown situation that held promise of becoming ideal.

At any rate, there were a considerable number of us who had a pioneering spirit. When the time came to leave there was no miraculous highway in the desert. Some people expected that, but after all, the Poet was a poet, and that is the way poets speak. It was a long, hard, grueling journey that we made, any way you take it. When we first saw the city we had highly mixed emotions. We knew Jerusalem had been sacked, but we were hardly ready for what we saw. It was in ruins, and it wasn't long until we realized that the only miracle that was going to restore the city was the miracle of human courage in the face of discouraging obstacles.

There have been many difficulties. Our own local rulers have

199

not been the best, and our religious leaders have left much to be desired. We have learned many things since we came here. For one thing, we have learned that discipline is the price of freedom, and discipline means law. In exile the laws were all made by persons outside our community. Now our laws must be made by those of us who are building a new society here in this place. Some of us are determined that it will be a society that assures righteousness, justice, and fair-play for everyone. This is more important to me than finishing the backbreaking task of erecting buildings and walls.

A Word About Isaiah 56—66

With the beginning of the study of chapter 56 it is necessary to consider the date and authorship of these chapters. There is a high degree of unanimity among scholars about chapters 40—55. However, the scholarly debate continues with reference to chapters 56—66. In 1892 Bernhard Duhm, a German scholar, wrote a famous commentary in which he argued that chapters 56—66 were written against a Palestinian rather than a Babylonian background. He detected differences in style, vocabulary, and point of view that led him to assign these chapters to a later era and another author, thus making a "Third Isaiah." This position, however, has been challenged by other highly competent scholars who emphasize the likenesses of 40—55 and 56—66 rather than the differences. Although I have no firm position on the matter, I am inclined to feel that these chapters do have a Palestinian background, whatever the authorship, and will so interpret them. If you wish to discuss the matter of date and authorship of chapters 56—66, you may ask your teacher to do some research and report to the class as a whole. Perhaps you would like to dig into the matter for yourself.

So far in our studies attention has been given to a verse by verse consideration of the assignments. In the remaining studies only selected passages will be given special attention. I sincerely hope that each student will make it his business to study the wider context in which these passages are located. In each study a brief outline of the whole passage will be given to aid you in your study.

An Outline of Isaiah 56—59

(1) A house of prayer for all peoples, 56:1–8
(2) A rebuke of watchmen (prophets) and shepherds (rulers), 56:9–12
(3) A rebuke of idolatry, 57:1–13
(4) The mercy and judgment of God, 57:14–21
(5) The futility of formalistic fasting, 58:1–5
(6) The fast of the righteous, 58:6–12
(7) The proper observance of the Sabbath, 58:13–14
(8) The rebuke of unrighteousness, 59:1–8
(9) The disappearance of justice, 59:9–15a
(10) The Lord will come as Judge, 59:15b–19
(11) The Lord will come also as Redeemer, 59:20–21

Before giving particular study to the passages which will be taken up below, spend the time that is necessary reading through Isaiah 56—59, noting the divisions of the material suggested above. *Does this reading help answer the critical question as to the date and authorship of this passage? How are these chapters different from or similar to Isaiah 40—55?*

A House of Prayer for All Peoples, 56:1–8

The exiles who returned to start a new life in Palestine faced many problems incidental to the establishment of a new community in what was to them a foreign land. One of the most pressing problems was that of deciding who should properly participate in the religious life of the community.

In Deuteronomy 23:1 eunuchs, probably because of their inability to reproduce themselves and thus help maintain the nation, were excluded from religious fellowship. In the Exile the foreigner, who had his own religion, did not generally mix with the Jewish minority in the observance of religious rites. He probably was not welcome because of the fear that there might be a resulting deterioration of the religious faith and practice of Israel if they were swamped by non-Jewish peoples. In view of the strong statement of Isaiah 56:1–8 there must have been considerable feeling that eunuchs and foreigners should not be welcomed in the religious rites of the new community.

But the teaching of the Prophet of the Exile had been highly influential. There were many who had grasped his vision of the gathering of all nations to Zion. The missionary emphasis of his message was still ringing in their ears. When the time came for the establishment of the new religious community and its worship, the prophetic voice directed that the eunuch and the foreigner be admitted to full fellowship on certain conditions. Read 56:1–8 at this time, noting the conditions that are set forth.

The conditions themselves (keeping the Sabbath, keeping one's hand from evil, choosing the things that please the Lord, holding fast the covenant, etc.) reflect a greater emphasis on keeping the law than is characteristic of Isaiah 40—55. This tendency in subsequent centuries contributed to the development of a rigid community of law in which the missionary emphasis of the Prophet of the Exile was either rejected or forgotten or both. Later generations came to reject the idea that the Temple was "a house of prayer for all peoples," as the prophet calls it in 56:7, and made it a house of prayer for the Jewish community. The important thing to note in 56:1–8 is that the message of the Prophet of the Exile was at that time still accepted as embodying the highest and clearest expression of God's will for His people.

This passage is especially important to Christians, since it was quoted by our Lord in connection with his cleansing of the Temple.

> And they came to Jerusalem. And he entered the temple and began to drive out those who sold and those who bought in the temple, and he overturned the tables of the money-changers and the seats of those who sold pigeons; and he would not allow anyone to carry anything through the temple. And he taught, and said to them, "Is it not written, 'My house shall be called a house of prayer for all the nations'? But you have made it a den of robbers." And the chief priests and the scribes heard it and sought a way to destroy him; for they feared him, because all the multitude was astonished at his teaching.   (Mark 11:15–18)

Jesus, by his words and actions, criticized two aspects of the elaborate temple worship of his day. It is frequently noted that he criticized the crass materialism of those who profited by the opera-

tion of the Temple. It is sometimes overlooked that he also criticized the fact that the Temple had become essentially a Jewish institution rather than an international institution. It is true that
Gentile proselytes to the Jewish faith were admitted to certain parts
of the Temple, but their membership in the community was definitely second-class. They were rigidly excluded and segregated from
the more sacred precincts of the Temple. They entered the inner
court only at the risk of life itself. Such was the race prejudice of
the Jews of Jesus' day!

Jesus came to open up the worship of God to all people of all
races. The true worship of God, he taught, has nothing to do with
sacred places or a person's racial background, but rather with
"spirit and truth." Jesus remembered a part of the Old Testament
that had been long forgotten by his fellow Jews, namely, the great
missionary passages of the Prophet of the Exile. Israel as a nation
could not bring herself to accept the foreigner (the non-Jew) and
for this reason, we believe, forfeited the rich legacy of Old Testament
promises. The valid people of God were those who remembered
that God's redemptive purpose included those to whom the Prophet
of the Exile referred again and again in the phrase, *"the ingathering
of the nations."*

Now this passage has certain implications for the people of God
today. If we consider the church in the world in its broadest dimension we behold the whole spectrum of humanity. It is not a white
man's religion, though it is sometimes so identified. It is not a
Western religion, though Christianity has been stronger in the Western hemisphere than in the Eastern. However, when the church
is viewed in its more limited denominational and congregational
dimensions, Jesus' words often become painfully applicable. Are
there members of more than one race worshiping in your congregation week after week? Are persons of races other than that which
predominates in your congregation welcome at the Lord's Table?
History testifies to the fact that the church, or any part of it, dies on
the vine when it discriminates against persons on the basis of race. If
you feel that you cannot or will not participate in interracial worship,
if you put racial homogeneity above the clear statement of the Word
and will of God, then there is reason to doubt the reality of your membership in the community of faith, whatever your official ecclesias-

tical status may be. The Lord's house in any age is "a house of prayer for *all* peoples." If it becomes anything other than that it ceases to be his house and the prayers that are offered are empty verbiage.

The Right and Wrong Kinds of Fasting, 58:1–12

If we follow the hypothesis that this prophecy was written after the return of the exiles from captivity in Babylon, we can surmise something of the prevailing moral, spiritual, and religious climate of that era. To say the least, the community established by the returning exiles was far from perfect. Upon their return they had no doubt conscientiously begun to worship God in a way that had not always been practical in a country in which they were a small and scattered minority. Isaiah 58:1–12 would suggest that a superficial, if not downright hypocritical, piety had sprung up. Sabbath observance was promoted in a way that had not always been possible during the years of captivity. Also, fasting had become a very popular religious exercise. Since only one fast a year was prescribed by the law (that in connection with the Day of Atonement) any other fasts must have been motivated by a desire to give the impression of a sort of super-righteousness on the part of those fasting. Perhaps it was to incline God to rebuild by a miracle the walls and the city that these fasts were observed (58:12).

Outwardly Israel seemed to be serving the Lord. What with the frequency of fasting and other religious observances a casual observer might conclude that this was a very religious and godly people. It must be said to the credit of Israel at this period in her history that she was going through the motions of religion in a very conscientious way. But there was something lacking.

The prophet who wrote Isaiah 58:1–12 manifested something like disgust as he appraised the popular religious exercises of the day. He had no praise for the skin-deep piety that people were trying to substitute for righteousness, justice, social concern, and common charity. *The time has come for you, the student, to read this passage for yourself. As you do so, note the following things:*

(1) the urgency with which the people are addressed, 58:1;
(2) the outward show of piety of the people addressed, 58:2;
(3) the fallacy of their kind of fasting, 58:3–4;
(4) the characteristics of the fasting that was so popular, 58:5;

(5) the kind of fast that God chooses for them, 58:6–7;

(6) some of the unresolved social problems in the postexilic community, 58:6–7; and

(7) the spiritual results of the fast of the righteous, 58:8–12.

If you have studied the passage with the outline above in mind certain enduring principles must have become apparent to you.

(1) Formalism in religion (going through the outward motions of piety, but lacking inward reality) makes no impression on God. Going to church, saying prayers so others will notice, observing the seasons of the ecclesiastical year, fasting, etc., if done merely to impress others with your religiosity, are a positive affront to God.

(2) It is entirely possible for people to delude themselves and possibly others into thinking that they are very religious people, when in fact they are far from pleasing God.

(3) God is concerned about such things as slavery, oppression (political or economic), poverty, and hunger. Sometimes the prophetic voice is challenged by those who say, "Stick to the gospel and quit preaching about social problems." The prophet in any age, to be true to his call and mission, must address himself to these matters for the simple reason that they are important to God.

Jesus was speaking in the prophetic tradition when he said:

> "Woe to you, scribes and Pharisees, hypocrites! for you tithe mint and dill and cummin, and have neglected the weightier matter of the law, justice and mercy and faith; these you ought to have done, without neglecting the others. You blind guides, straining out a gnat and swallowing a camel!
>
> "Woe to you, scribes and Pharisees, hypocrites! for you cleanse the outside of the cup and of the plate, but inside they are full of extortion and rapacity. You blind Pharisee! first cleanse the inside of the cup and of the plate, that the outside also may be clean.
>
> "Woe to you, scribes and Pharisees, hypocrites! for you are like whitewashed tombs, which outwardly appear beautiful, but within they are full of dead men's bones and all uncleanness. So you also outwardly appear righteous to men, but within you are full of hypocrisy and iniquity."
>
> (Matt. 23:23–28)

The relevance of Isaiah 58:1–12 to the church today is apparent. We do not practice fasting in many of our Protestant denominations, but we have the equivalent in other religious observances with which we sometimes endeavor to cloak our lack of compassion for the needy and of concern for justice in society. God is not content with many prayers spoken in the proper words, nor with many meetings well attended, nor with our observance of special days. He is concerned that his people be the instruments of his justice and his love in the world.

Judgment and Mercy, 59:15–21

This passage reiterates the truth that when God comes to men, he comes in *judgment* and in *redemption*. In his confrontation with mankind these two aspects of his coming reflect his *righteousness* and his *steadfast love*. These are not to be viewed as isolated and unrelated aspects of his nature. His righteousness is loving and his love is righteous.

God's coming in judgment is set forth in 59:15b–19. Read these verses noting the absence of justice in the land; the warrior image of the Lord; his vengeance upon the unjust; and the consequent fear of the Lord. *If God were to come to America today, what injustices in human relations would he condemn in our society?*

But God never comes in judgment that he does not also come in the role of Redeemer. In 59:20–21 we see this aspect of his nature. As you read these verses note the people who are objects of his redemptive love, the condition of his redemption, the undergirding basis of his redemption, and the scope of his redemption. This passage is especially meaningful for those who place a great emphasis on the importance of the covenant relation in the redemptive purpose of God.

God's coming (in judgment and mercy) is not to be relegated to some far off future moment in history when history as we know it shall end. He is forever coming to the world. He came in the law and prophetic word of the Old Testament. He came in the Advent of Jesus Christ. He came at Pentecost as the Holy Spirit. He comes in the events of history in every age. And he always comes in judgment and in mercy.

12

The Hope of Glory

A DISPLACED PERSON SPEAKS

There has been much discouragement among those of us who returned. You see, life here in this place has been anything but what we expected; it's been one long night of darkness and despair. But I, for one, feel that a new day is about to dawn. We have made a start, as you can see, on clearing away the rubble and rebuilding some of the more important buildings. Here and there you see proud little homes that our people have erected. It is true that it is far from magnificent, but you have no idea of the hopes and dreams that lie behind these modest beginnings. We have only made a start. We shall continue our work, and when we are gone others will take up where we shall leave off. One day the glory of this place will outshine all her former magnificence.

The Poet used to tell us that we were men with a mission. We have been fulfilling that mission since we came to this land. The Maker has plans for us, and a part of that plan is to rebuild this city. I guess you might say accomplishing this has become a sort of symbol for us. This city is more than a dwelling place for those of us who have returned. It is a holy city, the possession of the Maker, and we intend to build a city which will reflect his glory. Yes sir, the darkness of our long night is passing at last. Believe me, a new day of hope and promise is dawning.

Light of the world, we hail Thee,
Flushing the eastern skies;
Never shall darkness veil Thee
Again from human eyes;
Too long, alas, withholden,
Now spread from shore to shore;
Thy light, so glad and golden,
Shall set on earth no more.

Light of the world, Thy beauty
Steals into every heart,
And glorifies with duty
Life's poorest, humblest part;
Thou robest in Thy splendor
The simple ways of men,
And helpest them to render
Light back to thee again.

Light of the world, before Thee
Our spirits prostrate fall;
We worship, we adore Thee,
Thou Light, the Life of all;
With Thee is no forgetting
Of all Thy hand hath made;
Thy rising hath no setting,
Thy sunshine hath no shade.
—*The Hymnbook,* 138

A Survey of Isaiah 60—62

These three chapters contain three related poems that deserve to be treated together as a unit. The poem in chapter 60 returns to the theme of the glorified Jerusalem. The darkness of sin and judgment is driven out by the light which dawns upon Israel. The future splendor of Jerusalem is sketched; the regathering of all her children is predicted; the subjugation of her enemies is described; and the gathering of the wealth of the nations to her borders is prophesied. This chapter is reminiscent of chapters 49—50 which were treated earlier. *Read chapter 60 now for its poetry and symbolic message.*

The second poem, in chapter 61, contains a proclamation of glad tidings to Zion (Jerusalem). The speaker, whom most scholars identify as the prophet rather than the Lord, states the nature of his commission with reference to the afflicted, the heartbroken, and the captives. His is a message of encouragement to a people who have returned to the desolation of what was once the great city of Jerusalem. The poem tells of the coming restoration of the ruined city. Israel is assured that she shall be a priestly people among the peoples of the world, and that other nations shall serve her. The suffering of the people of God will be repaid by a double portion which shall be meted out to them. The poem closes with exultation over that which has been told Israel concerning her future. *Read the chapter now, using this paragraph as an outline of the contents.*

The third poem, in chapter 62, contains further predictions of Jerusalem's coming glory. Kings and nations shall witness her vindication. She shall be a beautiful jewel which adorns the hand of her Maker. No more shall she be called *Forsaken* and *Desolate,* but rather she shall be called *My delight is in her,* and *Married.* The poem asserts that watchmen have been placed on Jerusalem's walls who shall never be silent through unfaithfulness to their mission. Israel shall never again be subjugated and exploited as she has been in the past. The poem closes with a call to clear the way for the coming of the Lord. The salvation of God is with Israel and she shall be called the holy people. *Now read the chapter for yourself, trying to fathom what it has to say to the church today.*

The Lord Will Be Your Light, 60:1–3, 19–22

Someone has said that Isaiah 60 is a chapter that is literally drenched with light. Notice the frequency with which the words *light* and *glory* appear. These passages are important to Christians in view of the extensive use of the symbolism of light and darkness in the New Testament. Consider a few significant passages.

And suddenly there was with the angel a multitude of the heavenly host praising God and saying,

"Glory to God in the highest,
and on earth peace among men
    with whom he is pleased!"   (Luke 2:13–14)

In him was life, and the life was the light of men. The light shines in the darkness, and the darkness has not overcome it.

There was a man sent from God, whose name was John. He came for testimony, to bear witness to the light, that all might believe through him. He was not the light, but came to bear witness to the light.

The true light that enlightens every man was coming into the world.   (John 1:4–9)

Again Jesus spoke to them, saying, "I am the light of the world; he who follows me will not walk in darkness, but will have the light of life."   (John 8:12)

"As long as I am in the world, I am the light of the world."
                                 (John 9:5)

For it is the God who said, "Let light shine out of darkness," who has shone in our hearts to give the light of the knowledge of the glory of God in the face of Christ.
                             (2 Cor. 4:6)

. . . for once you were darkness, but now you are light in the Lord; walk as children of light . . . Take no part in the unfruitful works of darkness, but instead expose them.
                       (Eph. 5:8, 11)

And the city has no need of sun or moon to shine upon it, for the glory of God is its light, and its lamp is the Lamb. By its light shall the nations walk; and the kings of the earth shall bring their glory into it, and its gates shall never be shut by day—and there shall be no night there; . . .
                     (Rev. 21:23–25)

And night shall be no more; they need no light of lamp or sun, for the Lord God will be their light, and they shall reign for ever and ever.   (Rev. 22:5)

These are only a few of the scores of references to light and darkness in the New Testament. In the symbolism of the New Testament, God and Christ are the source of the light of truth and goodness which has shone forth from heaven upon mankind in the Christian revelation.

Bring your New Testament perspective to the study of Isaiah 60:1–3 and 19–22. *What did these passages mean to the people to whom they were originally addressed? If you had been a citizen of Jerusalem during the terribly difficult period of the return and the rebuilding of Jerusalem, how would you have interpreted the prophet's words?*

When in history do you think this prophecy was fulfilled? If Christ is the "Light of the world," what is he, and what does he do in this capacity? What evidences of darkness are there in the world today? Name those that come to mind most readily. What challenge to the church do you find in Isaiah 60:1–3? Do you think the light of God will ever be extinguished again in the world? If not, what does this imply for that part of human history before us?

Study the two passages from Revelation above in their respective contexts. Do you think that the writer of Revelation had Isaiah 60 in mind? If so, what was he trying to say through the use of symbols?

Make this an occasion for a very forthright self-examination. *Are you living in the light of Christ, or do you love darkness more than light?*

Proclaim Liberty! 61:1–4

And he came to Nazareth, where he had been brought up; and he went to the synagogue, as his custom was, on the sabbath day. And he stood up to read; and there was given to him the book of the prophet Isaiah. He opened the book and found the place where it was written,

"The Spirit of the Lord is upon me,
because he has anointed me to preach the good
tidings to the poor.
He has sent me to proclaim release to the captives
and recovering of sight to the blind,

to set at liberty those who are oppressed,
to proclaim the acceptable year of the Lord."

And he closed the book, and gave it back to the attendant, and sat down; and the eyes of all in the synagogue were fixed on him. And he began to say to them, "Today this scripture has been fulfilled in your hearing." (Luke 4:16–21)

Jesus' text for his sermon in the synagogue at Nazareth was the passage here under consideration. The Old Testament throws light on the mission and ministry of Jesus. By taking this text from Isaiah, Jesus set the tone for his ministry of compassion and love. For this passage is an emancipation proclamation. When Abraham Lincoln, the Great Emancipator, made his famous proclamation there was not an immediate liberation of all of the slaves in the South. The important thing was that the legal basis of their freedom had been irrevocably established. More than a hundred years later the implications of the Emancipation Proclamation are only now beginning to be fully realized. So, also, the proclamation of our Lord two thousand years ago is yet to be fully implemented, but the basis of human liberty has been established for all eternity.

Our Lord's "emancipation proclamation" declares human freedom on two levels. It would be an error to completely spiritualize what Jesus said at Nazareth and have it refer only to spiritual freedom. When the prophet of the Old Testament originally penned these words he was speaking of freedom of a political and social character. Jesus meant that too! Christ and his emissaries have struck many blows for the freedom of mankind throughout the history of the church. In fact, Christianity has been the great liberating force in the world for two millenia. But there are those who suffer from *spiritual* poverty to whom he came to proclaim good news, and there are those who are *spiritually* blind and captive to whom he assured *spiritual* sight and freedom. The Christian gospel, proclaimed beforehand by the prophet and reiterated by Jesus in his sermon in Nazareth, is neither "this-worldly" nor "other-worldly." It speaks to the needs of the whole man, body and spirit. It proclaims relief for both economic and spiritual poverty. It gives hope to the physically and spiritually blind. It strikes off the shackles of both body and spirit. It is good news to man in his human condition.

If this passage is to be more than an intellectual exercise we must see its relevance for the church and the world today. Christ's mission must be the church's mission if she is true to her Lord. Who are the afflicted, the broken-hearted, and the oppressed captives in your community today? What contact do these people have with your church and your church school class? It is not enough to merely talk about the church's mission to those classes of people mentioned by the prophet and by Jesus. The tragedy of too many inner city churches is that they have no communication with their immediate neighborhoods, which are usually economically deprived. The tragedy of too many suburban churches is that they live in splendid isolation from racial minorities, slum dwellers, and moral and spiritual decay. The tragedy of our nation is that we are woefully unaware of the great mass of hungry, sick, and suffering humanity both inside and outside our national boundaries. We cannot afford the luxury of irrelevancy in a world like ours. The politically oppressed, the economically distressed, the morally sick, and the spiritually blind peoples of the earth demand what Jesus came to give them, a gospel of hope and a declaration of freedom. *What is your church doing specifically to implement the mission of Christ in the world at your doorstep? in the world that lies beyond your immediate purview?* In your class session you may want to consider these questions seriously with your fellow students.

The Covenant People, 61:8–9

This brief passage identifies Israel as the blessed people of the everlasting covenant. This was an important word of encouragement for a people facing the long, hard task of rebuilding a ruined city and reestablishing a new community of faith amid the hardships incidental to resettling a strange land. Note how God describes himself.

> For I the LORD love justice
>   I hate robbery and wrong.
>   (Isa. 61:8*a*)

Israel had suffered much injustice and many robberies and wrongs at the hands of her oppressors during the time of captivity. Though these things were divine retribution which God permitted, as we have noted in other passages, the fact remains that God himself never ceases to hate injustice and wrong. He will recompense his people for all they have suffered during the chastening years of exile. Then comes the supremely important announcement: ". . . I will make an everlasting covenant with them." This covenant will involve not only them but also their yet unborn offspring. In generations to come all men will recognize them to be a people whom the Lord has blessed.

It is the New Testament conviction that the New Israel, the people of God in the New Testament era, are participators in this "everlasting covenant." When the church is true to the covenant it is indeed a people "whom the Lord has blessed."

> O Zion, haste, thy mission high fulfilling,
> To tell to all the world that God is Light,
> That He who made all nations is not willing
> One soul should perish, lost in shades of night.
>
> Behold how many thousands still are lying
> Bound in the darksome prison house of sin,
> With none to tell them of the Saviour's dying,
> Or of the life He died for them to win.
>
> Proclaim to every people, tongue, and nation
> That God, in whom they live and move, is Love:
> Tell how He stooped to save His lost creation,
> And died on earth that man might live above. . . .
>
> —*The Hymnbook,* 491

13

The New Creation

A DISPLACED PERSON SPEAKS

We are a troubled people, sir. We came to this place intent on making a dream come true. With high hopes and aching backs we gave ourselves to the task of rebuilding this ruined city. Many of us felt that it was even more important to restore the ancient faith and practices of our religion. But not all have felt this way. As you see, we have no Temple in which to worship, and all sorts of strange new practices have sprung up in our midst. Questionable sacrifices are being offered. The ancient laws concerning clean and unclean foods are openly violated. People who practice these things are not content with the old ways. They consider themselves superior to those of us who follow the ancient practices, and they wish to have nothing to do with us. They say we have not been initiated into the rites and ceremonies which they have developed and they withdraw from us. A sharp division has developed. The rank superstition of some is repulsive to those of us who wish to worship as the Lord has directed us. I am convinced that something dreadful is going to come to our people because of what is happening.

Those of us who refuse to take part in the new ways are confident, however, that the Lord will vindicate us and judge the others. We are having a time of trouble and confusion now, but believe me, it will not always be so. The day is coming when the Creator will separate true from false worshipers and will re-create for himself a people who will not stray from his ways. We believe that the future is with us. When the great day comes there will be no more calamities, heartaches, and trouble. Peace will reign in our midst, for we shall all be of one mind and heart. The Lord, who sometimes seems remote, shall then draw near and shall dwell forever in our midst.

A Survey of Isaiah 63—66

In this concluding lesson we shall study in a very general way Isaiah 63—66, giving particular attention to chapter 65, which ends on a high note of Messianic expectation. This should be good preparation for the next series of studies in the Gospel of John. *For the sake of the completeness of your study of the whole of Isaiah 40—66, and in order that you may view chapter 65 in context, you should take time in your study at this point to read chapters 63—66 in a single sitting, using the paragraphs immediately following as a study guide.*

Isaiah 63:1–6 contains a striking poem that pictures God as a bloody warrior returning from a battle in which he has visited judgment upon offenders. The imagery of the poem is captured by Julia Ward Howe's famous "Battle Hymn of the Republic."

> Mine eyes have seen the glory of the coming of the Lord;
> He is trampling out the vintage where the grapes of
>   wrath are stored;
> He hath loosed the fateful lightning of His terrible,
>   swift sword;
> His truth is marching on. . . .

In this passage from Isaiah judgment is meted out specifically upon Edom, the ancient enemy of Israel, but the idea of judgment is one that has wider application.

Isaiah 63:7—64:12 is a liturgical prayer for a renewal of God's former gracious dealing with his people. The days of old are remembered with thanksgiving, and an ardent prayer is uttered that God manifest himself anew in the life of the nation. The prayer closes with an appeal to God to moderate his wrath and forget the iniquity of Israel.

Chapter 65, which will be taken up in detail later in this chapter, reflects the fact that at the time of writing there were two parties among the Jews who returned to Palestine. One group deviated sharply from ordinary modes of worship while the other adhered strictly to ancient forms and practices. This chapter condemns the innovators and confirms the party that remained true to standard practices of worship. The passage ends with a beautiful Messianic poem which looks, we believe, toward the advent of the Christian era.

Chapter 66, which is closely related to chapter 65, sets forth the eternal blessedness of the true Israel and prophesies the doom of those who deviate from right practices of worship. A house made with hands and a multitude of sacrifices do not guarantee the reality of worship. The remainder of the poem (66:5–24) is difficult to analyze, and many commentators feel that this is a result of dislocation of parts of the text. Study the remainder of the chapter keeping in mind two great emphases, God's blessing upon the faithful and his judgment upon the apostates.

A Liturgical Prayer, 63:7—64:12

This is one of the great prayers of the Bible. It is typical of the highest tradition of Israel's devotional life. It combines religious sensitivity with an awareness of the meaning of history. Notice how the writer heaps up words and phrases that denote the goodness of God in relation to his people in 63:7–9. As the author of the prayer reflects on the uneven relation of Israel to her God he is overcome by a sense of the love and pity of God that permeates all of God's dealing with his people.

In 63:10–14 the author reveals his sense of history. The rebellion of the people of God and their grieving of his Holy Spirit is contrasted with the faithfulness of God as manifested in his mighty acts of deliverance in the days of Moses. Even when it is necessary for God to assume the role of the enemy of his people and fight against them he remembers the days of old when he was their deliverer.

In the next strophe (63:15–19) the author of the prayer calls upon God to look down from his glorious habitation in heaven and to behold the present lot of his people. Even in her forsakenness Israel is conscious of the Fatherhood of her Lord and Redeemer. Verse 17 is hard for the modern reader to understand, for it seems to say that God is the cause of Israel's moral defection. We must try to understand the theocentric viewpoint of the Old Testament, that sees God as the absolute and sovereign Lord of history. This in no way lessens the moral obligation of Israel when she sins against her Lord. Verses 18 and 19 are a cry to God to return for the sake of his servants who have shared the glory of the sanctuary of God for a season, but who now, to all outward appearances, have been forsaken by their God. In a time when many modern philosophies are saying to God's people that "God is dead," this is a highly appropriate prayer.

Chapter 64 is a plea for God to enter the stream of history with a great show of his power and righteousness. There is nothing in the moral life of Israel that warrants such an intervention. The author of the prayer is aware of the relation between sin and judgment. Yet, in spite of Israel's unworthiness, the author can still call God Father and look upon Israel as the pliable clay in the hands of the great Potter. He pleads the desolation of Zion and the disrepair of the Temple, and asks God to restrain himself no longer from acting on Israel's behalf. The prayer ends with a question, "Wilt thou restrain thyself at these things, O LORD? Wilt thou keep silent and afflict us sorely?"

This is a beautiful prayer that might be prayed by the class in an antiphonal fashion, two groups alternating in the reading of the strophes (paragraphs) well-defined in the R.S.V. At a time when "Zion has become a wilderness" in the eyes of the world it is a highly appropriate prayer.

A New Creation, 65:1–25

As indicated above, there are evidences in chapter 65 that there had arisen in the Jewish community a new religious viewpoint that was in conflict with the party who worshiped God in traditional ways. Some scholars have argued that this schismatic and unorthodox group is to be identified with the Samaritans, the descendants of those who were left in the Northern Kingdom after the Assyrian captivity. During the time of the Exile the Samaritans carried on a form of worship of the God of Israel, but it had become so corrupt that the Samaritans were rejected by Ezra and other leaders during the time of the return. This rejection was carried over into the New Testament period when "the Jews had no dealing with the Samaritans."

While this is a possibility, there is a greater probability that the unorthodox group was made up of the descendants of the few who remained in Palestine after the fall of Jerusalem. During the time of the Exile this group had absorbed a great deal of paganism and this constituted a real danger to the perpetuation of the true faith of Israel. This deviation seems to have manifested itself in connection with the practice of worship. The heresy, as we shall see, is condemned by the prophet, and the orthodox group is commended and confirmed in its point of view.

Read 65:1–7, noting: first, God's continued readiness to make himself accessible to a rebellious people who do not ask for him or seek him; second, indications as to the nature of the heretical worship which was being practiced; and finally, God's reaction to such worship. The sin of the heretical party lay not so much in the way in which they worshiped as in their rebellion against God. This passage presents a picture of God with his hands outstretched in supplication to his people, and the people in haughty rebellion against the very God they professed to worship. This may appear to be a strange situation, but does it not sometimes prevail in the church today? Can you think of situations in which people who profess to worship God are actually in rebellion against him?

Isaiah 65:8–16 contains a sharp contrast between the redemption of the faithful (verses 8–10) and the condemnation of the apostates (verses 11–15). Verse 16 is a conclusion of the whole matter. *Read this passage now, observing this division of the material.* Though the word *remnant* is not used in 65:8–10 we have here what is commonly called the doctrine of the remnant. Though

God punishes and destroys a part of Israel, he will always preserve a remnant of his people with whom he will keep his covenant. God will not destroy all the clusters in the vineyard, but will preserve that which has "a blessing in it." The inheritance will be given to the remnant which is preserved. Mere membership in the historical community is no guarantee of redemption. This is no less true of the church today than it was of ancient Israel. The true church which shall receive the inheritance is that part of the church which "has the blessing in it."

The apostates and their destiny are portrayed in sharp contrast in 65:11–15. They forsake the Lord and his holy mountain (the place of worship). They worship the gods Fortune and Destiny in drunken orgies. They are destined for destruction because they have not answered when God called, nor listened when he spoke. They have chosen things in which God does not delight. Verses 13–15 contain a telling contrast between the respective destinies of the faithful servants and of the apostates. If blessing is to come it must be a blessing that comes by the God of truth, and when oaths are taken this too must be by the God of truth (verse 16). The time of trouble and distress which accompanies the punishment of the apostates is forgotten by God and hid from his eyes in the time of blessing of his faithful servants.

The strong Messianic flavor of 65:17–25 and 66:22–24 makes these important passages for Christians. These passages are eschatological in tone. The words eschatology and eschatological may be unfamiliar to some readers. The Greek roots of these words are *eschaton,* meaning "last thing," and *logos,* meaning "word," "doctrine," or "teaching." Eschatology, therefore, means the teaching or doctrine concerning the last things. The biblical view of history contemplates a beginning of all things (Creation) and an end of all things (*eschaton*). Between the beginning and the end lies the story of man's fall and the whole, long process of his redemption. The last or end time will be one in which there will be a restoration of the innocence and harmony of the Creation. It is therefore a "re-creation." The re-creation which is anticipated involves not only man but all nature. Paul spoke of this when he wrote to the Romans:

For the creation waits with eager longing for the revealing of
the sons of God; for the creation was subjected to futility, not
of its own will but by the will of him who subjected it in
hope; because the creation itself will be set free from its bondage to decay and obtain the glorious liberty of the children of
God. We know that the whole creation has been groaning in
travail together until now; and not only the creation, but we
ourselves, who have the first fruits of the Spirit, groan inwardly
as we wait for adoption as sons, the redemption of our bodies.

(Rom. 8:19–23)

The new creation, while incomplete, has already begun. Thus
Paul says:

Therefore, if anyone is in Christ, he is a new creation; the
old has passed away, behold, the new has come.

(2 Cor. 5:17)

The writer of 2 Peter must have certainly had Isaiah 65:17 in
mind when he wrote:

But according to his promise we wait for new heavens and
a new earth in which righteousness dwells.

(2 Peter 3:13)

It is of the nature of God to create. When his creation is marred
by human sin it is his nature to re-create. The New Testament
picks up the Old Testament insights concerning the new creation
and carries them to an even higher peak of anticipation. Henry
Sloan Coffin puts it thus:

. . . *Behold, I create* emphasizes God's activity. This is a
new beginning. The present world is to be entirely renovated
and transformed as the setting for the new redeemed community. The Bible regards the physical creation as the background for the history of men and women under God. A new
stage in history, the final stage, requires a new setting. The
"newness" consists primarily in God's closeness to his people.
Irenaeus writes of the coming of Christ: "Learn that he
brought every new thing by bringing himself." He brought a
new covenant, a new man, a new hope, a new Jerusalem. Here

it is God's joy in his people which alters the fact of heaven and earth. Christians have found the world remade for them by the renewal of their spirits in Christ. . . .[1]

The idea of *new creation* is deeply rooted in biblical thought, but were it not, I think that man would probably have manufactured it. There are deep hopes and aspirations that spring up perennially in human consciousness that make re-creation a psychological and spiritual necessity. There is a wistful longing on the part of man for his original, uncomplicated situation. He is aware in some vague way that he is a fallen creature, and that his proper destiny is bound up with regaining the height from which he has fallen. He longs to recapture his proper status in the universe. He seeks to rediscover a lost relationship to whatever or whoever lies at the heart of things. Efforts to achieve human progress are in a way an inverted effort on man's part to go back to that from which he came and for which he was made. Man is not content for the story of his earthly pilgrimage to end as a tragedy. It must somewhere, somehow have a happy ending. In the eschatology of both the Old and New Testaments man's story does have a happy ending in which wrongs are righted, hopes fulfilled, and dreams realized. Whatever strife and conflict may have marked the pilgrimage, the end is marked by peace.

Eschatological ideas frequently find apocalyptic expression. The word *apocalyptic* comes from a Greek word meaning to disclose, lay bare, reveal, or make manifest. "Apocalypse" is thus simply another name for the book of Revelation. Apocalypticism is a type of thought which apparently originated in Zoroastrianism, by which the Jewish mind was considerably influenced during the Exile. Through Judaism it was mediated to Christian thought, and it is still with us today. It views history as the scene of a cosmic conflict between good and evil, or, to put it another way, between God and Satan. In biblical apocalyptical teaching, contrary to Zoroastrianism, the outcome of the struggle is not uncertain, for the ultimate victory of God is assured.

The apocalyptic mind, however, takes a pessimistic view of this present age, which may be expected to grow worse and worse until the end. The apocalyptic hope is fixed on a coming age which will be ushered in by the ultimate victory of God over the forces of evil. Those who hold this view earnestly scan the horizons of the times to discover signs of the coming end. The watchword is wait more than work. Pessimism about the present age virtually eliminates motivation for social action for the moral improvement of this world. Those who are deeply influenced by the apocalyptic elements of the Bible tend to be grossly literalistic in their interpretation of these passages. The dangers of this kind of interpretation become apparent when one enters into dialogue with Jehovah's Witnesses or Seventh-Day Adventists. Among these and similar groups there is a strong tendency to interpret all of Scripture in the light of the relatively few apocalyptic books and passages of the Bible.

The presence of the apocalyptic element in biblical literature makes it necessary for us to find a place for it in our theology, even though we must reject the gross literalism which is characteristic of most of the groups that put a high value on this type of thought. John Bright gives this wise admonition:

> But our evaluation of this [apocalypticism] must not be one-sided. To point out the pathology of it is all too easy. It is easy to laugh at airy speculations which, then and now, see signs of the end in every day's news, and find the personification of the arch-Foe first in this, then in that actor in present events. It is easier still to feel irritation at what can only be called the impudence of those who would draw diagrams, and even set dates, for the "times and the seasons" which Christ himself said that neither he nor the angels in heaven knew— but only God (Matt. 24:36; Mark 13:32; Acts 1:7). It could be pointed out, too, that there lurks here a rather fundamental pessimism regarding this earth which might, and on occasion has, cut the nerve of all effort toward its redemption. One could even say that there is something here which is not even very moral; it exhibits very little compassion, but rather seems actually to long for the destruction of millions of wicked if only a few righteous are saved.

> Yet strange though this "apocalyptic mind" is to us, we must not forget that there lived in it a great faith which even those who sneer at it would do well to copy. For all its funda-

mental pessimism about the world, it was in the profoundest sense optimistic. At a time when the current scene yielded only despair, when the power of evil was unbroken beyond human power to break it, there lived here the faith that the victory of God was nonetheless sure: God holds the issues of history; he is a God *whose kingdom comes.* Let those of us to whom the prayer "Thy kingdom come" has become a form to be rattled off without meaning, who find the Apocalyptic amusing, yet who tremble every time a Communist makes a speech—note it well. The Apocalyptic further insists that the world struggle is neither political nor economic, but essentially of the spirit and cosmic in scope. Behind all earthly striving it sees a continuing combat between good and evil, light and darkness, the Creator God and the destructive power of chaos, which summons men to take sides. There can be no neutrality. Whoever decides for the right, however humble he may be, has struck a blow for the Kingdom of God in a combat of decisive significance. In any case, there was in the Apocalyptic a faith that strengthened thousands of little men to an obedience unto the death, confident that their reward was with God (Dan. 12:1–4). Let all who scoff ask themselves if their more polite religion does as much.[2]

With these thoughts and the light of the New Testament revelation in mind, read Isaiah 65:17–25 and 66:22–24. Do not try to find a literal interpretation for these verses. These are human words and figures that endeavor to describe that which defies literal description. It must become apparent to you as you read that apart from Christ these passages would remain forever a fond but vain hope.

In an ecstatic vision the Seer of Patmos views Isaiah 65:17–24 through the eyes of one who has beheld the glory of God in Jesus Christ.

> Then I saw a new heaven and a new earth; for the first heaven and the first earth had passed away, and the sea was no more. And I saw the holy city, new Jerusalem, coming down out of heaven from God, prepared as a bride adorned

for her husband; and I heard a great voice from the throne saying, "Behold, the dwelling of God is with men. He will dwell with them, and they shall be his people, and God himself will be with them; he will wipe away every tear from their eyes, and death shall be no more, neither shall there be mourning nor crying nor pain any more, for the former things have passed away."   (Rev. 21:1–4)

A LOOK BACK

What has happened to you as a result of studying Isaiah 40–66? The following questions are for individual and group use, to help you review the insights that have come to you during the past weeks of studying God's Word:

1. *How has your conception of God grown or changed as a result of this study? Explain.*

2. *How has the study of this book helped you better understand the message of the New Testament? Explain.*

3. *What light has this study thrown on your understanding of the nature and mission of the church? Explain.*

4. *How has this study helped you better understand the meaning of history and the meaning of events in the life of mankind today? Explain.*

5. *What to you are the major religious ideas of Isaiah 40—66?*

6. *How has this study deepened and enriched your personal religious experience?*

7. *How would you apply the idea of servanthood to a Christian's life in the world today?*

8. *At what points in the study did you feel most the need to pause longer and study at greater depth?*

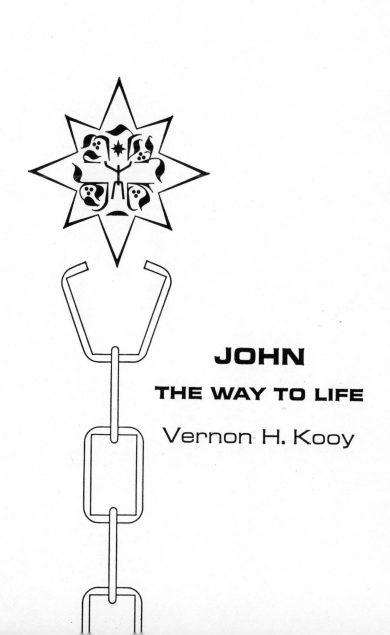

JOHN

THE WAY TO LIFE

Vernon H. Kooy

A Man with a Message

... I dreamed, and behold, I saw a man clothed with rags, standing in a certain place, with his face from his own house, a book in his hand, and a great burden upon his back. I looked, and saw him open the book, and read therein; and as he read, he wept and trembled; and, not being able longer to contain, he brake out with a lamentable cry, saying, "What shall I do?" ...

I saw also that he looked this way and that way, as if he would run; yet he stood still, because (as I perceived) he could not tell which way to go. I looked then, and saw a man named Evangelist coming to him, who asked, "Wherefore dost thou cry?"

He answered, "Sir, I perceive by the book in my hand, that I am condemned to die, and after that to come to judgment ..."

Then said Evangelist, "If this be thy condition, why standest thou still?"

He answered, "Because I know not whither to go." ... Then said Evangelist (pointing with his finger over a very wide field), "Do you see yonder wicket-gate?" The man said "No." Then said the other, "Do you see yonder shining light?" He said, "I think I do." Then said Evangelist, "Keep that light in your eye, and go up directly thereto: so shalt thou see the gate; at which, when thou knockest, it shall be told thee what thou shalt do." [1]

The world of our day, like John Bunyan's Pilgrim, is perplexed as to which way to go. Caught in a morass of problems of war, race, and poverty, summoned by the voices of isms that are at cross purposes, it is in need of an evangelist who with clear directions can show it the way to life. The author of the Fourth Gospel is such an evangelist. He is a man with a message about the way to life.

The gospel story is told in more than one way. Mark takes the reader over the events of the life of Jesus and lets the story make its own impression. Like a participant in the drama that is unfolding, the reader comes gradually to the confession that "Jesus is the Christ, the Son of God." John tells the story backwards. He begins with the disclosure that Christ is the Son of God (1:18; cf. 20:31). [Where no book is named, the scriptural reference is to John.] Then he retraces the steps of Jesus so that in every event the reader can behold the Christ of glory. He makes sure that each incident will be interpreted correctly and will manifest, as Filson says, who Jesus is—the Christ; what he offers to men—eternal life; and how this gift may be received—by believing in him.[2]

The Approach to the Gospel

The best way to begin the study of John is to read the Gospel through in a single sitting. This can be done in a little over an hour. As you read, note the author's emphasis on the identity of Jesus, on life, and on believing. It would be well also to review what Arnold B. Rhodes has written about John in his student's book, The Mighty Acts of God, *pp. 262–265.* [Some study suggestions and questions are *italicized* in each chapter. Your understanding of John and your experience in the study group will both be enriched if you carry out these suggestions or answer the questions through your personal study of the Gospel.]

John has been for many Christians their favorite Gospel. In it one meets the most profound truths described in the simplest terms; in it one meets the personal Christ; and in it one hears God speaking directly to the heart.

Yet John's Gospel is the most difficult to outline. Even though it contains fewer incidents than the other Gospels, there is no single pattern running through the whole. The author begins with a series of acts of Jesus (chapters 1—2), proceeds to some private discussions (chapters 3—4), and then continues with a number of public disputations at festival periods, interspersed with miracles (chapters 5—10). All this makes outlining difficult and I have not attempted it.

John interweaves history and interpretation. Much is symbolic and there are many side roads one could profitably explore. We shall be concerned chiefly with the aim of the author as expressed in 20:31. Consequently, our approach is topical, exploring what it means to believe and to have life. Such study calls for the rereading of some passages many times and the slighting of others. It is hoped, however, that after going through the various lessons, the student will have a good knowledge of the content of the book and of its message.

The Background of the Book

We do not know when John was written but it was probably toward the end of the first century. Tradition names Ephesus as its place of origin.

Four things stand out about the world to which John wrote.

(1) The world of John's day was a world of change. The age of the Apostles was passing into history; the expected return of the Lord was long delayed; the church was firmly established as an institution; and, the links with Judaism being severed, the church now sought its future in the great Gentile world.

(2) It was a time of controversy between the church and the synagogue. Jesus' Messiahship, his relation to God, his resurrection, and his ability to save were all matters of debate. Christianity was no longer viewed as a Jewish sect and hence a legitimate religion in the Roman Empire. It may well be that the Jews were responsible for instructing Rome on the differences between Judaism and Christianity. Note that in this Gospel the enemies of Jesus are "the Jews," not a particular sect or group within Judaism.

(3) There was a renewed interest in John the Baptizer. Many were contending that John and not Jesus was the true Messiah. For these the author reinterprets the mission of John. He plays

down John's message of judgment as preparation for the coming Kingdom and stresses that John is the first witness to Jesus as the Messiah.

(4) It was an age when the church was in danger of being torn asunder. Various abuses were creeping into its life and a variety of conflicting views were proclaimed, all of which claimed to be Christian. Some held Jesus to be no more than a phantom man, denying that Christ had come in the flesh or had a real body. Others denied his deity by claiming that the Spirit had joined the man Jesus at his baptism and left him on the cross.

In response to all this change and controversy John sets forth the truth as to Jesus' identity and the nature of his gift to men.

Today also we live in an age of change, more rapid and drastic perhaps than any the world has previously known. Christianity is losing ground; church membership and missionary efforts are on the decline when viewed in terms of population increase; other religions are on the rise; and a great wave of agnosticism is sweeping the world, abetted by political philosophies and scientific discoveries. It is a day when the church has been forced to reevaluate herself, to reexamine her Scriptures, to rewrite her creeds. It is also a period of the renewal of spiritual gifts, of increased literary activity directed toward the layman, and of vigorous efforts to unify Christendom. It is a time when the battle between faith and unbelief is being waged anew both within and without the church. In such a time this Gospel is intensely relevant.

The Man

This Gospel contains no clue as to the name of the author. Ancient tradition, almost without exception, ascribed it to John the son of Zebedee. This view has held sway in the church until the modern period. Bishop Westcott has given a fine defense of this position in his *Commentary on the Gospel According to St. John.* Arguing from details in the Gospel, he concludes step by step that the author is a Jew, from Palestine, an eyewitness, an Apostle, John the son of Zebedee.

Others have taken their clue from the absence of the name John in the book and its ascription in 21:20–24 to "the disciple whom Jesus loved." For most scholars this points to one of the inner three (Peter, James, and John): Is it likely such a favored disciple would not be mentioned in the other Gospels or found among the Twelve? Peter and James were martyred early (James in A.D. 44 and Peter in 64), which leaves only John. There have been other guesses as to "the disciple whom Jesus loved": the owner of the Upper Room (Acts 12:12 indicates that John Mark's home was the meeting place of the disciples in Jerusalem, and many think it was therefore the house of the Upper Room. By this theory, John Mark or his father was the beloved disciple.), the rich young ruler (from Mark 10:21), Lazarus (from John 11:3, 5, 36), or Matthias, who took the place of Judas (Acts 1:26). Few scholars would contend that any of these was the author, although recently Floyd V. Filson has made a case for Lazarus (see the *Layman's Bible Commentary*, Vol. 19, pp. 22–25).

The chief arguments against the Apostle John's having written the Gospel are these:

(1) John the son of Zebedee was a Galilean fisherman. Would he be likely to slight Galilee where so much of Jesus' ministry was conducted? The author of John stresses instead the Jerusalem ministry of Jesus.

(2) There is a kinship between this Gospel and the Letters of John. If by the same author, it is noteworthy that in 2 and 3 John the author designates himself as "the elder." Papias, an early church father (about A.D. 130), seems to distinguish two Johns among the disciples of Jesus. One is John the Elder; the other is John the Apostle, whom he mentions with the Twelve. Some suppose that John the Elder is the true author.

(3) The certification, "*we* know that *his* testimony is true" (21:24, author's italics; cf. 19:35), may indicate a publisher (or publishers) other than the witness responsible for the information in the Gospel.

(4) The ascription to "the disciple whom Jesus loved" would be an arrogant claim for an Apostle to make but most natural when coming from one of the Apostle's followers.

(5) There is no early testimony that John the Apostle lived or labored at Ephesus, the traditional place of origin of the Gospel.

The problem of authorship is not easily solved. The Gospel and tradition seem to point to an apostolic eyewitness. The most likely author, then, is John the son of Zebedee, even should the Gospel prove to have been edited and published by another.

We learn a good deal about the author from the Gospel itself. He was beloved by and especially close to Christ. He was a retiring individual, always placing himself in the background that Christ might have the center of the stage; nowhere did he care to be obtrusive, so that to Christ alone might be the glory. He was undoubtedly a Jew, perhaps a disciple of the Baptizer, well-acquainted with the geography of Palestine, with an intimate knowledge of, or access to, the details of the events in the life of Jesus. He mentions, for example, the cord whip used at the cleansing of the Temple, the hour of the conversation with the woman of Samaria, the young lad with the five loaves and two fishes at the feeding of the five thousand, the weariness of Jesus at the well, his weeping at the grave of Lazarus, and his washing of the disciples' feet. He alone gives us insights into the characters of Andrew, Philip, Nathanael, Thomas, and Judas.

The author was a theologian. He desired to give the meaning of Jesus rather than tell the story of his life. His book is

a theological commentary upon the Synoptic tradition. . . . St. John . . . is concerned not so much with the bare recording of 'what happened' as with the saving meaning of the truth of history itself . . . At every point the Fourth Evangelist is concerned with the interpretation of history, because *saving* truth is not historical knowledge as such . . . but is belief that the Father sent the Son to be the Saviour of the world.[3]

The author considers himself a witness. Have you ever been a witness? A witness is called to testify to what he has seen. He is sworn to tell the truth. A good exercise would be to trace the emphasis on witness in this Gospel. Note how the author emphasizes this element at the beginning and end of his book (cf. 1:15, 18 and 21:24). He witnesses to Christ so that the reader will come to faith and in turn become a witness.

The Message

John wants us to know three things about Jesus.

(1) Jesus is the Christ. This confession in one form or another runs throughout the Gospel (see chapters 1, 4, 6, 11, and 20 and note the variety of ways this confession is made). Jesus came to challenge men with his presence. Whenever he appears there lurks the question, "Who am I?" Each event and discourse seeks to help the reader answer this question. Keep this in mind. After studying the book see if you can state who Jesus is in terms that will be significant to a man of today who is biblically and theologically illiterate.

(2) Jesus is the revealer of God. He alone truly discloses the nature of the Father (1:18). He is the one sent (6:38; 7:29; 8:42 *et al.*), who does nothing of himself but only what God is doing (5:19). The glory of the Father is revealed in Jesus, especially in his miracles (2:11; 11:40) and on the cross (12:23 f.; 17:1). Moreover, the character of God is revealed in Jesus' attitude toward men.

(3) Jesus is the giver of life (5:21, 24; 10:10). The life he gives is not some future experience but a present reality. Note how the entire Gospel can be interpreted in terms of this figure. "In him was life, and the life was the light of men" (1:4); he speaks to Nicodemus of eternal life, he offers the Samaritan woman the water of life. He is the bread of life, the Good Shepherd who lays down his life. Himself the resurrection and the life, he calls the dead to life. What he offers is the more abundant life (10:10), eternal life, which one receives by believing. It is also the concern of the author that the reader may have life (20:31).

A Different Story, Yet the Same

Have you noticed how different this Gospel is from the others? The four Gospels present distinct portraits of Jesus while telling the same "good news." Mark is a reflection of apostolic preaching and presents Jesus as a doer of mighty works, the Son of Man who gives his life as "a ransom for many." Matthew's interest is teaching or catechizing; thus Jesus becomes the new Moses who presents the new law for the guidance of the New Israel. Luke concentrates on the compassion of Jesus, showing him to be the Great Physician who heals all who are sick in body or soul—the Savior of the world. John stands apart from this. His Gospel differs from the others both in pattern and in content.

JOHN	THE SYNOPTICS
Jesus' ministry covers three Passovers.	Jesus' ministry includes one Passover.
The center of activity is Judea. Here most of his ministry is conducted.	The center of activity is Galilee. Here most of his ministry is conducted.
Jesus is openly the Messiah, confessed so from the beginning.	Jesus' Messiahship is kept secret. Those who recognize him are forbidden to speak.
Personal experiences of Jesus are omitted or drastically altered.	Personal experiences of baptism, temptation, confession of Peter, transfiguration, agony in the Garden, cry from the cross are central in the story.
He gives his teaching in lengthy discourses on a single theme, using no parables.	He gives his teaching in short, pithy statements or simple stories, using many proverbs and parables.
Miracles are extraordinary ones. No exorcism of demons.	Has a wide variety of miracles with exorcisms prominent.
Most of ministry is concerned with individuals. When he meets crowds he usually engages in controversy. Jesus is aggressive and militant, making bold claims which are the main point of dispute.	Much of ministry is concerned with multitudes upon whom he has compassion. Jesus is meek and lowly, avoiding controversy as much as possible. His attitude toward the traditions is the main source of dispute.

From the contrasts listed on the preceding chart, you can see some of the ways in which John is different from the Synoptics (the first three Gospels). Have you noted other differences?

Yet the story is the same—"Jesus is the Christ, the Son of God" (20:31): Compare how Mark opens (Mark 1:1) and how the confessions are worded in the other Gospels (Matt. 16:16; Mark 8:29; Luke 9:20). In the Synoptics Jesus keeps his Messiahship secret because he did not want to cater to the nationalistic hopes of the Zealots. Compare what he says about his Kingdom in John 18:36. In the Synoptics much of his activity is the result of his compassion for those in need. Compare what he has to say about love in John 15:13. What other areas of agreement can you find? Is the story really so different? Note John's acquaintance with apostolic preaching and the gospel tradition as given in the chart appended to this lesson.

John has taken the portrait of Jesus during Passion Week and extended this over the entire Gospel. (Note that he sets the cleansing of the Temple at the beginning.) Thus the active Messiah, the crucified and risen Lord of glory, is the Jesus whom you meet early in the pages of his story.

The message centers in Jesus himself. The words and deeds of Jesus cannot be separated from his person. As John Baillie says:

> Christianity is, when fundamentally regarded, not a law but a gospel. It was as a gospel that it was preached from the very beginning. The word 'gospel' or (in its original Greek form) 'evangel' means good news; and good news is precisely what Christianity sets out to be. The little wireless listener who, on being taken to church for the first time, remarked that she 'liked the music better than the news,' well understood what the sermon was meant to be, however just or unjust may have been her estimate of its quality on that occasion.[4]

The gospel is the good news that God gave his Son so that the world through him may have life (3:16). The message is Jesus Christ, who and what he is. This John has grasped.

Note from the following chart how much of the material in the Synoptic Gospels is repeated in John in one form or another:

JOHN'S ACQUAINTANCE WITH APOSTOLIC PREACHING AND GOSPEL TRADITION

SYNOPTIC GOSPELS	JOHN'S GOSPEL
Introduction and infancy stories	Prologue (1:1–18)
Ministry of Baptizer and baptism of Jesus	Ministry and witness of the Baptizer (1:19–34)
Temptations of Jesus	Early disciples (1:35–51)
Early preaching and call of disciples	Signs and cleansing of Temple (2)
Mighty works and popularity	Personal teaching (3—4)
Controversies (Mark 2—3)	Controversy (5)
Teachings (Matthew 5—7, 13)	Feeding of 5000 and confession (6)
Confession at Caesarea Philippi	Controversy and claims (7—10)
Transfiguration	
Journey to Jerusalem	Raising of Lazarus and anointing (11—12)
Entry and cleansing of Temple	Entry, coming of Greeks, temptation, and transfiguration (12)
Teaching and debate	
Eschataological discourse	Footwashing (13)
Upper Room and supper	Word to disciples (14—16)
Garden prayer and arrest	High priestly prayer (17)
Denial and trial	Arrest, trial, and denial (18)
Crucifixion	Crucifixion (19)
Resurrection and commission	Resurrection and commission (20)
	Epilogue (21)

"And the Word became flesh and dwelt among us . . ."

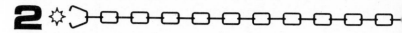

The Word Made Flesh

John opens his Gospel with a poem about the Word. Some scholars think that he took an older poem and revised it to fit this book. It is more likely, however, that it was written for this Gospel itself.

This poem is John's substitute for Matthew's and Luke's birth stories and for Mark's voice at Jesus' baptism. In Jesus Christ God and man come together. Jesus unites God and man in his own person. He also brings the believer face to face with God. In the Gospel which follows, the relation of the Son to the Father will be made clear. That men come in contact with God in and through Jesus Christ, that by faith they receive life which is in Christ, and that God prepares them for the coming of the Spirit through whom they receive this life, will also be stressed.

In this lesson we are concerned with the first eighteen verses of the Gospel, commonly called the Prologue. It would be well first to read Genesis 1:1–8 and Proverbs 8:22–31 and then to read these verses. (Note: "Wisdom" in the Old Testament language of Proverbs means much the same thing as "Word" in the New Testament Greek of John.) This will prepare you for some of the ideas here. Note the way the writer begins, how and when he introduces Jesus Christ, what he says about him. Mark the main themes mentioned. These themes you may expect to meet throughout the Gospel.

The Prologue is not formally an introduction; it is more like the theme of a symphony. In one brief sketch the author presents all the major motifs of the Gospel—Word, life, light, witness, glory, grace, and truth. He concentrates, however, on the Word.

He presents the eternal Word active in Creation; the Word incarnate, hidden but nevertheless received; and the great purpose of the Word. Here in cryptic fashion he describes Jesus Christ. The most important affirmations about him are to be found here.

The Background of "the Word"

By the term "Word" (*logos*) John is interpreting who and what Jesus is to Jews and Greeks alike.

For the Jew the Old Testament stressed the idea of the speaking God. His word was an expression of himself, carrying his authority, energized with his power, furthering his purpose (Isa. 55: 10–11). It was God's mode of action. God called things into existence by his word. He spoke to Noah and saved him and his house in the time of flood, summoned Abraham and sent him forth, delivered Israel from the hand of Pharaoh, addressed Israel to make a covenant with her, and laid his word on her. Through the priest he gave instruction (Torah or law) revealing his holy will; through the prophet he directed the course of history by his word of promise and judgment; through the later sage he gave counsel which became personified as wisdom (Prov. 8:12–36). Among the rabbis "word" became a substitute for the divine name. Thus for the Jew "word" and God were closely identified.

To the Greek the term translated "word" (*logos*) signified reason—that by which the Supreme Being contemplated the world, planned it, and brought it into existence. It stood for the principle of order, the power to think and know, the intermediary between God and his world which made the world rational and comprehensible. At the same time, by it men could understand the world and gain knowledge of God. All this would come to the mind of the Greek hearer of the Prologue.

For John and the early church, Christ was the divine agent of activity in the world (John 1:3; compare also 1 Cor. 8:6; Col. 1:13–20; and Heb. 1:1–3). He therefore could be identified with the "Word" of the Old Testament and the *logos* of Greek thought.

The Nature of a Word

Have you ever asked yourself what a word is? Certainly it is more than an utterance of syllables, a name by which objects are recognized, or an element of speech. Words call up mental pictures of objects, actions, or ideas in the mind of the hearer. They move the heart to rejoice and to weep. They arouse to anger and they quiet the troubled spirit. They bring understanding and they bring perplexity. They prompt to activity and they bring a halt to activity.

How much often hangs on a word! Two lives are intertwined and a home is formed by a word. A man is acquitted and another is confined to prison for life by a word. In the New York City transit strike of 1965 a whole city was thrown into confusion, traffic was snarled, small shops and restaurants were forced to close, stores and industry lost huge sums, all because of a word. Again, our words disclose our background, our way of life, our hopes and dreams. We make ourselves known by words.

So also with God's word. It reveals the divine personality, his will and purpose, his nature and activity, his glory and power. The following excerpt from the musical, *For Heaven's Sake,* illustrates this. Note the emphases in this poem.

> I open my mouth to speak
> And the word is there,
> Formed by the lips, the tongue,
> The organ of voice. Formed by
> The brain, transmitting the word
> By breath.
>
> I open my mouth to speak
> And the word is there,
> Traveling between us—caught
> By the organ of hearing, the ear,
> Transmitting the thought to the brain
> Through the word.
>
> Just so do we communicate—
> You and I: the thought
> From one mind leaping to another,
> Given shape and form and substance,

So that we know and are known
Through the word.

But let me speak to my very small son
And the words mean nothing,
For he does not know my language.
And so I must show him: "This is your foot,"
I say; "and it is meant for walking."
I help him up: "Here is the way to walk!"
And one day "walking" shapes in his brain
With the word.

God had something to say to Man,
But the words meant nothing,
For we did not know his language.
And so we were shown: "Behold, the Man,"
He said, "This is the image, the thought
In my mind—Man as I mean him, loving and serving.
I have put Him in flesh. Now the Word
Has shape and form and substance
To travel between us. Let Him show forth love
Till one day 'loving' shapes in your brain
With the Word." [1]

God Speaks in Jesus, 1:1–3

". . . the Word was God. . . . in the beginning with God; all things were made through him . . ." (1:1–3). The Bible takes it for granted that God acts by his word. In the opening of the Prologue, John emphasizes the relation of the Word to God. What do you suppose John means by "the Word was with God, and the Word was God"? Note how the writer avoids introducing Jesus by name at the very beginning: he speaks not of Jesus or of Christ, but of the Word. Now undoubtedly in the background of his mind is the idea that Jesus Christ is the Word of God, but he begins by describing the relation of the Word and God, and only after that does he describe the incarnation of the Word in Jesus. What does this suggest about the emphasis with respect to Jesus? (See 1:14 and 1: 18.)

The writer begins like the book of Genesis. Do you think he had this portion of the Bible in mind, "In the beginning God created . . . .And God said . . ." when he penned these words? Is that which in Genesis is ascribed to God here ascribed to Jesus? (Cf. John 1:3.) Or, is the writer saying that the God who created all things by his Word is now acting anew, speaking a word of redemption in Jesus Christ? How does this compare with what the writer of Hebrews says (Heb. 1:1–3)?

I think that part of the emphasis here is that the Creator God is the Redeemer God, the creative Word is the redeeming Word. (Does this imply anything about the relation of the New Testament to the Old?) The God who brought order out of chaos is now re-creating all things—making them alive—by redeeming them, by bringing order out of the chaos of men's minds, men's hearts, and men's lives.

Again, the opening words of this book seem to certify that Jesus Christ came from God. He was a unique person. He didn't suddenly appear as an exceptionally religious man or a great teacher who knew more about God than anyone else. The author is concerned to point out that in Jesus God is at work in a special way and that Jesus stands in a unique relationship to the Father. Thus Jesus is termed God's Son (1:18). This is John's way of saying what Paul says in the phrase, "God was in Christ" (2 Cor. 5:19). All that follows in this book is to be read in the light of this. God is not enthroned silent over the heavens. He turns to man with heart and mouth; he addresses him in Jesus Christ and calls him to obedience and faith. In Jesus, then, God is speaking to his world.

God Speaks in the Life of Jesus, 1:4–5

"And the Word became flesh and dwelt among us . . ." (1:14). So John tells the story of God's coming to earth in Jesus of Nazareth. The divine Word takes on human form. What do you suppose John means by the words, "the Word became flesh"? Why doesn't he say, "God became flesh"? Is he perchance trying to avoid the errors of Greek religious thought in which the gods were conceived of in human form and all the emotions and passions of men were attributed to them? Is he speaking from a Jewish background which held God to be one and invisible, so that an extension of the divine personality, such as Spirit or Word, is used to describe God's activity in Jesus? Is this a way of saying that God has now drawn near to mankind in a more personal way; he walks among men as one unknown; he meets man where he is and shares his life—all the experiences of human life? Is this a way of saying that God's word (his message), and thus God himself, comes to us in the life of Jesus?

Have you ever thought of the significance of Jesus being born as a child and growing to manhood? All the experiences that come to a person were shared by him. There is no stage of life from infancy to adulthood which Christ has not shared. He knows what it is to be a man—an infant, a child, a youth, an adult. People of all these ages can feel that Jesus understands them and knows their problems, for he had a similar experience.

Again, that God became man—as the Word made flesh—means that the ultimate revelation of God is not spoken from a mountain or given in a book, but is written in a life. The deepest truths of life, to be forcefully presented, must be embodied. The early Hebrews and later Jews (as they are usually called after the Exile) were almost never given to abstract thinking or abstract teaching. For them truth had to be set in concrete form. Thus Jesus spoke in parables, told stories, or used symbols to create a living situation in which the truth of God was set forth. He did not speculate on who a neighbor is, or what love is, or what faith can do. He illustrated these by parable, story, or his own actions, so that his hearers could see the truth embodied. So God came to the world in Jesus Christ. Howsoever God phrased his message of old, or by whatever person he spoke, people never seemed to hear or understand the depth of God's concern for the world or the limits to which he was willing to go to redeem it. Consequently God joined the lot of men, and as a man in Jesus Christ both revealed to men the way of life and opened the door to it.

Finally, Jesus is the message of God to man. In him God is not only acting but speaking. *Have you ever contemplated what God tried to say in Jesus Christ? How would you phrase this?* This sets the life of Jesus apart from every other life. His every word and his every act came as a message from God. This made men wonder who he was. They were perplexed and offended by him; finally they sought to get rid of him, for he was out of place in the world. He was in the world but not of it, and the people detected this. So they killed him. But the early church affirmed that the very death of Jesus was the heart of God's message to the world in his life.

God spoke in Jesus in a personal and exclusive way. This constituted the uniqueness of Jesus. This appears in three verses in John:

> No one has ever seen God; the only Son, who is in the bosom of the Father, he has made him known (1:18).

> "I am the way, and the truth, and the life; no one comes to the Father, but by me" (14:6).

> ". . . and I, when I am lifted up from the earth, will draw all men to myself" (12:32).

These are tremendous statements. They set Jesus apart from the rest of men.

God Speaks About Himself in Jesus, 1:16–18

"No one has ever seen God; the only Son . . . has made him known" (1:18). What do you think John means to say by this statement? Note, he does not say, "No one has ever known God." Why do you suppose he connects "seen God" with "made him known"? Part of the meaning surely is that in Jesus men come face to face with God. One of the reasons why it is so difficult to distinguish between Christ and God in our devotional life is that for most Christians God is best known as he is in Christ.

God reveals himself in Jesus Christ. His promises are not only relayed through a messenger or written in a book, but also embodied in a life. So John writes, ". . . the law was given through Moses; grace and truth came through Jesus Christ" (1:17). Jesus represents the faithful God, true to his promises and to himself, coming to reconcile men to himself. God is not subject to the emotional whims of the Greek gods who were made in the likeness of men. He is ever faithful and true to his covenant, to himself, and to his people.

God reveals himself as a God of love in Jesus. So Christ comes to men, helps them, and submits himself to love's demands, including the cross (15:13; cf. 13:1).

God reveals his yearning heart in Jesus. So Christ visits with a Pharisee at night and with a Samaritan woman at noonday and speaks to them about life and God's Kingdom.

What other things can you think of that God reveals about himself in Jesus? In Jesus men can know what God is like and what he wants to do for men. Do you think that we by God's Spirit also reveal what God is like? Is this why God is so concerned about a Christian's life? In what way are we like Christ in this? In what way are we different?

Finally, this means that what God has to offer to man is not some word, some rule to live by, some ideal to strive after, some key to unlock the mystery of the world. What God has to offer is himself in Jesus of Nazareth, and not just himself as a friend in need or a helper in difficulty: he offers man his life. Do you suppose this is why John calls the life that Jesus gives "eternal life"?

The implications of this emphasis in the Prologue are that God has uniquely joined us in our history. A new era has begun with Jesus. God is now directly and personally involved in the affairs of the world in a different way, first in the life of Jesus of Nazareth, and then in the life of Christians by his Spirit. John desires that men should have a real, living encounter with God in and through Jesus. Whatever salvation may mean and whatever the gift of life may imply, they demand first of all that a person come into encounter with God, with all that this signifies, in and through Jesus Christ. How easy God has made it for man to meet him! He has joined us in our humanity and in the world where we live so that we can come to know him.

"... among you stands one whom you do not know ..."

3

The Unknown in Your Midst

When God became man in the life of Jesus of Nazareth he was unrecognized. God laid aside the robe of his divinity, took the garb of a man of flesh, and hid himself among the men of the world. Part of the offense of the gospel and the mystery of the Incarnation (the "coming in flesh") is this simple fact. The difficulty which arises is that Christ, being in human form, is not recognized as divine. This is the basic problem of this Gospel, the chief source of controversy with the Jews, and the main cause of unbelief.

This difficulty is increased in that when God became man he did not appear among the most culturally advanced people of the day. He came as a member of a despised race—the Jews—a people culturally poor who had little to commend them. Neither did God appear among the leadership of the Jewish people. He came as a peasant from a despised corner of the land. It would have been difficult enough to recognize him had he come as a Nicodemus or a Gamaliel. But that he should appear as one of "the people of the land," the despised folk who were reputed to not know the law, and certainly not to keep it (7:49), as a poor peasant from Nazareth, made it virtually impossible to recognize him. Nathanael expressed the popular opinion, "Can anything good come out of Nazareth?" (1:46.) The Pharisees submitted the official position, "Search and you will see that no prophet is to rise from Galilee" (7:52). How hard it is to overcome the forces of prejudice and tradition!

We do not expect God to come as a man, to have a human form, to grow up among us, to look and act like a man. Would you be able to call even the most saintly man God, were God to appear in human flesh today? It was as difficult for the people of Jesus' day.

No wonder most people rejected him and wanted to be rid of him! The wonder is that any were led to believe on him and to confess him. Those who did, did not do this of themselves. They had help from above.

Read 1:19–51 and mark how various people came to recognize Jesus as the Christ—the Baptizer, his disciples, other men. Also note the various ways by which Jesus is confessed to be a Messianic figure. Why was it hard to recognize him as the Messiah? What things helped John the Baptist and the disciples to know him? In this chapter John relates the calling of five disciples. In the Synoptics also the call of only five disciples is given and the Jewish Talmud in its description of Jesus mentions that he had five. This, of course, does not mean that these were the only disciples Jesus had. Matthew mentions twelve (10:1–4); Luke, seventy (10:1); and after the Resurrection there were at least a hundred and twenty (Acts 1:15).

In this lesson we will study the strangeness of Jesus, the one well-known and yet unknown. This is really the problem of the human and the divine in Jesus. We will also note how men came to recognize him. This will enable us better to appreciate those who do not believe and better to understand their position.

The Strangeness of Jesus

Jesus was an enigma to the people to whom he came. They professed to know him. "Is not this Jesus, the son of Joseph, whose father and mother we know?" (6:42.) And again, ". . . we know where this man comes from; and when the Christ appears, no one will know where he comes from" (7:27). To this Jesus responds in surprise with a question: "You know me, and you know where I come from?" (7:28.) The Jews later had to acknowledge, ". . . as for this man, we do not know where he comes from" (9:29).

The stories about Jesus give evidence that the people did not know *him*. They knew his name, his parents, and his hometown, but they did not really understand *him*. About him there was always an air of mystery.

Men were intrigued by his miracles. These were signs which no one could gainsay. They prompted all kinds of answers to the question, "Who am I?" Nicodemus presents the scholar's view: "Rabbi, we know that you are a teacher come from God; for no one can do these signs that you do, unless God is with him" (3:2). Others hazarded other opinions. Some said, "This is indeed the prophet who is to come into the world!" (6:14) or, "This is really the Prophet" (7:40). Others were more bold in their claims: "Can it be that the authorities really know that this is the Christ?" (7:26); "This is the Christ" (7:41); or like the Samaritan woman, "Can this be the Christ?" (4:29.) Others denounced him: ". . . we know that this man is a sinner" (9:24); or, more vehemently, "Are we not right in saying that you are a Samaritan and have a demon?" (8:48; compare 8:52); or "He has a demon, and he is mad . . ." (10:20).

You can see the uncertainty as to who and what Jesus was. The Jews were torn between various opinions. In desperation and sincerity they said to Jesus, "How long will you keep us in suspense? If you are the Christ, tell us plainly" (10:24). All this shows that Jesus was well-known, but very much unknown. Something more was needed than an acquaintance with Jesus to know who he really was.

Why do you suppose Jesus seemed strange and the Jews had difficulty in recognizing Jesus? Was it because he was a peasant, a country boy, who acted like a rabbi? Was it the fact that the power of God was alive in him? Was it because he presumed to be an authority? Was it because he was more spiritual than others? Was it that he had prophetic insight, an ability to see what was in the mind and heart of a person, or to foresee the future? Note what he says about Peter (1:42) and Nathanael (1:48*b*), how much he knows about the Samaritan woman (4:17–18) and Judas (6:70), how he knows the nobleman's son will live (4:50) and that Lazarus is dead (11:14). Or was it perhaps that Jesus was more than a man? Would you have accepted his claims without question? Do you suppose it was any easier for the people of Jesus' day? What part do you think prejudice or tradition played in the failure of the Jews to accept Jesus? (See 1:46; cf. 7:52; 9:16.) Can it be that no one by himself comes to an understanding of Jesus? Is there something more required than human knowledge and human wisdom?

How Jesus Becomes Known

It is the author's conviction that, to know who Jesus really is, more is required than a knowledge of Jesus' life and an acquaintance with what the church believes about him. There is a plus which we call revelation (see Matt. 16:17, Gal. 1:12). It is a divine insight, an understanding above and beyond what the mind can provide. It furnishes a key to the understanding of Jesus' words and Jesus' deeds.

When Peter makes his great confession, according to Matthew's Gospel, Jesus responds, ". . . flesh and blood has not revealed this to you, but my Father who is in heaven" (16:17). This thought underlies the whole of the Fourth Gospel. That Jesus is the Word of God, or the Son of God, is not something men arrive at through meditation or speculation. It must be revealed to them. Throughout the Gospel there is expressed the need for someone to point men to Christ and to reveal his identity.

In this Gospel men come to know who Jesus is in the following ways.

(1) God has given the initial revelation. He disclosed the identity of the Messiah to the Baptizer. Note how the latter described the event (1:32–34); note also what he did as a result of it (1:36). John the Baptizer was given the task of making Christ known. Thus he became the first one to confess the Christ (1:34) and the initiator of the Christian movement. For us today, perhaps, the Bible performs the function of the Baptizer. Here the revelation of God is given.

(2) Another way by which men are led to see in Jesus the Christ is for Jesus to make his identity known. Most of the Gospel is concerned with this. Jesus revealed himself to Philip (1:43); he became a disciple and summoned another. Jesus revealed himself to the Samaritan woman (4:26), and she in turn brought the townspeople. Later he revealed himself to the man born blind (9:37).

We do not know what Jesus said or did to reveal himself to Philip. It took place, at any event, in a face to face meeting. Some

clue as to the way Jesus reveals himself is given in 4:7–26 and 9:
35–38. Note in each instance how what had previously taken place
prepared the individual for the self-disclosure of Jesus. How does
Jesus make himself known today?

(3) Jesus' words and works, as we shall see later, were also
means by which Jesus revealed himself. The miracles of Jesus were
manifestations of his glory as emphasized by the first and last of
those recorded in John (2:11 and 11:4). They were for John the
ultimate proof of the truth of the gospel and the identity of Jesus
Christ (20:30–31). Here the message is verified by a miracle. Perhaps John wrote at some distance from the earliest Gospels, where
the miracles are pictured as mighty works manifesting that the
power of God is at work in Jesus for the good of mankind.
   *Does Christ speak and work today? Do his words and works
still reveal his identity? Is it easier for us to recognize him through
his words and works than it was for the Jews of Jesus' day?*

(4) A final way by which Jesus becomes known is by one person witnessing to another. John the Baptizer pointed two of his disciples to Jesus; they spent a day with him, and one of them found
his brother and said to him, "We have found the Messiah" (1:41).
Philip was called to follow Jesus and he brought Nathanael. The
woman of Sychar brought the inhabitants of the village. And so it
went. Personal witness was one of the most effective means of making Christ known in the early church. This aspect of Christian life
has in some measure disappeared from the modern scene, but it is
being recaptured by the lay movement in the church. The emphasis
on a lay ministry is in part an attempt to inject the element of personal witness again into the Christian movement. A Christian is a
witness and testifies to others about the things that have happened
to him, or, more correctly, about him who has come into his life
and changed it.

Christian Witness

Christian witness is simply one person telling another about his
Christian faith. Often people think that this is the task of the minis-

ter alone. Or else they think that witness is given in the church building, and so they consider their obligation in this regard fulfilled when they have invited or brought another to the church. I wonder why this element of Christian life should often be neglected. Can it be we have never experienced the joy of salvation and therefore what we have to say about Jesus does not sound like "good news"? Can it be we have resented the street corner evangelists and the revivalists who come to us asking, "Are you saved," and so we seek to avoid offending others by being silent about our faith? Do we omit it because we do not know how to go about witnessing and have never been taught to do this in the program of the church?

Many people are hungry for someone to talk to. We cannot become intimately acquainted with our neighbors without having them at some time or other open up to us and lay bare their hearts. It is quite possible that the backyard or the kitchen may yet prove to be the best place for evangelism. A number of churches are sponsoring coffeehouses for students and others as places where discussion can take place and Christian witness can be given.

Since Christian witness is so important it is well to explore what John can tell us about it.

(1) Note first that the witness comes with a message. The Baptizer brings the initial message, "Behold, the Lamb of God, who takes away the sin of the world!" (John 1:29.) This is also part of the portrayal of Jesus as John understands him. Jesus is the lamb of God; as such he is crucified at the same time the passover lambs are slain (13:1; 18:28; 19:42), and not a bone of him is broken (19:32–36). Note what message the other witnesses bring: Andrew (1:41), Philip (1:45), the woman of Sychar (4:29).

(2) The message takes many forms, but mostly it is a confession: "We have found the Messiah" (1:41), or "We have found him of whom Moses in the law and also the prophets wrote, Jesus of Nazareth, the son of Joseph" (1:45). Sometimes it is in the form of a tantalizing question, "Can this be the Christ?" (4:29.)

(3) In each case something is said about Jesus which appeals

to the hearer. For Simon, a Galilean longing for the Messiah, the message came as a simple statement, "We have found him" (1:41); Nathanael, a student of the Scriptures,[1] was told of "him of whom Moses in the law and also the prophets wrote . . ." (1:45); to the Samaritans, who also awaited the coming of the Messiah to end their dispute with the Jews, it was a simple question, "Can this be Christ?" with the added incentive, he "told me all that I ever did" (4:29). In each case the witness is direct, personal, and confessional, as all testimonies must be. No sentimentality is expressed here, no elaborate calling attention to the self; only a simple, straightforward statement made directly and personally to the one encountered.

(4) The testimony also contains an invitation to meet Jesus. Perhaps this is expressed most forcefully in Philip's word to Nathanael when the latter presents his prejudicial disbelief, "Can anything good come out of Nazareth?" (1:46.) Philip does not argue about the merits of Nazareth, nor does he point to some great men who came from small villages. He gives the simple invitation, "Come and see" (1:46). This is ever the invitation in this Gospel (1:39; 1:46; 4:29). There is no arguing, no attempt by the witness to prove his statement, no effort to convince any individual that he is telling the truth. There is just the plain invitation to "Come and see," with the assurance that if one will meet Jesus he will know the truth of what has been said.

This Gospel is nothing more or less than such an invitation. John does not attempt to overwhelm the reader by heaping up evidences or by rational argumentation. He presents to the reader, rather, an earnest invitation to make a spiritual pilgrimage to meet Jesus, spend some time with him, and see for himself whether or not Jesus is the Christ. And the reader is assured that, be he as biased as a Nathanael (1:46) or as skeptical as a Thomas (20: 25), he will find in Jesus his Lord and his God (cf. also 4:27–30, 39–42).

This has some implications for the conduct of the church's mission of evangelism at home and abroad. The essential task of the mission is to bring men in contact with Jesus·Christ. *What ways can you suggest in which this can be done?* Through contact with the Bible? the church? the individual Christian? What part do the services of the church play? Is a Christlike life essential? Is one duty bound as a Christian to introduce men to Jesus? What does this imply for daily living? Do the agricultural, educational, and medical mission programs of the church have this as their central task?

It is well to note that we do not convert anyone. We do not save them. We rather point them to the Christ, who alone can save. We set men on the road where they can meet him. We introduce them to Jesus and, in the words of Peter Marshall, say, "Mr. Jones, meet the Master." It is Jesus alone who saves. He must be allowed to be free to deal with people in his own way. There is no one method alone by which he helps people.

With all that has been said about the simplicity of the gospel it still remains true that men need someone to bring them to Christ. There is need for someone to assume the role of Evangelist in *The Pilgrim's Progress,* so that men can find the wicket gate and walk the road that leads to the cross where they encounter the Christ who saves.

Jesus remains a stranger until his identity is disclosed to us. Cyril Richardson has emphasized in his book, *The Doctrine of the Trinity,* that both Jesus and the Holy Spirit represent the nearness of God. This means that God is now present in his world and near to his people. But he may not always be recognized. Jesus remains unknown until we come in contact with him. To know God in Jesus demands a sincere desire to meet him and a willingness to accept him for what he is. Jesus does not commit himself casually to men (see 2:23–25). To a sincere seeker he will manifest himself. To the rest he remains hidden. There may be many guesses as to his identity but no certainty. To the extent that a believer entrusts himself to Christ, to that extent Christ entrusts himself to the believer. This is why some individuals are closer to Christ than others and why some are more advanced in their Christian life. This is not a matter of intelligence, of background, or of influence. It is a matter of faith, for it is forever true, "According to your faith be it done to you." This should caution us against speaking too glibly about Jesus or pretending that we know all about him.

It is thus true that Jesus can be near and yet go undetected. For it is only to those who have "eyes to see and ears to hear" that he makes himself known.

> We would see Jesus, Mary's Son most holy,
> Light of the village life from day to day;
> Shining revealed through every task most lowly,
> The Christ of God, the Life, the Truth, the Way.
>
> We would see Jesus, on the mountain teaching,
> With all the listening people gathered round;
> While birds and flowers and sky above are preaching
> The blessedness which simple trust has found.
>
> We would see Jesus, in His work of healing,
> At eventide before the sun was set;
> Divine and human, in His deep revealing,
> Of God and man in loving service met.
>
> We would see Jesus; in the early morning
> Still as of old He calleth, "Follow Me";
> Let us arise, all meaner service scorning:
> Lord, we are Thine, we give ourselves to Thee![2]
>
> —*The Hymnbook,* 183

". . . Jesus did not trust himself to them . . . "

4 ✧ ⊃━❏━❏━❏━❏━❏━❏━❏━❏━

The Nature of Faith

John writes his Gospel that men may believe and have life (John 20:31). To most Christians "to believe" means "to express or to exercise faith." This entire Gospel is the story of the growth of faith and of unbelief. The opening incident in the ministry of Jesus leads to faith on the part of the early disciples (2:11). At the climax of the story the most skeptical of the disciples comes to profess his faith in Jesus as Lord and God (20:28).

Faith is a word in every Christian's vocabulary. It is taken for granted that everyone knows what it means. *But have you ever tried to define faith? What do you think of when you think of "believing"? Do you think of acknowledging as true what the Bible says about God and Jesus, ourselves, and the way of life? Do you think of the doctrines of the church, which you are asked to accept as a true statement of what the Scriptures teach? Do you think of trusting and relying upon God?* When you try to put in a brief statement what you mean by faith, it isn't easy, is it?

The church has defined faith in the following ways:

Faith in Jesus Christ is a saving grace, whereby we receive and rest upon him alone for salvation, as he is offered to us in the gospel (The Westminster Shorter Catechism, Q. 86).

[True faith] is not only a certain knowledge by which I accept as true all that God has revealed to us in his Word, but also a wholehearted trust which the Holy Spirit creates in me through the gospel, that, not only to others, but to me also God has given the forgiveness of sins, everlasting righteousness and salvation, out of sheer grace solely for the sake of Christ's saving work.[1]

Compare these definitions with the following modern ones:

Faith is belief in something or trust in some person . . . man's Yes to the Word of God.[2]

Faith is the state of being ultimately concerned . . .[3]

I have also seen faith defined as "betting your life on God." How do these definitions compare with that of the writer of Hebrews (Heb. 11:1)? with your own definition?

The aim of this lesson is to study what John has to teach us about faith. We will study some of the stories of the Gospel in which faith is called forth. In these stories we will take notice of the different kinds of faith. This will help us to express what we mean when we say, "I believe."

Read the two stories in chapter 2 of John and the story in chapter 9. In each instance the event led to faith. As you read see what you can discover about faith, about what led men to believe, and why in the last story the same event led to opposite effects in different men. You will meet many interesting ideas here. Note the details, the actions, the references to future events. Remember we are studying these to learn something about faith. What different types of faith are represented here? Why are certain types incomplete? What more is required?

Some Observations on Faith

(1) Faith is an activity. In the Gospel of John the noun *faith* is never used. Instead John uses the verb *to believe*. This describes action. Faith is something the Christian expresses, something he does, not something he passively lets happen. It is not simply knowledge or assurance. It is a response to God and Jesus Christ in which the whole person of the believer is involved. This response may be interpreted as obedience, commitment, surrender, receptivity, but it demands action on the part of the whole being of the individual. It is not merely a matter of the mind.

(2) Faith has a person as its object in John. Faith is directed to Jesus Christ. John does not ask men, "What do you believe?" but, "In whom do you believe?" This involves a relationship, a certain attachment, a commitment. This question becomes pertinent

when asked of ourselves, "In whom do I believe?" in God? in Jesus? in the Devil? in myself?

(3) Faith involves believing something about the person in whom you believe. You are not inclined to believe anyone and everyone. There must be some knowledge of a person—of his identity, his capabilities, his character, the cause for which he stands— before there can be any kind of commitment. This is the information about Jesus which John gives in his Gospel.

Certain aspects of the development of faith are given in chapters 2 and 9 of John. It will be impossible to discuss all the details or emphases in these chapters; we shall look at them to see what they tell us about faith.

Faith in the Miracles, 2:1–11

John opens his portrayal of the ministry of Jesus with a miracle at Cana of Galilee. It took place during the festivities of a wedding to which Jesus and his disciples had been invited. During the course of the feast (they usually lasted several days) the wine gave out. Jesus' mother asked him to do something about the lack. Note his response. Jesus never acts in this Gospel because another asks him to act. There is a divine plan and time schedule which he is following, and he acts only in accordance with it. No one can tell God what to do!

However, Jesus, in response to the need of the newly wedded pair, had the servants fill with water six huge stone jars which were used to store water for ceremonial washing and then draw out some of the contents and bear it to the guests. The steward of the feast, upon tasting it, declared it to be the best wine of the wedding. Thus, John says, Jesus manifested his glory, as though for a moment he removed the veil of flesh and enabled his disciples to see something of the brilliance of his true nature. In some ways signs like this in John are what the Transfiguration is in the Synoptics.

What was it in this story that led to faith on the part of the disciples? Was it Jesus' power over nature? Was it Jesus' helpfulness in getting his host out of an embarrassing situation? Was it something about the nature of the miracle itself?

The church has always been perplexed as to the meaning of the changing of water into wine at the wedding of Cana. Some have seen the story as exemplifying Jesus' blessing of marriage, others as manifesting Jesus' mastery over nature and using it to bless mankind, and still others as evidencing Jesus' concern for man and his ability to bring joy to life. Wherever Jesus is invited he becomes a true friend. He takes men's problems upon himself and bestows on men joy. He uses the power of God for the blessing of men in their time of need. He supplies what is lacking to bring joy and happiness. But he does this in his own time and in his own way.

Modern scholars tend to see some hidden meaning behind the miracles in John. They look upon these signs as symbolic. Some see here an allusion to the sacraments. They see the miracle of wine as similar to the miracle of bread in chapter 6, which is interpreted in terms of the Lord's Supper. In the Cana incident the sacrament is seen as a joyful feast—a foretaste of the marriage feast of the Lamb and the Bride in the age to come (Rev. 19:7, 9; 21:9). Others see the water made wine as a symbol of the Holy Spirit. Jesus supplies the new wine of the Spirit which brings joy to life and replaces the ceremonial washings and cleansings of the Jews. Still other scholars feel that John meant to show the replacement of Judaism in this manifestation of the glory of Jesus. What Christ has to offer is better than what went before. The new wine of Christianity is better than the old of Judaism.

One notes that in performing the miracle Jesus only uses the creative word. Can it be that the creative word of God, used in response to human need, is that which leads to faith, and that John wants the reader to see this creative word in action?

Faith in this instance is the result of a sign which Jesus performed. It is directed to Jesus as one who uses the power of God for the benefit of men. Perhaps this is where all faith begins. Note the number of references in this Gospel which link faith to signs, such as in the statement of Nicodemus (3:2), the reason given for the crowds following Jesus (6:2), and the response to the healing of the cripple (7:31) and to the raising of Lazarus (11:47).

Yet John seems to suggest that such faith is not perfect. While faith for some developed from a belief in signs, for others it did not (12:37). And Jesus did not trust himself to those in whom faith came simply from seeing signs (2:24). *Why do you suppose faith prompted by signs (or miracles) is insufficient?* Is it because such faith always seeks to be nourished by new and greater miracles? Is it because there is an inherent danger in such faith, that men are tempted thereby to think of Jesus only as a helper in time of need? How many think of Jesus only in this fashion! Does such faith also tempt men to call upon Christ to escape from what is distasteful? Is there a tendency to use Jesus for one's own ends? In this miracle Jesus acts only in accordance with the will and purpose of God. What does this imply as to our seeking help of God in time of need?

Faith in the Mission, 2:13–25

John places the cleansing of the Temple at the beginning of Jesus' ministry. It is possible that Jesus did this twice, but the accounts in the Gospels are so similar as to suggest that they are relating the same incident.

Amid all the details of the story—the whip of cords, the righteous indignation, the concern for the Father's house that it should not be a place of merchandise—the climax comes with the saying about the destruction of the "temple" and its being raised anew (2:19). John understands this saying to be a prediction of the Resurrection (2:21). The Temple itself must give way to a new dwelling place of God by his Spirit—Christ's body. (Compare what is said here with what is said about worship in John 4:20–24. Note how both passages envision a worship separated from the Jerusalem Temple.)

The opening story is a story of grace. This story is one of judgment. Jesus as Messiah brings a judgment upon the existing center of worship. I wonder how Jesus would judge our church? How often the church takes the place that belongs to Christ! We direct our attention to the church rather than to Christ. How often we crowd God and his Christ out of the church! The prayer meeting ceases and the building becomes a place of business. How much of the energies of the members and the business discussed at meetings are concerned with the raising of funds and the selling of merchandise. Against all this Jesus casts his judgment. *What is the legitimate business of the church? What things have a valid place in church? Where in our church would Jesus swing his whip?*

The point of this story is that the building where men have access to God is replaced by Jesus Christ. A young woman whose son was seriously injured by an automobile hunted desperately for an open church so she could pray to God. When she found no Protestant church open she finally went to a Roman Catholic one. She felt that in such great need the place to meet God and receive help was a place of worship. Yet if what is said here about the point of this story is true, Jesus has made it possible for men to meet God anywhere: the true temple of God is his body. Since the church is called Christ's body, is it also true that in fellowship with one another we meet Christ and have access to God?

This story of the cleansing of the Temple is, in accordance with the purpose of the Gospel (20:31), also meant to lead the reader to faith. Here Jesus assumes a Messianic role and pronounces judgment upon existing religion. Here he points the way to a new approach to God. Faith then means to accept Jesus as the way of approach to God. Why do you suppose John placed this story at the beginning of his book? Does he intend the story to verify the fact that Jesus is the Messiah? Does he mark by it the end of Judaism and its replacement by Christianity? Does he suggest that the Resurrection is the supreme proof of the identity and authority of Jesus?

I believe John uses this story to show Jesus' authority as Messiah and the nature of his Messianic mission. Jesus comes not as a zealot, a political revolutionary prompted by religious motives, but as one who is concerned about man's relation to God. Jesus himself is the new meeting place of God and man. By a display of his authority and by an act of judgment he summons men to faith in him.

Here faith is directed to Jesus as a Messianic figure. This is the second step in the development of faith. Faith in Jesus must include the understanding that he acts for God: he brings the judgment of God and ushers in a new way of life. Such faith is not without its danger. For men readily forget the nature of Jesus' Messiahship and tend to use Jesus to foster their political hopes and social dreams. The Jews would have been willing enough to accept Jesus as Messiah if he would have fulfilled their hopes for a new Israel (6:15; cf. 6:66). *Do we sometimes look to Christ to fulfill our political and social dreams and bring in our kind of world? Can it be that the reason the Kingdom progresses so slowly is that we are always getting our plans mixed up with his?*

Faith in the Man, 9:1–41

This incident in the central part of this book is the best illustration of the growth of faith and unbelief. It is a drama in eight parts: Jesus and his disciples (9:1–5); Jesus and the blind man (9:6–7); the neighbors and the blind man (9:8–12); the Pharisees and the blind man (9:13–17); the Jews and his parents (9:18–23); the Jews and the blind man—a second encounter (9:24–34); Jesus and the blind man—a second encounter (9:35–38); Jesus and the Pharisees (9:39–41).

Here a man born blind is healed by Jesus. Pressed by the Jews, he argues from his experience and progresses from naming his benefactor as "the man called Jesus" (9:11) to believing in him as the Son of Man (9:35–36). ("Son of Man" was Jesus' favorite title for himself. This title, while acknowledging Jesus' relation to God, emphasizes his oneness with humanity.) The Jews, arguing from their traditions, depreciate the miracle and see in Jesus a sinner (9:16); finally, because of their obdurate stubbornness, they are condemned by Jesus as sinful (9:41).

There are some interesting reversals in this story. An unlearned man becomes a teacher, and the teachers manifest their ignorance (9:29–34). The man born blind is exonerated from guilt, and the Pharisees who claim to see are charged with it (9:2–3, 40–41). What others can you name? Note the progress of the faith of the man born blind. What statements does he make about Jesus? (9:11, 17, 33, 35–38.) Note also the variety of ways the Pharisees seek to make light of the event in order to maintain their tradition (9:16, 18–20; cf. 9:22, 24, 26, 34). Notice how the blind man comes from experience to an encounter of faith. Yet not by his own effort does he come to faith. Only by means of a second confrontation with Jesus does he understand that God has been addressing him in the event. Then he commits himself to Jesus and worships him. Note that commitment involves more than knowledge; it also involves an act of decision and of worship.

Worship is the stance of the committed. *What lesson can we learn about faith and unbelief from this story? What is involved in commitment? Can one be a Christian without committing himself to Jesus?*

In these stories we have illustrated three types of faith: faith in Jesus as one who is able to work miracles for man's benefit; faith in Jesus as one who has a Messianic mission; and faith in Jesus who meets us in our experiences and reveals to us his identity. Faith begins often with an acknowledgment that Jesus is a helper in the time of need, that he brings the power of God to bear on our daily lives. We must see such experiences, however, against the broader background of Jesus' mission in the world as Messiah. Ultimately we must come to see that in the events of our lives God is addressing us in Jesus and summoning us to worship him.

> Strong Son of God, immortal Love,
> Whom we, that have not seen Thy face,
> By faith, and faith alone, embrace,
> Believing where we cannot prove;
>
> Thou seemest human and divine,
> The highest, holiest manhood, Thou.
> Our wills are ours, we know not how;
> Our wills are ours, to make them Thine.
>
> Our little systems have their day;
> They have their day and cease to be;
> They are but broken lights of Thee,
> And Thou, O Lord, art more than they.
>
> Let knowledge grow from more to more,
> But more of reverence in us dwell;
> That mind and soul, according well,
> May make one music as before.
>
> —*The Hymnbook,* 228

"You must be born anew."

5 ✧ ⊃━◻━◻━◻━◻━◻━◻━◻━◻━◻

The Demands of Faith

To be a Christian involves change. You may come to Jesus just as you are, as the old hymn has it, and enter the fellowship, but you cannot remain as you are. You must be changed and be willing to be changed further.

Faith always carries with it some obligations. There are certain requirements for becoming a Christian, certain elements which are involved in believing: there must be an acquaintance with Jesus, a knowledge of his true identity, a willingness for inner change, and a decision to accept Jesus Christ. I have called these the demands of faith. They are also the requirements for becoming a Christian.

In John 3—5 we have a number of stories each of which presents some demand by Jesus.

(1) Nicodemus—a new birth—baptism of water and the Spirit (3:1–21).
(2) The woman of Sychar—a felt need—the gift of God and who gives it (4:1–42).
(3) The nobleman's son—taking Jesus at his word—the life-giving word (4:46–54).
(4) The crippled man—a will to be whole—Jesus the Life-giver (5:1–18).

All these stories in one way or another are related to salvation. To be born anew, to ask Jesus for the gift of life, to take him at his word, to want to be whole, are essential for faith to blossom and bear fruit.

In these narratives Jesus deals with four types of individuals: a Pharisee, a Samaritan, a Roman, and a poor invalid. They repre-

sent opposite extremes religiously and socially. Jesus is concerned
about each, and to each he ministers. Each episode is intended in
some fashion to assure the reader that Jesus is the Christ, so that
he may have life. Some scholars feel that chapters 3 and 4 mani-
sion of the work of Christ in accordance with the
f Acts 1:8—from Jerusalem (3:1–21), Judea (3:
ria (4:1–42), to the ends of the earth (4:46–54).
may have been borrowed from Luke, who uses it in
his Gospel and the Acts, or it may be pure coincidence. In either
case the stories show the concern of Jesus for every man.

The New Birth—Nicodemus, 3:1–21

*As you read the story of Nicodemus, note the pattern which
John uses for many of his stories: a conversation, a word of Jesus
which is misunderstood, and then the discourse of Jesus. What can
you learn from this story about what the Christian faith requires
of us?*

It is possible that the Nicodemus story is John's substitute for
the Sermon on the Mount. This is the only place he mentions the
Kingdom of God and the requirements for entrance, which is a
theme of the Sermon on the Mount. The thrust of the story revolves around the saying: "Truly, truly, I say to you, unless one
is born anew [born of water and the Spirit (3:5)], he cannot see
the kingdom of God" (3:3). The remainder of the story explains
what this statement involves. The phrase "born anew" in Greek
has a double meaning: "to be born again" (a second time) and
"to be born from above." Nicodemus takes it in one sense while
Jesus takes it in the other.

"You must be born anew." This is an arresting statement to
address to one of the most pious religious leaders of the day! It
declares that no one can come to Jesus and partake of the new life
of the Kingdom unless he is radically changed at the very center
of his life. Herein is the offense of the gospel: even the best of
men, the most religious, are not good enough. Each one needs a
new birth of water and the Spirit. Does this suggest baptism? Note
what John says about baptism (1:33).

John describes the new birth much as Paul describes baptism

in Romans 6:1–11. The references to water and the Spirit call to mind baptism—the washing away of sin and the receiving of the gift of the Spirit. Baptism in the early church signified a new beginning, a radical change involving a break with the past and a new start in life. Paul described this change in terms of a participation in Christ's death and resurrection, the dying to sin and the rising to newness of life. John describes it in terms of a new birth from God (cf. 1:13). What elements do these two figures have in common? This change is not simply a change of habits or intentions. It is a complete change and an entirely new orientation of life. The Christian is a new creation, a new man in Christ (2 Cor. 5:17). The Spirit takes up his residence at the very center of one's life and the desires of the flesh must give way. Without this there is no seeing the Kingdom of God.

Herein lies the basic truth of the gospel. The Kingdom does not come by a change of the world round about us or with a change of our views. It comes with the change of heart and life which God brings about when we come to faith in Christ. There must be a death to self and a new birth to life with Christ before there can be any participation in the Kingdom of God. This was marked in the early church by baptism, at which time faith in Christ was confessed.

The new birth from above is not of a believer's own making. It comes from above even as Jesus comes from above. Nicodemus' consternation at this demand of Jesus is expressed in a serious question: How can a man be changed when he is old, when his habits are formed and his character and personality are set? Is it really possible for an adult to be changed? The response of Jesus is a straightforward Yes. A new birth is possible for man by the Spirit.

This change implies at least the following:

(1) Beginning life anew, with the past forgotten and a new future ahead.

(2) Entering the realm of Christ as a child with an adventurous spirit to explore a whole new world: the power of prayer, faith, love; the cultivation of meekness, patience, compassion; the imitation of Christ's life, his character,

his concern; the reception of the promises, power, and inheritance of God; and much more.

(3) Growing in Christian love and conduct, with an ever-deepening understanding of what it means to be a Christian and the steady development of a Christlike character.

(4) Developing and exercising new-found talents for the benefit of man and the glory of God.

(5) Conquering personal sin and bringing every thought into subjection, into obedience to Christ.

At which of these five are you working the hardest?

The new birth is the first requisite of faith. It is fruitless to ask whether faith comes first or the new birth. They go together and both are an act and a process. Here one cries, "I believe; help my unbelief!" (Mark 9:24.)

An Awareness of Need—the Samaritan Woman, 4:1–42

Read the story in 4:1–42. Note how the style is the same as that of the Nicodemus story: a conversation, a misunderstanding, and a discourse. A number of themes are woven together in this story: the living water which Christ gives (4:2–15); Jesus' prophetic insight and the disclosure of his identity (4:16–26); the discussion on worship and the true nature of God (4:20–24); the coming of the disciples and the word about the harvest (4:27, 31–38); the witness of the woman and the faith of the Samaritans (4:28–30, 39–42). Note how one theme leads to another until the whole of the story is told. This may be an illustration of apostolic preaching which often followed the same procedure. It illustrates how Jesus dealt with people according to the needs of the moment. What kind of demand is placed on this woman?

What is significant about the story is that Jesus was concerned about this woman. Her presence at noon at the well may have been due to her conduct; most women came early in the morning to draw water for the day. Her discussion with Jesus was perhaps due to her hunger for conversation. As the Pharisee had represented the best of Palestine, this woman may have represented the worst. About both Jesus was concerned.

Note how Jesus goes straight to the heart of the matter. Having asked for a drink, Jesus utters the all-important word, "If you knew the gift of God, and who it is that is saying to you, 'Give me a drink,' you would have asked him and he would have given you living water" (4:10). Jesus desires to give the woman living water. For her to receive this gift there must be an asking. But to ask she needs to know what the gift of life is—that which she had been seeking to no avail; and who can give it to her—in this instance he who is speaking with her. The conversation with the woman centers on these two needs.

Verses 1–15 have to do with the gift of life which Jesus gives, which satisfies the thirst of all who drink of it. Life, in John, is almost always connected with the idea of a flowing spring. What is the significance of this figure? What is the gift of life which Jesus offers: salvation? the Spirit?

Verses 16–26 deal with the one who can grant this new life— the Messiah. Jesus reveals himself to this woman. While the topic of conversation is the ancient controversy between the Jews and the Samaritans about the true place of worship, Jerusalem versus Gerizim, the real concern of Jesus is to disclose his identity. This he does, and from what follows it appears that the woman obtained what Christ wanted to give her.

As all of Nicodemus' study and meditation on the Scripture could not fill his soul's deep need, so here a life of pleasure, with a variety of men, could not satisfy human need either. Neither the religious nor the secular can satisfy without something more. One needs the gift of God. In John 3:16 the gift of God is Jesus himself. In this story it is something that Jesus gives—either salvation, or the Spirit who brings about the new life and constitutes the new life of the Christian (cf. Luke 11:13). *How are John 3:16 and 4:10 related?*

One of the prime requisites for faith, and for eternal life, is just this awareness of the soul's deep need and who can fill it. Christ can do nothing for the person who has no sense of need (Mark 2:17; 6:1–6). Further, the need Christ has come to fill is not some physical need, some desire or fancy of ours. It is the need of the soul for that which can make life full, meaningful, and joyful. One of the most significant verses of the Bible is Mark

10:45, "For the Son of man also came not to be served but to serve . . ." This is the whole purpose of his life. Thus Jesus asks in Mark the arresting question, "What do you want me to do for you?" (10:51.) This question will not receive the same answer from everyone. But it calls the individual to examine himself for his soul's deep need and then to voice it to Christ so that he may satisfy it. What is your answer to Jesus' question?

Taking Jesus at His Word—the Roman Nobleman, 4:46–54

As you read the story consider: What kind of demand is placed on this Roman? How does he respond to it? How does his response affect his family? What does this say about faith?

This story is different from the others in this section of our study: it contains no discourse of Jesus. As a story it is much like the events with which John begins the story of the ministry of Jesus.

The central figure in this story is a Roman. Note how John has progressed. He has described Jesus' relations with a Jewish teacher, a Samaritan woman, and now a Roman official. Jesus is concerned about all types of people from all walks of life. He is truly the universal Savior. How does this story compare with the similar narrative recorded in Matthew 8:5–13 and Luke 7:1–10? Has John perhaps told the same story in a more personal form by transforming the servant into a son? Often the same word, *pais,* was used in Greek for servant and child (see Acts 3:13, 26, noting R.S.V. margin).

In this instance the emphasis is on the life-giving word which Jesus speaks. He simply says to the desperate man, "Go; your son will live" (4:50). Without question or argument the official accepts the word and leaves for home. *Could you have done this?* As he is approaching Capernaum his servants meet him and inform him that his son lives. Determining the hour of healing, he discovers it to be the same in which Jesus said, ". . . your son will live." This convinces the official of Jesus' identity and he believes, together with all his house.

A new element is introduced in this healing story. Jesus heals at a distance. All the miracles in this Gospel are remarkable ones.

John has selected the most wondrous of Jesus' works around which to weave his story. Here Jesus simply speaks a word at a considerable distance from the sick child, yet healing takes place. Jesus has the words of life. He speaks the word and healing goes forth. How is this related to the prayers for healing today? What Jesus demands, as so many of the stories of healing in the Synoptics manifest, is faith on the part of the petitioner (Matt. 8:10 ff.; cf. Matt. 9:28f.; 15:28; 17:20; 21:21; Mark 2:5; 9:23; 10:52; Luke 7:50; 17:19). *How would you define faith in the light of this episode?* For me, faith means to take Jesus at his word, to recognize that Jesus speaks the word of life and that when he speaks the power of God goes forth. Jesus' word demands not questioning but action, not discussion but acceptance. It is of the nature of faith to believe that with God all things are in the realm of possibility, that the Creator can re-create, that the Giver of life can bring life to the dead (John 5:21, 25–29; cf. Rom. 4:16–25; Heb. 11:11–12). I am not contending here that all that is required for something to happen is a conviction that it will occur. I am only pointing out that Jesus demands to be taken at his word. The word of God is not to be questioned, it is to be believed; it is not to be discussed, it is to be received. Can you imagine what might happen if we took Jesus at his word, if we trusted the promises of God, accepted them, and laid claim to them? No more and no less than this is what Jesus demands.

A Will to Be Whole—the Crippled Man, 5:1–18; 7:14–24

As you read these passages consider: What kind of demand is placed on this man? How does he respond to it? Note how others responded to the miracle. Why do you suppose the man told the Jews that it was Jesus who had healed him? Does this indicate a lack of faith? How did this affect the Jews' attitude toward Jesus?

The last of the stories dealing with the demands of faith is that of the man at the pool of Bethesda (Bethzatha). Here John uses the story of a Sabbath controversy to make his point. A discourse follows the incident, in 5:19 ff., and it is resumed in 7:14–24.

As in the second story above, this passage has a number of themes:

(1) A Sabbath controversy in which Jesus shows that he is Lord of the Sabbath, and that as God's Son he works even as God (5:16–18; cf. Mark 2:23—3:6). John discloses that the two causes of controversy between Jesus and the Jewish leaders were his attitude toward the Sabbath and what they considered to be his blasphemy—he identified himself with God.

(2) Jesus' concern with a cripple who lived off the compassion (or lack of it) of society (5:1–9). He selects the most hopeless case of all the sick lying at the pool, an utterly helpless and neglected piece of humanity as seen in the man's lament, "Sir, I have no man . . ." (5:7).

(3) A discussion on the work of God and Jesus' mission (5:17–30).

(4) A discussion on the witnesses which verify Jesus' claim to be intimately related to God (5:31–47). We shall deal with this section elsewhere in this study.

An important element in faith comes to the forefront with Jesus' soul-searching question, "Do you want to be healed?" (5:6.) This is a startling approach, for the man seemed to be there for that very purpose. His response to Jesus, however, indicated that he had given up hope. He was at the point of blaming others for his condition. He had become a victim of self-pity, feeling nothing but reproach for his fellowman. He says in reality, "Does it do any good to want healing? No one cares about what happens to me" (see 5:7). The whole burden and guilt of his condition is thus laid upon the shoulders of society. How readily people with illnesses or handicaps tend to feel forsaken, blaming others for their condition.

"Do you want to be healed?" is a startling question. It places the onus on the individual. It asks whether he is ready to give up what has become a way of life and, in many respects, a source of comfort. Do you really want to be healed, to put an end to the complacency of misery, to feelings of self-pity, to the longing for sympathy, to living off charity? Are you ready for a life of activity and responsibility, to be a whole person, to work for a living, to become responsible for the weak and infirm, to shoulder the burdens of life of one's own and others' making? Do you want to be healed?

Spiritually this question is all-important. Do you want to be changed, to be good, to live the life of a disciple, to be a witness, to walk the way of the cross? Sometimes we are all too satisfied with being sinners and even place the blame for our condition on society. The hectic days in which we live, the stress of the times, the nature of our environment, the unconcern of society, or the prejudices of others, we say, are responsible for our lethargy and spiritual sloth, our sin and love of sinning. Jesus summons us to an act of will, an exercise of faith. Do you want to be good? Is this what you really want? Well, is it?

If so, the answer is simple. "Rise, . . . and walk." It is as easy as that. Make your decision, heed Christ's command, and do the impossible. Jesus wanted this man to desire something because God desired to do something for him. He asked for faith. Faith is always a venture, a daring step into the unknown, a rising and walking. No situation is ever hopeless, nor is the power for newness of life lacking. It is readily available in Jesus Christ. The real question is, Do you want it? If so, then rise and walk! This is another way of saying, "Come, follow me!"

These four stories illustrate four basic demands of faith: a birth from above (Nicodemus), asking for the gift of God from the right person (the Samaritan woman), taking Christ at his word (the Roman official), and desiring to be changed and transformed (the cripple). Can you think of any others which might be added to these? Note how John weaves into the question of Jesus' identity the nature of the response demanded by him. The author insists that faith be directed to the person of Christ, the One who meets us in the experiences of life, who speaks to the deep needs of the soul, and who seeks to bring us to the possession of life.

"...they ... bear witness to me ..."

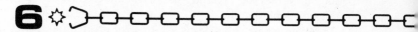

Aids to Faith

Faith is a complex Christian experience. It is not a human accomplishment, even though it is a human activity. John says that no one can come to Christ except the Father draw him (6:44; cf. Eph. 2:8). Insofar as faith is a response to the divine activity in Christ it is a human response: it involves a decision to surrender the self to Christ. But insofar as it is a work of the Spirit, it is the work of God and a gift he makes available to man. Thus there is a divine and a human side to faith.

Faith in the Christian sense is always directed to God or to Christ, the Son of God. When faith is directed to Christ it includes an acknowledgment of his intimate relationship to God (cf. 17:8; 20:31). One is challenged to believe that Jesus is the Son of God who speaks the divine word and does the divine work, and who was sent by the Father into the world for this very purpose. In this lesson we shall study the aids to faith which God has provided to enable us to see God in Christ reconciling the world to himself (2 Cor. 5:19).

For this lesson read John 5:19–47; 7:1–52; and 8:12–59, paying special attention to 5:30–47, in which Jesus gives a list of the things which verify his relation to the Father and lead to faith in him. What answers can you find in these verses to the question: How do you know Jesus is the Son of God?

These chapters center on Jesus' discussions with the Jews and are concerned with their lack of acceptance of him. Some have suggested that, instead of the discussions of Jesus with the Jews, they represent the frequent discussions between the church and the synagogue in the area of Ephesus during the latter part of the first century A.D. They contain, however, six sayings which begin, "Truly,

truly I say to you," which is a style of speaking unique to Jesus. Whether the discussions are from Jesus' life or from the later church period, they may be regarded as an accurate statement of what Jesus said about himself.

In telling others about Jesus, a Christian is often faced with the questions, "How do you know Jesus is the Son of God? What proof do you have?" How would you answer these questions? What evidence could you give for this confession? Perhaps you would list the Bible, the experience of the nearness of Christ in prayer and worship, the presence of Christ in the sacraments, the experience of salvation in our lives, the inner witness of the Holy Spirit, the influence of Jesus upon our world. John enumerates the following: the witness of the Baptizer, the works of Jesus, the witness of the Father, and the witness of the Scriptures. These are the evidences which he believes will lead to faith.

The Witness of the Baptizer

Jesus says to his opponents, "You sent to John, and he has borne witness to the truth. Not that the testimony which I receive is from man; but I say this that you may be saved. He was a burning and shining lamp, and you were willing to rejoice for a while in his light" (5:33–35).

In the Gospel of John it is the Baptizer who gives the first testimony about Jesus. Note the passages which refer to him: 1:6–8, 15, 19–34, 35–36; 3:25–30 (perhaps the passage 3:31–36 is also meant by the author to be the words of the Baptizer). How does John regard himself in these passages? How does he regard Jesus? What does he say about Jesus?

Today the role of the Baptizer is assumed by individuals who have helped us to know Christ. Most of us have been influenced in one way or another to look upon Jesus as divine through the witness of others—religious authors, teachers, ministers, parents—who have interpreted Christ for us and have helped us to see God in him. Among those who have revealed to me the Christ have been Johannes Amos Comenius, Giovanni Papini, G. A. Studdert-Kennedy, Pierre van Paassen, James Muilenburg, and Helmut Thielicke. These have broadened my understanding of the gospel and have helped me to know Christ as the Savior.

Whatever else it may have been, the biblical witness was direct. There were no veiled allusions, no mere suggesting or hinting. There was a simple, direct statement which came from conviction. So often we shy away from direct testimony. We talk about the church, the cause of justice and right, the Golden Rule, the Christian character, but so seldom about what Jesus means to us. In John's Gospel everyone uses the direct approach: the Baptizer, Jesus, the author himself. Witness, to be effective, needs to say plainly what Jesus means for the sinner.

Witness should have the ring of conviction. It is said that the testimony meeting is becoming a thing of the past. In some ways the testimony meeting as it existed in prayer meeting or in revivals was ineffective. Often the same ones participated and the testimonies were formal and stereotyped and not convincing. For the most part they were given before the "saints." The witness in the Gospels came with conviction to those who did not believe. John spoke to two disciples, they to others, and so on. They met people where they were and told them about Jesus. None of the witnessing was in a church building. As was said earlier, it may be that the best evangelism will take place over a cup of coffee, across some back fence, or while relaxing at lunch. But we need to recapture the boldness to speak about Jesus.

The first Christians went on a determined mission. They had good news and they were intent on publishing it to the world. So they went and found others and told them about Jesus. They "gossiped" the gospel. So much casual conversation today is trite and meaningless. It is a way of passing time or of promoting one's ego, but nothing of value is communicated. Not so with these Christians and the gospel. They were eager to speak and there was an urgency about them. They found that people were hungry for the Good News, the word of life.

Many people today are troubled by a deep need and desire to find meaning in life. Much of modern literature and drama evidences this concern. While it may be a difficult time for religion, it is an opportune time to "gossip" the Good News. One wonders how many churches have a planned program of evangelism. *Does your church have such a program? Outside of the every member canvass of your own members for finances, is there a visitation program in*

*which an urgency is felt and a real effort is made to reach men with
the gospel, to bring them face to face with Jesus Christ?* The first
Christians told what Jesus meant to them. They brought strength
to the weak, courage to the cowardly, hope to the despairing, joy to
the sorrowful. It has happened before. It can happen again. It can
happen where you are.

The Witness of the Works of Jesus

A more effective witness than the testimony of others was Jesus'
works. His very works bore witness that the Father had sent him
(5:36). In John, the miracles, signs, or works of Jesus are the ultimate proof of his identity, and they validate his message. Men can
know its truth because they see its power. Though Jesus refused to
give a sign to prove that he was Messiah, John says that his works
can be such a sign for an unbeliever. Do you see here a connection
with what Jesus says in Matthew 11:2–6? Note that the things Jesus
was doing testified that God was at work: evil was being cast out
of the world; men's lives were being changed; and God was establishing his rule. Is not this what John is trying to communicate in
this passage?

In 8:31–59 we have a good example of this. Jesus says there
that one's actions betray one's spiritual parentage. The Jews seek
to kill Jesus; they lie about him and heap abuse on him. This kind
of thing Abraham never did. Neither does God do it. These very
acts prove their spiritual parentage to be demonic. Jesus goes about
doing good and giving life, which proves his spiritual parentage is
from God (cf. Matt. 7:16, 20). What do our actions reveal about
our spiritual parentage?

The Jews charged Jesus with breaking the Sabbath and blasphemy (5:18; 9:16; 10:33; 19:7). These points are throughout
the Gospel the main source of the Jewish opposition to Jesus and
are the reasons for the crucifixion. Jesus responds to these charges
by declaring himself guiltless. On the Sabbath he is doing the work
of God. God is working on the Sabbath (sustaining the world), so
Jesus works (5:17). As for blasphemy, Jesus speaks the truth of
God (8:31–32, 42–47). If you are going to believe, you must
judge Jesus by his words and works, not by traditions, prejudices,
or the walls men have thought to build around themselves and God.

The change wrought by Christ and the good works done in his name verify and validate the truth of the gospel. True, the history of the church has not been without scandal. Nor is any parish perfect; the history of your own parish and its members' lives may have many skeletons and unfavorable items. But that Christ still does the work of God can be affirmed. Some of this work is seen in changed lives, evil habits conquered, an interest in the things of the Spirit, a new attitude toward life, an abundance of good works. Surely every church has evidence of such things among its members. *What evidence can you find in your church that Jesus is the Christ?*

There are also the great social reforms which Christianity has helped to foster. The church encouraged education and established the first universities. The church inspired concern for the poor, the aged, the handicapped, the diseased—a concern which we now take for granted as a part of the American way of life. Begun by the church also was the concern for social justice and for morality, and good government has been sponsored and influenced, directly or indirectly, by Christianity. That society as a whole—in contrast to the institutional church—has now taken over most of these activities may in some way be regretted, but the church can be proud of having so leavened society that these concerns have become a part of our way of life. Now the church can turn her attention to new concerns and new areas of transformation where the structure of life must be brought under the Lordship of Jesus Christ. *What new areas of transformation can you suggest?*

The Witness of the Father

Jesus claims also that God has borne witness to him (5:37). You have never seen God's form or heard his voice, but had you known him you would have recognized him in Jesus (see 5:37–38). John has such a deep understanding of the intimacy that exists between Jesus and God that he is convinced that if you know and see the one you know and see the other (cf. 14:7, 9–11). If men know God, they can recognize him in Jesus, for he speaks the divine word and does the divine work (8:19, 28, 38, 42, 47). Thus the Father witnesses to Jesus.

John seems to say things that are contradictory in this Gospel. "No one has ever seen God; the only Son . . . has made him known"

(1:18). Yet only by knowing the Father can one recognize him in the Son (8:42, 47). Doesn't this place man in an impossible situation? Paul reminds us in Romans 1:19–23 that all men have some knowledge of God. The fact that every people have some form of deity proves this. Men may have little gods fashioned after their own pattern, confined in power and limited in character so that they can use them to further their own ends. But all people have some conception of deity. The Christian also begins with the fact that there is a God, but he allows God to be God. He knows that what God does is good, has purpose, and is for the blessing of mankind. He does not pretend to know all about him, but accepts whatever brings wholeness, healing, order out of chaos, deliverance, forgiveness, newness of life as coming from God.

In the days of Franklin Delano Roosevelt a radio commentator in speaking on the Roosevelt family began with the words, "It makes all the difference in the world who your father is." He stressed that a father's position and prestige carried over to his family and that the family became a very special family because the father was a special person. This holds true spiritually also. It makes a lot of difference who your father is. The spirit that motivates you denotes your parentage. Hatred, meanness, brutality, lying, cheating, selfishness, willful destruction, libel, slander, deceit, fraud, graft, bribery, theft, murder, rapacity do not and cannot stem from God. These actions are not prompted by the Holy Spirit.

I wonder how our lives would stand this test? *What in your life can you point to as the work of God? What indicates that your spiritual parentage is of God? In the passage Jesus calls attention to the making of a man whole, to the saving of life. This is God's work and God thus witnesses to the Son. What other kinds of acts are motivated by God and are his work?*

The Witness of the Scriptures

We have noted three of the witnesses John says help us to know who Jesus is: John the Baptizer, the works of Jesus, and the Father himself. In 5:39, 45–47 it is stated also that the central theme of Scripture (in this case the Old Testament) is Jesus Christ. The Old Testament looks forward to him and finds its meaning in him. The

New Testament flows forth from him and looks back to him. This is why the theme of apostolic preaching was simply Jesus (Acts 8: 35; 2:22–24, 32–36; 4:10; Rom. 1:3–4; 1 Cor. 1:23–24).

The Scriptures do not always say so explicitly that their true meaning is found in Christ. The Jews had the Scriptures but failed to recognize Jesus. The Bible can be read as literature or as history without any awareness that its true meaning is to be discovered only when it is interpreted in terms of Christ. Men need a guide in reading the Bible, someone to open up its meaning. This Jesus did for the disciples (Luke 24:27), Philip did for the Ethiopian eunuch (Acts 8:35), and FROM BONDAGE TO FREEDOM seeks to do for you.

The Old Testament is the story of God and his effort to gather a people to himself. God created a world and put man in it. By the abuse of his freedom man became estranged from God. Sin set in and permeated the world. So God started over again with Noah. But sin was still there. He chose Abraham and his family and sought to establish a people. He brought them to Egypt where they became a great nation, led them forth, bound them to him, and brought them to Canaan so they could bring the world to God. But Israel was rebellious. She wanted to be like the nations. She served other deities besides the Lord. So God brought her into captivity. When she was duly punished he brought her back to her land. Israel was cured of idolatry but evil was not rooted out of the heart. Someone was needed to purify her heart and teach her the way of God so that she could become a servant people. Thus the Old Testament awaits and prepares for the coming of Jesus Christ.

James Sprunt in the first section of this book has shown how the Passover (p. 52), the covenant (p. 75), and redemption in the Old Testament (pp. 111–112) all find their fulfillment in Jesus Christ. It would be well to review what he says. Similarly all the Old Testament institutions and practices find their fulfillment in him. John makes mention of the fact that Abraham (8:56), Moses (5:46), and Isaiah (12:41) all saw from afar Jesus Christ and gave testimony to him.

The key to Scripture is not some theologian, not some system of theology, not some confessional statement; rather, it is Jesus Christ.

Furthermore, all of Scripture points to him, and our knowledge of Christ comes to us from the Scriptures. *Can you think of anything we know about Jesus which doesn't come from the Bible?*

Here then are the witnesses which Jesus felt should verify the truth of his words and provide the key to his identity: men who stood close to God and had received the truth; his own works; the Father; and the Scripture. *What other proofs would you offer today? How would you phrase these in meaningful terms for men today?*

All these proofs ultimately stem from God himself. They do not have their origin in man. They have not come by meditation, reason, or an interchange of ideas. They have come by revelation. They all demand acceptance. The Baptizer (or men) must be believed, the signs accepted, God known, and the Scripture believed. Here, as Paul has so nobly said,

> But as it is written,
> "What no eye has seen, nor ear heard,
> nor the heart of man conceived,
> what God has prepared for those who love him,"

God has revealed to us through the Spirit. For the Spirit searches everything, even the depths of God. For what person knows a man's thoughts except the spirit of the man which is in him? So also no one comprehends the thoughts of God except the Spirit of God. Now we have received not the spirit of the world, but the Spirit which is from God, that we might understand the gifts bestowed on us by God. And we impart this in words not taught by human wisdom but taught by the Spirit, interpreting spiritual truths to those who possess the Spirit.

> The unspiritual man does not receive the gifts of the Spirit of God, for they are folly to him, and he is not able to understand them because they are spiritually discerned. (1 Cor. 2: 9–14)

"I am the bread of life."

7

Claims and Controversies

The central issue of the Gospel and the major question it asks is, Who is Jesus? He claims to be from God, to speak God's word, and to do God's work. These claims Jesus now puts in the form of symbols—bread, light, door, shepherd, resurrection, way, and vine. These symbols say what Jesus means to the Christian. They are given in the form of "I am." All these claims are meant to lead readers to see and confess Jesus' relation to the Father—Jesus is the Son of God. John never says in so many words, "Jesus is God," but he comes closer to this than any other Gospel writer when he says, ". . . the Word was God" (1:1), "I and the Father are one" (10:30; cf. 10:38, 17:11, 21–22), and "He who has seen me has seen the Father . . ." (14:9.)

The essence of these claims is also the subject of controversy. Jesus makes himself equal with God (5:18; 10:33–38; 19:7). This he does by calling God his Father in such an intimate way as to suggest that he is God's physical Son (cf. 19:7).

In order to feel the full weight of the claims of Jesus you should read chapters 6 through 11. Note how in this central section John takes the question at Caesarea Philippi, ". . . who do you say that I am?" (Mark 8:29) and expands it, making it the central question and making its answer the central affirmation.

Jesus often uses the phrase "I am . . ." to describe himself (6: 35, 48; 8:12; 9:5; 10:7, 9, 11, 14; 11:25; 14:6; 15:1, 5). Be sure to read at least these verses. Note how some of the words are uttered twice by Jesus as though for emphasis. Having read these verses try to put in your own words John's answer to this question, Who is Jesus?

281

In one instance (8:58) Jesus uses the statement "I am" by itself. Here there was particular reason for the animosity of the Jews. Jesus was applying to himself the special name for God in the Old Testament (Exod. 3:14), a name so sacred that in Jesus' day the Jews did not even pronounce it for fear of profaning it. They used substitutes for it, the most common of which was "Lord," a title afterwards ascribed by the church to Jesus. In the Exodus passage "I AM" signifies the living God who is known by his activity. In the Exodus event God revealed himself as the Deliverer. Wherever "I AM" appears in the Old Testament it always recalls this activity on the part of God. The cryptic word of Exodus 3:14, "I AM WHO I AM," also indicates that there is a consistency in the nature and activity of Israel's God. What he proved to be in the Exodus event he would always be. This is his very nature. God is the Redeemer. Jesus, the Savior of the world, was totally correct in applying this title to himself. But is it any wonder the Jews were offended by this daring claim of Jesus?

John does not argue the matter as to what Jesus means or can mean to men. He lets Jesus speak for himself. Jesus' words about himself follow as the natural interpretation of his actions. Most of these claims are presented at festival periods. Thus there may be a relation between Jesus' words and certain aspects of the chief festivals of the Jews.

The Bread of Life—Manna, 6:35, 48

Following the feeding of the five thousand, Jesus gave a discourse on the "bread of life" (6:25–59). It was Passover time, the Jewish festival of independence. The people had been fed; they saw in Jesus one who could provide for them and so came to him again, on the other side of the sea, perhaps with the ulterior motive of making him their king (6:26; cf. 6:15). What better leader could men desire? He could feed an entire army with the meagerest of rations. What better man to lead a revolt? Further, there was a tradition that when Messiah appeared he would duplicate the feat of Moses, leading Israel through the wilderness and feeding her upon manna from heaven. This time they asked for manna, not a few loaves multiplied.

Manna was a white substance left by the dew every morning from which the wandering Israelites in Moses' time made bread (Exodus 16:4–36; see p. 62 above). Note what is said about manna in John 6:25–59. How does John describe it? How does Jesus describe himself? What do you suppose Jesus meant by this figure of speech? Does "from heaven" give us a clue (6:31; cf. 32–33)?

Bread for the Hebrew was a gift from God. It was the basic sustainer of life. Crumbs and crusts were never thrown out or allowed to remain on the ground to be trampled under foot, but were placed on a stone where some bird or hungry man could find them. For bread was precious; it was God's gift.

Jesus' use of this figure stresses that he is God's gift of food for the Christian. He is essential to Christian life, as essential as bread, and he must be eaten (6:50–51, 53). Eating Jesus is to receive him into one's life. How often we feed on other things and fill our lives with trivialities. How many such things can you mention? What a judgment this can be on our lives. If there is to be any Christian life then Christ must be our daily diet.

Do you suppose John had the sacrament of the Lord's Supper in mind when he wrote this discourse? Note there is no discussion of the Last Supper in chapter 13. Does John imply that partaking of the Lord's Supper is one way of feeding on Christ?

The Light of the World, 8:12; 9:5

The ceremony of lights at the Feast of Tabernacles may have prompted this word of Jesus spoken at that festival. Each night of the feast huge *menorahs* (lampstands with four golden bowls) fitted with wicks of worn-out priestly garments were filled with oil and lit. Under these the celebrants danced a torch dance to the music of flutes and the singing of the Levites. Note the appropriateness then of the figure, "light of the world."

Light, in the Old Testament, was associated with God (Ps. 27:1), with his word (Ps. 119:105), and with his glory. The faces of those who like Moses had seen the glory of the Lord shone (Exod. 34:29). So, in the Holy of Holies and in the New Jerusalem there is no lamp, for the "glory of God is its light . . ." (Rev. 21:23;

cf. Exod. 40:34; Lev. 16:2; 1 Kings 8:11). What God is and what his word is, that Jesus claims to be. He supplies knowledge, guidance, holiness—whatever a man requires to walk uprightly in obedience to God. *Can you think of other blessings we associate with the light which Jesus supplies to men?*

The Good Shepherd, 10:11, 14

In chapter 10 Jesus applies two symbols to himself, door (10: 7, 9) and shepherd (10:11, 14). Both of these must be understood against the background, given in chapter 9, of the healing of the man born blind. The picture is taken from a Palestinian sheepfold, which was surrounded by a wall with a gate or door for entrance. A gatekeeper guarded the door and let enter only the shepherds whose sheep were within. The door stresses that Jesus is the way of access to God. By this figure he contrasts his mission with that of the would-be messiahs of the times who sought to establish the Kingdom by force and only bathed the country in blood. This is not the way of God or of Jesus. Jesus gave his own life for his sheep. *To what would-be messiahs of our day would Jesus contrast himself? Are there ways in which those in the church may be thieves and robbers, preying upon Christ's sheep?*

The figure of the door also expresses the uniqueness of Jesus. He alone is the way of entrance into the Kingdom (10:7–9; 14: 6). He who enters by Christ is nourished and nurtured. Yet men ever seek to enter the Kingdom by some other way—by influence, good works, violence, stealth—to no avail. You cannot buy, beg or steal your way into the Kingdom. As the Negro spiritual has it,

> My Lord, it's so high, can't get over it;
> So wide, can't get around it,
> So low, can't get under it;
> You must come in at de door.[1]

By the Good Shepherd image Jesus contrasts his work with that of the Pharisees, especially in their dealings with the man born blind. The Pharisees were more concerned that the Sabbath had been broken than that a work of God had taken place (9:16). Persisting in their opinions they sought to discredit Jesus. When this failed, they excommunicated the one who had been healed. In all this they manifested that they were not interested in God's sheep. They were interested in exercising authority and safeguarding status.

For this attitude Klara Svensson castigated her husband Albert, associate pastor of the Sjöbo parish, because he spent his time with statistical reports when he should have been visiting his parish and giving comfort to a dying woman filled with anxiety over her destiny. She says:

> I asked if he really meant that Christ had had any help from his office work that week. Did he really mean that he would have hindered Jesus from visiting his parish if he had postponed his statistics for a day? . . . "It was the 7th," said Albert, "and the report was due on the 8th. You know how hurried I was." . . . He defended himself against an implied accusation. But it did not remain implicit long. I stopped and looked him straight in the eye. "Albert," I said, "you don't believe in the Last Judgment. You believe only in the provincial office and the Central Statistical Bureau. If you neglect your statistics, you may get a rebuke from some bureaucrat in Stockholm. If the negligence is repeated, it may even go so far that the rebuke is repeated by the diocesan chapter, and that shame you cannot bear. But if you do not prepare those people for death who later appear in your obituary statistics, you will not be criticized, for this does not appear in any columns and is not noticeable in any statistic. Such matters are only recorded in heaven and will be known only on the Day of Judgment. And for that you don't give a farthing, Albert. It doesn't concern you. Hence, the only sensible conclusion is that you believe in the Central Statistical Bureau, but you do not believe in the Last Judgment. But if there is a Last Judgment, you will be accused for the murder of Kristin's soul and you cannot clear yourself, for there are witnesses to your conduct." [2]

What marks Jesus as the Good Shepherd is that he lays down his life for the sheep (10:11, 15, 17). These words were spoken at the Feast of Dedication, celebrating the cleansing of the Temple and the restoration of worship under Judas Maccabaeus. It hailed God as Israel's true Shepherd and looked forward to a reunited Israel under a new David. Here Jesus claims to be that Shepherd.

The shepherd image emphasizes the divine call (10:3–4, 16, 27), the divine guidance and protection (10:10, 14, 28), and the nourishment unto life (10:9–10, 28). The characteristic of sheep is that they follow the voice of the shepherd and no other (10:3, 5, 8, 16, 27). A rather searching question is, Admitting Jesus is the Good Shepherd, are we his sheep or only a pack of wolves? Do we follow his voice or a thousand and one other voices beguiling us? *How does the shepherd image here compare with that in Psalm 23 and Ezekiel 34:11–16?*

Jesus also says that there are other sheep—helpless, a prey to wild beasts—who need to hear a voice, who need to be sought and brought that there may be one fold, even as there is one Shepherd (10:16). Here the mission of the church is expounded. *What are the implications of this for today? Are denominational and national churches consistent with this goal? How can we manifest the oneness of Christ's fold in our own church?*

The Resurrection, 11:25

The Lazarus incident is the climactic sign in this book. Not only is it the ultimate proof that Jesus is the life-giver, but it is also the incident, more than any other single one, responsible for Jesus' death (11:45–53). It also looks forward to the resurrection of Jesus and becomes a veiled prophecy of that event.

Probably the most enigmatic words Jesus ever spoke are contained in this account, ". . . he who believes in me, though he die, yet shall he live, and whoever lives and believes in me shall never die" (11:25–26). Was there ever a bolder or more sweeping assertion? Yet the incident vindicates this claim of Jesus to be the giver of life. A man dead four days was brought back to life at the call of Jesus. The Jews believed the spirit of a person would hover near the body of the dead for three days hoping to gain reentrance, but after that it would depart forever. Hence the significance of the fourth day. The man was really dead, without hope, already decomposing. Yet at the call of Jesus he came forth (11:43–44). Such is the power of the person and word of Jesus.

Jesus' bold claim was made in response to a statement about the final resurrection (11:24). What does this tell us about the life Jesus gives?

For the Jew, to be cut off from family fellowship is to be dead. This happens when a Jew marries outside his faith or in some way disgraces his faith. He is cast out and then treated as dead—in some cases a symbolic funeral is even held for him. He no longer exists as far as the family is concerned. So also here. He who is separated from fellowship is, as it were, dead (cf. Luke 15:24, 32), but in Christ he is made alive again, restored to fellowship. Consequently, to be saved is to pass from death to life (5:24). To be alive is to be alive to God, to have the breath (Spirit) of God in one, to have Jesus as the source of one's life, to be a member of God's family and to be in communion with him. Such a person is sensitive to human need, goodness, the cause of God, spiritual devotion, mission.

The final mystery is that life comes through the portal of death. Here is a preview of the resurrection, the ultimate and final vindication of Christ's identity and his oneness with God. Jesus has power not only over nature (as in the first sign), or disease (as in the second sign), or over men, but also over death itself. Now there will be no stopping him (11:48). No one of Jesus' day had displayed such power and authority. The Jews, instead of accepting this miracle as the work of God, found it expedient that Jesus should die (11:50). But even though he died, he became alive again. Jesus thus is a force to contend with in the world, a force which the world cannot be rid of.

The Way, 14:6

The last two "I am's" Jesus spoke privately to his disciples. The first one sums up what he said to the Jews: "I am the way, and the truth, and the life; no one comes to the Father, but by me" (14:6). Jesus is the way even as he is the door. He is the truth even as he is the light. He is the life even as he is the resurrection.

As he described himself to his disciples by the figure of the way, Jesus no doubt looked back to the prophetic emphasis on the way (Isa. 35:8; 40:3; Mal. 3:1) and claimed to be the fulfillment of it. He also knew himself to be the way of access to God, opening the heavens to the worshiper (1:51). Further he was an illustration of the way of conduct that is becoming to a child of God. The Christians early became known as "those of the Way" (Acts 9:2; 19:9, 23; 22:4).

Jesus was the truth, the true representative of man and the true revealer of God. He was the life. As the Eternal One he came to share that life with men (10:10, 28). What is said here is that if one desires entrance into the Kingdom, to know God and to live with him, he must come through Jesus Christ.

The Vine, 15:1, 5

The prophets often referred to Israel as a vine (Ps. 80:8; Isa. 5:1–7; Jer. 2:21; Hos. 10:1). It is probable that Jesus is here contrasting himself with the vine of the Jews which had become degenerate (Jer. 2:21). He was the true vine—the true Israel, representative of the true people of God. What is significant in Jesus' use of this image is that he emphasizes the necessity of abiding in him. The disciples draw their life from him. Those who do not are cut off. As in the figure of the church, the body of Christ, where Christ and his people make a unit, so here Christ as the vine and his disciples as the branches make a unit. *What are the implications of this figure of the vine and branches for today? What does it mean to abide in Christ? In what way do we draw our life from him?*

The real concern of Christ is that he and his disciples may become one, even as he and God are one (17:11, 23). This demands that Christ's people be one (17:11, 21, 22, 23). We are all branches of the same vine. So often we act as though we belonged to different vines. *In what ways can we express our kinship with one another and our relatedness to Christ?*

In these symbols Jesus interprets what he means to believers. He is bread, light, door, shepherd, resurrection, way, vine. He is necessary and vital: he is nourishment; he is protector, provider, and guide; he is the source of life. The Christian's entire life is bound up with and flows forth from him.

All these claims are meant to lead to the conviction that Jesus is the Son of God. Back of the words is the bold claim that Jesus is for men what God is. On this the whole Gospel stands or falls. The Jews understood these claims but charged Jesus with blasphemy (5:18; 10:33; 19:7). They never received him. Can you really tell whether or not Jesus is speaking the truth in all these claims unless you put them to the test? Can you tell whether Christ is bread unless you feed on him? Can you tell whether he is the Good Shepherd unless you follow him? Is not this what it means to believe in him?

"... why do you not believe me?"

8

Barriers to Faith

Over against Jesus' question in the Gospel, "Who am I?" and the answers of the people and of Jesus himself, comes another, equally important, "... why do you not believe me?" (8:46.) Here John seems to have in mind not only the people to whom Jesus spoke but the people of his own day. His Gospel comes out of his experience in proclaiming through the church the good news of Jesus.

Why do not men accept Jesus' words? Why do they not believe him? And why do they not believe us when we speak about him? John presents a number of answers which we shall now study together. Such a study will be valuable in analyzing some of our unbelief and also the reaction to our mission efforts.

In preparing the lesson scan the section, chapters 3 through 12, and note the various reasons given in the discourses of Jesus as to why men do not believe. Look especially at John 3:19; 5:44–47; 6:60; 8:19; 8:43; 10:26. Now make a list of reasons that come out of your own experience. This should give you an insight into the obstacles you have to face in presenting the gospel to others.

While some may take comfort in the fact that if men do not believe us neither did they believe Jesus when he was alive, it remains that Jesus said, "... I, when I am lifted up from the earth, will draw all men to myself" (12:32). This is a promise which puts responsibility on us.

Barriers the Bible Mentions

Among the reasons for lack of faith mentioned throughout the Bible, the following stand out.

(1) Men love "darkness rather than light," 3:19. Any daily newspaper will verify that men are evil. They do not casually come to Christ. Rather, they avoid him because he reveals what they are. Tillich has said somewhere that evil cannot stand sheer goodness; it always seeks to be rid of it. This is undoubtedly one of the reasons why Jesus was crucified. Have you also noticed how difficult some people make it for others to be good? Goodness always places a judgment on evil.

Also, they cannot stand reproof. They take offense at Jesus because he points out their sin. So many of us really do not know ourselves as we are. It is more comfortable to live an illusion. So we wear masks, pretend, put on an act, seek approval and applause, to cover up what we are like inside. Those whose deeds are evil will ever find difficulty in the presence of Jesus. They have nothing in common with him. Something has to give. Either they will have to change or Christ will have to go. They cannot exist together.

(2) Men seek glory and praise from one another, 5:44; 12:42–43. Not all are really Christian who show some goodness of heart. They may do good deeds for praise, their whole purpose being to promote themselves. This is why they do not recognize Jesus. They don't want to be like him; that demands humility and self-denial. (Note how Jesus described some of the Pharisees in Matt. 6:2–18 and in 23:2–7.) Such people could not believe. They were vying with Christ.

The glory motive is strong indeed, and we are all more or less affected by it. It is enhanced by the lure of prizes and of special privilege, the glamour of having one's name in print, the excitement of publicity and popularity, and the gathering of "fans" to bask in our light. All this Jesus disavowed.

In the Christian faith Christ is to be all in all. No one can say Christ is wonderful and promote himself at the same time. As Browning said, "How very hard it is to be a Christian!"

(3) Men do not believe Moses (the Bible), 5:45–47. That this word is spoken to religious people, people who have been faith-

ful in their religious devotions, makes it all the more significant. For Jesus charges them with a lack of understanding and acceptance of that in which they claimed to be expert. They do not take the Bible seriously, accepting it for what it says. Thus they do not know the God of the Bible, nor yet the work of God as revealed in the Bible, and so they do not recognize the Messiah. Had they believed Moses they would not have found Jesus himself, and his words and deeds, so strange.

The Bible for all its popularity is to many an unknown book. It may appear to be simple and its message uncomplicated, but men do not often understand its meaning without someone like Philip to guide them (Acts 8:30–31). One wonders, why this element of mystery? Why this difficulty? Is it that we have lost the fine art of reading? Or do we come to the Bible with preconceived notions as to what it says? Or do we dislike what it says and hence find fault with it? Or do we read it like a novel and consequently not take seriously what it says?

I suspect that today much of the problem lies with us. Many homes have forsaken the custom of reading the Bible as a family. Consequently the Bible is no longer a part of our life. It has become foreign to us and we no longer recognize its language.

To meet God and Christ in the Bible requires more than a casual or an occasional reading. It requires study and searching. One of the purposes of these Bible studies is to give you some exercise in studying the Bible. They seek to help you see the Bible as a living Word applicable to your life today. They also attempt to show you how Bible study is done so that you can study other books of the Bible on your own. But if you are to benefit from them you will need to be diligent and spend time with the Bible. A quick look at the lesson will not be of much help. The only way to know the Bible and to receive benefit from it is to read it and study it. Otherwise it will be a forgotten book, and when the Bible is forgotten God and Christ become less familiar, faith grows dim, and Christianity becomes a formality.

Behind the Bible there is an element of mystery, for God's ways are not man's ways nor his thoughts man's thoughts (Isa. 55:8–9). Its basic message is not a demand that men do great things, win great honors, overcome great handicaps. Rather in it we learn that God has done what is needful for man, what man could not do for himself. This is one thing that makes it so difficult for men to accept it. Men do not like to be beholden to one another; much less do they like to be beholden to God.

(4) Men are prejudiced, 7:41. There was a fervent and deep-seated prejudice among the Jewish leaders against the peasantry, especially against those who lived on the fringe of Palestine. Here one meets the snobbery of the "spiritually elite," of the privileged, of those who took pride in their religious devotions. There is also here the common prejudice of the city dweller against the villager, the rich against the poor, the educated against the peasant, the official against the ruled. How hard it is to get ahead, to gain recognition, when one is born on the wrong side of the tracks! How easily one "from the right side" assumes a superior air. A peasant, untrained, from a despised district—how could he be the Messiah? So professors have looked down on their students, city dwellers on their country cousins, white on black, master on slave, rich on poor, denominations upon sects, churches upon mission stations, etc. How can we recognize the Lord unless we have an open mind? There are so many reasons, which sound sensible, why we don't like a person, a group, a color, or a class that it is difficult to see that we have a built-in prejudice which has colored our view. So it was with the Jews. *How strong a hindrance to faith do you think prejudice is today?*

(5) Men do not know God, 8:19; cf. 8:33–59. There are two elements to this reason for the unbelief of men: they have not maintained a close fellowship with God, so that he has become a stranger; and they have not allowed God to motivate their lives. Their motivations come from elsewhere. These two elements go together, for an estrangement from God means an attachment to someone else. The Bible understands man as an incurably social creature. There are no solitary men in the Bible. Neither are there spiritually neutral men in the Bible.

Paul, in Romans, makes plain that men are in bondage either

to the Devil or to Christ (Rom. 6:15–23). There is no one who is not in bondage to one or the other. As all good Jews of his day, he believed that spiritual forces were in control of each man and were responsible for his actions. It was either Christ, who through Paul performed the good (Rom. 7:4; Gal. 2:20), or the Devil, who through him worked the evil (Rom. 7:8, 13, 17). There were no other alternatives.

Biblically, to know is to be intimate with. Thus to know God is to obey him, to do his will, to keep his commandments. What actions on the part of the Jews showed they did not know God? What knowledge of God is necessary to see Jesus as God?

The actions of many men betray a parentage different from God. Men bent on evil, inhuman, bestial, brutal; men doing harm for kicks or out of hatred; men making a living by using other people, dragging them down to debauchery—how can such recognize Christ? They don't even know God. If, as many have contended, we are living in the time of the death or absence of God, how much more difficult will it be for men to believe in Jesus!

(6) They cannot hear Christ's word, 6:60; 8:43. The problem here is not a malfunction of the organ of hearing. The Jews cannot bear to listen to Christ's word (6:60); he irritates them and disturbs them, and they do not want to be disturbed. They do not like what they hear, so they do not respond.

Why do you suppose the Jews could not stand to listen to Jesus? Did he say things which did not agree with their theology? Was it because he, a peasant, claimed to stand closer to God than they? Was it the nature of the response demanded of them? Why do Jesus' words offend people today? Is it the absoluteness of their demands, the magnitude of them, the urgency of them? Is it the insistence on self-denial, or cross-bearing? Or is it that men do not trust Jesus and therefore do not believe his words? What do you think?

(7) They are not of Christ's sheep, 10:26; cf. 6:44. This reason for the lack of faith is rather disturbing. Jesus seems to imply that these Jews were not among the called, that God had destined

them for destruction; consequently they do not believe in him. Something similar seems to be implied in John 12:37–40, where the disbelief of the Jews is said to be in fulfillment of Scripture. *If a person is not a Christian is it God's fault? What does it mean to be a Christian, one of Christ's sheep?*

It may be that what Jesus is saying is not so much that they are not *his* sheep, but that they are not *sheep*. Pierre van Paassen tells the story of a hunchback named Ugolin who from youth had been an outcast. He had a sister three years his elder who was falsely accused by a farmer for whom she worked of stealing some money and was sent to prison for three years. When she returned she could find no work and paid for the medical and living expenses of her brother by working in a house of ill fame. One night the hunchback, returning to his home, was set upon by a crowd of persons who made sport of him, beat him, tore his clothes from him; after this humiliation the hunchback went to the river and drowned himself. Following the report of his death his sister shot herself. The pastor of the parish church, Monsieur de la Roudaire, assured the author that they would have a Mass of requiem and be buried from the church. The day of the funeral the church was crowded; shops were closed, and most of the villagers were there. Then Van Paassen continues:

> After the absolution the Abbé mounted the pulpit and stood there for a moment in his lace chasuble with its black stole, looking intently at the congregation and slowly turning his head from left to right as if he wanted to recognize every man and woman present.
>
> Then he said: "Christians!" and the word had the effect of a whiplash. And again: "Christians! When the Lord of life and death shall ask me on the Day of Judgment, 'Pasteur de la Roudaire, where are thy sheep?' I will not answer Him. And when the Lord shall ask me for the second time: 'Pasteur de la Roudaire, where are thy sheep?' I will yet not answer Him. But when the Lord shall ask me the third time: 'Pasteur . . . de . . . la . . . Rou . . . daire, where . . . are thy . . . sheep?' I shall hang my head in shame and I will

answer: They were not sheep, Lord—they were a pack of wolves!" [1]

As long as men are worldly and love to be so, are evil and relish it, are proud and arrogant and not desirous of change, are satisfied without Christ, they will not believe in him. To come to faith, one must have a need he wishes Christ to fill.

This is John's explanation of why men did not believe in Jesus (cf. 12:37–41). Those the Father gave him he kept (17:12); others were not of his sheep. John does not say that they cannot be, but that they are not. This means that at present they are not concerned about God. Paul also writes that carnal (or unspiritual) men cannot understand the things of the Spirit and are not concerned about them (1 Cor. 2:14).

Twentieth-Century Barriers

These are the chief reasons given by Jesus as to why men did not believe on him. *What others could you add today?* I have asked myself that question and have come up with the following. Perhaps your list will be different.

(1) The Christian faith is irrational. To believe is to trust God to be and do what seems impossible. The Christian replies: to try to approach Christianity strictly by reason, to try to avoid all mystery, does not lead to faith. There is ever an element of mystery, of awe and wonder, of beyondness, of astonishment, of miracle, of the unexpected, of the manifestation of divine glory. So Jacob came upon God at Bethel, and so we come upon God in Jesus. Without an openness to such phenomena there can be no faith.

(2) Christians are not attractive. Church people are not perfect, and there is a mixture of God and the world in their lives. Going to church doesn't seem to have made them any better. There are too many hypocrites to be found in church. The Christian replies: they are there, to be sure, but redemption takes place within the church, not outside of it, and they at least are where redemption may take place.

(3) Christians do not seem happy. There are so many "Thou shalt not's" that Christians do not appear to have any zest for living or to get any joy out of life. The Christian replies: the concern of Jesus is that men's joy may be full. It may well be we have been too repressive, unwilling to allow within the church the natural outlets for exuberance, so that Christians do not know how to express joy. Christians ought to be the happiest people in the world. Read 2 Corinthians 6:3–10 and Philippians 3:1—4:7 and see what Paul says about rejoicing.

(4) People are too busy with other things. People are busy. There are clubs and civic programs that demand and deserve attention. Television, golf, sports, all kinds of entertaining, friends, an automobile, a boat, the home, and the garden all demand and deserve attention. There is little time left for the church and God.

(5) Men look to science to bring in the new day. Descartes, a sixteenth century French philosopher, long ago predicted this. Many feel that science will bring the good and government will restrain the evil. What more is there to expect from the Kingdom of God?

(6) The church and Christ have become irrelevant. Other agencies have now taken over the work by which the church benefited society in former days. Charity drives, care for the aged, medical research, the Red Cross, the government, and others have taken over so much that there is no longer any real need for the church. How would you answer this?

(7) The language of faith is outmoded. Words such as king, priest, lord, servant, and bondage are out-of-date in our world, for men want freedom and individual expression. Again, such words as heaven, hell, justification, and grace need interpretation in order to be understood by modern man. Moreover, concepts such as Messiah, Son of God, and Son of Man have no place in the vocabulary of the average person. How can the church with

its outmoded language communicate with the world of the twentieth century?

Perhaps John never intended to list all the reasons for unbelief but only enough to let the hearer know that it was his own fault. Nowhere is the blame placed upon anyone else.

"If I do not wash you . . ."

9

A Royal Servant

This section, chapters 13—17, constitutes the most intimate and personal discourse of the Gospel. Here Jesus bares his heart to his disciples in private. He communicates to them what it means to be a disciple and prepares them for events to come. This is his farewell, his last will and testament. After this he will speak to them no more until after his resurrection.

The farewells of the Bible are significant. We have recorded the last words of Jacob (Gen. 49), of Moses (Deut. 33), and of David (2 Sam. 23; 1 Kings 2). For the most part they constitute a blessing and a charge. So also with Jesus, who is the true Israel, the true Moses, and the true David. He speaks to his own, blesses and commissions them, and prepares them for the future, pointing them to the way of life.

Read carefully chapters 13—17. Try to put down the main themes of these chapters. Note what is upon Jesus' heart and what he commands his disciples. Keep in mind the gospel story as we know it from the other Gospels and note how, while aware of the main course of events, John places a different emphasis upon them and uses them as a background for Jesus' final teaching of his disciples.

Much of what John relates here has parallels with other events in the Gospels. The chart on the following page points out many of these between the Synoptics and John's Gospel.

While not all parallels are exact, John manifests sufficiently a dependence on apostolic tradition as recorded by the Synoptists. Note here that the sayings parallel what is spoken primarily to the disciples in the other Gospels.

JOHN	THE SYNOPTICS
Washing of disciples' feet 13:1–20	The Last Supper—lesson on humility Luke 22:24–27
Revelation of betrayer 13:21–30	Revelation of betrayer Luke 22:21–23
The new commandment 13:31–35	Sermon on the Mount Matt. 5:21–26, 43–48
Revelation of denier 13:36–38	Revelation of denier Luke 22:31–34
Announcement of departure; disclosure of Self; coming of Comforter 14:1–31	Passion announcements Mark 8:31; 9:31; 10:33–34
Vine and branches—choosing and appointing 15:1-17	Mission of the twelve Matt. 10; cf. Luke 22:28–36
Coming of persecution 15:18—16:4	Discourse on the end Matt. 24:9–14; Mark 13:9–13
Coming of Counselor and judgment 16:5-15	Discourse on the end Matt. 24:36–44; Mark 13:24–27
Weeping and rejoicing 16:16–33	Passion announcements Lament over Jerusalem Luke 13:34–35; 19:41–44 Parable of fig tree Mark 13:28–31
High-priestly prayer 17:1–26	Supper discourse Luke 22:28–30 Garden prayer Luke 22:39–46

In this section Jesus is preparing his disciples for his departure and for the work that lies ahead. Undoubtedly a number of themes of his ministry will reappear. One notes that the discourse is a composite of his teaching. It may have been given at one time, or, in keeping with the nature of John's Gospel, it may be that John summarizes here what Jesus said to his disciples in private throughout his ministry. For this is the first and last time Jesus addresses his disciples at length in John.

The Footwashing, 13:1–20

John does not repeat events he has given before. While the scene is the Upper Room and the meal the Last Supper, John does not mention anything about the meal. Two reasons may account for this:

(1) The meal, for John, was not the Passover. It did not represent Jesus as the Lamb of God. Jesus' death on the cross portrayed this role of Jesus in John's Gospel.

(2) He has explained the significance of the Lord's Supper in chapter 6.

The footwashing is the focal point of attention for John. It is a lesson in humility for those who, according to Luke, were disputing which of them was the greatest (Luke 22:24–27). Perhaps they were vying for chief seats around the table or discussing the relative merits of their respective positions. No one undertook to perform the servile task of footwashing. Perhaps like children they were arguing as to who should do it. Thus Jesus' act becomes a call to servitude, a dramatic portrayal of the whole spirit of Jesus' ministry, climaxed in the cross.

Further, it is a cleansing. At Qumran (where the Dead Sea Scrolls were produced) the members of the community had to bathe before partaking of the sacred meal. This practice may have prevailed among the early Christians. According to the Didache, an early Jewish-Christian document, only those baptized were allowed to partake of the Supper. A remnant of this may be found here: "If I do not wash you, you have no part in me" (13:8). Whether or not this has reference to baptism, it is a needful cleansing, apart from which one has no part in Christ or the fellowship founded by him. Here then is the secret of the cross and the meaning of Jesus' ministry. It also attests that the servant's role is the mark of the disciple.

Jesus' Concern for His Disciples

In this passage Jesus ministers to his disciples' needs.

(1) He cleanses them (13:5–10).

(2) He gives the disciples a new commandment (13:34; 15:12–17).

(3) He reveals the source of strength—abiding in Christ (15:4–7).

(4) He commissions them to carry on his work (13:20; 14:12–14).

(5) He prepares them for persecution (15:18–27).

(6) He promises them his presence by the Spirit (14:18–19, 26; 16:13).

(7) He prays for them (chapter 17).

This ministry to his disciples is preparatory to Jesus' departure. When it is accomplished, Jesus goes as it is planned.

The Mark of a Disciple

Jesus' concern for his disciples, in view of their tendency toward jealousy, is that they be motivated by love (13:34–35). This is to mark off his disciples from all others. The members of the embryonic church were to be known by their love for one another.

It is significant that this follows the lesson on humility. The question, Who is the greatest? bothered the disciples. In this they were human. They vied for position and status. Jesus had to instruct them constantly about the way of humility. Note the request of James and John and the jealousy of the Twelve (Mark 10:35–45; cf. 9:33–37); the emphasis on cross-bearing (Mark 8:34–35); the argument about greatness and the jealousy expressed toward a man not a member of their own band (Mark 9:33–41); and the lessons on entering the Kingdom as a child and being concerned about God's little ones (Mark 9:33–37). Thus, much of Jesus' effort was spent in trying to mold the disciples into a fellowship where love abounded.

If love is the test of discipleship, how does our church stand the test? How do you? How many are willing to do menial tasks without praise, to be servants for all because of love for them? Here Jesus' own example becomes the pattern (15:13).

This is what it means to be Christlike, and it is so difficult because so often love is unrequited, unreturned. So many are unlovable. To love the unlovable—how difficult!

First there is a cleansing, then the commandment to love, and finally the concern that the disciples would remain true in the face of persecution. They were not to expect life to be easy, but to anticipate the same treatment Jesus received. The world acts thus because it does not know God or that God sent Jesus (15:21). Those who hate Christ will hate his disciples. But the Spirit will bear witness with them so that they are not left alone (15:26). Thus they are nerved for this hour.

The Counselor

While John presupposes the presence of the Spirit in a number of his sayings (3:8; 4:14; 7:37–39), this is the first occasion in which he speaks directly about his coming. Note what light Jesus sheds on the Holy Spirit here.

(1) Jesus speaks of the Holy Spirit in terms of a Counselor. (In Greek the word is *paraklētos*. A paraclete was a lawyer who would assist a defendant by his wisdom and counsel in presenting his case before the courts.)

(2) The Spirit takes the place of the physical presence of Jesus (14:16), and he will be with the disciples forever.

(3) The Spirit will teach the disciples all things and help them to recall the words of Jesus (14:26).

(4) The Spirit will bear witness to Christ (15:26).

(5) The Spirit will convince the world of sin and of righteousness and of judgment (16:8–11).

(6) The Spirit will guide the disciples into all truth, declaring what he has heard and especially the things that are to come (16:13–15).

Note that the Spirit is termed the Spirit of truth (14:17; 15:26; 16:13). What does John say about truth in 14:6 and 18:37? Does John's title for the Spirit indicate that God and Jesus and the Spirit are all related?

The Spirit, who is the Spirit of Christ, is the eternal, abiding Presence who takes the place of the historical Jesus of Nazareth. He interprets the events and words of Jesus and foretells the future. He assists the disciples in their work and confronts the world with the judgment of Christ. In other words, the Spirit carries the redemptive work of Christ to its completion. He takes up where Christ left off. While Christ was only on earth for a few years, the Spirit is ever present. Thus the power and help of God are always available to those who are committed to Christ and engaged in carrying on his work.

The Legacy of Prayer

Along with the Spirit the church is given the legacy of prayer.

There runs through the discourse like a thread the promise, "Whatever you ask in my name, I will do it . . ." (14:13–14; 15:7, 16; 16:23–24, 26–27). As Jesus commissions his disciples he equips them with what will be necessary for carrying out his work. He gives them the Spirit and prayer. *Can you think of anything else that might be required?*

A tremendous promise is made in 14:13–14. It seems to give the disciples a carte blanche for the future. It further ties the future work of the church to Jesus, as he has promised to grant the disciples their requests. The condition is simply that prayer be in his name. In his name means in the spirit of Christ, as if Christ himself were praying. How many of our prayers meet this qualification?

Note how in this entire section the style of John 3, 4, and 6 is reproduced, as Jesus sets forth his teaching to correct the misconceptions of his hearers.

The Commission

This passage is not simply a farewell; it equips the disciples for the future. It concerns the life of the disciples without Jesus' physical presence, but it also concerns their future task of carrying on his work. The disciples know the Father (14:7) and they know the way (14:4, 6). Therefore they are assigned a part of Christ's work. They are to do greater works than Jesus (14:12). They are to bear fruit for God (15:5, 8), to reap the harvest which Christ's death brings (12:24). Christ has chosen and appointed them for this very purpose (15:16). To help them in this work he gives them the Spirit and the promise of answered prayer.

Witness and prayer go together. I wonder how much of our testimony is undergirded with a prayer in Christ's name on behalf of the work to be done or of the persons to be confronted with Christ? This is a cooperative venture. It is not accomplished by witness alone, nor by prayer alone, but by both together. Thus Christ through his Spirit completes his redemptive work. This way of life brings joy to the believer (15:11; 16:24).

The secret of fruitbearing is to abide in Christ and to have Christ's word abide in you (15:7, 10, 14; cf. 14:21). What is the word to which Christ refers? (Cf. 13:34; 15:12–17.) Does this guard against divisive elements among the disciples? What are some other results of abiding in Christ which are valuable for mission?

Jesus' Prayer for His Own, John 17

The prayer of chapter 17, often called the High-priestly Prayer, takes the place in this Gospel of the prayer in the Garden. Note that here there is no wavering or desire to be spared from the cross. The only request that Jesus makes for himself is that God will restore to him the glory he laid aside when he became man (17:1, 5). He makes this request because his work on earth is finished (17:4). This verse seems to imply that the work God gave Christ to do was not merely to die on the cross. Jesus appears to say that his work is finished before that event. Here his work is interpreted as manifesting God's name to men (17:6), giving the disciples God's words (17:8), helping them to realize that God sent Jesus (17:8). Eternal life thus is spoken of as "knowing the only true God and Jesus Christ whom he has sent" (17:3). Do you suppose these words were spoken with the cross in mind? Is there a relation between this passage and John 1:18 which states that Jesus has made God known? Does Jesus express his work here in terms of making God known, speaking his words, performing his works, and convincing men that what he has done is the work of God? In what way is the cross the seal to all. this? How does the cross make God known? Is it possible that our view of the atonement will have to be broadened so as to include both his life and his death?

Jesus' prayer is for his disciples. He asks that they be kept in God's name (17:11) and kept from the evil one (17:15). Jesus asks that God should do for them in the future what he did for them while he was on earth. He kept them in God's name, guarded them so that none was lost ". . . but the son of perdition . . ." (17:12). For the disciples there is no escape from hardship, difficulty, persecution; only deliverance from the evil one. So many try to escape the former when the important thing is not to fall in with evil.

Jesus' further concern is that the disciples may be one even as God and Jesus are one (17:11). This word, along with the lesson on humility and the new commandment, implies that there must be no divisions among Jesus' disciples, no jealousy, hatred, antagonism, or any other divisive spirit. There is rather to be a common spirit of humility, service, and obedience to Jesus Christ. The relation of Jesus and God, the nature of their life together, is to be the pattern for the relation of the disciples to each other, and for this Jesus has given the church his Spirit. *In what ways are Jesus and God one? How does this apply to the disciples?* Note Jesus also asks this for all who should believe through the efforts of the disciples (17:20–21). Note what Jesus gives as the reason for his concern for the oneness of Christians (17:23). What are the implications of this for our church? For the churches in our community? For worldwide Christendom? Have you noticed that practically the whole of Jesus' prayer is concerned with the future of the work he has laid upon his disciples?

> Strong Son of God, whose work was His that sent Thee,
> One with the Father, thought and deed and word,
> One make us all, true comrades in Thy service,
> And make us one in Thee with God the Lord.
> —*The Hymnbook,* 288.

Jesus' final request in this prayer is that the disciples may be with Christ to behold his glory (17:24). Here is a parallel to sharing in Christ's resurrection. Those who share his work on earth, his suffering and cross, shall also share in his resurrection and behold the fullness of his glory. From this point on John proceeds to tell the story of the cross.

This discourse presents the sum and substance of Jesus' words to his disciples, for the most part as concerns their future. There is a lesson on humility, a new commandment, and a commission, for the carrying out of which the disciples receive the gifts of the Holy Spirit and of prayer so that they may bear fruit; and finally there is Jesus' own prayer that they may be preserved from evil and maintain a unity like that which exists between Jesus and God. Thus Jesus provides for the future. The disciples will be in the world what Jesus himself was. In his First Letter John has expressed it this way:

> Here is the test by which we can make sure that we are in him: whoever claims to be dwelling in him, binds himself to live as Christ himself lived. (1 John 2:6, N.E.B.)[1]

Or, as Philips has translated the same verse:

> The life of a man who professes to be living in God must bear the stamp of Christ.[2]

For this task Jesus does not leave the disciple to his own strength. He blesses him with the help and protection of God himself. It is hard to be a Christian! But one does have help!

". . . I, when I am lifted up . . ."

10 ✧⟩□□□□□□□□□□□

His Finest Hour

Winston Churchill, shortly after Dunkirk and a month after becoming Prime Minister, in rallying a shaken and battered empire, spoke these memorable words:

> Let us therefore brace ourselves to our duties, and bear ourselves, that, if the British Empire and its Commonwealth last for a thousand years, men will still say, "This was their finest hour!" (Speech, House of Commons, and later broadcast, June 18, 1940)[1]

So Christ faced the cross! In the midst of rejection and hatred, when his cause seemed lost, a call came from an unexpected quarter: "Sir, we wish to see Jesus." To this call, that might seem to be an invitation to flee, to start anew in another place, to begin again with a new people in a new clime, Jesus said, "No!" He would choose his own battleground and it would be here. "Now is my soul troubled. And what shall I say? 'Father, save me from this hour?' No, for this purpose I have come to this hour. Father, glorify thy name. . . . I, when I am lifted up from the earth, will draw all men to myself" (12:27–32). Never was there a bolder defiance of enemies; never a more courageous stand to duty; never a more determined effort to fight evil here and now and be done with it. And the Christian church after nearly two thousand years still says, "This was his finest hour!"

This is a tremendous claim about a Man whose future seemed to draw him inevitably to a cross, a tremendous claim for a church whose Lord had been crucified! The wonder of the cross is that the disciples did not fall apart. They went forth and said of their leader's crucifixion, "This was his finest hour." This hour made all others take on meaning. This hour determined the future. This hour set down the ruler of this world once for all. This hour made millions of individuals—a countless multitude—ready to lay down their lives for him whom they heralded as King of kings and Lord of lords.

It may be that the world has become more secular as science is enthroned. Christian missions are declining; many members are only loosely tied to the church; many others have no use for it. Perhaps a post-Christian era has begun. But it is still true that Jesus will draw all men unto himself.

This is a strong claim. Is it true? This question is particularly significant when other religions, such as Islam and Buddhism, are experiencing a revival. What can one make of this? That Christianity would capture the world was the hope and dream of the disciples. It would not take long, they thought, for the world to be won for Christ. Now, can it be that the cross, instead of being his finest hour, was a victory for the world? Was an upstart crusader removed, so that, after a few centuries of prosperous activity, in the end Christianity will die out, just as did the ancient religions of Egypt and Mesopotamia?

Read chapters 12, 18, and 19 for today's lesson. Note especially the emphases in these chapters—the hour, the question in the garden, Jesus' protection of his disciples, the trial, and three cries from the cross, which are different from the three recorded in the Gospel of Luke. What do the cries from the cross reveal about the character of John's Gospel and the meaning of the cross for him? Observe how John weaves other themes into the story—the drinking of the cup (18:11), the passion announcements (18:32), the nature of the Kingdom (18:36). Note the relation between the cross and mission which comes to the fore here. This is more than a home-going.

The Concept of "the Hour" in John

By use of the word "hour" John discloses his view of the cross. It is God's act accomplished in God's time. There are four different phrases in which the term "hour" appears:

(1) "... his hour had not yet come" (7:30; 8:20; cf. 2:4).

(2) ". . . the hour is coming when . . ." (4:21; 5:28; 16:2).

(3) ". . . the hour is coming, and now is . . ." (4:23; 5:25; cf. 16:32).

(4) "The hour has come . . ." (12:23; 17:1; cf. 12:27; 13:1).

Note what is said in each reference. Which phrases have to do with the cross? What does the contrast between "My hour has not yet come" (2:4) and "The hour has come . . ." (12:23) imply about the cross of Jesus? Is there any sense of tragedy here? What do you suppose John intends when he characterizes the "hour" as one of glorification? Note what he says about departing to the Father (13:1).

For John, the harvest of the life and ministry of Christ comes after his death and resurrection, as the work of the disciples and the Spirit. Jesus came for a moment to manifest the divine glory so a few would know the way to God. These few he gathered into a close-knit fellowship and entrusted to them the responsibility for relaying to the world what they had seen and heard (1 John 1:1–3). What Jesus was unable to do in his life would be accomplished by the disciples after his death. The death of Christ is not tragedy: the cross is part of a whole scheme of events which end in victory (12:32). A similar emphasis appears in the Letter to the Hebrews:

> . . . let us run with perseverance the race that is set before us, looking to Jesus the pioneer and perfecter of our faith, who for the joy that was set before him endured the cross, despising the shame, and is seated at the right hand of the throne of God. (12:1–2)

Thus, for John, Jesus' bitterest hour became his finest.

The Meaning of the Cross

In John we are a long way from the early sermons in Acts which often treat the cross as plain murder, the effect of which was undone by God (as in Acts 2:23–24; 3:13–15; 5:30; 7:52; 10:39–40; 13:27–30). Note how in all these sermons the emphasis is the same: The Jews murdered Jesus, but God raised him from the dead and exalted him. John stresses the exaltation. The cross for him was a lifting up, a means of return to the Father and glory. It marked the end of Jesus' humiliation (his emptying himself, his laying aside the prerogatives of deity, Phil. 2:6–11). From now on Jesus is Lord.

John interprets the cross in terms of the Passover. The Passover celebrated all the events surrounding the Exodus from Egypt, especially the Lord's victory in the deliverance of Israel and the defeat of Pharaoh and his host. (See the discussion earlier in FROM BONDAGE TO FREEDOM, pp. 49–59.) It became the Jewish "Independence Day."

Central to the feast was the sacrifice of the paschal lamb. The lamb was without spot or blemish; it was killed without breaking any bones (19:33); it was Israel's substitute for the death of the firstborn. The rite itself marked God's judgment on the powers of evil and his deliverance of his people. It was thus an appropriate symbol for Jesus who, as God's only Son, was slain so that the rest of mankind could go free. In this death judgment and grace come together.

Grace is manifest in the cross in that Jesus is God's special gift to the world for the deliverance of man (1:29; 3:16). There is also judgment in the cross (12:31). Jesus does not come to judge, but his presence is a judgment (3:17–19). Jesus does not die to condemn, but his death is a condemnation. Men love darkness (3:19); they reject goodness. Thus the cross marks the lengthened darkness of the world.

Further, in the judgment, the ruler of this world will be cast out (12:31) and Jesus will reign as Lord. Here evil is defeated and loses its hold on humanity. Does this also include the fear of death? Is the enticement of the world broken? Has John written with the experience of Acts 2:37 in mind—when men see the result of their evil deeds will they be conscience-stricken and turn to him whom they crucified?

Jesus' Acceptance of the Cross

While the cross was interpreted for the disciples as Jesus' means of departure to the Father (13:1; 14:12, 28; 16:5, 17, 28), there was more to it than that. Here is a man who believes his cause to be the cause of God, who will not be swayed by opposition, by threats and schemes, by stones or name calling, by accusations, by false testimony, beatings, abuse—nor by the cross. If this be his lot, to the cross he will go, assured that then he will draw men to himself.

Jesus believed in God's love and concern for man. This was his cause. He would let no person or thing move him from it: no appeals from his disciples, no threats from the priests, no summons from the Greeks. He asks no quarter; he seeks no escape. He will do his task to the end (13:1). Here he will make his stand; here he will reveal his glory.

He was a man with a purpose. He felt called of God, sent for this very task. God's will must be done. It was precious, dearer than life itself. Man must have a purpose to live for; he cannot stand meaningless existence. This was Jesus' purpose: to fulfill God's plan.

There was love. Jesus would not forsake men; he would not leave them to human cruelty, pride, passion, lust for power (13:1). Once for all he would draw them. Let them do what they would, he would not curse them, damn them, seek vengeance upon them, call heaven to rain fire on them, consign them to hell! He loved them. If someone must die, he would die 10,000 times rather than show hatred to one soul. So he kept a betrayer's secret and let him do his devilish work (13:27). So he let his disciples escape (18:8), and took care of his mother (19:26–27). When he breathed his last he could say, "It is finished" (19:30). This was his finest hour!

Jesus' deliberate acceptance of the cross is shown by John's description of the events:

(1) Jesus protected his own. The cross was God's will for him alone. He made it possible for the disciples to depart (18:8).

(2) Jesus did not defend himself before the high priest. Others could tell what he had said and done (18:20–21).

(3) At the trial before Pilate, Jesus does not struggle to gain acquittal, for his Kingdom is not of this world.

(4) Pilate is only a tool in God's hand. He would have no power over Jesus were it not given to him from above (19:11).

(5) Note also the references to the fulfillment of Scripture (19: 23–24 and 19:36–37).

All this verifies that the cross was God's plan. Yet it was also man's act. All who had a part in it were responsible for it.

Who was the guilty? Who brought this upon Thee?
Alas, my treason, Jesus, hath undone Thee!
'Twas I, Lord Jesus, I it was denied Thee;
I crucified Thee.[2]

The Effect of the Cross

The direct effect of the cross was twofold:

(1) The gathering of the church (10:16; 12:32; 17:20).

(2) The sending out of the church to convert the world (12:24; 15:16; 20:21).

There were other effects, however:

(3) The cross brought boldness to the disciples. Following his resurrection, Jesus gathered his little band of discouraged and defeated men, commissioned them, and sent them forth (20:21) on the same mission he had had. And they went,

> . . . treated as imposters, and yet are true; as unknown, and yet well known; as dying, and behold we live; as punished, and yet not killed; as sorrowful, yet always rejoicing; as poor, yet making many rich; as having nothing and yet possessing everything. (2 Cor. 6:8–10)

(4) The cross won over the power of Rome. The disciples went to city after city, were beaten, suffered hardships, and faced constant danger (cf. 2 Cor. 11:26–27). Yet in each place they captured the hearts of some and established churches. Idols were abandoned, books of magic were burned, and men found release in a new way of life. They could be threatened and tortured, but they willingly endured, joyously confident of victory. And at last, under Constantine, Rome itself made obeisance to Christ and confessed him Lord.

Jesus needed to give himself completely to the cause. Anything less would have thrown suspicion on it and on him. Now it is our turn, not merely to gape or even to tell others, "There's a man on a cross!" but to join him there. He went about doing good, ferreting out evil. He wouldn't give up when his life was threatened. How many compromise their principles, how many allow themselves to be used by forces of wickedness, because they are afraid to take a stand! How many, when the battle lines are drawn, throw down their arms and run! Women give up virtue, men their honor; they lie, cheat, steal, become addicts, because they are afraid to stand up for the right, to take the side of Christ, to join him on the cross.

Had Jesus given in, his life would have been a failure, no longer able to serve any useful purpose. Therefore he would not give in. He would fight it out to the bitter end. Should not the disciple do the same?

> Were the whole realm of nature mine,
> That were a present far too small;
> Love so amazing, so divine,
> Demands my soul, my life, my all.
>
> *—The Hymnbook,* 198

Undoubtedly this Gospel was written after the initial wave of success on the part of the disciples. It was in anticipation of the continued spread of the gospel that it was written to encourage the church to faithful witness. Does Jesus' attitude toward the cross inspire faith in him as a Leader? as a Savior? as the Son of God?

Some Further Thoughts on the Cross

I have added some additional thoughts for your contemplation on the reason for the cross. Perhaps you can think of others.

(1) The cross reveals the true nature of evil. There sin did its worst, taking an innocent life in a brutal display of injustice. This Jesus endured without any complaint or demand for vengeance; he gave men no occasion for their cruelty. Man needs to see evil in its ultimate form, as at Calvary. We become too accustomed to evil, accepting it as a part of life without being horrified at it. The Romans rejoiced at the brutalities of the arena; the women of France did their knitting while watching the heads roll from the guillotine; people in America become spectators to rape or murder, refusing to help the victims; they even encourage would-be suicides to jump. We need to see evil in all its ugliness.

(2) Was not Jesus officially put to death as a rebel, a threat to peace? Then, he has not come to help men to adjust to their en-

vironment, to relieve tensions, to give peace. He creates tension wherever there is evil. Jesus had to die because he claimed men's loyalties, and Rome would have none of this. Christ cuts across the common ways of men. He challenges men to loyalty above that due to the state or to the world.

(3) What Caiaphas means as a word of worldly wisdom (11:50) has a deeper spiritual meaning and is a prophecy of the means of redemption. The cross is a divine necessity.

(4) The world needs a sense of justice. It cannot stand a God of grace alone. Men cry out, like the elder brother in Luke's parable (15:29–30), that it isn't just to be gracious to a prodigal! They need a feeling that justice is at the heart of the world, that when the prophets cry, "But let justice roll down like waters, and righteousness like an overflowing stream" (Amos 5:24), they are calling for something that is of God. Men cannot live with mercy alone. This tends to chaos. So to give men a sense of justice the cross was planned. *How does the cross point to justice?* See Romans 3:21–26.

(5) Man needs to be changed, transformed. Whatever goodness there may be in man is in bondage to the demonic. Men are tired and helpless; when they want to do good, they cannot, and so they cry out like Paul, "Who will deliver me from this body of death?" (Rom. 7:24.) God says, "I will." Thus the cross.

(6) The world needed to know and see one Man who could be totally dedicated, utterly loyal to God, come what may. Men needed to see that there is a power available to do the things they dream of doing and be the persons they dream of being. Very few want to be evil. But many are discouraged and in despair and need to see the glory of a fully dedicated life. God will not let such a life be destroyed.

(7) Men need to know the value of human beings. So often life is considered cheap; here we see its value. God values men so dearly that he gave his Son.

"My Lord and my God!"

11 ✧ ⊃▭▭▭▭▭▭▭▭▭◁

The Great Confession

The twentieth chapter is more than John's report of the Resurrection; it is the climax and consummation of his Gospel. In it he compresses the concluding events of Jesus' life: the empty tomb (1–10), the resurrection appearances (11–29), the joyous confession on the part of the disciples (25), the commissioning of the disciples (21), and the gift of the Spirit (22).

The purpose of the book is that men "may believe . . . and . . . have life" (20:31). One is prompted to ask what men are to believe? Or, if believing involves a relationship, in whom are men to believe? This chapter gives the answer to that question (20:28).

To understand the full significance of the confession of Thomas it is necessary to read this chapter of John and compare the confession of Thomas with the confessions elsewhere in the Gospel. What does Thomas here call Jesus? How does this compare with what Jesus has been called by Philip (1:45), Nathanael (1:49), the Samaritans (4:42), or Peter (6:68–69)?

The Form of the Confession

The form of the confession is at once striking. Suetonius, a Roman historian, informs us in his book, *Twelve Caesars,* that Emperor Domitian ascribed to himself divine titles and

> began as follows in issuing a circular letter in the name of his procurators, "Our Master and our God bids that this be done." And so the custom arose of henceforth addressing him in no other way even in writing or in conversation.[1]

Domitian reigned from A.D. 81 to 96. If this Gospel was composed during or soon after his reign the confession of Thomas is the more significant. It separates the Christians from the Romans and Christ from Caesar. To the Romans the emperor may be Lord and God, but to the Christians only Jesus is Lord and God. This confession then must be understood as asserting Jesus to be divine. The ascription to Jesus of titles boldly assumed by secular rulers has nothing comparable to it today. Can this be one reason why some were reluctant to believe in Jesus?

Note the personal element in the confession. Jesus is not called Lord and God of the world, nor even of all Christians, as in the phrase, "our Lord," frequently used by Paul. This is more personal —*my* Lord and *my* God. This implies that a personal relation has been established between Jesus and the believer.

The Confessions of the Gospel

According to the purpose of this Gospel (20:31), the confession of Martha (11:27), and the confessions in the Synoptics (Mark 1:1; Matt. 16:16; 26:63; Luke 9:20), men are to believe that Jesus is the Messiah, the Son of God. Confession of faith in Jesus Christ takes many forms in John's Gospel. Jesus is the Lamb of God (1: 29, 36); the Messiah or the Christ (1:41; 4:29; 7:41); the Son of God (1:34, 49); the King of Israel (1:49); the Savior of the world (4:42); the Holy One of God (6:69); and, more personally, "My Lord and my God" (20:28). Probably early Christian confessions took a number of forms. The most common were "Jesus is Messiah," "Jesus is the Son of God," and "Jesus is Lord." Lord became the most popular ascription for Jesus, and Messiah became more a name—Christ—than a title.

All these confessions say who and what Jesus is. Some emphasize his relation to God—Son of God, Holy One of God. Others stress his relation to Israel—Messiah, King of Israel. Still others are more extensive and describe his relationship to the world—Lamb of God, Savior of the world.

Two elements seem to have been a part of such confessions: First, one confessed something about Jesus' relation to God—his deity. This comes to the fore especially in Jesus' discussions with the Jews in chapters 5, 7, and 8. Secondly, one confessed Jesus' relation to men. He is Messiah, Savior, King, Lord. Note how all these have to do with redemption.

How early in the church the duality of Christ and the mystery of the Incarnation comes to the fore! Jesus is Son of God and Son of Man, not one more or less than the other. Both aspects must be confessed. He saves as the God who became man, who became part of our world and part of our life. Thus the mystery of the Word made flesh is made to permeate the whole Gospel as it permeated the entire Christian faith of the first century.

The Meaning of the Confession

(1) Christ. While the confession of Thomas does not use the word Christ or Messiah, John was well aware of the use of this term among the early Christians. It is linked with Son of God in his statement of purpose (20:31). It is also given in the confession by Martha (11:27), and its significance is seen too in the Samaritan incident (4:29; cf. 1:41; 7:26, 41–42).

The word "Christ" is a Greek translation of the Hebrew word *Messiah,* meaning "the Anointed One." In the stories of Saul and David such anointing was accompanied by a gift of the Spirit which enabled the anointed one to deliver Israel from her enemies (1 Sam. 10:1; 16:13). At the close of the Old Testament period, the Jews expected a new deliverer from the house of David to destroy Israel's enemies, restore her kingdom, and usher in the reign of God and a new era of prosperity. This hope was particularly strong among the Zealots of Jesus' day. Their ardent patriotism and nationalism, along with their desire for violence, made Jesus hesitate to apply this title to himself. By the time John wrote, Messiah, under Christian reinterpretation, denoted one who would redeem man from sin and establish God's rule in the heart. While among the masses many materialistic elements still were retained in this hope, the New Testament is free from such descriptions in its discussion of the Messiah.

The Messiah is one anointed by God to deliver his people and usher in his Kingdom. The New Testament makes plain that the Messiah does not cater to the selfish hopes of men, nor is his Kingdom comparable to those in which men contend for power. When Jesus accepts the term Messiah, he reinterprets its meaning (compare Matt. 16:21; John 18:33–37). For Jesus, the Messiah is one who brings to men deliverance from sin, promotes the rule of God over the world, and gives new life to men. This Messiahship in John, however, is not otherworldly. It has to do with this world and with this life (cf. John 10:10).

A new and better world and a new and better life have been the constant dream and ambition of mankind throughout history. Some like the Zealots have sought to establish this by force. The efforts of Germany, Japan, and the Communists of our time are living witness to the persistence of such attempts. What has been tragic in so many of these efforts is that they have fostered some would-be messiah with a thirst for power who has not been concerned with God's rule of justice and love for men.

The new order Christ brings comes from above. It is God's gift to the world, breaking into the old and bringing new life. It makes a great deal of difference *from what* men desire to be delivered. Some want deliverance from the tyranny of men; others want deliverance from want, fear, war, disease, misfortune, servitude—in short, from everything disagreeable and unpleasant. God's concern is not mainly with such, but with sin. His Kingdom does not promise ivory palaces and golden streets, but persecution and crosses. It deals with the unpleasant, not by removing it, but by inspiring a devotion to a higher aim for which no sacrifice is too great. Note Paul on this:

> . . . I count everything as loss because of the surpassing worth of knowing Christ Jesus my Lord. For his sake I have suffered the loss of all things, and count them as refuse, in order that I may gain Christ and be found in him, not having a righteousness of my own, based on law, but that which is through faith in Christ, the righteousness from God that depends on faith; that I may know him and the power of his resurrection, and may share his sufferings, becoming like him in his death, that if possible I may attain the resurrection from the dead.
>
> Not that I have already obtained this or am already perfect; but I press on to make it my own, because Christ Jesus has made me his own.　　　　　(Phil. 3:8–12)

(2) Lord. One of the earliest and by far the most popular confessions was simply, "Jesus is Lord" (Rom. 10:9; 1 Cor. 12:3; cf. Acts 2:36; Phil. 2:11).

"Lord" has various meanings. For the Jew it was a substitute for the divine name, *Yahweh*. Fearing to violate the Third Commandment, the Jews did not say the divine name, but used such substitutes as Strength, Rock, Heaven, or the Blessed; the most popular was "Lord."

"Lord" was also a polite form of address, like "sir" or "mister." The Gospels still preserve this usage of Lord (John 4:11, 15; 5:7; in each case the R.S.V. rightly translates the word as merely "sir").

Again, "Lord" suggests authority and dominion. A teacher was called Master and Lord, and noted men were addressed by this title (as in Matt. 20:25; 23:10; 1 Cor. 8:5). Perhaps the term "Lord" as used in Matthew 7:21 is meant in this sense.

All these ideas may be present in the confession of Thomas. "Jesus is Lord" means that Jesus is the divine Master, to whom belongs all authority, dominion, and power. By this confession we acknowledge our subservience to him. He is our Master and Teacher. We sit at his feet to listen, to learn, and to obey. He is our Ruler. He sends us forth, telling us when and where to go. It is his perogative to command, ours to obey. His is the plan and program. He sets the goal and marks out the way. It is his work that is to be done. He sets the hours, assigns the labor, gives the reward. He is Lord.

This Lordship of Christ has many facets. He is Lord of the individual, "My Lord." He is also Lord of the church, "our Lord": all its aims, efforts, goals, programs, drives, services come under his control. Jesus is Lord of the world (1 Cor. 15:24–26; Phil. 2:10–11; Col. 1:15–20; cf. Rom. 8:18–21). All creation is included in the redemption of Christ; there is nothing over which Jesus is not Lord. Part of our Christian task is to bring everything into subjection to Christ. This is a long, slow process and often we are tempted to give up in despair. But for the Christian there can be but one Master, Christ (Matt. 23:10).

(3) God. In his confession Thomas declares, "Jesus is my God." John intends this word to be the climactic word on the identity of Jesus. Thomas declares that he finds God revealed in Jesus. The worship and service which belong to God Thomas is

willing to give also to Jesus. How Jesus could be termed God and yet distinguished from him John does not explain. He never faced the problem; he simply sets God and Jesus in a relation of Father and Son.

G. A. Studdert-Kennedy has somewhere described one's god as one's master passion, that which commands all one's energy, utilizes all one's talents, holds all one's allegiance. Your god is what you live for. Some live for food, others for drink, sex, wealth, fame, status, family, home, church, country, hobby, sport, work, security, science, art, or music. Whatever dominates the whole of life becomes one's god. One may not have an altar to it, but he serves and worships it nevertheless. For the Christian, Jesus is that master passion, dominating every thought and action and infiltrating every part of life.

How simple and how difficult that is! So much of life is lived without taking Jesus into consideration. We live as though he had never lived and as though he had never died. Even in our Christian homes and churches so much activity is planned and so much money is spent without taking Jesus into consideration. He is seldom in our thoughts. We live for self or the church more than for Christ. We often don't let our friends know of our faith, seemingly proud to be able to hide the fact we are Christians.

There is a great deal of difference between living for Christ and living for the church. Christians are not safe from idols, for they can easily make an idol out of the Bible or the church. What do you think Jesus would say about our large, ornate churches; our expansive educational units; our round of conferences, retreats, and institutes; our efforts to get the greatest number involved in running the program? Not that this is wrong in and by itself, but one wonders whether the world gets the impression in all this that Jesus Christ is Lord and God. It is much easier to get people interested in the church than in Christ, much easier to get them involved in the church than in confrontation with Christ. The church is a place to meet Christ but it should never become an end in itself.

That Christ is God means that nothing else must take his place. No other program, no matter how necessary and helpful, may claim our first allegiance. In whatever we engage, whether civil rights, the political arena, the social welfare sphere, a service club, a youth movement, or another of the hundred and one worthy patriotic and social organizations, we must through our service leave the witness: Jesus is my Lord and my God.

Some Remarks on This Confession

John comes to the end of his story by bringing the extreme skeptic among the disciples to faith. As the story begins with the bringing of the prejudiced Nathanael to confession, so it ends with the confession of one who wants visible and tangible proof. For Thomas, seeing is believing. He requires more than the testimony of others, which may be no more than idle gossip or wishful thinking which has taken on the veil of truth. He is akin to the scientist and rationalist. He is not gullible, ready to believe anything; he won't even accept the word of reliable witnesses, his own companions. He demands to be shown. So Jesus shows him.

The ultimate proof for Thomas are the scars in Jesus' hands and side—the wounds of Christ. Thomas wanted to be sure the companion he knew and the Christ of faith were one and the same person, that the Christian faith was built on no idle dream but was founded on fact, on verifiable evidence. From our standpoint he had it easy. Jesus gave him his desire and manifested himself to him. *What can one say to the skeptics of today that will convince them? Are the wounds of Christ still the marks by which he is known?*

> Hath He marks to lead me to Him,
> If He be my Guide?
> "In His feet and hands are wound prints,
> And His side." —*The Hymnbook,* 264

Must the church and the Christian bear the marks of Christ to manifest him to the world?

There is a mild rebuke in the final word to Thomas, "Blessed are those who have not seen and yet believe" (20:29). There is also a great challenge to men today because Jesus is no longer visibly present. But the Holy Spirit, according to John, takes his place. Through the Spirit the Christian continues the ministry of Christ and even performs greater deeds than Christ (14:12). Further-more, Christ has promised to do for the disciples whatever they ask (14:13–14).

This confession is personal—for me he is God—and each must speak for himself. This Gospel has this personal emphasis through-out. Jesus is concerned with persons, confronting them individually where they are and according to their own temperament and makeup. He deals with each in accordance with his peculiar per-sonality. Thus this confession may have different implications for different people.

Again, it is the risen Jesus who has been crucified who is Lord and God. Now he appears in his true glory. Now he truly manifests the Father. The warning against the making of images in the Bible was given not only because the representation of what is spirit (4: 24) is impossible, but also because spirit must manifest itself in something living. The contrast between God and idols of old in-volved just this point (see Ps. 115:3–8; 135:15–18; Isa. 44:9–20; 46:5–7). The idols were not living; only what is alive can adequately express the deity. Thus the marvel and wonder of the Incarnation, and the double marvel of the Holy Spirit.

John met the unbelief of his day with this Gospel or testimony. It may not have the same effect today as then. We may require a new terminology and new illustrations for conveying the meaning of Christ. Can you think of any? But what John demands is still the major demand. You must see Jesus related to both God and the world of men. He must become the Master of your life, the center around which the whole of living revolves. If there is to be any de-liverance and any transformation, it will come through your rela-tionship to him and by his power.

". . . do you love me? . . . Follow me!"

12 ✧ A Parting Word

John closes his Gospel in a strange and touching way. Having come to the end of his story and having completed his purpose, he wouldn't lay down his pen. It is as if he were not satisfied with what he had written, as if something were missing. He could not leave men just coming to believe. It was necessary to add one final word.

The disciples, even the most skeptical of them, were convinced that Jesus was alive and was their Lord. Jesus had given them the Spirit. Commissioned to go forth in his name, they were fully equipped. What more was necessary? This question is particularly important for the Christian. Having been confronted with Jesus Christ and having come to faith, what more is there?

Read John 21. As you read it try to answer this question: Why do you think John added this chapter? Did the author find a few more stories after writing the Gospel and add them at the end? Was the author trying to harmonize his tradition of appearances at Jerusalem with another tradition of an appearance in Galilee, as some scholars suggest? Was this chapter written by an editor who wanted to do two things—to say that Jesus gave the pastoral office to Peter, appointing him shepherd of Christ's flock, and to correct a misunderstanding of what Jesus said about the "disciple whom Jesus loved"—as Filson suggests? Whether by the author of the first twenty chapters or by an editor, the addendum closes the story on a different note, a more direct and challenging note, which suggests that bringing a person to confession is not the sole purpose of the author, and that confession of faith is not the ultimate goal of evangelism. What new emphasis does this chapter add to the story?

Do You Love Me?

This story has received many and varied interpretations. The individual details are often used to teach lessons not found in the story itself. While John often uses symbolism, compressing many ideas within the context of a single event, there is always a basic purpose which controls the story and provides a clue to its intended meaning. Details should be interpreted in relation to this meaning. Thus it is fruitless to search for meaning behind the number of fish caught. Jerome presents a tradition that according to the ancient world there were a hundred and fifty-three species of fish, which suggested to him the universal scope of the Gospel. But John makes nothing of the catch except that it is the miracle through which the "disciple whom Jesus loved" recognizes the Lord. The number may be no more than a detail of tradition.

It would also be improper to make much of the different words for love used in the question to Peter, ". . . do you love me?" (*agapas*); and his answer, "Yes, Lord, you know that I love you" (*philo*). Such variation in language is totally in keeping with the linguistic variations throughout the Gospel. The point of the story is the reinstatement of Peter.

The story is about a resurrection appearance. The disciples, at least seven of them, were fishing. This had been their trade, the means whereby they earned their living. After they spend a fruitless night at it, Jesus, unrecognized, asks them whether they have caught anything and advises them to cast on the right side of the boat. This they do, and now they have a capacity catch. By the miracle Jesus is recognized. Note Jesus' prophetic insight, its effect, and his strangeness after the resurrection.

The ensuing breakfast takes the form of a communion meal. Jesus takes bread, breaks it, and gives it to them, and so with the fish, much after the pattern of the episodes of the feeding of the five thousand and of the four thousand. After the meal, as in the Upper Room stories, Jesus speaks to his disciples. Here the question is simple and direct: "Do you love me?" On the surface the story shows the reinstatement of Peter and his investment with the pastoral office. As Peter three times denied Christ, so he is now asked three times whether he loves Christ. But has the story a further intent? Is there a suggestion perhaps that not only for Peter but for every Christian this is the all-important question, even after we have confessed Jesus as Lord?

Jesus is concerned that men should love him. This is in keeping with the whole tenor of the Gospel. John concentrates on love. It was love which prompted God to send his Son into the world (3:16). It was love that encouraged Jesus to lay down his life (13:1; 15:13). His commandment to his disciples is that they love one another (13:34; 15:12–17), and love is the mark by which they are to be known (13:35). Love is the all-important concern of Christ. Is it any wonder then that this Gospel should end on this note? The lack of this emphasis in chapter 20 may have prompted the author or an editor to add this final note, so that the Gospel might be true to the concern of Christ.

"Do you love me?" Jesus does not ask whether Peter loves the sheep, or whether he loves the world, or loves people. Because a person loves people is no sufficient reason for his becoming an evangelist. One must love Christ. Christ does not ask Peter either whether he loves the work or the mission of Christ. The people to whom he is sent may be quite unlovable, and the work at times distasteful. The question is whether he loves Christ. This will enable him to suffer and to endure. Paul was keenly aware of this. To the Galatians he writes:

> I have been crucified with Christ; it is no longer I who live, but Christ who lives in me; and the life I now live in the flesh I live by faith in the Son of God who loved me and gave himself for me. (2:20)

No one can go on a mission for Christ unless he loves him. The mission needs a driving force which only love can supply. To love Christ is to be able to love those for whom he died.

Note what Paul says in 1 Corinthians 13 as to love. List what he says it is and what it is not; what it does not do and what it does do. Love never fails. This was Paul's experience. By love we must live; it is more necessary to manifest love within the church (and elsewhere!) than any other spiritual gift one may possess.

Love in the Christian sense is not based on physical attraction or kinship. It takes its pattern from God's love for man. The neighbor, the stranger, the enemy, are the objects of one's concern and care. Love acts with no regard for the self. It does not count the cost. It treats the other with dignity and respect. And it binds men together in such a fashion that what affects one affects all. Note it is John who wrote, ". . . God is love" (1 John 4:8). Over against the holiness of the priests and the Essenes, over against the legalism of the scribes and Pharisees, Jesus placed love. It became the mark by which Christians were known.

Love binds individuals together, and thus the church is bound together as Christians are attached to one another. What happens to one is the concern of all. Think what this means for discipline within the church. How easy it is to blame, to heap abuse and ridicule upon another. Can it be that one reason Jesus failed to condemn sinners, to the chagrin of the righteous, was that he loved them? So he joined himself to them and made their problems his own. This does not imply that to love is to condone; to love is to build up and not to tear down; it is to save and not to destroy.

"Do you love me?" This is an arresting question, for it distinguishes Christ himself from what he has to offer. It is noteworthy that in this Gospel God's gift to men is not deliverance from sin, nor yet salvation, nor yet restoration, but a Person. Can it be that what is responsible for the lifeless Christianity of some people is that they have come to love what Christ has to offer but have not learned to love him?

The story is told about a woman in France who went through the streets of her village with a torch in one hand and a bucket of water in the other. When the people asked her why she carried the water, she said, "To put out the fires of hell." And all acknowledged that that would be a good thing; if one did not have to fear hell how much pleasanter life would be! Then they asked, "But why the torch?" To which she responded, "To burn down heaven." For she wanted to teach men to love Christ for himself and not because they feared hell or wanted to get to heaven. There is much truth in the story. For the one who loves, nothing else matters than to be close to his beloved and to please him.

Follow Me!

The Gospel ends as it began. In the opening story two disciples of the Baptizer follow Jesus and he asks them, "What do you seek?" When they inquire concerning his lodging he responds, "Come and see" (1:37–39). In reality they are seeking Jesus and he invites them to follow him. Now after the story of Christ is told, the disciples express their faith and, if Peter is representative, their love. The future path is laid bare and Peter can look forward to a cross. To this future Jesus now invites Peter with a simple straight-forward command, "Follow me" (21:19). This is the final word, the word after all other words have been spoken. After faith and love comes the invitation to follow.

This was the consistent invitation of Jesus throughout the Gospels. It was his word to Peter and Andrew, James and John (Matt. 4:19; Mark 1:17). It was the summons to Philip (John 1:43), and the invitation to Levi or Matthew (Matt. 9:9; Mark 2:14; Luke 5:27). It was the word to would-be followers (Matt. 8:22; Luke 9:59), and his general invitation to all who would come after him (Matt. 16:24; Mark 8:34; Luke 9:23; cf. Matt. 10:38). Here it is his final message to Peter and through him to all Christians.

What is implied in following Jesus? Sheldon, in his book, *In His Steps*, took it to be the imitation of Christ by asking in every situation, "What would Jesus do?" Francis of Assisi understood it as the renunciation of riches for a life of poverty and service. Others have understood it in other ways. How do you understand it?

Following Jesus means that his life is the pattern of life for the Christian. Paul stressed this in 1 Corinthians 11:1 (cf. 1 Thess. 1:6). Thomas á Kempis provided the church of his time with a guide to *The Imitation of Christ*. Perhaps the Gospels are meant to be such a guide. Redemption not only provides deliverance from the past—the forgiveness of sins, but also involves the development of a new life. For this new life Jesus is the pattern. As Paul Harrison has said in his meditations on the Gospel of John, anyone who seeks to make any aspect of Jesus' life or ministry his own by imitating it will find a whole new life opening up to him.

Following Jesus defines the work of the Christian: it is the work of Christ. Note the form of the Great Commission in John (20:21). The task of the Christian and the church is no more and no less than the completion of the work of Christ. For the accomplishment of that task Jesus endowed the disciples with his Spirit. The Spirit is not given for the Christian's or the church's enjoyment; he is given for mission. The Spirit carries on the work of Christ through the individual Christian.

Following Jesus implies fellowship with him. The word for "follow" is an interesting one in Greek. It means "to walk the same road together." To follow Christ is to walk the road he walked in fellowship with him. It is our fellowship with him, our daily communion through meditation and prayer, that strengthens us and shapes our spirits for the performance of his task. What a tragedy, then, when this fellowship is neglected!

There is also a mild rebuke in the summons to follow Jesus as related in the story. Christians are tempted to judge their lives by others. Note this tendency in Peter (21:21). Such comparisons often become the basis for status-seeking or complacency and inactivity. It invites the praise of self and the condemnation of others. Or it sets forth an example which is less than perfect. This is not the way of Christ. Note also the emphasis in the stories of the talents (Matt. 25:14-30) and of the pounds (Luke 19:11-27). Each person is called to account for the mission entrusted to him. Is this not a part of the priesthood of believers?

In every church there is a tendency to follow ministers who have served effectively. As in Paul's day, men say, "I follow Paul," "I follow Apollos," or "I follow Cephas" (see 1 Cor. 1:12). How Christians have wasted their resources and retarded the progress of the Kingdom by such divisions. Here the rebuke of Christ is pertinent. He is Lord; we must fix our eyes and hearts on him.

Our daily life is often highly competitive. It is no wonder that at times we carry this spirit over into the church. How often we gauge our church program by that of another church! How often we place our giving on a comparative basis! How often we determine the extent of our participation in church activities by that of others! How much of this do you think would come under Christ's rebuke? What does following Christ imply as to our daily life? Does it mean turning the other cheek, walking a second mile, losing our coat and giving our cloak? Does this place the Christian at the mercy of selfish and aggressive individuals? Is there a limit to following Christ? Are there some aspects of Christ's life which cannot be duplicated in our modern day? Name some of these. In what sense then are we to follow Christ?

In this final chapter John summarizes his understanding of the Christian life. The Christian's response to the redemptive act of God in Jesus Christ is faith. Faith manifests itself in love; and love manifests itself in service. Wherever Christ comes he brings with him the Kingdom, which John equates with the gift of eternal life. Where faith, love, and service abound in the name of Christ, there the Kingdom manifests its presence. Yet we are not so much builders of the Kingdom as built into it. As John Knox says:

> Our part in the building will be allowing ourselves to be "built in," yielding ourselves without reservation—without care for a single vested interest, without self-righteous fidelity to a single ancient prejudice—to the mighty working of the Spirit, who alone can break down all dividing walls of hostility and can reconcile us all to God in one body.[1]

SUGGESTED REVIEW

This concludes our study of John's Gospel. After having spent a number of weeks with this book it would be helpful to pause and see what you have learned from it. All good study calls for a review. One way to do this is to turn to the Table of Contents and to recall the things that stand out in your mind about each lesson. Another way is to ask yourself some questions about John. To help you in this I have selected the following questions:

1. *State in your own words what it means to have faith, to believe in Jesus.*

2. *What did Jesus mean to John and the early church? State in your own words what Jesus means to you. How does your confession compare with those in this Gospel?*

3. *What is the importance of Christian witness? How can it best be given? How does Jesus help to witness?*

4. *What are some of the aids to faith that will help the modern man to believe? What are some of the hindrances that prevent him from believing?*

5. *What is the meaning of the cross? What is its significance in the purpose of Jesus' life?*

6. *What characterizes the life of a believer? How are Christians known in the world?*

7. *What does it mean to follow Jesus?*

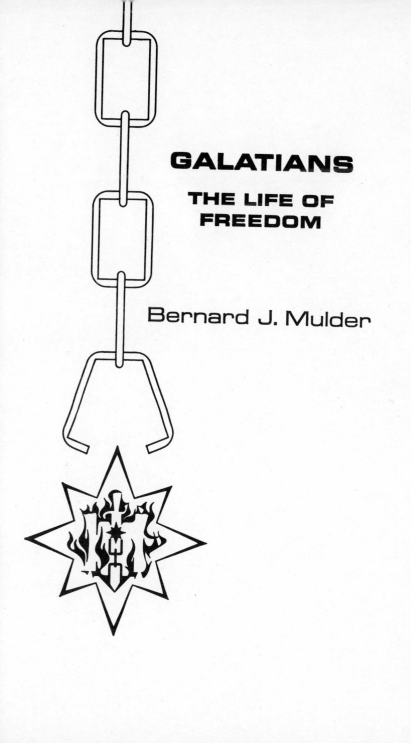

GALATIANS

THE LIFE OF FREEDOM

Bernard J. Mulder

1 The Gospel Reaches Galatia

ADVANCE STUDY

For background for your study of Galatians read Luke's account of Paul's visit to Galatia, Acts 13:1–3, 13–52. What happened to Paul in Galatia? What ideas did he preach there?

"I will not eat with you," said Shylock in Shakespeare's *Merchant of Venice*. "I will buy with you, sell with you, talk with you, walk with you, and so following; but I will not eat with you . . ." The bard presents Shylock as the Jewish moneylender who attempted to exact from Antonio's body, the forfeit, of the pound of flesh which the latter had pledged for a loan to Bassanio. Shylock could do business with Gentiles, but he could not eat with them because the meat or fowl which Gentiles ate was not "kosher" meat —that is, from animals or birds killed in the presence of a rabbi by cutting their throats and draining out the God-given life blood.

Had Shakespeare read Paul's Letter to the Galatians? We do not know, of course, but we may surmise that as a baptized Christian who showed considerable theological insight he may well have done so. Certainly one of the major concerns that prompted the writing of the Letter to the Galatians was also Shylock's problem— could Jews and Gentiles eat together? The Christian congregations in Galatia were composed largely of Gentile converts. Happy in their new way of life, they were soon disturbed by Jewish teachers who said that the Gentiles could not be truly Christian until they had first become Jews—that is, submitted to the rite of circumcision and agreed to obey the Jewish food laws. And until these Gentiles thus became "first-class Christians," the Christians of Jewish background would not eat with them.

There was similar confusion elsewhere. The notable Peter, leader of the apostolic preaching-teaching team, had come to Antioch and had not hesitated to sit down to dinner with the Gentile Christians. Then when other Jews came from Jerusalem, Peter, "fearing the circumcision party" as Paul puts it, changed his attitude and, like Shylock, said, "I will not eat with you." No wonder that the ordinary lay men and women in the Galatian churches were confused and upset. Both to reassure them and "straighten them out" Paul writes the letter. How he answers the questions and solves the problems is in the letter. Do you wonder that Paul, the fiery evangelist, got "hot under the collar" when he saw what Peter was doing and what was happening to his Galatian converts? How will you react as you read the story and find its relevance in this present day?

Galatia and Its People

To better understand these events, we need some background information. Take a look at the map on p. 337 and refresh your memory as to where Galatia was in Asia Minor. Think of it in relation to Jerusalem in Palestine with which we are more familiar. This will tell us where Paul traveled as messenger of the good news to the Gentiles. The early history is not too clear, but we do know that in about 300 B.C. the area was conquered and settled by descendants of wild Gallic tribes. Greeks and Persians in turn ruled the land. Then came Rome in 25 B.C., forming the country into a Roman province. The Roman conquerors allowed the people of the country to maintain their own local government as well as their religion. This religion was mainly Cybelene worship.

Cybele, in mythology often called the mother of the gods, was the goddess of nature. Primarily she was thought of as a deification of the earth, reproducing and sustaining the life of nature. Secondarily, she was the nourishing mother of man. It was said that she haunted mountain and forest vastnesses accompanied by trains of wild attendants. She was ministered to by eunuch priests who were called Galli. The people practiced orgiastic rites and revelries in honor of her and of her lover Attis. Phrygia was early the chief center of her followers (see map). By 204 B.C. the Romans had imported her worship directly, and in their mythological system she

became the mother of Zeus, the king of Roman gods. When the Romans later conquered Galatia they settled some 10,000 Jews in the area.

The Galatians themselves were an excitable people. Earlier they had been described as barbarians, the men being known as "raiding warriors." Because they loved excitement, the Romans had often used them as mercenaries. Fortune changed often for them; they were now for and now against the Roman rulers, until the day came when Rome finally put an end to the maneuvering, made Galatia a Roman province, and appointed a "king of Galatia." It was among such people that Paul lived and preached and won converts on his first great missionary journey.

The First Missionary Journey

Paul's trip to Galatia is history. Luke tells the story in Acts 13 —14. The scene in itself is graphic, for the missionary zeal of the congregation at Antioch in Syria will always be remembered. This was an amazingly unselfish church, befitting a people who were the first to be called by the name Christian (even though the name may originally have been used in a scoffing way). As a Christian church they tried the novel experiment of sending their own best preachers into the world untouched by Christianity to wrestle with evil and to bring the good news of the gospel. In this way Paul and Barnabas started out as a preaching team.

How did Paul approach his work, a task in which he would be engaged all the rest of his life? We can get some understanding of the matter by taking a closer look at Acts 13. For instance, examine Acts 13:1–3. What do these verses say to you about the church at Antioch? Do you think that there is any significance in the fact that fasting is mentioned twice in three verses?

Verses 4–12 tell of the exciting events that took place as Barnabas and Paul visited the island of Cyprus. In verses 13–14 we see the missionary team landing on the coast of Asia Minor and then pushing on inland to Antioch of Pisidia, which lies in the Roman providence of Galatia. On the Sabbath they attended the synagogue and, according to Jewish custom, after the law and the prophets had been read, the visitors were invited to speak. In verses 16–41 Luke gives us Paul's sermon. Of course, Luke was not there, and surely there was no modern day stenographer or tape recorder in the house. The sermon is likely an illustration of Paul's preaching style, the content of which Luke must have heard many times on later missionary journeys. What Paul preached at Pisidian Antioch was the same good news which ultimately led to the conversion of the readers of his Letter to the Galatians.

The Missionary Sermon

Undoubtedly Paul said more than is here recorded. You can read the sermon in three minutes. Most people today would not be happy if their preacher was that brief. What did the Apostle say in this first sermon as a missionary? Did he follow today's generally accepted sermon structure plan of three major points or "memory pegs"? As you outline the sermon and look at its content, remember that the congregation was made up of Jews, "men of Israel," and of a number of Gentiles who had accepted the Jewish faith, "you that fear God" (Acts 13:16). Compare your outline now with the following, and do not be afraid to differ:

(1)   A brief review of the history of Israel from the Exodus to
       King David (Acts 13: 17–22).
(2)   The announcement of great David's greater Son (Acts
       13:23–37).
       (a)   His forerunner; his life, trial, crucifixion, and bur-
              ial; the Resurrection.
       (b)   A fulfillment of Scripture: Psalm 2; Isaiah 55;
              Psalm 16.
(3)   The application (Acts 13:38–41).
       (a)   This is the gospel, "the good news . . . promised to
              the fathers."
       (b)   Here is freedom from the burden of the law of
              Moses.
       (c)   In Christ there is forgiveness of sins.
       (d)   A solemn warning against unbelief (a free quota-
              tion from the prophets).

*Would you think that this was a good sermon if your pastor
used this outline on a given Sunday morning? Why did Paul call
special attention to Israel's history and put emphasis on King
David? How did the Scripture quotations help to present Jesus?*
[Some study suggestions and questions are *italicized* in each chapter.
Your understanding of Galatians and your experience in the study
group will both be enriched if you carry out these suggestions or
answer these questions through your personal study of the letter.]
In Romans we read that "through the law comes knowledge of sin,"
as Paul emphasizes here also. Note carefully that when Paul says in
verse 39 that "by him every one that believes is freed . . ." he is
talking about justification by faith, which is a central theme of the
Galatian letter.

How was this first missionary sermon received? Verses 42–48
of Acts 13 tells the story. A visiting preacher is often told as he
shakes hands with the congregation, "Please come again." This was
true for Paul and Barnabas. The people begged the team to come
back the next Sabbath, and many, both Jews and Gentiles, followed
the missionaries down the street and continued to ask questions.

When the next Sabbath came, the synagogue was packed and
the crowd overflowed into the street. ". . . the whole city gathered

together to hear the word of God." There were no loudspeakers, of course, but it would have made little difference. No sooner had Paul begun to preach than hecklers interrupted the sermon. These were jealous leaders who had tried hard to fill the synagogue but had never succeeded. They called Paul names and contradicted his teaching. Have you ever heard a preacher heckled in the middle of his sermon? I have been heckled, but only once in more than forty years of preaching. As I was preaching a man stood up and shouted, "I don't believe it," and with that stalked out of the church. I continued the sermon.

Paul, however, could not go on, for the hecklers did not leave. Unafraid, Paul announced that since the Jews would not listen, the team would now turn to the Gentiles as God had commanded his servant (Isa. 49:6). The Gentiles were glad and, as the evangelists continued their work, many believed. However, in mistaken religious zeal, devout Jewish men and women continued the persecution so that the missionaries "shook off the dust from their feet" and went on to the next town, Iconium.

What did all of this mean for the church of Jesus Christ of which we are members? Up until that second Sabbath in Antioch, the mission of the church had been to "the lost sheep of the house of Israel" and to Gentiles who had been converted to Judaism. But in Pisidian Antioch there were Gentiles who had never been in the synagogue before. At best these people worshiped Greek and Roman gods and reveled in myths and legends. But at the same time they were fearful because they believed that the gods often caused suffering and laughed when men were in misery and pain. Paul, in the name of Christ, brought freedom from fear, and the people quickly responded. Considering the nature of the Galatian people, the response was probably in part impulsive, and there certainly was not a full understanding of the gospel. Yet the new sense of freedom brought unrestrained joy. Through this first missionary sermon and God's blessing, the church had become the church for all people.

Why Study Galatians

How long the missionary team remained in each town we are not told. But it must have been a comparatively short time, for the entire journey took only a little more than a year. Try now to imagine yourself in the position of a person who has heard Paul and has had as a result a rich and transforming spiritual experience. Your heart has been touched by the story of the Savior, Jesus, of his death for you and his Resurrection. Your feelings of guilt or frustration or hopelessness have been relieved by the good news of God's love for you. You have listened to Paul and Barnabas, prayed with them, sung with them, and your heart is full of joy. You are determined to be God's faithful servant. But now Paul is gone and you have only the memory of his words and the certainty of your own wonderful experience. What do you do now? What does it mean to be a faithful servant of God in your own particular situation? You really need some advice and there are those who offer to answer your questions. You want an answer, but do they have the right answer?

We will look in detail in chapter 2 at the "help" that was offered to the Galatian Christians. Paul writes this letter to warn them against false helpers and to put before them in unmistakable terms how men become Christians and how men are to live the Christian life once they have accepted Jesus Christ. This is why Galatians speaks to our needs today.

There are many leaders and causes offering "life." There are many voices saying to the Christian, "To be a first-class Christian do this . . . or that . . . or the other." Here in the Letter to the Galatians is a word with authority that speaks to these great issues of life. And this is our reason for studying Galatians or any of the sixty-six books of the Bible. For it is a legitimate question to ask, Why should we study the Bible at all?

The Bible is an ancient book. In its language it is a reflection of the culture of its day. Its people are largely rural, and its stories are of shepherds and sheep, of cattle and oxen, of tents and wells of water. Its universe is a three-decked world, with heaven and the stars above, the earth under a great canopied dome, and the great deep beneath. The history of its people is but a line here and there in the stories of such world dynasties as Egypt and Persia and Rome.

Yet most of the history of these world powers of the past is but a record in libraries, studied now and again by collegians to gain a credit and perused by researchers who are writing new books for

Ph.D. degrees, but unknown to the multitudes of earth's peoples. But the stories of this little people, Israel, and the spiritual interpretation of these events by those who have lived within the Christian community, are known throughout the whole wide earth. We call the record of these events plus their interpretation the Word of God.

We come back to the question. Does this 3,000 word letter, written 1900 years ago, have any relevance for us who live in this space age? As seekers after the truth and as Christians, we are interested in such questions as these:

(1) How and when was Christianity born?

(2) When is one really a Christian? What are the qualities of a genuine Christian?

(3) What is the relationship of law and Christian freedom?

(4) What is the relationship of discipleship and discipline?

There are a host of other questions and problems that touch us where we live today, for ancient heresies often have parallels in present ones, and human need and the human situation change very little.

Driving along a Tennessee road I saw signs saying "Get right with God!" How does one get right with God? How is the sinful record written on the slate of our lives erased? When is the "fullness of time" for me? What does it mean to forgive? When are we free to do just as we please, if ever? Do I ever like to give up things? Do I have to make sacrifices? What does the cross mean to me?

Relevant? you ask. Does it touch me where I live? Let us get on with it. The answers are in Galatians. This letter is a "revelation of God." It tells us not only what a man can do for God but what God has done for him.

REVIEW

1. What do you hope to learn from this study of Galatians?

2. What ideas in Paul's sermon to the Galatians (Acts 13:16–41) mean most to you?

3. How do you think Paul's sermon would be different were he to preach in your own town today?

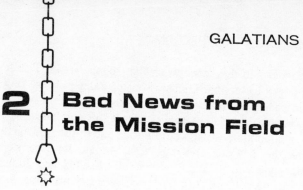

2 Bad News from the Mission Field

ADVANCE STUDY

Before you read further in this book take fifteen or twenty minutes and read Paul's Letter to the Galatians. What ideas in its first five verses do you find developed elsewhere in this letter?

The Disturbing Preachers

Do your fellow church members sometimes listen to preachers, perhaps via radio or TV, who bring an unsettling influence? Some ask questions which they do not answer and present problems which they do not solve. Others cause confusion, or raise doubts, or even contradict what the pastor of one's church is teaching.

This last was the case in the Galatian churches. Just where these visitors came from we are not quite certain. It is possible that they were from the Jewish community itself. Some ten thousand Jews had been settled in the Galatian area when Rome conquered that part of the country, but according to Roman custom of the time they had been allowed to maintain their own religious practices and faith. Whatever their origin, these men said to the newborn Gentile converts that they were not really Christian at all. "You must first become a Jew before you can be a Christian," they said. What this implied we will see as we get deeper into the letter. But let it be said here that this declaration flatly contradicted what the minister-evangelist, Paul, had preached. Do you wonder that his ire was up or that he dashed off a letter with hot-headed haste?

The Problem

How long the evangelists had remained in Galatia is uncertain.

343

But no sooner had they gone when the trouble began. The Jewish teachers began to say that Paul was out of order in suggesting that one could change from pagan to Christian in one step. As we said earlier, whether these false teachers came from the outside or from the Jewish community itself we do not know. But they strongly insisted that the new converts must first become Jews before they could possibly become Christians. We call these teachers Judaizers.

The idea that Gentiles could become Jews was not without precedent. Isaiah had talked about Jews becoming "a light to the nations" (see Isa. 49:1–6). The prophet Zechariah too had prophesied that "ten men from the nations of every tongue shall take hold of the robe of a Jew," and walk with him into the Holy City (Zech. 8:23). There are no records, but without doubt there were understanding Gentiles who appreciated the moral teachings and promises of the prophets above the myths and legends of the Greek gods, and who embraced the Jewish faith. In Acts we meet also the "God-fearers," who accepted Jewish doctrine and morals, but who did not actually become Jews. They attended the synagogue (see Acts 13:16), and they often responded enthusiastically to the Christian gospel when they heard it.

When many of the recent converts turned so quickly from the simple faith in Jesus which Paul had taught them, he was both angry and astonished. He was angry because the Jewish teachers belittled the authority of the gospel he preached. Of this more will be said later. He was astonished that many of the converts listened so readily to the false teachers and were about to conform to their teaching. This astonishment reflected displeasure, it is true, but there was much more of sorrow in it. Paul understood that it was difficult for a new convert to hold to a sound faith, especially when a contrary teaching came so soon after his conversion. Therefore in calling them back to the gospel he writes in the spirit of restoring one who has been overtaken in a fault. These Galatians of quick enthusiasms and quickly cooling emotions were not deliberate evil-doers. But their eyes had been blinded; now they did not see clearly. They were suffering a great loss in changing so quickly from the freedom which Christ gives to the ritual and yoke of the Jewish laws. Paul was sad and distressed and deeply perplexed.

Who Were the Judaizers?

Dare we sit for a moment where the Jewish teachers sat? These men held the law in high regard and as God-given. They were thus offended by Paul's ignoring of the law and by his teaching that the Gentiles could become God's people without circumcision and performance of the law.

These teachers were undoubtedly Christians who were zealous to preserve Jewish customs and to graft the gospel onto the law of Moses. What they taught can be determined on the basis of Paul's answer to them. They did not deny the Messiahship of Jesus nor his Resurrection. They apparently also agreed that faith in Christ was necessary for salvation. But faith was secondary. First it was necessary to become a Jew—that is, to accept circumcision as a religious rite and to keep the law of Moses. Thus the Judaizers said that salvation is by faith and works. They boasted that they were descendants of Abraham, and they may have claimed to have been trained by the Apostles in Jerusalem. They also suggested that Paul was a heretic and that, as a former persecutor of the church, he was out of step with the Apostles, while the good news which he had brought could not possibly be the whole truth. Did not Christ observe the law? Did not the Apostles in Jerusalem continue to live as Jews lived? Were not both the Sabbath and Sunday observed in worship?

When many of the new converts wavered, Paul did not hesitate to put the false teachers in their place. His sorrow for the too-easily-swayed new converts is balanced by righteous anger against the false teachers. The Galatian letter, dictated in great haste and under severe pressure, was the first effective step to halt the influence of the Judaizers. Paul argues that this "contrary gospel" was in reality no gospel at all. The issue was and continues to this day to be clear-cut. Are we saved through faith alone or by faith plus good works? And if salvation comes by faith alone, what is the relationship of works to faith as one seeks to live the Christian life?

The Nature of a Letter

A letter is not an essay. The latter is a treatise in which both a proposition, with its discussion and argument, and a conclusion are fully presented. A letter, on the other hand, is but one side of a dialogue. The writer assumes that the recipient of a letter will understand what the talk is all about. The problems or questions or situations are understood by the reader, who is himself the partner in the dialogue.

The translators of the K.J.V. in 1611 called Galatians, as well as all the other writings of Paul, "epistles." The translators of the R.S.V. say that the writings are "letters." Is there a difference? An epistle is usually considered a rather formal letter, but Galatians has very little that is formal about it. It is a hot-under-the-collar document. It is like a sword flashing in a swordsman's hand.

We, however, are reading this letter nineteen hundred years later and almost certainly not in Galatia. And Paul was not thinking of us when he wrote. As a friend and teacher he was writing to his friends in the churches of Galatia. Nor did he have any thought when he wrote that one day his letter would be selected by the church under the guidance of the Holy Spirit for a chosen place in the holy Scriptures and that generations of people would look upon the words of this letter as the Word of God, as we still do today.

Galatians was not written as a general essay in theology, but to deal with a particular situation. The problem it confronts, however, is by no means unique to Galatia.

A Study of Galatians 1:1–5

These five verses form an introduction to the letter. Read the verses carefully, possibly in several translations, and then try to answer the following questions:

(1)   *The very first word reminds us of what obvious difference between ancient letters and modern ones?*

(2)   *What one point does Paul make about his apostleship?*

(3)   *Is there a relationship between the end of verse four and the main thrust of verse one?*

(4)   *Why does Paul mention his brethren in verse two?*

(5)   *What does the New Testament mean by an apostle? grace? peace? "the present evil age"?*

Not all of these are easy questions, obviously, but real Bible study takes time and thought and, where they are available, some additional resources.

If an author is an able writer, he gives you a clue to what he thinks is important by emphasizing it in some fashion. Paul in these five verses mentions several key words—see question five above—and we need to learn what these words mean. Apart from these words, what thoughts does he set forth in two almost parenthetical sections, that which follows the word "apostle" in verse 1, and verses 4–5? Over one-half of the words in these five verses are found in these two parenthetical passages, which suggests that to Paul these ideas were extremely significant. Can you relate them to the problems that caused Paul to write this letter?

Finally, if this passage is a faithful introduction, what is Paul going to write about? In all his letters the Apostle follows the same style. In this letter he begins with a personal note, the defense of his apostleship; then comes the doctrinal section, on justification by faith; it is followed by the application of the doctrine to personal and church life. As you read and study the letter you will discover the lines of this broad outline.

Several of today's scholars have concluded that this letter is the first from the pen of the Apostle. I share in that conclusion. However, many commentators, especially the old, established ones, feel differently about it. But whether first or not, this letter has by its content changed the course of history. That is why it is often called the Magna Charta of the Christian church.

REVIEW

1. With this much introduction, now what do you hope to learn from this course?

2. In what sense is the problem of the Galatian church one which concerns you? your church?

3. In what way does Christ "deliver us from the present evil age" (verse 4) of the twentieth century? In what ways does he not do so?

4. Suppose you were a Galatian Christian. Some have said that you must keep certain laws in order to live up to your new faith. Paul says you need not. How would you know which was right?

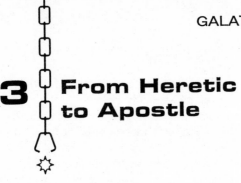

3 From Heretic to Apostle

ADVANCE STUDY

Before you read what follows, open your Bible and read Galatians 1:6–17. Look for answers to these questions:

1. What is the main point Paul is trying to make by telling about his call?

2. How does Paul know that what he has been preaching is true?

3. How do these verses compare with Acts 9:1–22?

"I'll be damned!" What a startling exclamation with which to begin! One hears it now and again when someone is suddenly surprised or when something quite contrary to the expected has taken place. But if you are surprised to have the words used here, read Galatians 1:6–9. For Paul, in writing to the Galatians, said exactly that, referring both to the troublemakers and to himself as well. Even angels from heaven are not spared. "If I, or angels or anyone else preaches a contrary gospel, let him be damned," he says, in effect.

The R.S.V. translates the word "accursed." The N.E.B. uses "let him be outcast."[1] And the K.J.V. says "anathema," a word which is almost like the original Greek word. Martin Luther suggests that this damnation was a curse pronounced by church authority.[2] The word itself originally meant "devoted to God," in the sense that a dove or a sheep was so dedicated as a sacrifice. But in the act of sacrifice the bird or animal died, so the word came to mean "a curse." It was in this sense that the cross of Christ was "an accursed thing." The N.E.B. use of the word "outcast" makes one think of

Jesus' reference to Gehenna, the place of casting out, where there was "weeping and gnashing of teeth." Paul undoubtedly meant that spiritual state in which one is alienated from God by sin.

The preacher of a contrary gospel exposed himself to divine anger, for by him "The divine gospel is branded as a lie, the lying Gospel is offered as the truth; the double falsehood leads souls to destruction," says Lenski.[3] If I do this, or others do so, or even angels, let him be damned, says Paul.

Before we face the natural question, How could Paul be so certain about the true gospel? Let us see how the occasion for the use of these strong words developed.

A Flashback

This technique is often employed by television and motion pictures to establish the background for a present experience. That the method is older than the modern screen is well attested by Paul in this letter written almost 2000 years ago. Paul had not shared the earthly life of Jesus as Peter and others had experienced it, yet he understood the significance of our Lord's life, death, and Resurrection more clearly than any other. He knew that his apostleship and the ability to lead his own and others' lives in a new direction had come to him on the basis of the manifestation of the risen Jesus Christ. How could he convince these false teachers, as well as the confused Galatians and all of us, of the genuineness of his present zeal and the reasonableness of his amazing confidence? The answer is this very ancient but still used technique of the flashback.

Paul, the Persecutor

Some years ago I worshiped one Sunday morning with a congregation of one of the so-called sects. The minister publicly acknowledged that he was uneducated. This surely was no disgrace, except that he tried to put himself in a class with "the Apostle Paul, who was also an uneducated man but a great preacher of the gospel." Here the minister's lack of education showed all too clearly, for Paul was undoubtedly one of the best educated men of his time.

Saul, as he was called in his youth, was born in Tarsus of Cilicia (see map) in a Jewish family. Mark Anthony had given all of Cilicia's citizens Roman citizenship, a matter of which they were very proud (read Acts 22:22–29). As a child and teen-ager Paul must have had all the advantages of the synagogue school and the best teachers in Tarsus, as he studied not only the Mosaic law but the traditions built around it as well. Although his family probably had some wealth and position, Paul as a student also learned a trade (Acts 18:3). It has been suggested that he studied harder than anyone else: "His was a zeal that never slept," says one commentator. He did nothing by halves. Then he went to college in Jerusalem, became a special pupil of Gamaliel, and was "thoroughly trained in every point of . . . ancestral law" (Acts 22:3, N.E.B).

At college the pupil became more zealous than the teacher. Professor Gamaliel, the first to bear the title of *Rabban* (our master, our great one) rather than the ordinary *Rabbi* (my master), was an honored Pharisee and member of the Sanhedrin. It was he who advised care in the trial of Peter and the other Apostles (read Acts 5:34–39). Paul, in the zeal of his youth, became a rabid traditionalist and a fanatical defender of his belief. In his mind the followers of Jesus were heretics.

What was his basic problem? Fantastic as it may seem, it was a question of love. *Paul hated Jesus because he loved Christ so much.* Think about that sentence for a while. To Paul the followers of the Way, as he called it, were heretics. The freedom of the Christians was the opposite of all that the sacred law demanded. This sect must at all costs be destroyed.

Consider the ends to which his fanatical zeal drove Paul; some of these are his own words:

(1) He "laid waste the church" (Acts 8:3).

(2) He "dragged off men and women and committed them to prison" (Acts 8:3).

(3) He breathed "threats and murder against the disciples" (Acts 9:1).

(4) He planned to bring Christians "bound" to Jerusalem (Acts 9:2).

(5) He "persecuted this Way [Christians] to the death" (Acts 22:4).

(6) " . . . in every synagogue [he] imprisoned and beat those who believed" (Acts 22:19).

(7) He voted the death penalty for heresy (Acts 26:10).

(8) He tried to make Christians blaspheme, going even to for-
    eign cities in his zeal (Acts 26:11).

Then God stepped in. "It is time to stop," God said. "It's time
that you discover that Jesus whom you hate and Christ whom you
love are one and the same Person." What did God do?

On the Road to Damascus

As I rattled along the road from Beirut to Damascus in an old
Ford car, I thought of Paul and his experience. He was likely
traveling on foot to this old city, there to beat, imprison, and possibly destroy some of his fellowmen for their heresy in following
Jesus and the Way. In his pocket he had letters of authority from
the chief priests in Jerusalem.

Then suddenly a light flashed. He was blinded by its intensity.
He had a vision. And he was converted. There on the Damascus
Road, by a sudden illumination, Paul understood that the Jesus
whom he persecuted was the Christ whom he loved, that Jesus
Christ was God's Son. Can we explain what happened?

The Conversion Experience

We have only Paul's own story as he insists that the source of
his gospel is God. As Luke tells of Paul's conversion (Acts 9:1–9),
there was a flash of light; Paul heard a voice, was blinded, and was
by this voice instructed to enter the city and wait for his commission. His companions on the road heard the voice too but saw no
one. On seeing that their leader had been blinded, they led him into
the city. The experience raises several interesting questions.

The first is, did Paul at this time know anything about Jesus?
Considering the fact that Paul thought of the followers of Jesus as
heretical enemies, he surely, as a persecutor, must have studied
their beliefs and observed their way of life. We have detailed information about one specific case. While Paul was in Jerusalem the
number of the disciples grew, and it became necessary to appoint
deacons to handle the charity work of the church (read Acts 6 and
7). One of the seven men elected was Stephen. The latter was more
than a deacon, however, as we tend to think of the office today.
". . . full of faith and of the Holy Spirit," says Luke, he began to
preach and to work miracles.

Then the leaders of the synagogue tried to trap him, arguing with him and bringing false accusations against him. And when nothing succeeded they summoned him before the Council. Here Stephen made his defense, but for his manifest heresy he was stoned to death. Those who threw the stones shed their coats, and young Paul became a coat-holder. He lifted no hand to save the young deacon; rather, approving of murder, he became a murderer in his heart *in the name of his religion*. But how much, even unconsciously, of what Stephen testified concerning Jesus had found its way into Paul's heart and slightly softened that flintlike man for the revelation that was to come? Only God knows, even as only God knows what goes on in any man.

But what impression do you get from reading 1:13–14 [Where no book is named, the scriptural reference is to Galatians.] *about Paul's attitude as he went toward Damascus? Would you imagine him to be burdened by a sense of guilt, anxiously looking for deliverance? Or was Paul a successful young man, doing his job effectively, admired by his friends? Was Paul in anguish or was he whistling?* Don't guess or say what you have always heard—see what Paul says in this passage from Galatians.

Conversion and Paul's Revelation

A second question concerns the conversion experience itself. Paul did not call it conversion, he called it a revelation (1:12).

What is conversion? As we think of it in the Christian faith, conversion is a spiritual and moral change which comes with a definite and decisive adoption of the Christian faith. It is a change of attitude involving both repentance and faith; it means a turning from sin to God and coming to God in full surrender and trust. Psychologically, many have a sudden and highly emotional experience, one which does not always last. If it does not, this is not true conversion. According to the Reformed faith, there is no backsliding for the truly changed person.

Not all of this happened on the Damascus Road. Paul was not changed from a bad man to a good man. He had tried to live such a good life that he could claim blamelessness before men (Phil. 3:6). Neither was Paul converted to a totally different religion, as a person might change from Hinduism to Christianity. He continued to hold to the Old Testament, but he insisted that the gospel had always been in the plan of God, the law being a teacher to lead one to the Savior (3:23–24). It seems that he had long known this but had fought against it with all his might. His fanatical persecuting zeal was but an over-compensation for his own inner restlessness, until God said, "Stop."

Paul describes his experience as an act of God. It was not a theological proposition which he had worked out in study and thought, but a personal deliverance from darkness into light. This revelation had in it all the elements of what some call the *Ordo Salutis* (the order of salvation): regeneration, conversion, illumination, and calling. On the Damascus Road Paul faced at one and the same time his *destiny* as one set apart before birth; his *call* by God's grace to see God's Son; and his *mission* to preach him among the Gentiles (1:15–16). Nor was his revelation for his individual salvation alone. It was to fit him to herald the gospel which had been given to him.

This claim that he had received his call directly from God meant to Paul that his call did not come because of his holy life, his intense Pharisaical faith, his prayers, or his work, but only through God's grace. This election to high office from before his birth, his conversion and call, and the beginning of his ministry in fulfillment of the call (Act 9:20) are all set before the Galatians to guarantee the authority of the gospel he had preached. All of this had been God's doing; therefore his gospel, and his gospel alone, is God's truth.

To what extent would you say that Paul's conversion was a typical one? Has there been an experience in your life that could be compared in any way to what happened to Paul on the Damascus Road? Do you have a sense of destiny? call? mission? Does Paul suggest that others should expect an experience similar to his?

After the Revelation

The Damascus Road experience must have made a profound impression upon Paul's sensitive mind and heart. Instead of rushing out to talk it over with others he went into Arabia to think through what he had seen and heard, to consolidate in his own mind the relationship of his past attitudes to his present feelings. But it is also quite possible, considering Paul's natural zeal, that he soon began his missionary work by preaching in Arabia, east of Damascus, to the descendants of Abraham by his wife Keturah and by Hagar (Gen. 25). It was thus that he would have incurred the enmity of the Arabian king, Aretas (2 Cor. 11:32–33). It has also been suggested that as he began his ministry with these whom the Old Testament shows to be cut off from the covenant, though with a claim to it by blood ties, so he at the end of his life was anxious to go to Tarshish (Spain), the land which Jonah was providentially kept from visiting. It would certainly not be strange for him thus to root his missionary effort in the Old Testament.

Who Is a Disciple?

Our Lord's last command to his followers was to "Go . . . and make disciples of all nations" (Matt. 28:19). Paul was obedient to this command as he brought the gospel to the Galatians. This directive of the Christ has not been cancelled. It is still on the books and must be heeded now more than ever. World population is increasing faster than church membership is growing. We need disciples of Jesus. What and who is a disciple?

A disciple is a learner. He is one who accepts the doctrines of his teacher and assists in spreading them. Almost all famous leaders have had or do have disciples: Socrates, Plato, Kant, Marx, John the Baptist, Jesus, and hosts of others yesterday and today. In the biblical record the word is used 260 times in the Gospels and Acts (see for instance Matt. 22:16; John 1:35; 9:28).

What did Jesus say about the nature of discipleship? He said that the true disciple cannot escape the false accusations and slanders that come to his master (see Matt. 10:24–25). The disciple must also be prepared to give up all that he has when it is necessary (Luke 14:33). This is illustrated by the classic story of the disciple of a Roman master who heard that enemies were seeking the master's life. He at once clothed himself in his master's garments in which he was found by the enemy and killed. To his memory the master erected a monument of gratitude for a disciple's loyal affection.

In another place, Jesus says that a disciple must carry a cross in order to follow the Savior (Luke 14:27), and also that if he "gives to one of these little ones even a cup of cold water because he is a disciple . . . he shall not lose his reward" (Matt. 10:42).

The words disciple and discipline are closely related. While the latter does have a secondary meaning of punishment and is often so used when we talk of church censure, its major meaning is "a course of study." This textbook itself, FROM BONDAGE TO FREEDOM, and all of the Covenant Life Curriculum compose a discipline of the Christian church for the instruction and training of disciples in the art of assisting in the spreading of the gospel.

Do you think Paul could have kept still after his conversion? Look again at verse 10 where the Apostle stresses that his loyalty is to Jesus Christ alone. Can a true servant of Christ be a man-pleaser? Have you thought through the quality of your personal discipleship?

REVIEW

1. How did Paul know his understanding of the gospel and the Christian life was true? How do we know our understanding is true?

2. How is Paul's encounter with Christ like our own, and how is it unique?

3. When Paul was converted he went through much discipline in order to become the disciple he later was. What discipline do you personally expect to go through in order to learn, as a good disciple, what message God has for you in this course?

4. What message from God, if any, have you gotten from your study so far?

4 The Unity of the Early Church

ADVANCE STUDY

Before reading the commentary which follows read these verses. Answer:

1. *What is the main point Paul is making about his gospel?*
2. *What is the main point Paul is making about himself?*
3. *What is the main point Paul is making about the church?*

Telling the Truth

"By God, I am not lying. I am telling the truth." Strong words coming from the pen of Paul as he writes to the Galatians! But here they are in the letter (1:20). Calvin explains that an oath of this nature was employed only on weighty occasions. It was a direct appeal to the judgment seat of God by a man determined to maintain the integrity and truth of his words and actions. Swearing to "tell the truth, the whole truth, and nothing but the truth" in a court of law before a judge is today's counterpart.

Paul is maintaining that the gospel he preached was not from men but was a revelation of Jesus Christ. So condemnatory were his accusers and hecklers that the Apostle felt it necessary to swear before God he was telling the truth: he did not go up to Jerusalem to be instructed by the Apostles nor to get their official approval (we will go into this in more detail on pp. 357–360).

What in the world had happened to cause this outburst? Part of the issue at stake was the unity of the church. Paul had started off considering Jesus a heretic. Now he was being accused by the Judaizers of perverting the gospel. And he in turn was calling them heretics. Confusion compounded!

Heresy is defined as adherence to a religious opinion opposed to the authorized doctrinal standards of a church or to generally accepted beliefs. In former days, when religion was a state matter, heresy was a crime. A classic example for churches of Reformed theology is the burning of Servetus in 1553 by the city council of Geneva, because he had denied infant baptism and the Trinity. Calvin approved of the death sentence but not of the method of execution, but the Council outvoted him, being at that time dominated by his enemies.

In a heresy the character of the heretic is always involved. Does he know what he is talking about? What are his motives? What motivated Paul when he called Jesus and his disciples heretics? And now the tables have turned! Paul writes to solve the problem and swears to the truth of his words.

The Purpose of This Chapter

The Scripture passage is a personal statement by Paul of what he did following his conversion. The false teachers had accused him of having hurried to Jerusalem to be instructed by the Apostles, and thus they claimed that he was preaching a secondhand gospel which he misunderstood. Paul's usefulness as a minister was at stake. He felt it necessary to convince the Galatians that his gospel was the word of Christ which he had learned from Christ himself, not from any man. That's why he writes about where he went, what he did, and how he was received.

To study this passage we must begin with the last verses of the previous passage to see just what Paul did when God said to him, "Stop!" *Read 1:17—2:1 carefully and list the five things Paul says he did, following him on the map.* What was the time span? What do you think the Apostle was doing during the long "silent" years? And before you read further in this text, ask yourself what 1:1—2:10 says about the unity of the early church in its theology and practice. What evidence is there for unity? Is there evidence of some disunity? What are the practical results of unity? What are the implications of all this for today?

Going Up to Jerusalem, 1:18–24

Of course, Paul was no stranger to Jerusalem. Here he had been in school under Professor Gamaliel. Here he had joined the party of the Pharisees and had become a rabid defender of every jot and tittle of the Jewish law. From here he had set out towards Damascus to persecute the Christians. In Jerusalem itself his name was a fearful byword in the Christian community. It must have taken courage to go back there with an entirely different story. His former friends, the Jewish leaders, would hate him as a traitor; the Christians would shun him, for he had tortured and killed their relatives and friends and it would be hard to believe that he was now one of them. Our past often rises up to haunt us and we meet it only by facing it squarely.

This *first* visit to Jerusalem as a believer came three years after his conversion (1:18). He came, as he says, to visit Peter who was the head of the apostolic band. He did not hurry there as soon as he was converted to receive instruction, that is, to be taught the gospel, for he had received the latter directly from Christ himself. Neither did he come to receive Peter's apostolic benediction, or to seek, by association with the "first" Apostle, to gain prestige for himself. He simply tells the Galatians that he came to *visit* Peter, and he stayed for fifteen days. Lightfoot quotes Chrysostom (A.D. 347–407), the eloquent preacher-bishop of Constantinople, as saying that the word "visit" which Paul used is "A word used . . . by those who go to see great and famous cities,"[1] like one of us in America going to visit Rome or Tokyo or Cairo. Paul simply went to see a great hero of the faith.

What did they talk about? I wish that there had been a tape recorder under the davenport in Peter's house. But neither one ever told, so far as we have any record. Picture them in your imagination as they tell each other about their experiences with the living and risen Christ, of their mutual joy in the gospel, of their respective missions, and of God's blessing upon their work.

It is in connection with this visit that Paul takes the oath mentioned earlier in this chapter (1:20). One wonders why this was necessary. Paul does not say, but undoubtedly the criticism of the false teachers had caused other eyebrows to be lifted; people were asking, "Is that really all there was to that visit to Jerusalem?" This was a friendly visit to a great man and nothing more, swears

Paul. It is unfortunate that many people are so mistrustful that oaths must be taken to guarantee integrity.

On this visit Paul says that he saw "none of the other apostles except James the Lord's brother" (1:19). James, who had become a disciple after the resurrection of Jesus, was the pastor of the Jerusalem congregation. Paul calls him "the Lord's brother" but this does not necessarily mean that James was the son of Mary. Some think he was Joseph's son by an earlier marriage and thus a half brother of Jesus, but John Calvin argues that he was the son of Cleopas, the husband of Mary's sister, and thus a cousin of our Lord. In eastern lands all relatives are "brothers and sisters" in a family, something like our "kissin' " cousins in the Southland.

Whichever way it was, the fact is that he was an important person and Paul does not hesitate to tell his hecklers that James was in full agreement with him in both his theology and his mission. This was very significant. If anyone was going to feel that Paul was not Jewish enough in his doctrine and practice, it would be the head of the Jerusalem church. The fact that James voiced no complaints showed that it was not Paul, but rather his opponents, the Judaizers, who did not preach the gospel aright.

The same testimony comes from the reaction of the Judean churches. These churches were composed of Jews who had accepted Jesus Christ as their Savior-Messiah; it is most unlikely that there would be any Gentiles in them. Did they feel, from what they had heard of Paul's ministry from Peter and James, that he was a heretic who did not give adequate place in Christianity to Jewish faith and practice? No! On the contrary, ". . . they only heard it said, 'He who once persecuted us is now preaching the faith he once tried to destroy.' And they glorified God because of me" (1:23–24).

Paul's exit from the Holy City was in a hurry. He does not tell the Galatians about the incident, but Luke in writing Acts does tell the story (Acts 9:17–30). Paul's bold preaching had stirred up the Greek-speaking Jews, the Hellenists, who sought to kill him, but his Christian friends hustled him out of town to Caesarea, where he took a ship to Tarsus in Cilicia, his old hometown. Once more he took the hard road. What do you think his former friends in Tarsus would think?

Now for about eight years we do not hear from Paul or about him at all. Was he preaching and teaching and doing missionary work? We do not know, for there is no record, but it seems very likely that he was. Emil G. Kraeling suggests in *I Have Kept the Faith* that some of the things Paul refers to in 2 Corinthians 11: 23ff. may well have taken place during this period of the Apostle's ministry.[2] In the meantime Barnabas had become a leader in the church in Antioch of Cilicia. When the congregation grew, Barnabas needed help and remembered Paul. The pastor brought the latter to Antioch as co-pastor and for the next five or six years they worked together in this growing church.

The First Church World Service

Church World Service, in which the major denominations share and the proceeds of which go to relieve hunger in famine-stricken countries, is not a new principle. It all began when Paul, in company with his fellow pastor, Barnabas, made another visit to Jerusalem to deliver the contributions which had been raised in the Gentile churches for famine relief in Judea (Acts 11:27–30). The visit came fourteen years after the first one and was "by revelation" (2:2). This probably refers to the prophecy of famine which had been made by Agabus and the consequent feeling within Paul that God wanted him to take part in the effort at famine relief.

The Apostle did not tell the Galatians about the famine in the letter; his concern in mentioning this visit was its relationship to the attacks of the Judaizers. So he tells how, when he was in Jerusalem, he used the occasion to explain carefully to the leaders, the men "of repute" (2:2), in private conversation the content of the gospel which he was preaching. He wanted to make certain once more that he was doing the right thing and not "running . . . in vain."

Not all Bible students are agreed that this Jerusalem visit in 2:1 is the same as the famine relief visit of Acts 11. Some contend that this occasion in Galatians 2 was the meeting of the first church council in Jerusalem, described by Luke in Acts 15, and that Paul held his private conversations with Peter before the main meeting. But at that council important decisions were made with regard to the Gentile Christians, as you will see if you read Acts 15. These decisions touched directly upon the very problems with which Paul deals in the letter. Surely Paul would have quoted the conclusions of the council in his letter and thus stopped the slandering tongues of the false teachers if the decisions had already been made. The decisions were circulated by a general letter to all the churches and, as John Calvin says, "Undoubtedly this one word [if quoted in Paul's letter] would have shut their mouth. . . ."[3]

It is the position of this text that Paul wrote to the Galatians before the Jerusalem council referred to by Luke in Acts 15 was held, and also before Luke wrote the Acts. This view is also held by Arnold B. Rhodes in *The Mighty Acts of God,* and is ably explained by Archibald M. Hunter in the *Layman's Bible Commentary, Vol. 22.* It is also the position of that eminent Bible scholar of Reformation days, John Calvin. Students have long sought to reconcile the apparent inconsistencies in various narrative sections of the Acts and Galatians. To me, as a former newspaper reporter, these present no problem. This does not mean that they are not there or could just as well be swept under the rug. But a reporter will remember that Paul and Luke were writing from different viewpoints. Paul in the letter is telling the Galatians a personal story in order to validate before them the gospel he preached and the apostleship he held, both of which God had given him. Paul was an actor in the story which he tells. Luke, on the other hand, wrote the story of the mighty acts of the church for a different purpose. Writing from different positions and with different purposes, they often stress different facts which sometimes to the reader today seem to be inconsistent with each other.

Titus, the Greek

In talking privately with the leaders in Jerusalem, Paul was concerned to know that they approved the gospel which he preached to the Gentiles. If they too, for instance, had said that all Gentiles must be circumcised, there surely would have been disunity in the church and Paul's work would to that extent have been "in vain." However, Peter and James and John approved heartily of all that Paul and Barnabas were doing.

But more than nice words seemed to be necessary. Paul had brought with him a test case in the person of Titus. The latter was Greek and thus a Gentile and uncircumcised. What would the Jewish Christians of Jerusalem itself do when a Gentile Christian was brought into their fellowship? Would they demand that he conform to Jewish law, including above all circumcision? The Judaizers would have the Galatians think so. But Paul explains that this simply did not happen. Titus was not compelled to be circumcised, though there were some who did raise this issue. But, says Paul, ". . . we did not yield submission even for a moment, that the truth of the gospel might be preserved for you" (2:5). And in this stand he had the full support of Peter and James and John. He adds, these were men "who were reputed to be pillars"—by which he was not questioning their stature in the church, but slyly putting pressure on his critics: do you Judaizers consider them reputable? If so, why don't you do as they do?

(It should be recognized that there is some uncertainty about the text of 2:3, as reflected in its rather awkward translation in both the K.J.V. and the R.S.V. Some manuscripts indicate that Titus was circumcised. But Paul's point would still be valid, that this was not done *under compulsion;* it was not required by the pillars of the Jerusalem church. If Titus were circumcised it would rather be an act comparable to the circumcision of Timothy in Acts 16:3, by which Paul sought to remove any cause of offense to the Jews that might keep them from responding to the gospel; cf. 1 Cor. 9: 19–23.)

In making Titus a test case, Paul did not condemn circumcision as such. He simply protested its being made a condition of salvation. In many of our Protestant churches a prospective member is asked something like this: Do you believe in Jesus Christ and depend upon him alone for salvation as he is offered in the gospel? The answer must be in the affirmative. The need for defending this truth continues so long as men are told by some that salvation can only be obtained by believing in Christ and in addition doing something else. The "something else" in Galatia was circumcision and obedience to Jewish rules. Today it may be joining a certain church, or receiving a certain baptism, or having a certain emotional experience, or—what other requirement have you heard laid down?

The Christian gospel is not an easy thing to accept. It is most difficult for a sinful, prideful man to see that outside of the love and grace of God he is lost. It is equally difficult for us to take it in that by God's grace in Christ and by it alone we are saved; we don't have to add anything and we cannot add anything. This is the good news of the gospel. All of this Paul seeks to explain to the Galatian disciples who were confused by the false teachers.

Home and Foreign Missions

The end of the visit was a happy one, as Paul tells the Galatians. The "pillars" (2:9), a common reference to VIPs (Very Important People), shook hands with Paul and Barnabas and by this act said that the Gentile converts did not need to be circumcised or to obligate themselves to keep the Jewish laws in order to be first-class Christians. There was unity in both theology and practice in the church. (Note: this private act was later confirmed in the first ecumenical church council held in Jerusalem as set forth in Acts 15. The problem which Paul faced in Galatia had later become a general problem and needed to be settled once and for all time. That it was not, however, settled "for all time" is evidenced by today's proponents of a legalistic religion rather than Christian liberty, of salvation by grace plus works rather than salvation by grace alone.)

When the handshaking was over, home and foreign missions had been definitely established as a principle of the work of the church. There are those who argue that here was evidence of disunity in the early church, that Peter and Paul were not really in deep agreement. The truth is that all recognized that the gospel is one, but that their spheres of influence and areas of service were divided by divine appointment: Peter to the Jews and Paul to the Gentiles. Well and good, says the advocate of disunity, but what does this do to the command of Jesus to the Twelve to "Go therefore and make disciples of all nations . . ." (Matt. 28:19–20)? This command of Jesus was not to the individual Apostles, for each did not travel into all the world in his day. This command of Jesus was a general directive to the preaching and teaching office of the church, as applicable today as it was then. Nor did Paul and Peter confine themselves exclusively to one race. Wherever Paul traveled he always went first to the synagogue and offered the gospel to the Jews. Peter and the other Apostles likwise offered the gospel to the Gentiles, as we see Peter doing, for instance, to Cornelius and others (Acts 10:1ff).

Should Christians be interested in each others' needs? Paul had come with a gift from the Gentiles for the needy in Jerusalem, and Peter asks that this be continued (2:10). The church is one, irrespective of nation or race, and need of one is of concern to all. (Just why the church members in Jerusalem were in dire straits is uncertain. There presumably was famine in the area, as Agabus had said. Add to this the possible boycott measures imposed by the strict Jews against their fellow Jews who had become Christians and one can readily understand the need for help.)

The Unity of the Early Church

As you have studied the scriptural passage assigned in this section, undoubtedly the marks of the unity of the early church have become self-evident. Does what you have noted agree with the following?

(1) The reception of Paul, the former persecutor, by the Christians of Damascus.

(2) The warm reception of Paul and Barnabas by Peter and James, the leaders of the mother church in Jerusalem, and their sense of oneness in the gospel.

(3) The approval of Paul's ministry to the Gentiles both theologically and in practice by the Christians in Judea, even though they did not know Paul personally but only by hearsay.

(4) The giving of the right hand of fellowship by the "pillars" —Peter, James and John—in Jerusalem, and their mutual concept of the work of the church as *mission,* with its several spheres of influence and areas of service.

(5) The recognition that Jews and Gentiles alike are saved by Jesus Christ and are one because of their common faith.

How is all of this relevant for the church of today? If there is a lack of unity now, how can we bring about a closer and a better relationship in order that the church's mission may be fully realized?

REVIEW

1. *What things divide the church in our own day?*

2. *What truths, attitudes, or actions set forth in this chapter might help unite the church?*

3. *Why should the church be united? Does it really matter that we are all split up, so long as we are sincere?*

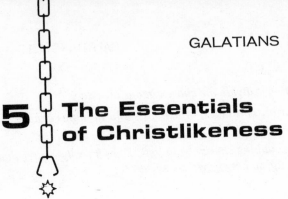

5 The Essentials of Christlikeness

ADVANCE STUDY

Before reading this chapter read 2:11–21 and give your own answer to the following:

1. What is the main issue in the controversy between Peter and Paul described here?

2. From the context in this passage what do you think Paul means by dying to the law and living by faith?

3. Exactly what does Paul put in place of laws as the guide for the Christian's life?

When Peter Came to Visit

From delivering the collections for famine relief in Jerusalem to a church supper in Antioch is a long jump. But in writing to the Galatians Paul makes it between verse 10 of the last section and verse 11 with which the study of this chapter begins. Paul and Barnabas had returned to the church at Antioch with the good news of the unity of the church. The matter of Christian Jew and Gentile convert working and walking along together seemed to be settled. There must have been real joy in the Antioch congregation that all members could sit down to their common meal without qualms of conscience or mental reservation. Then the church heard that they were to have a visit from Peter, the recognized head of the apostolic group. This was a high honor for the congregation. Paul must have been happy too, for he remembered with pleasure his earlier visit in Peter's house and the recent cordial handshake in Jerusalem. But on the first evening of Peter's visit there was a sharp clash. What happened?

In reading the Scripture passage remember that Paul now is not in Antioch but is writing to the Galatian churches. He is still defending the truth of the gospel which he had preached and the quality of his apostleship. In the serious crisis which had arisen in the Galatians churches, Paul was the one person who could clearly state what the gospel says—that one is saved by faith and lives by faith. He alone could keep the new-born church from slipping back into the ceremony and legalism of the law.

The preachers of the "contrary gospel" were not non-Christian or pagan. They believed in Christ as Savior, but said that men must also keep the Old Testament law. Some of them probably said that obedience was actually necessary for salvation; others that Christ saved but that the Jewish law was the pattern for the Christian life, and that a "good Christian" should be circumcised, obey the food laws, keep the Sabbath, etc., etc. And when the converts in Galatia quoted Paul to the contrary, these teachers insisted that Paul's gospel was not the same as that of the Apostles and that Paul did not have the authority of an Apostle.

Paul's answer is in this letter in chapters 1 and 2; we need to hear it. From Paul as he writes we must also learn again that a Christian church cannot practice any kind of class or racial distinction; we must remind ourselves of what the truth of the gospel is and what it means to be really Christlike. And then we must take a look at ourselves to see in what measure we have had this essential Christian experience.

Here, in effect, is what Paul says on these points: My conversion was entirely due to God's act of revelation; it took me totally by surprise. It certainly did not come through my obedience to law, though at that I was an expert (1:14). My pattern of living is likewise controlled by God and not by the law. In obedience to God I went to work preaching the gospel as soon as I was converted. When I finally got around to checking with some of the Christian leaders of the church like Peter and James, I found they agreed with me. They preached the same way of salvation and followed the same pattern of Christian living. There was no compulsion to keep the law. Even when I took the Gentile Titus to Jerusalem, no one compelled him to be circumcised so that he would be a first-class Christian.

And now I have heard that in Galatia there are attempts at compulsion. Some Jewish Christians are saying: To be a Christian you must submit to circumcision. Others say: To be a really first-rate Christian, it is not enough to be saved by grace; you must go on to obey the Jewish laws. Once before, Paul goes on, there had been on attempt at compulsion—at a church supper at Antioch. Let me tell you what happened and what I did about it.

Sitting Down to Supper, 2:11–14

This church supper to which the Apostle refers had been held as much as a year or more before Paul even got to Galatia. It was held at Antioch, and it will be remembered that this was a Roman city, very cosmopolitan in its population. It was a city where the citizens combined big business with much pleasure and a hedonistic philosophy of "Let us eat, drink, and be merry." The gospel had come to Antioch at an early period, likely brought by refugees. As the church grew, the Jerusalem church had sent Barnabas to guide the new church as its teacher, and he in turn had called Paul out of the obscurity of Tarsus and brought him in as his helper. It was this congregation, made up of converted Jews and Gentiles, who were first called Christians. It was also this same people who, in their enthusiasm for the gospel, had taken their Lord's word very literally to "Go into all the world . . ." and hence, under the guidance of the Holy Spirit, had sent their own pastors, namely Paul and Barnabas, into Galatia as an evangelistic missionary team.

To this thriving church Peter had come from Jerusalem for a visit. He was still aglow with the direct vision which he had received (read Acts 10:9–23). He felt deeply that what God had cleansed he must not call common. In this sense the vision had taught him how needless for Christians were the various traditions such as the food laws and circumcision. Coming to Antioch he was invited to have supper at the church.

This church supper was probably the familiar *agape,* a Greek word meaning "love" used to denote the love feasts of the early Christians. On these occasions the members of the congregation ate together, and all brought their own food except the very poor and the widows. At these "pot lucks" the people would dine in groups, such as members of a family or a congenial group of friends, much as we do at a church supper today. Likely there were some among the Jewish Christians who brought only kosher food, which was their privilege as long as this was not made a regulation for all, for this eating together was a recognized bond of brotherhood for the members of the church. Slave and free, male and female, Jew and Greek—all ate together.

Then it happened. Other visitors arrived from the Jerusalem church; Peter saw them coming and "drew back and separated himself" from the Gentile table; that is, he turned coward in his heart; probably he joined a Jewish group. The visitors, who were members of the "circumcision party," were converts to Christ but belonged to the sect of the Pharisees, to whom the prohibition against eating with the impure (Gentiles) remained a major principle (see Luke 15:2). Shame on Peter, we say. How could he have acted in this manner?

Coward and Hypocrite

These two words are often used in conjunction with each other. We must conclude that at this love feast Peter was both. A coward is a person who shows a marked lack of courage in the face of danger. Peter certainly was not a timid man, yet it was fear that made him act against his better conviction—"brave" Peter, who once proclaimed loudly that he would die with Jesus (Luke 22:33), and then, when it came to the test, lied three times about even knowing the Master! Now at the church supper he slinks slowly away from the Gentile table, shunning and disparaging them in the presence of his colleagues. Peter's fear was not of physical violence but of possible scorn and ridicule. He thought only of himself and what others would think of him. Let us each ask, What would fear do to me in like circumstances? How much am I afraid of harm to what I call my good name?

Peter was also a hypocrite. That's a strong accusation to make about anyone and should not be made lightly. A hypocrite is one who, for the purpose of winning approval, tries to appear to be other or better than he is. Often we hear it said that "actions speak louder than words." At the supper Peter acted in one way when in his heart he believed another. Unfortunately, one does not always sin alone. In this case others of the believing Jews also left the Gentile tables. Even Barnabas followed Peter's example. All of them transgressed against their better convictions and by their actions gave unwarranted and undue deference to prejudice.

This is why Paul opposed Peter "to his face" (2:11). The rebuke was not for transgressing the law. Nor was it a question of eating and drinking as such. The public chastisement was for the acted-out claim that by refusing to eat with Gentile Christians one became more righteous before God. The rebuke was no mountain-out-of-a-molehill matter. Here was one of the first principles of the Christian faith. Although Peter was the dean of the apostolic church, Paul paid no regard to either the dignity or the position of the visitor. He did not speak behind Peter's back, but faced him openly and frankly and thereby also declared his own authority in the ranks of apostleship.

There are those who say that Paul was too hard on Peter, that the rebuke should have been made in private. Often we hear that a family of a church should not wash its dirty linen in public. There is much validity in the latter, but in the Galatian churches the Judaizers were playing Peter against Paul and doing it publicly. Peter by his act of leaving the table had cast reflection upon the Gentile Christians by his holier-than-thou attitude. John Calvin says that if Paul had not stood up to Peter on the spot the church would have been split, Christian liberty would have been in danger, and the doctrine of the grace of God would have been anathema!

The Truth of the Gospel, 2:14

The basis of Paul's rebuke of Peter and the other "cowards and hypocrites" was this travesty on "the truth of the gospel." By his action Peter was asking the Gentile Christians to "get right with God" by observing the law from which he himself had been set free by his vision. In the religious sense, righteousness is a state of acceptance with God. On his visit to Jerusalem Peter had given Paul the "right hand of fellowship" (2:9) when the former had heard about the manifestation of the grace of God among the Gentiles. The Gentile Christians were thus declared acceptable to God without observing the works of the law. But at Antioch Peter had by example withheld his hand, thereby perverting the truth of the gospel. And not only Peter, but the "rest of the Jews acted insincerely . . . even Barnabas" (2:13).

The argument which the Apostle uses seems to be somewhat mixed up in its metaphors. We remember that the letter was written in haste and under great stress. It seems for a moment that he is saying that Jews by birth are righteous and that Gentiles are sinners (2:15), but Paul is using Jewish language with Jewish inferences. Jews had always counted on the works of the law as the true source of getting right with God. But now we Jews, says Paul, have discovered that we made a mistake. We have found out that Jews are sinners just like Gentiles who never knew anything about the law. We know now that God does not favor us because we do something, but that we are declared acceptable through faith in Jesus Christ. Three times in succession Paul declares that righteousness is "not by works of the law." But, Paul writes to the Galatians, Peter by his actions said something different. He was not "straightforward about the truth of the gospel" (2:14).

What Is the Truth of the Gospel?

Paul sets down in a few sentences in the letter what he must have preached to the Galatians many, many times. To him the prayer of David was real, that in the presence of the righteousness of God "no man living is righteous" (Ps. 143:2). Paul speaks out of personal experience: He had really tried as hard as possible to win God's favor by obeying every single jot and tittle of the law.

The "truth of the gospel" is that acceptance with God does not come in this manner. It comes only by trusting completely in Jesus Christ in whose name we are declared righteous. We Jews, argues Paul, with all of our superior advantage by birth and all of our pretensions to being better than other people, have gained nothing. If we now insist that by obedience to law we are righteous, as the false teachers demand, we are recommending a way towards righteousness which we know to be wrong. It is a reflection on Christ himself if we insist that his followers, whether Jew or Gentile, lack something which the law can give.

It is remarkable in how many ways the experience of Martin Luther parallels that of Paul. Luther, too, was a devout churchman but destined for the service of civil law. One day while he was out riding a severe thunderstorm arose, and he took shelter under a tree. Lightning struck the tree, but Luther's life was spared. On the spot he promised God that he would devote his life to the priesthood and, changing his course, he began to study theology. He was a good student and was given special privileges in biblical studies. Paul's letters to the Romans and Galatians were his favorites. But through it all he had no peace in his soul. He did all manner of penance and spent long periods in meditation and prayer, but no peace came.

Then he was advised to go to Rome, climb the stone steps of the Sacred Stairs on his knees, and on every step say a prayer. But he never got to the top. Somewhere along the way it seemed as if the heavens were opened and a voice spoke saying that "not . . . by works of the law but through faith in Jesus Christ" (2:16) is one declared acceptable before God. Later, kneeling in the church, with a cross in his hands, as tears of gratitude flowed, he murmured, "For me, for me." Whether the story is fact or inspired legend, we do not know, but Luther had this sort of an experience with God and went on to become in time the leader of the Reformation, and the Letter to the Galatians became the guideline for the Protestant movement in the formation of the church of Christ.

"Crucified with Christ," 2:20

Having stated the principle of how one "gets right with God," Paul now tells the Galatians what he personally did. "I am dead to the law" he says; that is, he abandoned it completely and cast himself as a sinner upon the mercy of God. His avowed purpose is to "live to God," which Calvin describes as regulating "our life according to his will, so as to study nothing else in our whole life, but to gain his approbation . . ." So great was the change that had come over Paul that the best way he could describe it was by saying, "I am crucified with Christ." This was mystical language, of course, not literal, for Paul lived on for many years, and much of his important work was still ahead. What did the Apostle mean?

Here we have an *essential Christian experience*. This is not a mere figure of speech. ". . . the wages of sin is death," says God's Word (Rom. 6:23), but our Lord was crucified for our sin in our place. As the old fisherman replied when he was asked what the cross meant to him: "He swapped with me." Paul's statement is a declaration of devotion, a willingness to be literally crucified for Christ's sake if need be.

Would I be willing? is a real question to face. Living as we do in our self-satisfying culture and our affluent social order, the requirement may never come to actually lay down our lives for the sake of Jesus. But this was real for the Apostle. To others later he described (as in 2 Cor. 11:23–33) the beatings and stonings, the starvation and imprisonment, the accusations and persecutions. At the end in Rome Paul actually gave his life. But more difficult than even the willingness to die physically was the death of his old life: his passions, his habits, and his old associations.

Christianity is more than an educational system. It is not a scheme that warrants reservations. It was not easy for Paul to kill the old body. God had to strike him down with a flash from heaven. It is no light matter for anyone to destroy the life of sin. Sin is full of pleasant attractions. It is deeply rooted in our inner nature. And the perversity of the world (this "evil age," 1:4) favors all manner of crookedness. To make the change we must accept the Savior. Conscience will not dethrone the old life. The law will not kill the sin in man. It is only when we come to Calvary and reach out our hand to the dying Christ, entering into his experience by faith, that the old self receives its mortal wounds. This is essential Christian experience.

Paul adds that Christ must live in us, when he wrote about "Christ who lives in me." He feels that he has so given himself to the Savior that Christ has the complete ruling power over him. To live we must kill the old self. We die that we may live. When we bury the old life, new energies spring up from the grave. This given life is Christ's; its power comes from Christ; it is swayed by the will of Christ; it breathes the spirit of Christ; it seeks the ends which Christ sought; it is lived in personal communion with the Savior. Selfish aims and desires are gone, and all of life's values are changed into nobler conceptions and grander ideals. As Alfred Noyes, the late poet laureate of England, wrote

> Die to the little hatreds; die to greed;
> Die to the old ignoble selves we knew;
>
> . . . .
>
> And that's not done by sword, or tongue, or pen
> There's but one way. God make us better men.[1]

All of this, says the Apostle, is not something vaguely visible in the distant future. It is a present attainment.

What is *the secret of this essential experience?* Paul answers this way: ". . . the life I now live in the flesh I live by faith in the Son of God . . ." The Apostle had urged this faith upon the Galatians, and they had gladly accepted it. The false teachers had sought to discount this experience by demanding that it take second place to the works of the law. If the latter is true, cried Paul, then Christ died for nothing. For if a man could get right with God by obeying the law, then why did Christ have to die? And that's a good question to ask today in our "do this" and "don't do that" conceptions of religion. Test yourself honestly now; how much of your religion is determined by the pious doing of works and the observance of religious motions, by following man-made rules and the pressure of the crowd?

"Christ . . . Lives in Me," 2:20

The Apostle, in writing to the Galatians in defense of his right to preach the gospel of grace, says ". . . it is no longer I who live, but Christ who lives in me . . ." This is essential Christian experience. You see, the faith which a Christian professes is more than a series of propositions about Christ. It is relatively easy to set up a series of facts about him, and then begin to revere the facts. Soon we measure and judge and even condemn each other because of the acceptance or rejection of this set of facts about the Savior. In the past this has brought war in the church, causing destruction and death. Christian has fought and murdered Christian, men have suffered in the stocks, and "heretics" have been burned at the stake, all because of a difference in the interpretation of a set of facts. To-day "the body of Christ" is split into hundreds of fragments for the same reason. Good Christian men judge and condemn each other and it seems once more that Christ has died in vain.

Much later the Apostle wrote to his young friend Timothy the very secret of what he meant by "Christ . . . lives in me" (read 1 Tim. 3:16). Moffatt translates it this way, "And who does not admit how profound is the divine truth of our religion?—it is He who was 'manifest in the flesh . . .' "[2] Our religion—it is HE! Christ himself is the divine truth of the religion which bears his name. He constitutes its central meaning. He is the core of its facts; he is the circumference of its teaching. He personally carries the facts of Christianity into the field of credibility.

A modern Jew asked a Christian Jew, "Suppose there was born among us a son, and they said that he was virgin born, would you believe it?" "Yes," said the Christian, "if he were such a son."

Ask a Christian about the reality of the Resurrection. He believes it because it was Christ who was raised. The character of the Person testifies to the actuality of the events of his life. The essence of Christianity, the essential Christian experience, is utter devotion to Jesus Christ as Savior and Lord. Truly following him is the test of discipleship. We are not saved by agreement to a system of truth or set of facts. Salvation is a personal relationship of trust in a personal Savior.

A physician who had always been skeptical of religion was dying. A Christian doctor was at his side and urged the dying man to surrender to Christ. He listened with amazement as the light dawned on his mind. "All my life I have been bothered with what set of facts to believe, and now I see it is whom to trust!" Can we honestly say that we trust in the Lord Jesus Christ for strength and salvation and that we seek to live in total and exclusive obedience to him? This is essential Christian experience.

REVIEW

1.   What is the difference between living by law and living by faith in the Son of God in a modern kitchen, in industry, in school? Be specific in your answer.

2.   What modern parallels can you think of to Peter's refusal to eat with Christians of another race? What would Paul say to such a refusal? What would you?

6 Justification by Faith

ADVANCE STUDY

1. *From this passage make two lists of words. In one list put words associated with "faith," such as "Spirit," etc. In the other, list words associated with "law," such as "works," etc. How do those in the first list give us freedom?*

2. *How does the story of Abraham illustrate Paul's point?*

The Magic of the "Evil Eye"

"Look me right in the eye and say it" is a request frequently heard when one seeks to challenge a statement that has been made. Not unrelated is the belief that a snake can fascinate a little bird by its unwinking gaze, so that the bird does not run to safety but becomes the serpent's morning snack. These ideas and others stem directly from the ancient fear of the sorcerer who cast a spell by his "evil eye." Many of the Galatians, including some who had been converted by Paul's preaching of Christ, feared the evil eye greatly, even though they believed that it could have an effect only if the subject looked straight into the eyes of the bewitcher.

Paul uses this familiar analogy in his letter as he turns now from the vindication of his gospel and his apostleship to challenge the Galatians on their conduct. He says both in sorrow and in rebuke that they should have kept their eyes on Christ instead of looking into the faces of the false teachers and thus being misled. And in so doing he takes the opportunity to set forth a central truth of the gospel, the doctrine of justification by faith.

Paul, as missionary pastor of the churches, is surprised and

377

deeply disappointed. In effect, he says, everywhere I preached I painted word pictures of Christ crucified, as if I were hanging up large painted posters with pictures of Christ on the cross (this is what the Greek suggests very clearly in the words "publicly portrayed" in 3:1). If only you had kept your eyes on the Christ on the cross instead of being fascinated by the eyes of these false sorcerers, you would not now be in difficulty and confusion. What got into you?

The Galatians, of course, were not fully grounded in their faith and thus would the more easily listen to the beguiling preachers of the "contrary gospel." Paul quickly saw what is as true today as then, that grace and faith do not suddenly transform a Christian into a perfect person. Growth in grace is necessary. Sanctification takes time. And all the while the tempter sets his evil eye upon men, even the most self-assured, and bedevils them with falsehoods. In Galatia a drastic reprimand was necessary to bring the people to their senses, and therefore the sharp words in the understandable analogy of the evil eye.

In this vivid approach Paul seeks to jostle the memories of his Christian friends by appealing to their experience. He reminds them that the blessings of the Holy Spirit came to them in the form of signs and wonders, and he asks whether these special gifts were received by the works of the law, such as obeying the food laws and accepting circumcision, or by faith in Christ (3:2). How could it be the former, Paul asks, when as Gentiles you knew nothing about the law? Having been accepted by God through faith in Christ, can you now be made perfect by ritual and abstentions and fleshly practices? You were saved by looking in faith to Christ; should you not live also by looking to him, rather than to rules?

In his sorrow mingled with pastoral rebuke, the Apostle reminds the people that they suffered greatly with him when they accepted the gospel. Undoubtedly many were ridiculed by their pagan neighbors. Families were broken up and long-standing friendships were disrupted. Is all of this now for nothing? When Paul says "if it really is in vain" (3:4), he expresses the hope that the situation is not as bad as he feared; perhaps if he reminds them (and us) once more of what God has given them in Christ, they will pay no more attention to the sorcerers, but will look Christ in the eye again. For this reason he redeclares the teaching on justification by faith (3:11).

Purpose of Chapter 6

The purpose of this chapter is to help us understand as clearly as possible justification by faith, this central doctrine of the Christian gospel which Paul declares so succinctly in 2:16 and 3:11. The subject is not easy, for Paul moves quite freely in the letter between justification (what God has done) and sanctification (what we must do). But to live as Christians we must understand what God has done for us. He has *justified* us, as Paul says. What does this mean? Why is this needed? How is it brought about? What follows will help you find in Galatians the answers to these questions.

The Nature of Justification, 3:6–9

(1)   *Read Genesis 15:1–6. What was Abram's (Abraham's) problem? God's promise?*

(2)   *Did Abraham respond "by works of the law" or "by hearing with faith" (3:2)?*

(3)   *Did God approve of Abraham's response?*

(4)   *In the light of this passage, who among the Galatians are the true descendants of Abraham?*

In 3:1–5 Paul illustrates and defends the gospel he proclaims by speaking of the Holy Spirit. It is a hearing-with-faith kind of gospel, because the Holy Spirit came to the Galatian Christians when they heard with faith, not when they did the works of the law. Having started on this level, says Paul, why would you sink back to a lower level? Having been saved by hearing with faith, why do you not live by hearing with faith rather than by circumcision, Sabbath-keeping, etc.?

In 3:6–9 there is a second illustration, Abraham. Review your answer to question 2 at the beginning of the chapter in the light of your study of this passage using the four questions immediately above. To which Old Testament character would the advocates of the law most naturally point? Note how here, as in Romans 4 and elsewhere, Paul puts emphasis instead on Abraham. In the light of

Genesis 15:1–6 and Galatians 3:6–9 how would you define justification by faith?

To justify is to accept and receive someone or something as just. Justification is by its nature a judicial act, in this case the act of God. Abraham was neither sinless nor perfect, but because of his faith God treated him as if he were; he pronounced him righteous, and he began the long, and in this life ever incomplete, process of making him righteous. A justified man is by God's grace acquitted; he is not innocent of nor free from all sin by any means.

Some time ago I was driving through a small town in Ohio and failed to see a large stop sign at the end of the street. Soon a man on a motorcycle was alongside asking me to pull over. There were the usual questions and the examination of driving credentials. When the officer noted on my card that I was a clergyman, he implied that I should therefore have known better, but for the same reason he did not write out a ticket. By letting me go without fine or imprisonment he graciously treated me as if I were righteous. I was guilty but I was forgiven; I drove on justified in his sight. I did not have to pay the penalty I deserved.

To justify is to declare that the demands of the law are satisfied and the very grounds for the infliction of punishment have been taken away. It's like erecting a large chalkboard and writing on it the many sins of our whole lives. God now comes and for the sake of his Son washes the board clean and henceforth looks at it as if nothing had ever been written there at all. ". . . I will forgive their iniquity, and I will remember their sin no more," says God (Jer. 31:34).

There is often confusion and misunderstanding about justification because of the expectation that a person declared righteous should at once become a perfect person. But I look at my Christian neighbor and I see him sinning. In fact, I look at myself and I find that I am committing the same old sins all over again. I thought that I was a Christian, but if so, it would seem that I would be better than I am. Then I look at the Apostle Peter and see him leaving the Gentile table even though he knew better. What has happened to his righteousness? I look at Paul and he says, "I can will what is right, but I cannot do it. For I do not do the good I want, but the evil I do not want is what I do" (Rom. 7:18–19). Then what about me?

This I must remember about the nature of justification. This act of God does not immediately change the character of the sinner. It does not remove the pollution of sin nor the internal corruption from his heart. But it changes his status before God from that of a criminal to that of a child. Paul often used the figure of *walking* in the interpretation of a spiritual truth. To make this change of status clear, using Paul's figure of "walking," let me be personal. Before God touched my life I was walking in one direction. God's will was not my concern, and the problems of my neighbors were of no moment to me. I was interested only in the big I, without regard for anyone or anything else. Then God touched my life and I reversed directions. Today when I transgress God's law I am aware of it and am on my knees asking forgiveness, and I receive it. If today I offend my neighbor or a member of my family, before the sun goes down I seek to make things right again. I am a sinner, but I am justified; I am no longer an outcast; I am God's child.

The Need of Justification, 3:10–12

(1)   *What additional pair of contrasting words does Paul introduce in verses 10 and 14?*

(2)   *According to 3:10–12, is it possible for anyone to be saved by works of the law?*

(3)   *Does Paul argue from men's deeds or from theory or from both?*

(4)   *How would you relate the point Paul makes in these verses to what he has said in 3:1–9?*

The aim of all religious systems is to restore the sinner to divine favor. Man's sense of need is illustrated by a story told of Akbar, the great Mogul emperor of India. Near his tomb at Agra are the tombs of five of his wives. Akbar, a Hindu by birth, had married a Jewess, a Mohammedan, a Brahman, a Zoroastrian, and a Christian, in order to study the effect of these great religions, hoping to find an answer to his personal problem as to which of them was the greatest. In a further effort he had gathered the sacred books of these religions and had them translated for use in his private library. "How did it come out?" I asked a Dr. Metah, the former head of the public health service in India, as I sat next to him at a luncheon one day. "No one seems to know," he replied. But surely Akbar's desire was to lay hold of divine favor. The altars and shrines of peoples from the dawn of history until now are mute witness to the fact that men in all ages have sought to get right with God or the gods as they know them. Universally man is conscious that he is a sinner, that he is unrighteous.

A basic fact of biblical religion, as Abraham reminded God, is that "the Judge of all the earth [will] do right" (Gen. 18:25). The psalmist (Ps. 14:1-3) said that in contrast all men "are alike corrupt; there is none that does good, no, not one." ". . . all have sinned and fall short of the glory of God," said Paul (Rom. 3:23). The Bible says that "the soul that sins shall die" (Ezek. 18:20). This is the problem that faces man, which means that it faces you and me.

God himself has had to step in. In Isaiah 50:7-9, the far-seeing prophet promised that God would vindicate his people. Earlier he had quoted the Lord as saying, "I, I am the LORD, and besides me there is no savior" (Isa. 43:11). This Savior, whom Paul had preached to the Galatians, was the crucified One, God's only Son. In him alone is righteousness, and we receive righteousness only by faith; we cannot earn it.

The Means of Justification, 3:13-14

Bill was a good man, they said. Oh, yes, he drank a little, and he swore a little. Sometimes he even cheated a little, both on his family and on his neighbors. But he was a good man. He would give you the shirt off his back. So, when it comes to heaven's gate, "I'll take my chance with Bill."

This popular conception of salvation by means of good works is nullified by Paul when he says in the letter that "no man is justified before God by the law" (3:11), that is, by doing good deeds, worthy as these may be in themselves. Perhaps this is a good place to ask the question, Why are the good deeds of the law not the means to righteousness?

The answer is relatively simple. For one thing, we cannot earn extra credit by good works. All of our time belongs to our Creator. There is no such thing as overtime in the Kingdom of God. I remember a builder of roads, a Christian and an elder in the church. He had finished an exceptionally fine piece of work and received voluminous praise from the city councilmen. That he should have received a modest "Thank you" was certainly in order, but he disclaimed the excessive vocabulary for as he said, "My best is what God expects me to do. This I owe to God. There is no extra merit in it." Because a man pays one debt we don't cancel all his debts!

Further, our good works are not perfect; but the law demands perfection. In our imperfection our sin stands revealed, and the law, instead of being a blessing, brings a curse (see Deut. 27:26). The law must be kept perfectly or it brings us under condemnation.

Why is the law insufficient? Its moral standards are so high no man can attain them. And there is no power to help one attain except the power of God through Christ, whose atoning death put an end to the curse of the law when he "bore our sins in his body on the tree" (1 Pet. 2:24; cf. Gal. 3:13). Christ's cross fulfilled the original plan of God exemplified in Abraham and testified to by Habakkuk when he said that "the righteous shall live by his faith" (Hab. 2:4).

Justification, therefore, is by faith in Jesus Christ. We are not justified "on account of" faith, but "through" faith (3:11). Faith is not a virtue or a good work; it is itself God's gracious gift (Eph. 2:8–9).

In setting forth the principle, Paul went the teachers of the "contrary gospel" one better. They were always going back to Moses and the Mosaic law. Paul goes back to Abraham, the "father of the race." He reminds the Galatians that God had chosen Abraham and had promised that he would make of Abraham's descendants a great nation (Gen. 12:2), and that in him all the families of the earth would be blessed. The law, as such, did not then exist, but Abraham believed God's promise and it was "reckoned to him as righteousness" (Rom. 4:3). Faith as a means to righteousness did not begin with the New Testament or with Paul, as has sometimes been said. It is deep in the heart of all biblical religion.

Abraham's faith did not immediately change him as a person; it did immediately change his status before God. Faith became for him the instrument for appropriating the righteousness of Christ, so that Paul could even say that the gospel was preached before to Abraham (3:8). What could the false teachers now say, for Abraham was a revered ancestor? What God was now doing in justifying the Gentiles by faith was therefore not new. In God's sight the real descendants of Abraham were not, then, his blood relatives, but all those who followed his example of faith. Now in Galatia God's promise to bless all nations in Abraham has come true. Through Christ Jesus the blessing of Abraham came upon the Gentiles (and all of us) "that we might receive the promise of the Spirit through faith" (3:14).

What is the nature of this faith? Adequate faith is a deep sense of dependence upon God, ascribing all honor to God and seeking the glory of God. It is acceptance of the righteousness which God freely offers in Christ Jesus. Man's response to the Creator's gracious initiative is his faith. Adequate faith trusts fully in the sacrifice of Christ in our place, for God for our sake "made him to be sin who knew no sin, so that in him we might become the righteousness of God (2 Cor. 5:21). This same note of Christ being our substitute is found in 3:13—Christ "a curse for us."

Such faith is related to the covenantal faithfulness of God as first expressed to Abraham in the promise. This means that God is true and never fails, even though man may fall far short. As shown by all the conduct of Israel, man's faithfulness does not and cannot nullify the faithfulness of our Maker. God's message is true, and we receive the blessing of the promise by trusting fully in God's word. To seek righteousness through the deeds of the law is to distrust God and try to propitiate him as if he were not faithful to his promises. Christ's righteousness is imputed to us, freely given to us as his own. "To impute" means "to cover as with a cloak." On Sunday morning before I preach, I cover my suit completely with the pulpit gown, so that men no longer see the suit. In like manner the love of God covers me for the sake of Christ. I am declared righteous when I accept his love and trust in his promises for now and for the future.

REVIEW

1. Some psychotherapists sometimes speak of someone's having a guilt complex. How could this passage help such a person, weighed down with an awareness of personal unworthiness?

2. "Not everyone who says to me 'Lord, Lord,' . . . but he who does the will of my Father . . ?" says Jesus (Matt.7:21). Which do you agree with: Jesus' emphasis on deeds or Paul's on faith? Or how do you reconcile these two?

3. How would Paul reply to the man who says, "My religion is the 'golden rule' "?

7 The Purpose of the Law

ADVANCE STUDY

1. List the values of the law described in this passage.

2. In what ways does Paul say God's promise is superior to the law?

On Breaking a Will, 3:15–18

(1) What is the point of Paul's illustration about the making of a will?

(2) How does Paul indicate the superiority of the promise over the law?

(3) If our spiritual inheritance comes from God by promise, what is our part in this relationship?

A news story in the major newspapers of the country some time ago told of a sizable legacy left by an individual for the care and feeding of a dog that survived his master. Although the will seemed unnatural, it had been properly drawn, witnessed, and probated, and an administrator had been named to carry out its provisions in behalf of the animal. Some distant relatives, thinking that the whole thing was senseless, tried their best to break the will, but to no avail. It was legal in every aspect, and the court directed that the wishes of the testator be fulfilled. When a will is properly drawn and signed, our civil law does not allow a third party to alter its provisions.

It is interesting, therefore, that the Apostle Paul as he continues writing the Letter to the Galatians uses this very human illustration, one with which both Jews and Gentiles were quite familiar, to defend the doctrine of justification by faith which he had set before them. "To give a human example, brethren," he says, "no one annuls even a man's will, or adds to it, once it has been ratified." (Note in passing that he begins this argument by calling the Galatians "brethren," as if he felt that the rebuke in the first part of the letter had been rather harsh, so that he now wanted to soften the tone. Paul never meant that the Galatian Christians had deserted the faith completely; they were his brothers in Christ, but they were truly confused and needed help.)

The immediate problem was a misunderstanding as to the purpose of the law. Many of the false teachers did not deny the reality of justification by faith as a gift of the grace of God; they were saying that a person in order to be really and fully Christian should also observe such requirements of the law as Sabbath observance, circumcision, and the food laws.

Paul argues that God made a covenant promise to Abraham that Abraham's faith would be reckoned to him as righteousness (3:6–9). Just as a man's will cannot be tampered with by a third party, so God's covenant must be respected. (In Greek the same word means both *will* and *covenant*.) Something that happened at least 430 years later (the giving of the law) cannot annul an agreement that God had entered into. God does not go back on his promises.

Furthermore, the promise was to Abraham and his "seed"— which refers to Christ. So it is the man committed to Christ who stands in the line of the promise. He does not receive or increase his inheritance by keeping the law, for if that were the situation the word *promise* would not have been appropriate. But Genesis says clearly that the inheritance was given by God's promise, not earned by man's obedience.

However, the discussion itself raised a question, "Why then the law?" Before we try for the answer we must refresh our memories about the law itself.

What Is the Law?

A doctor of jurisprudence would reply that the law is a body of regulations and rules existing for the welfare of the body politic and for the maintenance of a well-ordered life in a community. This runs contrary to the usual conception that law is a restriction, a curtailment of our actions, an infringement upon our liberties. It is negative in the latter sense, but the law is not primarily negative, only secondarily so. Only when one transgresses upon the best interests of his neighbors or rebels against the will of God does law become restrictive and disciplinary and punitive. This conception of law in general is necessary to a better understanding of biblical law.

Rule and law have been present in the lives of people from the beginning of recorded history. If we take the first book of the Bible as a guideline, we are reminded of family and tribal laws, of rules for marriage and adoption, of directions for punishment and revenge, and of rules and treaties with regard to grazing lands and boundaries. These generally were administered by the heads of families, tribal chiefs, or the head of a confederation of tribes.

Other people than those we call God's people had their codes as well. Archaeology has uncovered, for instance, a code of laws which governed the Hittite peoples, who are mentioned fifty times in sixteen books of the Old Testament. We also have a collection of Assyrian laws, including perhaps the most famous in antiquity, the law collection of Hammurabi, discovered in 1902 in Babylon. There are others, but our chief concern is with biblical law.

Formal biblical law begins with Moses as the Bible presents him in his unique work as lawgiver. The Mosaic law is contained in the Hexateuch (the Pentateuch, the first five books of the Bible, plus Joshua), and in Ezekiel 40—48, where the prophet in a vision given to him in the twenty-fifth year of the Exile (Ezek. 40:1) draws an outline of the restored commonwealth of Israel. In the time of Nehemiah, the law of Moses definitely referred to the entire Pentateuch (Neh. 8:1).

Basic to Hebrew law is the covenant code made between God and Israel at Mt. Sinai (Exod. 19—24), which includes the Decalogue. This is treated in the study of Exodus in this series. Biblical scholars sometimes refer to the covenant code as the Book of the Covenant. These students of the Bible also refer to the Deuteronomic Code (the Book of Deuteronomy in the Pentateuch—for its importance see 2 Kings 22:8–13), and the Holiness Code, sometimes called the Priestly Code (Lev. 17—26). This Holiness Code implies again and again that Israel is to be a holy people because God is holy, that as a nation they are God's "own possession" (Exod. 19:5) and therefore must exhibit spiritual and moral qualities which all other people could see.

The Hebrew word *torah,* which basically means "to direct" or "to point the way," is the general Old Testament term for divine instruction and guidance through the law and is often translated "law." To the devout Israelite, from the days at Mt. Sinai on, the Torah was a joy and a help that God had given his people, teaching them to know his ways and to do his will. The psalmist praised God for the law because he loved it (read Ps. 1 and 19 and skim through 119). The law was a mark of God's favor, not a burden. Moses asked, "And what great nation is there, that has statutes and ordinances so righteous as all this law . . ." (Deut. 4:8), and the psalmist says that when God gave "his statutes and ordinances to Israel, he has not dealt thus with any other nation" (Ps. 147: 19–20).

God chose a people because he loved them (Deut. 7:8); he re-deemed them from slavery in Egypt and reconfirmed the Abrahamic covenant at Mt. Sinai. Here the Torah was added, not as a means of salvation, for Israel had already been set free by the grace of God, but as a pattern of response to God's gift. That is why Israel, as a free people, rejoiced in the gift of the law. It was for their well-being, for the maintenance of a well-ordered life in the community (read Deut. 30:15–19; 32:46–47). Luther says that the law was given ". . . that there might be in the world a special people, rigidly controlled by the Law, a people out of which Christ should be born. . . ."

Speaking broadly Christians often call the entire Old Testament the *Law,* much as they call the New Testament the *Gospel.* Mani-festly this is not correct, for while the New Testament is the good news of the grace of God, this grace was also there in the Old Testa-ment as God made his covenant with Abraham and renewed it with Israel. Paul makes this very clear in Galatians. But this misconcep-tion has by no means evaporated. One still hears it in various forms, largely because of a misunderstanding of the role of the original covenant law.

Facing the Problem

Where then is the problem? Why in his argument in behalf of

justification by faith does Paul seemingly discount the law? Not because of the nature and purpose of the basic Torah, for the giving of the law did not break the covenant. Rather he spoke as he did because of the misuse and misinterpretations the false teachers were making of the law in the presence of the Gentile Christians.

In the period of the Exile the remnant of Israel which hoped to return to Palestine knew that they had not kept God's law, and they set out to do better. To maintain themselves as a separate people in a pagan land, they began to adhere strictly to rites and ceremonies and to a legal code of strict do's and don'ts. Upon the return from Exile, this legal code was scrupulously observed, with the party of the Pharisees, of which Paul in his early days had been one of the most ardent members, leading the way. To this written legal code the interpreters added a vast system of oral traditions, which were soon declared to be equal to the written law in importance. Those who kept the code were the only godly people, and all this "doing" was done to win God's favor.

But Paul, looking back as a Christian, realized that the harder he tried the less righteous he had been. The Damascus Road experience had revealed to him that justification was by faith alone and not through the works of the law. The Gentiles, who had no love of the Old Testament law, gladly accepted the gospel which Paul preached.

Then rose up the false teachers. They did not discount the covenant promise, but they insisted that to secure its full value the law code must be observed; they seemed thus to put the law first and grace second. The Galatians were confused and Paul was angry. Paul did not undervalue the Mosaic law, as some have charged. He felt that these teachers misunderstood its place (3:15–19) in God's plan of salvation fulfilled in Christ. That's why Paul fought so earnestly against law-righteousness which the Judaizers sought to impose upon the Galatian churches. God would have nullified his own promise if he had added the law as a condition of grace.

Why Then the Law? 3:19–22

That's now the question and a good one. Paul may be forgiven if, in the light of what his opponents were trying to do to him, he now stresses the negative purpose of the law. The Apostle's word that the law "was added because of transgressions" is also stated in Romans 3:20 where Paul says that through the law comes the knowledge of sin. *The Heidelberg Catechism* quotes Christ's summary of the law (Matt. 22:37–40) and adds in Question 5 that no one keeps this perfectly: " . . . by nature I am prone to hate God and my neighbor" (see Rom. 3:10, 23; 8:7; and 1 John 1:8).[1] Surely sin existed prior to the law (Gen. 3), but, says Paul in Romans 4:15, "where there is no law there is no transgression." Then he straightforwardly tells the Romans that the law came "to increase the trespass" (Rom. 5:20).

The whole problem of human life is "to get right with God." The question is, How? The standards and regulations of the law can never be kept fully. Always there is imperfection and frustration. The negative purpose of the law is to show us our sins and sickness, but it cannot cure. The law is like a doctor who is an expert in diagnosis, but who is helpless to cure the disease. But what about the Gentiles who did not know the law? Were they not sinners too, since transgression was there from the beginning? Paul has answered this question for the Romans. "They show that what the law requires is written on their hearts . . . their conscience also bears witness . . ." (read Rom. 2:12–16). What does this say about the non-Christian at home and pagans in other parts of the world?

But, sir, you say, I still have a problem in the negative approach. A large newspaper display proclaimed the coming of a noted evangelist. A story in connection with it told of the depths of degradation from which he had risen, now to preach the pure gospel, with the implication that what he had to say of grace and salvation was all the better because of his real experience with the opposite. Is there virtue in sinning? I think of the man who arose in prayer meeting again and again to tell of the transgressions of his life from which he was now redeemed; there was a smirk in the telling. Shall we do evil that good may come? "Are we to continue in sin that grace may abound?" asks Paul (Rom. 6:1). The answer is No, says Paul, and the law can tell you why.

The Paidagōgos, 3:23–29

(1) *Does Paul, by what he has said, mean to eliminate any place for the law?*

(2) *What positive role does a custodian play? Is it a permanent or a temporary role?*

(3) *How does verse 29 serve as a climax to Paul's arguments in chapter 3? Put yourself in the place of the Galatians as you answer this question; then ask yourself what significance it has for you.*

The letter moves now to the illustration of a fact likely to be understood by all. The law in its purpose is like a *paidagōgos*, Paul says. This Greek word is the origin of our English word "pedagogue," a teacher of children and youth, a schoolmaster. But this is not quite the ancient meaning. In the Greek and Roman world of Paul's day, the more affluent citizens entrusted their sons between the ages of seven and seventeen to a trusted slave, usually a person of high character who had served the family for many years. It was his duty to lead the child to school and deliver him to the teacher. He also taught the growing youngster manners and guarded him against running into temptation and danger. He also carried a stick with which to punish if necessary, and he had full authority to do so. The growing boy often resented this training to be a gentleman, and sometimes openly rebelled against his guardian as the latter sought to keep his charge from getting into bad company.

The word has been variously translated as "schoolmaster," "guardian," and "tutor," but the nearest to the original is "custodian," so the R.S.V. says, ". . . the law was our custodian." The older translation of "schoolmaster" is not acceptable, for the slave was not a professor. His chief business was to attend to and safeguard the child until the latter attained maturity.

Applying this analogy to the question of the purpose of the law, what principles do we see? The first is that the custodian restrains and controls his charge. The characteristics that were common to these slave-guardians were several. One was rigid orders. Little was left to the direction of the child, and often no explanation was forthcoming as to whys and wherefores. Thus the guardian often restrained his charge. This literally means that he acted like a jailer. Usually the custodian was an old family retainer who probably no longer had young ideas. He often checked and repressed the young people in his care. Under the law too, there was little room for freedom of action. It was definite and precise in its "You shall" and "You shall not."

The custodian used compulsion if necessary. His own master had commanded him to use the rod if obedience was not given. Why do people obey the law? Ask yourself that question. Is it more from hope of reward or from fear of punishment? Is it not the latter, a desire not to get caught, although we would like to disobey? Large numbers of people are under compulsion; they do not act from love nor from willing obedience. But the custodian was suited to the age of his charge. Restraint and control were necessary. Implicit obedience must be learned before the conscience can function properly.

Thus the law was and is in reality a "tutor," as the N.E.B. says. It imposes checks on evil; it regulates outward actions; it guides our conduct. Law restrains the sins of society; it protects both the community and the individual by preventing transgressions by those who have no Christian motivation. If one is not able to say that "the love of Christ controls us" (2 Cor. 5:14), he is firmly reminded that "whatever a man sows, that he will also reap" (Gal. 6:7).

The custodian also prepared the growing person for manhood. Calvin says ". . . in training a child, the object is to prepare him . . . for maturer years." The child was being made into a man as habits of obedience were being learned. When elementary education had trained a boy he was then ready for higher education, for he had become a man. In this way the "law was the grammar school of theology, which . . . handed them over to faith to be completed," says Calvin. As Paul has indicated, the means is by developing a sense of sin. This sense of sin also brings a sense of need, a need which comes to full realization only when we know how great are our sins and their consequences.

The custodian finally discharged the son at the age of seventeen, usually coinciding with the end of his secondary school education. He was now graduating. So "the law was our custodian until Christ came, that we might be justified by faith" (3:24). But now that faith has come we are no longer under the custodian. The diploma is a parchment indicating our sonship which comes through faith in Christ, in whom there is justification. We are not Christians because we live in a Christian land, or because we have godly parents, or because we have joined a Christian church. The state cannot save individuals; the laws of a state are restraining and often punitive. But both the law and the gospel are from God. The law is our guardian while we are spiritually immature, but when we trust Christ we have become full-grown sons.

Baptized into Christ

Paul now tells the Galatians that they have been brought into this relationship of sonship through baptism (3:27). This sacrament was preceded by a confession of faith by which the candidate declared that Jesus Christ is Lord and Savior. "Putting on Christ" was a metaphor for having a toga or great cloak placed across the shoulders, entirely covering a person. It meant that one submitted himself completely to the will of Christ, with the resolve to serve him with devotion and obedience. Now all advantages or disadvantages of birth disappear. When one is a child of God it does not matter whether he is Jew or Gentile, man or woman, freeman or slave, all are one in Christ Jesus. If you are a Christian, then the legacy of the promise which God made to Abraham is yours.

REVIEW

1. "Love God and do as you please," said Augustine. What in this passage seems to agree and what to differ with this idea?

2. Abraham lived a good life without any laws, says Paul. Couldn't Christian America do so, too? Give reasons for your answer.

3. In what specific ways should Christians try to manifest more clearly their unity across lines of race, class, and sex as proclaimed in Galatians 3:28?

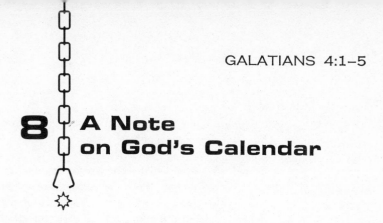

8 A Note on God's Calendar

ADVANCE STUDY

1. According to these five verses, what difference has the coming of God's Son made to us?

2. How are these verses related to the paragraph preceding them (Gal. 3:23–29)?

"Bells on the Horses"

About five hundred years before Jesus was "born of woman" (4:4), Zechariah was returning to Jerusalem from exile. Both a priest and a prophet, he was greatly instrumental in rekindling the hopes of a depressed people; he was especially effective in urging them to rebuild the Temple to the glory of God.

When the work was finished the prophet turned his thought to the future and to a spiritual Jerusalem. There is little hope, he said, for the fulfillment of God's promises except through the coming in of the Messianic age. "And on that day," he prophesied, "there shall be inscribed on the bells of the horses, 'Holy to the LORD'" (Zech. 14:20). The same is said for the pots in the kitchen, all of this meaning that in the day when God would send forth his Son the farmer in his field and the homemaker in her kitchen would dedicate their work to the glory of God.

In this section of the letter, Paul speaks of the day when this plan of God began to be fulfilled, the day when Jesus was born of Mary. It sounds like the Christmas story, and in many ways it is, as Paul presents facts of doctrine to his Galatian congregations.

From Minor to Heir, 4:1–3

(1) *What new emphasis does Paul make in these verses as he returns to the illustration of the pedagogue?*

(2) *Are any Americans enslaved today? By what?*

The Apostle has been writing about the purpose of the law. He uses the illustration of the pedagogue, the slave guardian of a son under age, and likens the functions of the law to the duties of the custodian. It seems that his defense of the doctrine of justification by faith is finished when, almost as an afterthought, he throws in a second but related illustration, a comparison which leads to the setting forth of God's greatest work, the commissioning of his own Son for specific service in the world of men.

The new illustration concerns the son of an affluent family and his rights from infancy to majority. Customs in this respect varied in the communities with which the Galatians were familiar. Among the Greeks, infancy ended at age seven, and the minor was then under the care of the custodian until age eighteen; he then served the state as a cadet until age twenty. The Roman system was variable. A son was an infant until age seven, reached puberty at age fourteen, and remained under the guardian until anywhere from seventeen to twenty-five, depending on the judgment of the father. Then the young man was brought to the forum by his family and, in a religious ceremony, was introduced to public life. Also on that day the male offered a ball, and the female a doll, to Apollo to show that childish things were now behind them.

For the Jewish boy it was once again different and perhaps more elaborate. Whether in Paul's family the Roman or Jewish custom prevailed, we do not know. Considering that the family was proud of both relationships, it is quite likely that both were observed. With regard to the Jewish customs there is some confusion with regard to the age factor. One custom says that a boy became the citizen of the Jewish commonwealth at the age of thirteen and a day, a girl at the age of twelve and a day. Another says that on the first Sabbath after his twelfth birthday, the father took the boy to the synagogue or the Temple for the ceremony. There is no story in the New Testament which is more familiar to all age groups than that of the boy Jesus in Jerusalem at the age of twelve (Luke 2: 41–52). At the presentation the father spoke a benediction, "Blessed be Thou, O God, who hast taken from me the responsibility of this boy." The boy also promised that he would truly seek to keep all of God's commandments and would assume full responsibility for all of his actions toward Yahweh.

By illustrations drawn from such familiar customs, Paul argues that all of us, Jews and Gentiles alike, were once minor children. We had no rights before God. Although we had a great inheritance coming to us, we were no better than slaves. We are familiar with the idea that the Jews were under the pedagogue, the law, despite their role as God's people. Calvin says that the Jews of the Old Testament times were free, since they are God's chosen in distinction from other people, yet they were not in full possession of the inheritance while they were still under the custodianship of the law. But in what sense had the non-Jewish Galatians been enslaved, and if such bondage rested upon them, does it rest on us today until we find true freedom in Christ?

Ruled by the Stars, 4:3

As the Apostle writes he uses one analogy after another. Having written about the minor being under the guardian and as such no better than a slave, though he would one day inherit all, he says that in this latter state "we were slaves to the elemental spirits of the universe" (4:3). The Apostle repeats the same phrase twice in his letter to the Colossians (2:8, 20). What do you make of this?

Scholars are not all agreed as to what Paul had in mind, but if the principle of interpreting Scripture by Scripture is correct (and it is), then the letter writer himself gives us a hint to his meaning in verse 10 of this chapter when he says, "you observe days, and months, and seasons, and years!" Pagan people ruled their lives by the stars. The sun and moon and stars were believed to be inhabited by spiritual bodies or powers which determined not only the wind and the rain, the thunder and the lightning, but also the day-by-day events in every man's life.

To these heavenly bodies, these "elemental spirits," the pagan Galatians had been enslaved, living their lives in superstitious fear and dread. Thus they were no better off than the Jewish Galatians who had been in bondage to the law, which could not save but simply kept them under a restraint. (And while it is taken for granted that men need to be restrained, it still is not a happy situation to be in!)

Is twentieth-century man free from enslavement "to the elemental spirits of the universe"? Our evening newspaper has a regular column on horoscopes, what to do when the stars are in a certain position in the sky if you are born in January, or if your birthday is under the sign of Taurus the bull. Some people must fear the stars still! Nor is this the only example of slavery. What is the effect on us when a black cat crosses our path in the pale moonlight?

Nor is that all. How many people's lives, or major areas of them, are controlled by social or business standards, cultural customs, alcohol, clothing fashions, family traditions, "the rat race," or tribal (community) taboos? How many of us who call Christ Lord are able to resist such pressures? Galatians may be an ancient document, but the problems Paul confronts are as contemporary as the record of your own activities and expenditures of the past week. The word of redemption and adoption (4:5) which is at the heart of Paul's gospel is good news to many a modern who yearns to break his chains.

God's Desk Calendar, 4:4

If all men need to be brought from bondage to freedom through Christ, why didn't he come sooner? If Jesus Christ was the fulfillment of the promise, why did God wait so long? John Calvin, the Genevan theologian, consoled himself with the thought that the answer to this question was hidden in "the secret purpose of God." Do you have a better suggestion? From the beginning there had been a note on the calendar of God and, when in the flight of celestial days "the time had fully come, God sent forth his Son . . ."

Taking a look at the world of that day from our human standpoint, however, many conditions made the time seem favorable for the coming of the Christ.

Politically the time was right. Roman law exercised its rule almost everywhere, with the result that trade and commerce flourished, and travel was relatively safe over a wide area. Paul and his associates thus could go almost anywhere as evangelists.

Culturally the time was also right. Greek civilization had reached many parts of the empire. The Greek language was understood by at least part of the population in all but the most remote villages. This not only gave a sense of unity among peoples which had not been experienced before, but also opened doors for the communication of the gospel.

Religiously the time was ripe. The ancient philosophies as developed by Socrates, Zeno the Stoic, and others had never been widely accepted. Belief in the old pagan gods, such as those of Greece and Rome, was dying. The faith of many Jews, too, had become anemic as the Jews of the dispersion had been settled among the nations. Yet this same fact of the dispersion would provide in many places a base through the synagogues for the first preaching of the gospel, as was true in the Galatian towns.

Into this situation God "sent forth his Son." When he was "born of woman" there in the cattle barn, his Jewish mother wrapped him in the customary swaddling cloths and cradled him in a manger.

Jesus Was a Jew

This statement has and will come as a shock to some, but Jesus was born a Jew, having been "born under the law," as Paul says. According to this law, he was circumcised on the eighth day (Luke 2:21) and given the name Jesus as commanded by the angel. Under this law he was presented in the Temple by Mary and Joseph (Luke 2:22–24) and then, at the age of twelve, he became a full member of the Hebrew commonwealth (Luke 2:41–51). Without doubt he attended the synagogue school at Nazareth, where he spent his time memorizing the law, working the rest of the day in the carpenter shop. With his fellow Jews he kept the Sabbath, worshiped in the synagogue, observed the feasts, and paid his Temple taxes. He was baptized by his cousin, John the Baptist, and at the age of thirty he began his ministry.

Jesus was "born of woman" that he might share the life of other men. He began with the helplessness and limitations of all human babies in order that a solidarity with all God's created world might be established. His was a full humanity, sharing with us in our sorrows and joys, our failures and achievements, our temptations and our victories. For him, like many others, life was short. At the age of thirty-three, he died.

Was this son of Mary dark in color? Travel in the Middle East today, as I have done, and see for yourself. The artists who have painted him a blond, with Anglo-Saxon features, are surely as inaccurate as are Japanese or African artists who gave him almond-shaped eyes or Negroid features (though each artist senses that Jesus belongs to every culture and to all people, and such portrayals show genuine insight in this regard). Jesus was a Jew, "born of woman" in the Middle East, and his features were undoubtedly those of his kindred according to the flesh.

This Jesus "born of woman" is the most radical and revolutionary character that has ever walked any road or suggested any course of action. He upsets all of men's accustomed ways of thinking, a procedure which is far more significant than his upsetting of the tables of the money changers. He disturbs the peace of the well-established and brings an end to the luxury of the comfortable. He was the unorthodox modernist of his day and continues to shake up the complacent.

The First Mission Board, 4:4–5

Paul, as he writes to the Galatians, says that "God sent forth his Son." If a missionary is one who is sent on a mission, then Jesus was a missionary, and the sending society was Heaven itself. How natural that the congregation at Antioch had sent their own best preachers as missionaries to the people of Galatia, when Heaven had sent its very best to a darkened world that was still God's world, and to a wayward people who were still God's people.

Why was he sent? "To redeem those who were under the law," Paul says (4:5). Have you ever asked yourself, Why didn't God just declare redemption, even as in the days of creation the worlds were made by the fiat of his will? It would have been so much easier. No cross would have been necessary; no more mission boards or missionaries would be needed. But no redemption could take place through a proclamation which set aside the law. God himself gave the law; it had divine validity. Any solution had to build on this basis; it could not bypass the law. So God sent his Son to fulfill the law as well as to redeem men condemned by it.

When we break down the reasons for his coming, the answer is something like this:

(1) That prophecy might be fulfilled. From the time that the covenant had been established with Abraham (Gen. 12:3; 17:7), God had renewed his assurance through the prophets that in his own good time the promise would be fulfilled. When Jacob met Joseph again in Egypt, he called his sons to him and, in a moment of exaltation, he gave them his blessing and predicted that the princely line would be through Judah. "The scepter shall not depart from Judah, nor the ruler's staff from between his feet, until he comes to whom it belongs . . ." (Gen. 49:10). Eight hundred years before the time, the prophet Isaiah said that "to us a child is born, to us a son is given . . . and his name will be called . . . Prince of Peace" (Isa. 9:6). In exile Israel was called on to "prepare the way of the LORD" (Isa. 40:3); later she was told of one "despised and rejected by men . . . wounded for our transgressions . . . bruised for our iniquities . . ." (Isa. 53:3–5). Micah speaks of a ruler to come out of Bethlehem who "shall be great to the ends of the earth. And this shall be peace . . ." (Mic. 5:2–5). And Zechariah prophesied that "your king comes to you . . . riding . . . on a colt . . . and he shall command peace to the nations . . ." (Zech. 9:9–10). Nahum too speaks clearly as to why he came. Writing to comfort Judah, the prophet sang the gospel of deliverance when he foresaw "on the mountains the feet of him who brings good tidings, who proclaims peace" (Nah. 1:15). When Jesus was born of Mary, the angel choirs sang of peace on earth through him whom the former prophets called "the Prince of Peace," and who came, as Paul says, with the good news of redemption. It seems as if the prophets dared men to believe as they did. Jesus himself asked the two on the way to Emmaus why they were so slow to believe all that the prophets had spoken (Luke 24:25).

(2) That God might be glorified. When Jesus was "born of

woman," there were shepherds in the field keeping watch over their flocks by night. To these shepherds the angelic choir sang the *Gloria in Excelsis,* glory to God in the highest. How well our Lord's mother, as she exulted in her gladness, could sing of God's mercy on "those who fear [love] him." The three-fold divine glory of might, holiness, and eternal mercy is fused into one through the Incarnation. In Jesus Christ there is power for our weakness; holiness is blended with forgiving love; and there is mercy for all. Christ came to bring glory to God by providing redemption for those "under the law."

(3) That "we might receive adoption as sons." This we will study in chapter 9. I ask myself, Do I give God the glory for all he has done for me? Or do I still think that I can do a little bit of my redemption for myself?

REVIEW

1. Where you work, how would a slave act differently from the owner's grown son? How is this difference like the difference between the way a non-Christian and a Christian live and work?

2. Just what is different in the house or office about the life of one who believes in God's Son and that of a good Jew who does not believe in Jesus but does sincerely try to live by the Ten Commandments? What would Paul in these verses say to this question?

3. The first century A.D. *was "the fullness of time" for God to set us free from the Jewish law and from "the elemental spirits of the universe." The twentieth century is the "fullness of time" for Christ to free us from what?*

9 Sons by Adoption

ADVANCE STUDY

Galatians 4:6–31 falls into three paragraphs: 6–11, 12–19 and 21–31. Before reading further see if you can put in one sentence each the theme of each of these paragraphs. What title would you give Galatians 4?

Moses, Prince of Egypt

How did Moses, who in history is known as the great deliverer and lawgiver of Israel, get to be a prince in Egypt? Many of you have recently studied the story in this textbook (pp. 28–33). But even if you have not, this historical event is familiar to every reader of the Bible, for it is one of the stirring tales of the early history of God's people. The sojourn and slavery in Egypt, the decree of the Pharaoh that all Hebrew male children must die lest the slave hordes become too strong, the hiding of the young baby in a basket in the bulrushes in the Nile, the discovery of the baby and arrangements for his care, his adoption as the son of Pharaoh's daughter— what story and what events are more stirring? It must have been recited at hundreds of camp fires and in countless homes as parents told and retold their tribal history to succeeding generations.

How did a slave-child become a prince? He was adopted! This act of the princess of Egypt is in itself an opening to the understanding of Paul's word in his letter to the Galatians when he writes that Christ came "to redeem those who were under the law, so that we might receive adoption as sons" (4:5). The N.E.B. puts it this way: "God sent his Son . . . to purchase freedom for the subjects of the law, in order that we might attain the status of sons."

Reread 3:23—4:7 and note the emphasis Paul puts on sonship and adoption. He evidently feels that these closely related concepts are significant and meaningful for his readers. Do you feel this way about them yourself? *Does the fact that you are a son of God through faith in Jesus Christ seem important to you? Would your offer of an opportunity to be adopted into God's family stir the imagination and invoke an eager response from the non-Christian who lives in your block or works at your factory or office? To what felt need, if any, does the invitation to adoption speak?*

Modern men are often accused of an unwillingness to get involved, and this is a fair criticism of many. But this fear of getting too closely tied to other people is balanced and probably exceeded by man's sense of alienation and loneliness. He feels that he lacks the support of fellow human beings on whom he can lean; he suspects, somewhat vaguely, that things are against him and that he lives in a hostile world. He is burdened with the constant pressure to do well, for there is no forgiveness if he breaks the rules, misses the opportunity, or "fouls up the job." Do you agree that many individuals and families today are lonely in that sense? Have you ever felt that way yourself?

Is it possible that this dual concept of adoption-into-sonship could speak to twentieth-century people in their loneliness? Be thinking along these lines as you study Galatians 4:4–31, in terms of yourself or specific people who may know loneliness.

What Is Adoption?

The general meaning of the word is the voluntary acceptance of a child of other parents to be as one's own child. So the princess of Egypt took Moses not only into her palace, but into her family; "he became her son" (Exod. 2:10). Among ancient peoples adoption was practiced by bringing an outsider into the family or tribe and giving to him the rights and responsibilities of a member by birth. Thus in our own early history American Indians now and again adopted a member of another tribe, or even on occasion a white person, into their own tribe.

Among all the rules and laws of the Old Testament, there is no regulation with regard to adoption, though we know that it was practiced: Mordecai, for instance, adopted Esther, the daughter of his uncle, "as his own daughter" (Esther 2:7). When the Apostle, therefore, used the metaphor of adoption, he did not turn to his Jewish heritage and custom but to the Roman, with which he was also familiar as a Roman citizen. Among the Romans, adoption was a legal method by which a wealthy, childless person often adopted a promising slave to become his son and heir; he then showered upon him all the perquisites and privileges of a natural-born son.

Benefits of Adoption, 4:4–7

What results of adoption does Paul mention in these verses? Why do you suppose he includes the Aramaic word, *Abba?*

Paul had written, even as he had surely preached, that God had sent his Son so that "we might receive adoption as sons" (4:5). We all have been slaves, he says in effect; the Jews to the Old Testament law, the Gentiles to the customs of the day and to their pagan practices. But now we have come to maturity as we have been redeemed by Christ, and we have been adopted as sons into the family of God. This act of adoption as children by God is the measure of the Father's love. While this graciousness of God is entirely unmerited, it is nevertheless genuine adoption whereby we become joint heirs with Christ.

It is natural that someone should ask, But how does one know for a certainty that he is a child of God? Paul seems to be answering that question when he says, ". . . God has sent the Spirit of his Son into our hearts, crying 'Abba! Father!' " (4:6.) If out of your heart you cry, "Abba, Father," you may be sure that the Holy Spirit has moved you. If the heart speaks, we know that we are sons.

"Abba" means "father" in Aramaic, the language generally spoken in Palestine in Jesus' day. Actually it is a word of intense familiarity like our word "daddy." No true Jew ever spoke to God in that fashion. He loved the word, but he did not dare use it in speaking to Almighty God. Nowhere in Jewish literature, apart from the New Testament, is it used in reference to God.

How did it get here, then? Only one answer is possible: Jesus used it (see Mark 14:36, for instance), and the sense of closeness to God and intimacy with God that it communicated made the very word an unforgettable part of Christian tradition. It is especially appropriate, then, that Paul includes it here to stress the glory and joy of adoption. It dramatizes the intimate ties of sonship. The law scolds us and convicts us until, in our weakness, the Spirit of God cries in our hearts, "Abba, Father." This cry to which we are moved by the Spirit simply says, "I am in deep need; I do not know what to do or where to turn, but I am your child."

Should we ever be kept in a state of uncertainty as to our status with God? There are those who believe we should. Paul says No. The gospel of the Son of God is reassurance for every sinner. To have received the Spirit of Christ is the sign that we as adopted sons are heirs of God's full blessing, for "the Spirit bears witness with our Spirit that we are the children of God" (Rom. 8:16).

One Step Forward, Two Steps Back, 4:8–11

Does Paul deny the existence of the forces which had enslaved the Galatians before they became Christians? What does he say about them? Why did Paul correct himself in verse 9?

The Apostle now pleads with the Galatian Christians, calling attention to the days before the gospel came to them when they were living in bondage and fear. Having accepted Christ, ". . . how can you turn back . . ." he asks. This is progress in reverse. This is one step forward and two steps backwards. Paul is once more expressing surprise and keen disappointment that they would return to non-Christian idols and practices which, though they may be worshiped, are no gods. They have been freed from such by their knowledge of God—or rather, as he quickly catches himself, because God has first sought them; Paul continues to insist that his gospel centers on God's work, not man's works.

The appeal is to not turn back to "the elemental spirits," which have been mentioned earlier. For the Gentiles these elemental things had not been the Jewish law. But now to go under the law, as the false teachers urged, would be to return to the old pattern of external rules and regulations from which they had been delivered. The law is weak in that it can define sin and convict the sinner, but it cannot offer a remedy. It is also beggarly when it is compared to the richness of God's grace: For every changing situation the law needed a new rule, whereas the grace of God is sufficient for all situations.

Special attention is called once more to "days and months and seasons and years," and advisedly so, for the principle of this matter is still with us today. *Days* then referred to the weekly Sabbath; *months* to special occasions determined by the moon; *seasons* to the annual feasts, such as the Passover; and *years* to the sabbatical year every seventh year. The Apostle surely is not condemning good order in religious worship, nor denying that there can be value in stated services and ceremonies. But the Judaizers had been urging the Gentile Christians, who had so recently come out of the ritual of pagan practices, as well as superstition and fear, to return to methodical observances in order to obtain favor with God. This is once more like worshiping gods which do not exist. By your conduct, Paul means to say, you indicate that you want to be slaves once more. Had the Apostle done all of his work for nothing? Was he exaggerating when he said, "I am afraid I have labored over you in vain" (4:11)? Not likely! Having come out of the law's slavery, he knew better than anyone else what was involved. Had the Judaizers succeeded in imposing this bondage on the early church, if a set of observances to gain divine favor had been saddled upon it, the gospel of grace would have been void and the conscience of man would not yet be free.

To what extent is legalism still a part of our lives today? Christianity is living the whole of life in obedience to Christ's will and in loyalty to his work. But men find such total demands burdensome and frightening. We seek to escape them by defining Christianity as going to church and keeping certain rules. Such things may be the sustenance of religion, but they are not its substance. *Yet who of us does not at times prefer to be regulated by standards, often of our own choosing, rather than to seek in our decisions the guidance of the Holy Spirit? To what extent is a certain amount of such legalism necessary? When does it become dangerous?*

"Follow Me," 4:12–20

Children often play a game called "Follow the Leader." As

Paul continues his plea in the letter, that is about what he is asking the congregation to do. He becomes very personal once more in calling them brothers and, a little later, "my little children." He reminds them of how they received him when he first came to them, a sick man. They could have scorned or despised him for his weakness, but instead they received him as Christ Jesus himself. They did him no wrong; in fact, they would have plucked out their eyes and given them to him. Now what has happened?

"Have I then become your enemy by telling you the truth?" Once Paul had first place in their hearts, but now others do. Why? Why? What are these false teachers after? Now "they make much of you" but only for the purpose of having you honor them later. In bringing Christ to you I travailed as a mother having her child. And now I feel the hurt all over again until Christ is formed in you once more.

All of this has been said in support of the Apostle's plea to imitate him. What is our usual thought of a person who says, "You must be like I am"? This can be and often is supreme egotism, but is this what Paul means? There was a time when Paul as a Pharisee thought he was blameless. He had everything and he knew everything. And then he discovered how empty and futile it all was, that he was nothing in himself, and that he had to look beyond himself to Jesus Christ in order to be given the gift of righteousness. Now, "brethren, I beseech you," cease to win your own righteousness, and like me, look away from yourself to our Lord for his gift. Become as I am, dependent upon God; weak in myself, my life is effective—as you know by experience (4:13–14)—only through God's power.

Sarah and Hagar: an Allegory, 4:21–31

Having made his personal plea, the Apostle, wishing that he might be with them instead of writing them a letter, says that he is all mixed up about them. But he also says that he wants to try once more to explain. For this purpose he used what in gospel history is called the Abrahamic allegory.

The Jewish rabbis said that Scripture, in addition to its literal, historical meaning, had a special spiritual significance, an allegorical meaning. This was even true of every word, figure of speech, and grammatical form. This method of interpretation had undoubtedly been used by Paul before his conversion and was surely familiar to the Judaizers. In this method the historical facts are not explained away but are invested with new meaning, the latter supposedly being the ultimate spiritual truth. In Galatians Paul treats allegorically an event in the history of God's people, not as original proof, but as confirmation of what he has already proved. *

The story itself as history is very familiar. God had made a promise to Abraham that he would be the father of a great nation. But both Abraham and Sarah were getting old and there was as yet no son or heir. Among ancient peoples, however, including the biblical patriarchal families, there was a custom that a man's wife who had no children could ask her husband to take one of her slave maidens to become his proxy wife. The regulation was that the baby born of such a union was to be delivered between the knees of the wife; it was then considered her own child.

Sarah chose her slave-maiden Hagar, an Egyptian girl, and to this union a son was born. But Hagar, instead of acting out her part, mocked Sarah for her shame in being childless. God planned otherwise and promised Sarah that she would have a son. Sarah laughed at the thought, but in due time Isaac was born. Trouble brewed in the household, however, and when Sarah saw Isaac and Ishmael playing together she asked her husband to send Hagar and Ishmael away. (There was a Jewish tradition that Ishmael was mistreating Isaac; cf. 4:29.) Abraham was displeased for, after all, Ishmael was his son. But God told him to do what Sarah asked because the promise was to be fulfilled through Isaac. God also said that for the sake of Abraham, he would make a nation of the son of Hagar. The two nations today are the Jews and the Arabs.

In giving this historical event an allegorical meaning, Paul draws a contrast between the false sonship of Ishmael and the true sonship of Isaac. Ishmael had been born naturally, but Isaac was the son of divine promise, born to Sarah when she was past the normal child-bearing age. The two women are now made to be the symbols of the two covenants: Hagar the representative of the covenant of the law made at Sinai, which put Israel in bondage to the law, and Sarah the representative of the new covenant of faith for Jew and Gentile alike. Hagar and her son are now cast out into the Arabian desert with God's approval, showing that God meant to replace the law with the new covenant. The thrust of the illustration was that Ishmael, the son of the slave woman representative of the law, could not inherit the promise given to Abraham. Neither could Ishmael and Isaac live together, as the Judaizers were trying to get the Galatians to do, for Judaism cannot combine with Christianity. One is a legalistic system, the other is free grace. Ishmael represents man's efforts, his attempt to do God's will by works; Isaac represents hearing with faith (3:2) the promises of God.

Paul's whole argument, as he closes the doctrinal portion of the letter, has been to show that there is no place for legalism in the church. Christians both then and now must not enslave themselves in legal bondage and forfeit the freedom of faith.

REVIEW

1. In what ways does Christ today set free "wage slaves"? men enslaved to drink? men enslaved by prejudice?

2. From what other kinds of twentieth-century slavery does Christ free men? How?

3. Which of Paul's qualities ought to be imitated (4:12) and which avoided?

4. A parent comments on rearing children: "I think some of us let them twist us around their fingers. I don't think we lay down the law. Isn't it possible to say, 'You cannot do that unless you do your homework first'?" Is this parent a legalist? How are law and freedom and Spirit related in rearing children? How does this illustrate Paul's point?

10 Obligations of Freedom

ADVANCE STUDY

1. Read Galatians 5:1–15. What is Christian freedom according to these verses?

2. Why does Paul feel such hostility in verse 12?

3. What restrictions do you find Paul placing on freedom, if any?

4. Where did Paul get the idea expressed in verse 14?

The Sandbox or the Classroom

There is a four-story school building on the edge of Greenwich Village in New York City called the Fifteenth Street School. It has two unusual things about it: it was established by TV panelist Orson Bean, and its students do not have to attend classes at all if they would rather play in a sandbox. The school is patterned after the famous Summerhill School in England, founded by Dr. A. S. Niell, a British child psychologist. In 1964 Bean bought the building, hired four teachers, and received a charter from the New York State Board of Regents. The school in 1965–1966 had forty-one students in nursery, kindergarten, and first grade, and the founder hopes to add a grade a year through grade twelve.

The curriculum follows the New York State plan, but the children are free to attend class or stay away. "The point," explained the founder, "is to get the children to take on responsibility for their own behavior. This is brought about by giving them freedom. We are not permissive. We have strict discipline and strong rules about respecting the rights of others. These rules are not arbitrary but based on common sense. We believe in freedom without license, that there is responsibility involved in all freedom."[1]

In writing to the Galatian Christians, Paul, in the section under discussion, tells them that they are "called to freedom . . . only do not use your freedom as an opportunity for the flesh . . ." that is, you are not to do as you please without any sense of obligation or responsibility. This doctrine of Christian liberty is the high point of the letter: all that has been said before has moved towards this climax. Galatians is often called "The Letter on Christian Liberty."

Galatians 3—4 has been called the theological part of the letter because of the Apostle's statement on the nature of justification by faith. Now he moves, as he does in all of his letters, from theology to ethics—how to live what we believe. The soundest and purest theology is of no value unless it is lived out in daily associations; to say, "I believe in God," and then disregard him in all we do and say is folly. This practical part is the final effort to persuade the Gentile Christians to stand fast in the freedom Christ has given us, and "not submit again to a yoke of slavery." The Galatians had accepted salvation as a gift. This strong warning against its loss has in it the implication that if they now add rites and ceremonies to gain added favor or as a substitute for the free gift, they are returning to the paganism from which they have come.

Stepping Back to Cybele

Circumcision was surely a key matter in all of the discussion on the law and the gospel. It was the initial rite of admittance into the Jewish commonwealth, baby sons being circumcised on the eighth day (see Luke 2:21). Practiced by many ancient peoples as a sanitary measure, the slight operation had taken on religious significance for the Jews at the command of God. It was a symbol of the grace of God. Proselytes to the Jewish faith accepted the rite as the the first step towards full fellowship with the Hebrews.

The problem was that the Gentile Christians had received the grace of God through faith in Christ, without having known anything about the law or circumcision. Many of them had recently come from the pagan worship of Cybele with its sexual perversions and its mutilation practices for priests and pious devotees. The false teachers were not asking that the Gentiles return to such practices, of course, but were saying that the Jewish rite of circumcision was a first step to full Christian citizenship.

It is understandable that this had a real appeal for some of the recent pagans. Their only Bible was the Old Testament, in which the rite was commanded by God. But Paul rejected the imposition of circumcision on ex-pagan converts because it was an attempt to gain spirituality "on their own." That is why Paul was so adamant. ". . . if you receive circumcision, Christ will be of no advantage to you." Be circumcised, and you lose everything, was Paul's clear-cut word. No wonder the Galatians were confused.

Paul's attitude could have been a problem to the Jewish Christians, for they had already been circumcised and this could not be undone. It reminds one of the problem facing missionaries among polygamous tribes. A man has three wives and now becomes a Christian. What must he do? Shall he send two of the women back into the bush, or what? For the Jewish Christian Paul solved the dilemma by clearly saying that circumcision for the Christian can do no harm; it simply does not matter, "For in Christ Jesus neither circumcision nor uncircumcision is of any avail, but faith working through love."

To the Gentile Christian Paul said in effect, Forget circumcision. It is not necessary; it will do you no good. To the Jewish Christian who had already undergone the rite he said, Disregard it; it may be good as a health measure, but it has no religious value, now that Christ is yours by faith.

The Apostle does not leave the Gentiles without logical reason. Take one step in legalism and then you must take a second, and a third, and so on *ad infinitum*. "I testify again to every man who receives circumcision that he is bound to keep the whole law." It is like a person from another country applying for citizenship in the United States. He cannot say that he will just keep one or two of our laws. If citizenship is granted he must promise to obey all of the laws of the country. John Calvin quotes Hugo Grotius, the Dutch jurist and theologian (1583–1645) who said: "If Judaism is the road to salvation, the whole of Judaism must be observed. You must not cull or throw away whatever part of it you think fit."

Paul certainly could testify to that, as he says. The harder he had tried in his earlier days, the more he realized the impossibility of it all. The law had only brought to him the knowledge of his sin. Not until he had cast himself upon the mercy and the love of God through faith in Jesus Christ did he experience any sense of freedom.

Paul's Galatian brethren had known this once, but now they were seemingly going back at least part of the way at the insistence of the Judaizers. Considering their background, the false teaching had a strong appeal. The inference seems to be that the first step had not as yet been taken by many, and therefore the well known proverb that a "little yeast leavens the whole lump," was an appropriate warning.

As a boy growing up on a farm in Michigan, I remember mother burying a yeast cake in a pan of dough up there on the warming oven of the cook stove. It was always a mystery, but in time the little bubbles would rise to make at last the bread that boys like. The leaven was a necessary ingredient for making good bread. In biblical times leaven generally consisted of a portion of dough preserved from a previous batch.

For the Jew leaven nearly always symbolized evil. There was no time for the leaven to work when the Hebrews left Egypt in great haste (Exod. 12:34–39). This use of unleavened bread continued in Israel's customs in connection with the Passover and does to this day. The objection to leaven was simply that fermentation of the yeast was a symbol of corruption. In Matthew's Gospel, "leaven" describes the unsound teaching of the Pharisees (Matt. 16:11–12); in 1 Corinthians, the loose living of the Corinthians (1 Cor. 5:6–8); and in Galatians, the false teaching on circumcision (5:9). Jesus used the symbol in a good sense when he talked about the silent but steady growth of the Kingdom of God among men (Luke 13:20–21).

In the use of the figure here Paul is referring more to the evil teaching than to the corrupting teachers. When he says "a little yeast," he seems to infer that the change of mind and heart is just beginning, that the fermentation has not as yet gone very far, but that there is great danger if the process is not stopped at once and the yeast rooted out. The Apostle has "confidence" that the Galatians will "take no other view" than his.

Paul's mind was jumping all over the place as he dictated to his secretary. From yeast to a race course was a long jump, but in his extreme agitation the Apostle had made it. Illustrations from the Olympic and other games were often used by the evangelist. Paul took the fight, the rules, the race, the prize, and the goal as good portrayals of Christian life and activity. The Galatians were running a good race, but now they were being "hindered" from obeying the truth. Someone was putting roadblocks on the race course.

One of the hurdles was the accusation that Paul still preached circumcision. He does not clarify this and it is difficult to see how the charge could be made against him. Could the fact that Paul was a Jew and did preach from the Old Testament have been the basis for the accusation? He does not explain but simply asks, Why, if what they say is true, are they then slandering him still? This is after all what they want. If it is true, then his preaching of the cross is no longer a stumbling block to them. In effect, Paul says, "The fact that I am still criticized by the Judaizers shows that I do not really teach what they now try to say I teach." And here his righteous anger flares at the accusation; where someone today might justifiably have said, "Go to the devil," Paul says to his tormentors, "Go become eunuchs! I wish those who unsettle you would mutilate themselves!" The reference is to the practice of castration by the priests of Cybele. The language was harsh and showed his utter contempt both for circumcision and for those who were seeking to saddle the rite upon the Gentile believers.

What Is Christian Liberty?

Liberty in general is freedom from restraint or compulsion. In the purest sense it is power to do as one pleases. In a city or state this freedom is limited by the requirements and the well-being of others. Christian freedom says, as Paul establishes in this letter, that a Christian is a free man because Christ has set him free. He is free from legal rules as conditions of salvation; he does not need ceremonies to aid him in getting right or staying right with God, and sin and evil habits and desires no longer have dominion over him. But as civil liberty is limited by the well-being of others, so Christian freedom is limited by the fact that a Christian has given himself completely to Jesus Christ, his Master and Lord.

Martin Luther, whose advice we are taking here, knew what he was talking about. "When I was a monk I tried ever so hard to live up to the strict rules of my order. I used to make a list of my sins, and I was always on the way to confession, and whatever penances were enjoined upon me I performed religiously. In spite of it all, my conscience was always in a fever of doubt. The more I sought to help my poor stricken conscience the worse it got. The more I paid attention to the regulations the more I transgressed them."

What is the exact role of the conscience in Christian liberty? Does it guide us helpfully—as to repay taxes dishonestly withheld —or does it torture us needlessly, as in the case of Luther? Or does it do one thing to one person, another to another? From what does grace set us free?

In the matter of freedom of conduct, the Christian looks to God in the knowledge that God is not angry but merciful, and that by his living Spirit he will guide us into the truth and into the right way. If fear assails us, if conscience accuses us that we have not done enough, if the wrath of God seems to descend, we are reminded that " '. . . with everlasting love I will have compassion on you,' says the Lord, your Redeemer" (Isa. 54:8).

Christian freedom, as Paul implies (5:13), is freedom from fear and from bondage, but not liberty to give ourselves over to the sins of passion and lust. We are not free to sin but free not to sin. Freedom gives us unlimited opportunity—to love and to act in love. It does not provide "an opportunity for the flesh."

"The flesh" here does not refer to the physical body but to those sinful impulses which seek to control the will and which often are expressed in the physical body in such sins as greed and lust. These impulses are tempted to use liberty as an occasion to go all out of bounds. This was especially true in Galatia: for those who had been so recently set free the pendulum had swung all the way over to license. Some find freedom incredible: in his book, *Thinking Black*, Dan Crawford said that ". . . we Missionaries are reaping the harvest of this oppression [the slave trade], for the worst type of convert is the redeemed slave. The man is still in a fog, and has not yet shaken off the chattel idea even in the glorious idea of the Gospel."[2] Others go to the opposite extreme of total license. We cannot just let the "set-free" sinner go. His release comes only when he comes under another law, the law of love.

The Paradox

The gospel is a paradox. It sets the sinner free from one law to place him under another. The gospel helps one to change places from being a slave to sin to being a slave to Christ. It gives freedom to servants only to make them servants to one another. Peter urges us: "Live as free men, yet without using your freedom as a pretext for evil; but live as servants of God" (1 Pet. 2:16).

In interpreting the paradox Paul tells the Galatians how this freedom is to be used. That always is the question anyway: not what we have but what we do with what we have. The lawful use of liberty is that it is regulated by love. Here the Apostle goes back to the heart of the legal code itself, when he quotes, ". . . you shall love your neighbor as yourself . . ." (Lev. 19:18). What a clever way to show the Judaizers that they were transgressing their own law! Jesus too had approved this law of God when a lawyer had asked him about inheriting eternal life (Luke 10:25), and Paul said that the "whole law is fulfilled in [this] one word" (5:14).

My Neighbor and the Obligations of Freedom

"Who is my neighbor?" is a question often asked and not too easily answered today. The classic answer is in our Lord's response to the same question, the story of the Good Samaritan (Luke 10:29–37). When the story had been told and the lawyer had replied that it was the Samaritan who showed true neighborliness because of the mercy he put in practice, Jesus said, "Go and do likewise." This says that everyone needing our help regardless of race or creed is our neighbor.

In the story the need was medical care, food, and hotel charges, and the Samaritan supplied all three. It was an immediate answer to an immediate need. But think of today's world with its millions who need medicine and bread. J. Paul Getty, rated as the world's richest man today, writing on "The World Is Mean to Millionaires" in the *Saturday Evening Post,* says that he receives 200 to 2000 letters a day asking for money. "If I were convinced that by giving away my fortune I could make a real contribution toward solving the problems of world poverty, I'd give away 99.5 percent of all that I have immediately. But . . . this is not the case. The best form of charity I know is the act of meeting a payroll."[3] Are needs met by either meeting a payroll *or* giving, or should those who can do so seek to do *both?*

Almost a more basic question is how much to love our neighbor. The ancient Levitical law, endorsed by Jesus, is to love the neighbor as much as I love myself. Love cannot be measured by the bushel, but it can be seen in kind. I am created in the image of God. Do I think of my neighbor in the same way? How do you think the priest and the Levite felt about the wounded man? Love for neighbor as for self says that we give everyone his right; that we neither do nor talk harm, but only good; that we truly feel that our neighbor's welfare is involved with our own. It is more than just being nice to other people. It means that we carry another's load if necessary (6:2). Right neighbor love implies the love of God, as Jesus said. Indeed, this is its first test and visible fruit.

Some of the church members in Galatia must have been seriously lacking in this love for one another. Paul speaks of their biting and devouring one another and warns that if they continue they will just eat each other up. The image is one of wild beasts, as when two bull moose lock horns in a fight and both perish.

REVIEW

1. "A Christian man is a perfectly free Lord of all, subject to none." "A Christian man is a perfectly dutiful servant of all, subject to all." So wrote Martin Luther. How can both statements be true? What would Paul say about Luther's paradox?

2. Some advocates of the so-called new morality say that we are bound by no absolute laws, not even the commandment against adultery, but that we are simply bound to absolute love of our neighbors in whatever situation we may be. In what sense, if any, would Paul agree? Would you?

3. *Dietrich Bonhoeffer, martyred under Hitler, once wrote:*
"Cheap grace is the deadly enemy of our Church. We are fighting
to-day for costly grace. . . . Cheap grace is the preaching of for-
giveness without requiring repentance, baptism without church dis-
cipline, Communion without confession, absolution without per-
sonal confession."[4] *Would Paul's doctrine of free grace agree with*
or disagree with Bonhoeffer's concept of "costly grace"? Which
verses support your answer?

11 Walking by the Spirit

ADVANCE STUDY

1. The word for the great Paul's great guide for life is repeated seven times in Galatians 5:16–25. See if you can find what it is and underline each occurrence in your Bible.

2. Draw a circle around each occurrence of the opposite word, "flesh." What is Paul saying about these two?

3. Which is Paul saying in Galatians 6:1–5, that we are to bear each other's burdens or that every man is to bear his own load?

Self-Torment

Martin Luther, in his commentary on Galatians, writes very plainly about one of his personal problems. "When I was a monk," he says, "I thought I was lost forever whenever I felt an evil emotion, carnal lust, wrath, hatred, or envy. I tried to quiet my conscience in many ways, but it did not work, because lust would always come back and give me no rest. I told myself: 'You have permitted this and that sin, envy, impatience, and the like. Your joining this holy order has been in vain, and all your good works are good for nothing.' If at that time I had understood this passage, 'The flesh lusteth against the Spirit, and the Spirit against the flesh,' I could have spared myself many a day of self-torment. I would have said to myself: 'Martin, you will never be without sin, for you have flesh. Despair not, but resist the flesh.' "

What comfort did Martin Luther say he found in 5:16–26? Why did he not find verse 21 fatal to his hopes of salvation, do you suppose? Write a paragraph setting forth the basic principles of Christian living that are found in verses 16–25. Write a second paragraph

*describing what practical influence these principles could have on
you as you face an ordinary day. What is the difference between
"live" and "walk" in verse 25?*

Thus far in the letter, Paul has explained what Christian liberty
is, and from what and for what the Galatian Christians have been
set free. His argument in calling attention to the basic Levitical law
of loving one's neighbor as one's self was exceedingly astute, for this
was a law which Jesus himself had quoted, one which the false
teachers could not set aside.

The question now was how the Galatians could use this liberty,
how this loving of one's neighbor as one's self could be expressed
in a practical way. Serious problems had arisen among the church
members in their personal relationships. In this new-found relationship, how should the matter of living together be resolved? Liberty
could be either used or abused, as money can be handled or mis-
handled. If liberty is misused, it brings nothing but a curse and in
the end destruction. As the ethical section of the letter continues,
therefore, Paul makes a strong appeal to the Galatian Christians to
stand firm in the freedom with which Christ has set them free. One
of the ways of doing this, says the Apostle, is to "walk by the Spirit,
and do not gratify the desires of the flesh" (5:16).

Spirit and Flesh

"Spirit" and "flesh" are not different elements of our human
nature, as is sometimes thought. By "the Spirit" the Apostle refers to
the Holy Spirit, the power of God available to all Christians since
Pentecost (Acts 2). The Christians in Galatia had already received
the baptism of the Spirit, as was evidenced by the signs and wonders which had been seen (3:1–5). All the good and gracious impulses within the believers came from the living Spirit. Whatever
there was of love and joy and good works came when the Spirit of
God moved the human spirit within.

"Flesh," as indicated in the previous chapter, is not simply our
bodies, but is the whole human nature as it exists apart from God.
It is the unregenerate nature of a person. It is human nature tainted
and despoiled by sin. Our body is a part of that nature, but there is
much beside that; "sins of the flesh" include such things as pride as
well as adultery.

This call by Paul to "walk by the Spirit" is in the nature of a battle cry. I can almost see him raising a banner and shouting a resounding challenge. The Judaizers had said, "Live by the law"; Paul cried, "Walk by the Spirit of God." This call repeats what has been evident all through the letter, the battle early Christianity had to fight between two tendencies of thought, prevalent even today. One view conceives of religion as consisting of outward obedience to law, a series of painful efforts to keep the rules; the other recognizes that the Christian religion is a new, divine life, a life from which the bondage to fear and sin has been removed, wherein one freely walks with the Lord in the light of his Word.

"Walk by the Spirit"

"To walk" is a phrase often used biblically to express the comings and goings of our everyday life. It refers more to the routine and the practical than to the special events and the extraordinary. It is "living from day to day in the usual way." The Spirit is to be our unseen companion as we travel the road to guide us in the direction we should go.

Most of us would agree that a Christian has within himself two natures, a lower and a higher. The lower consists of that part of us to which the sins of life make their strong, almost instinctive appeal. All the dry rot of life centers in this lower nature, as the Apostle shows in his catalogue of the sins of the flesh.

The higher nature is a person's better self. Both Luther and Calvin called it "the conscience," the instructing intuition that distinguishes right from wrong, an inner quality given to the man by the Creator, partially deadened by sin, but requickened by the Holy Spirit. Both of these natures desire to rule the whole man, the "flesh" desiring the loosing of all restraint, the spirit within man, as guided by the Holy Spirit, seeking to bring the body into subjection. The Apostle himself speaks on another occasion about the struggle in his own life in this respect. ". . . I pommel my body and subdue it . . ." he said (1 Cor. 9:27), which someone has described as a real prizefight, for freely translated it reads, "Daily I give myself a black eye." For the good to be dominant, we must change much of our thinking from the lower to the higher level.

Here is where many of us fail and come short. How much thought do we give to things of the Spirit in the average day? Before any step or any plan, do we deliberately open a door to the motivating power of God's Spirit? Walking by the Spirit is not automatic. He does not force himself upon us. He offers his companionship, but we have been created with the capacity to accept it or to reject it. His walking along with us must definitely be sought, and to many this is an unreality. The Spirit is to them at best a nebulous something, whose association with us as an infallible Guide may be something to talk about, but is rarely of practical significance.

On the other hand there is abundant testimony from men and women who speak of having been controlled and directed by God's Spirit. How can we know the Spirit is with us? What attitude on our part can make him more real? The Apostle says that "those who belong to Christ Jesus have crucified the flesh . . ." (5:24). For them the Spirit working with the human spirit has won the victory.

What Walking by the Spirit Does

Walking by the Spirit conquers the flesh, says the Apostle. Let it be said once more that the latter means more than the physical aspect of one's being. It was Grecian philosophy, not Christian teaching, which said that this part of a man was more base and less worthy. The Bible, because of the creation and especially because the Son of God assumed human flesh, has insisted that the human body is something worthy in God's sight, fit to be used in his service. By "the desires of the flesh" Paul means everything that is expressive of sinful human nature, whether or not the body is involved. One does not necessarily have to move a muscle to sin in the flesh.

To make the matter quite concrete and practical for the Galatians, Paul now lists a catalogue of transgressions. The list surely was not all inclusive, but pointed particularly to those practices and attitudes prevalent in the world of that day. The fifteen sins which are mentioned are in the nature of a measuring rod by which the church members could ascertain if they were walking by the Spirit. Such lists of vices were quite common in the Stoic writings of the day. Paul, too, in at least four other letters, makes a systematic presentation of the current evils. (See Rom. 13:13; 1 Cor. 5:10–11;

6:9–10; Eph. 4:31; 5:3–4; Col. 3:5, 8.) These, the Apostle says in effect, are so plain that everyone can see the evil.

Biblical scholars often divide this list of vices in the letter into four categories:

(1) Sensual Sins

(a) *Immorality*—This is the first in the list and means illicit sexual intercouse. In Roman days this was considered both moral and natural; it was even thought essential by many, as it is in some places today. The N.E.B. uses the word "fornication," which generally means sexual intimacy between unmarried persons, such as the premarital testing employed by many. The Christian is chaste, reserving the intimate love life for the marriage relationship.

(b) *Impurity*—This word refers to all sexual deviation such as homosexuality and lesbianism, as well as intercourse with animals. It is like the festering pus of an unclean wound because of which one is unfit to associate with his fellowmen. Impurity finally affects not only the physical being but the whole personality.

(c) *Licentiousness*—This includes the first two, but goes a step farther. Now all the bars are down, every restraint is removed, and there is complete abandonment to evil. Persons may try to hide their fornication or practice impurity in secret, but the indecent (N.E.B.) person does not care if he shocks people. There are no limits.

It must be noted that each and everyone of these three is in direct violation of God's seventh commandment.

(2) Idolatrous Sins

(a) *Idolatry*—The worship of godless images. Paul mentions this next in the list because idolatry was often associated with sexual sins in the pagan world, both male and female prostitutes often being a part of idol worship. For us idol worship takes place when material things or anything else become our god.

(b) *Sorcery*—This was the use of power gained supposedly by the assistance of evil spirits. This brand of idolatry was quite common in the ancient world. Luke tells of converted sorcerers in Corinth who brought their books valued at fifty thousand pieces of silver and burned them (Acts 19:18–20).

(3)   Sins of Personal Animosity—There must have been personal unfriendliness between members of the church to have produced such a list of shortcomings. This must have been a general condition then as now, for a number of these vices are mentioned in four other letters, as well as the Acts. How many of the same evils are present today in your congregation? (Dare I ask: in your heart?)

(a)   *Enmity*—This is ill will and antagonism towards others. A person who bears enmity is always hostile to his fellowmen. He has no real love for others.

(b)   *Strife*—To strive for the laurel wreath in the Olympian games in Paul's day was an honorable effort, but here Paul means quarrelsome rivalry.

(c)   *Jealousy*—This is a double-pronged vice. It is the desire to have what others have irrespective of whether or not one has earned the right to it. One who drives a low-priced car can be almost insanely jealous of a neighbor who owns a Cadillac, even though he himself does not have the means either to buy or maintain a large automobile. Jealousy also arises when there is fear or mistrust. In this sense married persons can be distrustful of each other, or students of the teacher, or workmen of the manager.

(d)   *Anger*—Paul here means sudden bursts of temper like a quick explosion, after which one just as quickly simmers down. It is like the uncontrolled temper tantrums of a child who the next minute smiles and plays again. For an adult this spells immaturity.

(e)   *Selfishness*—This is an egotism which causes one to give exclusive attention to his own interest. It is self-seeking without any consideration of others.

(f)   *Dissension*—This is discord or disagreement in opinion. As this is being written there is strong dissension between the Buddhist and Catholic groups in Vietnam without concern for the common fight against the Viet Cong. But this staying apart instead of working together serves to make impossible the unity of the country for the good of the whole. Near where I live is a city with many vices and public evils. The Protestants in the city are strong enough to control the civil government if only the so-called liberals and conservatives could cease their dissension; now they simply let the evil, their common enemy, have its way in the city.

(g) *Party Spirit*—This is stepped-up dissension in which people change from disliking each other's views to disliking each other. This is the root out of which sects and schisms are born. The Pharisees and the Sadducees of Paul's day were good examples of party spirit.

(h) *Envy*—The Greek Stoics of Paul's day said that envy was grief at someone else's good. An envious man may have no desire to excel; he just hates to see the progress and excellence of others. He begrudges another person what he has, even though the latter may have gained what he has by hard work or hard thinking.

(4) Sins of Intemperance

(a) *Drunkenness*—This vice was not too common in the Hellenistic world of Paul's day, because wine was a mild beverage usually consisting of three parts of water to two of wine. However, the worshipers of Cybele often indulged too much.

(b) *Carousing*—The N.E.B. translates this "orgies." The word first referred to the dancing and singing after a victory at the games. But the revelry often went out of control and degenerated into license, leading to every kind of intemperance.

There were more, for the Apostle adds, "and the like." The penalty was clear cut and unequivocal: ". . . those who do such things shall not inherit the kingdom of God." Is this to be taken as applying to single acts (no man who is jealous, for instance, can be saved) or is Paul talking about a pattern of life? Or is this question

—how close can I come to being lost and still be saved?—quite inappropriate for a Christian even to ask?

New Tastes and High Desires

Overcoming the sins of the flesh is a positive and not a negative business. Often our prayers to be rid of sin and evil seem to receive no answer until God's Spirit is allowed free course in the human spirit. It is then that we acquire new tastes and high desires. We go no further in the search of lower pleasures. The Spirit puts a bridle on our desires when the reins are in his hands. It is then that the fruit of the Spirit—love, joy, peace, patience, kindness, goodness, faithfulness, gentleness, and self-control—are the obvious by-products of walking with our unseen Companion.

A New Trap

From this high plane of "the fruit of the Spirit," Paul immediately comes back to a very practical problem. He has argued that our lives are not to be ruled by laws and regulations. However, when these are removed there is danger of falling into a new trap, that of regulating ourselves by comparing ourselves to others.

In one of my pastorates it was still the custom, when I began my ministry there, for the deacons to circulate among the homes of the congregation with a subscription list for the pastor's salary. Quite often one member would ask to see the list and then, comparing himself with his neighbor, would make his own subscription.

In 5:25—6:3 Paul does not talk about giving, but he does say in effect: Suppose a man is overtaken in a fault (that is, caught in a sudden temptation by one of the works of the flesh); he is not to be shunned, but the effort is to be made to "restore him in a spirit of gentleness." To "restore" is literally to "mend," as one would carefully set a broken bone. Worldly men seize on the fault of another to insult or to reproach him. Even some Christians experience a secret, inward glee at the downfall of another, thinking they will now look better by comparison. But a wise Christian gets under the burden with his fellowman to help him bear the load of moral responsibility. It is then that he walks by the Spirit.

This matter of bearing one another's burdens is not one of

moral responsibility only, but also has its very practical aspects. Think what Christians could do as individuals, families, or congregations to minister to illegitimate children, to children in homes where one parent is gone, to the alcoholic or dope addict and his family, etc. The tragedies of our days offer countless opportunities for burden-bearing in the name and spirit of Jesus Christ.

More good, practical advice is found in 6:4: test your own work. As a boy out on the farm in Michigan I often felt that my brother was not doing his share. "You just hoe your own row," my father would say. The tendency to take our eyes off our own work and to compare ourselves with how little or how much others do is all too prevalent. Ultimately, as Paul says, ". . . each man will have to bear his own load."

In dictating this thought of sharing with one another as Christians, Paul's rapidly moving mind suddenly turned in another direction, to the elders in the churches (6:6). Luke says that such elders had been appointed (Acts 14:23), and Paul now says that these teachers must be given a living by those who are taught.

Then, just as quickly, Paul turns to speak a very earnest warning (6:7). God's eye is upon us all, he says in effect. In our freedom from the law we cannot thumb our nose at God. God sees whether we sow to the flesh or to the Spirit. The reward of walking by the Spirit will be a holy life lived in communion with God both now and on into the other side of time.

REVIEW

1. One popular moral maxim is, "Let your conscience be your guide!" In what sense, as suggested by this chapter, does the Christian agree or disagree?

2.   Have you ever known a person who did so truly "walk by the Spirit" that he had the qualities described in 5:22–24?

3.   Can you recall times when Paul's advice in 6:1–2 was carried out by your own church or class members?

4.   Which verse do you agree with: Galatians 6:2 or 6:5? In what sense, if any, can both be true?

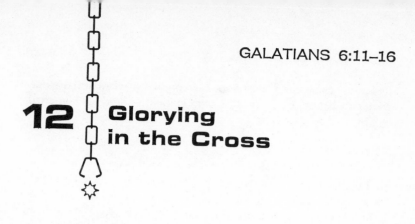

12 Glorying in the Cross

ADVANCE STUDY

1. Galatians 6:11–16 is a personally written postscript to the letter. Why do you think Paul added it?

2. In these verses Paul says certain things do not matter and certain things are of utmost importance. Which words in this passage fall in each category?

The Cross in the Colosseum

On my last visit in Rome I made a special trip to the Colosseum to touch the cross in that ancient ruin. This great sports arena was completed about A.D. 80 by Titus after his destruction of Jerusalem, with the help of 30,000 Jewish slaves. In a niche in the wall at the far end of the ruin stands a cross. It was placed there by the Italian government in the days of Benito Mussolini in honor of Telemachus, the Asian monk who, tradition says, died in the arena because he gloried in the cross.

Telemachus lived and ministered around A.D. 400. In a vision he had been instructed to go to Rome; he arrived on a day when a great celebration was in progress. There was rejoicing in a victory over the Goths, and 80,000 people were in their seats in the Colosseum. The gladiators stood before Caesar and cried, "Hail, Caesar, we who are about to die salute thee." With this Telemachus jumped into the arena and cried, "In the name of the crucified Christ, forbear!" There were titters and jeers, and finally one of the gladiators ran him through with his spear. As the life blood of the monk ebbed away and mingled with the sand, one by one the great throng left the arena. Soon the Colosseum was empty. No gladiatorial games were ever held there again. One who gloried in the cross had cried, "Stop!"[1]

A Postscript

To set forth this central theme of all his preaching once more, Paul concludes his letter with a postscript in his own handwriting. It was quite customary in that day to dictate to a secretary and then, with the signature, to add a personal P.S., even as we often do in business today. Sometimes only general instructions were given to the secretary, who then drafted the letter, and the author would add a postscript with his signature. The Letter to the Galatians, however, gives every indication of having been dictated by an agitated man who was pacing the floor and who, in his zeal, sometimes left a sentence or thought unfinished. In this spirit, Paul returns to the central issue with which he began, that of circumcision. In a few sentences, some of them very sharp and positive, he sums up the main thrust of the letter.

The K.J.V. in verse 11 suggests that Paul apologizes for having written such a long letter, but a more accurate translation indicates that he is referring to the letters that make up the words, not to the whole of Galatians. Paul's hand may have been hurt in the riots in Perga; or possibly his eyesight was poor (were his eyes permanently damaged on the Damascus Road?); and he therefore wrote as a child might, in block capitals. Whatever the reason, it does not temper the scorn with which he rebukes the false teachers for their insincerity and selfish motives. What were the specific charges so pointedly made in his own handwriting against the false teachers?

The first rebuke was for their cowardly actions in seeking to force the Gentile converts to practice circumcision so that the teachers would be protected from persecution. Galatia was a Roman province, you remember, and Rome recognized Judaism officially, allowing the Jews to practice their religion; circumcision was the symbol or mark of this faith. But the official standing of Christianity was not yet determined, and Christians might soon be subject to persecution. Having the mark of a Jew could then be a passport to safety.

At the same time, the fact that these teachers had accepted Christ would bring the scorn and hatred of fellow Jews, but urging converts from paganism to keep the ceremonial law would help appease the Jews. Making this "showing in the flesh" thus brought safety from both the Romans and their fellow Jews.

Paul's second charge is that the false teachers are inconsistent, for they themselves do not keep the whole law. Then, in similar vein to 5:12, he again attacks the Judaizers. Freely translated, he says that all they want is trophies of foreskins, so that they can boast about the number of people they have reduced to legalistic slavery. They are like the Indian with white scalps on his belt or the bounty hunter with notches on his gun. This is often the way of zealous partisans, whether in politics or government or religion. Many times the motivation is pure selfishness, and the means used are cowardly and underhanded. Can you possibly imagine any thrill to this kind of glory?

Glory in the Cross

In my college days it was quite the custom, when victory had been won either in athletics or on the debate or oratorical rostrum, for the students to declare a "glory day." On glory day there was joy and exultation and often a big bonfire on campus with songs and dances.

But as for me, says Paul, I glory in the cross of the Lord Jesus Christ, that death on a tree characterized by ignominy, shame, and degradation. "But God forbid that I should boast of anything but the cross . . ." as the N.E.B. translates it. What a strange paradox!

Crucifixion as a method of killing was borrowed by the Romans from the Persians and Carthaginians and meted out to slaves, murderers, and insurrectionists. It was the cruelest and most shameful and degraded form of death that could be given to anyone; hence, no Roman citizen could be crucified. Yet a little band of rebels against the established religious order of the first century chose the cross as the sign and symbol of their new faith! It is as if we took the electric chair or the gallows as the symbol of some newly founded order.

But as natural as it is to think about the physical aspects of the crucifixion, Paul was not thinking of the wooden cross or of the actual pain and suffering when he wrote his postscript. It was not in the physical aspects that Paul gloried. Rather he was saying, as Calvin transliterates, "May God protect us from such a fearful calamity!" as to boast in anything else than the atoning death of Jesus Christ.

To the Pharisees the cross was an offense, a scandal. Circumcision and the law were the glory of the Jew; these were the common standards by which men praised each other. To Paul, the former Pharisee who had been redeemed by Christ, there was no value in circumcision (6:15). To be or not to be circumcised made no difference. The new creation, the new life in Christ, was all that mattered.

The Alternative

Suppose for a moment that Paul had yielded to the request of the Judaizers. After all, they had accepted Christ! Why not give in a little? Why not compromise a bit, accept circumcision as an outward symbol and thereby escape all persecution, both from the Romans and from his fellow Jews? The mobbing and near murder that happened later in the Temple in Jerusalem might even have been prevented by just a little give-and-take (read Acts 21: 27–36). Paul might have accepted the subtle argument of the self-seeking teachers that they were merely trying to soften the offense of the cross so that it might the more readily be accepted, even as men today disavow the atoning purpose of Jesus and suggest that his death was but the effort of a martyr to retrieve as much of a lost cause as possible. Yield and compromise? God forbid such a calamity, no matter what persecutions follow. Paul was saying, "In the cross of Christ I glory."

The Way of the Cross

Paul could glory in the cross because by it the world was crucified to him and he to the world (6:14). The entire world of Jewish rites and ceremonies was no longer necessary, for the death of Christ was entirely sufficient. These rites had lost all claim and hold upon his life. They were no longer the basis of either hope or glory. What counted for him and counts for us are not ordinances or ceremonies but "a new creation." This new creation, or being "a new creature," is a complete spiritual renewal, a living union with Christ. Luther says that a "new creature" is one in whom the image of God has been renewed, and that not by good works, but by Christ alone. It is the work of the Holy Spirit who fills our hearts with faith and love.

There is an old hymn which says that "the way of the cross leads home." What is the way of the cross of which the Apostle was so proud to boast?

(1) Some feel that the cross pays the price of our redemption and leaves nothing to be done by us. This is both true and untrue. The truth is that the cross does for us what we cannot do for ourselves. We are bought with the ransom price which only Christ can pay. But all too often men sing, "Jesus paid it all," and then leave it with the singing.

The greatest fallacy in religion is that Christianity is free. It is instead the most costly thing in the entire world. To experience this "new creation" of which Paul speaks one must, for instance, pay the price of loneliness. The first Christians in Galatia had to leave their idol worship and its rituals, their old associations and habits, and many of their former friends and even members of their families. "He who loves father or mother more than me is not worthy of me," said Jesus. The late Samuel M. Zwemer, modern prophet to the Muslims, often told how a Muslim, having become a Christian, would also become an outcast and would frequently even as Paul, suffer persecution and sometimes death for his new-found faith. In many places in the world today one is scorned and shunned because he walks the way of the cross.

One must also pay the price of surrender. I do not like to yield, and very few people do. We may therefore be comforted by the thought that this had been a problem for Paul too. Pharisee of the Pharisees, he had exalted himself before God in his egotistical blamelessness under the law. He fought against his own conscience in his unwillingness to surrender until God had to strike him down on the Damascus Road. What a struggle to yield! But not until he did was a new creation possible.

Or take Jesus. What, you say, Jesus too? Certainly! ". . . in every respect" he "has been tempted as we are . . ." Take the moment on the mountain: the world was at his feet, if he would but bend the knee to the Tempter for just a second. Christ wanted that world, but he would not have it that way. He had to give it up. Or take the time the people sought to make him their king and their champion against the hated Romans. He wanted to be a king, but he would not be king that way. He had to give it up. Or consider the Garden of Gethsemane and his prayer to "let this cup pass." He was only thirty-three and he wanted to live. But God asked him to surrender his life to pay the price of redemption. Thus Jesus gave his life for us.

(2) Others conceive the way of the cross as an inspiring example. This is also both true and untrue. It is true if it leads us to deny self, take up the cross as Jesus requires, and follow him. But it is untrue if we lightly and easily accept the example theory as a complete interpretation of the atonement. To oversimplify, this theory says that God loves everybody and that all man needs is to be made better. Christ died as a noble martyr for a great cause, and his example of faithfulness leads one to the truth and duty of personal reformation. By following the good man Jesus Christ one also becomes a good man.

But, as most of us are willing to admit, we already *know* better than we *do*. More than an example is needed. Furthermore, our very standards are too low. Jesus said, "For if you love those who love you, what reward have you? Do not even the tax collectors do the same?" This touches all the merely tit-for-tat relationships of our daily living, which may be commendable in themselves, but are not the way of the cross. The cross spells complete sacrifice, or as Paul said, ". . . the world has been crucified to me, and I to the world."

(3) For still others, the cross is a great inspiration because it represents fidelity to a principle. This too can be both true and untrue. The cross was truly a great spectacle in that a life was given for a great principle, and that is always inspiring.

However, history is replete with the names of great people who have suffered for principle, and we honor such; but Jesus died for more than a principle. He died for sin-blighted, evil-distorted, passion-distracted men and women. A spectacle is soon forgotten, and a great inspiration fades, but the Son of God lays his strength beside weak and defeated humanity, loves us, and brings us to wholeness of life.

In the crucified Christ we see a noble example of devotion to the highest principles, and as Christians we are expected to try to be Christlike. But salvation itself does not come through "a good showing in the flesh" (6:12) but through "a revelation of Jesus Christ" (1:12). In the cross we see the redeeming love of God the Father and of his Christ supremely revealed. By faith we identify ourselves with Christ (2:20) and live now as "a new creation" (6:15) in him.

The Measuring Rod

Nearing the end of the postscript, the Apostle promises the twin blessings of mercy and peace upon all "who walk by this rule." The "rule" was a measuring rod to certify size or length. It was something like a surveyor's chain used in mapping out a district to determine an allotment for each person. Those who "walk by this rule" place their entire confidence for acceptance with God not in outward rites and ordinances such as circumcision, but in the redeeming work of Jesus Christ. For Paul this benediction was a prayer for those he loved. For him the "Israel of God" included all those who put their trust in Christ, who measured both faith and life by God's Son.

REVIEW

1. In what sense are such hymns as "In the Cross of Christ I Glory" (The Hymnbook, 195) and "When I Survey the Wondrous Cross" (The Hymnbook, 198) based on Galatians?

2. Dietrich Bonhoeffer once wrote: "Such grace is costly because it calls us to follow, and it is grace because it calls us to follow Jesus Christ. It is costly because it costs a man his life, and it is grace because it gives a man the only true life. It is costly because it condemns sin, and grace because it justifies the sinner. Above all, it is costly because it cost God the life of his Son . . ."[2] How are these ideas reflected in Galatians and in the above commentary?

13 Brands of Honor

ADVANCE STUDY

1. For a review, reread Galatians. (It will take only fifteen to twenty minutes.)

2. See if you can outline the book or give a title to each chapter of it.

3. What are the most important ideas of Galatians?

Once and for Always

The letter we have been reading and studying has concerned itself largely with the basic principle that vital religion does not consist in a set of external rites or outward obedience to a set of laws, but in a deep trust in the person of Jesus Christ, with one's life directed and guided by the Holy Spirit. In proclaiming this truth, Paul found it necessary to defend his apostleship and to explain fully the doctrine of justification by faith, the purpose of the law, and what it means to "walk by the Spirit." The heart of the gospel is the cross of Jesus, in which the Apostle glories to the exclusion of everything else. The entire letter is a trumpet call for Christian liberty, asking a person not to stay hedged about by the law, which only convicts one of sin and evil, but to come out of this dark prison house into the freedom of God's light through the person and work of the Savior. Concluding the dictated letter with a postscript in his own hand, Paul says in effect, "And now, once and for always, let us hear no more accusations. I am finished with my self-defense. Let no one in the future question my authority. For I bear on my body the scars of the Lord Jesus."

The Marks or Brands

What were these marks on his body? Biblical students have argued this question for years, and it is not settled yet. Was it a bodily weakness or physical infirmity of some kind? Those who advance this theory point to the letter itself which says, "you know that it was because of a bodily ailment that I preached the gospel to you at first" (4:13). Some have suggested that the ailment may have been malaria, an intermittent disease marked by chills followed by high fevers. Sholem Asch in his book, *The Apostle,* suggests that Paul contracted this malaria in Perga and that it would suddenly strike him as with fire when he was preaching, causing him to stumble or fall. The Apostle is happy, as he says in the letter, that "though my condition was a trial to you, you did not scorn or despise me . . ." (4:14).

Others argue that quite likely Paul had weak eyes, and they too quote from the letter, ". . . you would have plucked out your eyes and given them to me" (4:15); and also, "See with what large letters I am writing" (6:11), which also suggests poor eyesight. There are still thousands of people in the Middle East who suffer from ophthalmia, an inflammatory disease of the eye which comes from unsanitary conditions. It was my privilege to interview the late world-famous evangelist, Toyohiko Kagawa of Japan, whose vision was largely destroyed by this disease which he had contracted in the slums of Kobe where he lived and worked.

When and where shall we find a documented answer? At this date, probably nowhere. For me the "marks" were the scars and lacerations caused by the stoning at Lystra and being "dragged out of the city, supposing that he was dead" (Acts 14:19). We do not know how the dragging was done, but have you ever seen the scars on a man who has been dragged by a horse or a car? Paul bared his scars and bade the Galatians to look upon him, for these marks were received because he preached Jesus Christ and him crucified.

The "Stigmata" of Jesus

Some few believe that when the Apostle speaks of the "marks of Jesus" the reference is to the five wounds of Jesus, where the nails pierced his hands and feet and the spear was thrust into his side. A classic though legendary example of one marked by stigmata is Francis of Assisi, the famous and saintly Christian who lived in Italy from 1182 to 1226. This kind and gentle soul, the son of a rich merchant, lived in complete poverty in order to be able to minister to the sick, especially to those with repulsive diseases. He founded the Franciscan Order with its monastic vows of poverty, chastity, and obedience. By 1219 not less than five thousand followers had caught the mystic enthusiasm of their leader in whom they saw the life of Jesus again brought near to men. The legend says that once he fasted on a lonely mountain and in a vision saw the Son of God crucified on a cross as wide as the horizon. Deep pity touched his heart and, when the vision faded, the stigmata of Jesus, that is, the marks of the nails and the spear, were on his body, inflicted, so the story says, by the Lord himself. These marks remained until Francis died. Truth or legend, who can tell?

Some think that Paul, too, in being "crucified with Christ" passed through a like experience, so that he also bore the prints of the nails in his hands. But there is no other reference to this in any of his letters.

Brands of Honor

The literal stigmata in Paul's day were tattoos or brands used on people. Winston Churchill in one of his famous orations spoke of "each spotted name branded with marks of everlasting shame." This is not the way Paul thought about his scars. "I bear on my body the marks," he said—like some trophy or royal symbol or row of medals given for extraordinary gallantry.

Three classes of men were branded in the ancient world. One was the soldier who was so devoted to his commander that he voluntarily had the latter's name and insignia branded on his chest or forearm. The second was the temple slave in the service of Cybele, or perhaps a follower of the goddess so devoted that he had himself branded as a mark of his devotion. This idea is probably present in Paul's thinking, as a devoted follower of Christ. The third group consisted of slaves. The brand could be one of disgrace upon a slave who had run away and had been returned, the marks usually being burned on his forehead for all to see; or it could be a brand of honor upon the hand, indicating allegiance to a specific master and at the same time protecting the wearer against claims from other masters and from harm. In this sense, the Roman historian Herodotus said that the person on whom the stigmata marks were placed, had given himself to a god and could not be touched.[1] Paul was saying, "I bear on my body the scars. I have given myself to Christ. Let no one trouble me anymore."

Our Bondage Is Freedom

Paul all through the letter has called himself a slave of Christ. Translators have often made this to read servant of Christ. But Paul does not mean the ordinary relationship of servant and master, especially as it is understood today. A servant to us is one who is hired and is paid for his work; there is perhaps a contract, and obligations can be terminated by either party. But Paul considered that he was Christ's slave in the absolute sense. The relationship was one of complete authority and unconditional submission. A slave belonged to, was the property of, his master for the owner to do with as he liked. It is agreed that there is an atrociousness about this relationship between man and man. Human slavery, still present in places in the world today, is truly abhorrent. But Paul says that the relationship is beautiful and blessed when applied to a man and his Savior. He bore the marks on his body proudly.

In this bond-servant relationship, Jesus Christ has complete authority over us. All of our time, our talents, and our services belong to him. As servants of Jesus, there is no room for self-will or self-assertion or self-indulgence. That which in itself is degrading and barbaric between men becomes joyous. At least, this is the way Paul felt. These scars or brands were proof that he belonged wholly to Jesus. He was Christ's soldier, his devotee, indeed, his slave.

But a man will ask, and the world will ask, "Are we not free?" The answer is that we are slaves no matter what, either to sin, or to the devil (as Luther said), or to Christ. In this matter there is no neutral position. This is the paradox: we are set free the moment we become slaves of Jesus Christ. How can or does this happen? In the past men acquired slaves either by conquest in war or by purchase. The Bible says of us as Christians that "you were bought with a price" (1 Cor. 6:20) and the purchase price was Christ's life blood shed on the cross. But having paid the price, as the letter has so clearly shown all through, Christ set us free. Christian slavery, with its utter surrender to the Master, Jesus Christ, is in reality the highest freedom, for "if the Son makes you free, you will be free indeed" (John 8:36).

Marks of Ownership

It has already been said that the marks were scars from stoning and dragging through the dirt. Paul bore these proudly as a testimony to the gospel. These brands fully proved whose bond servant the Apostle considered himself to be. Suppose for a moment that Paul had compromised in the matter of circumcision? There would then have been no stoning and no marks, and so no badge of the Lord. "These scars proclaim that I am the bond servant of Jesus," Paul says in effect loudly and clearly.

But what about us? What about me? We have probably not been stoned for Christ's sake or dragged through the street and left for dead. Most of us are in good health and, if there are any scars, they are not likely to be a result of testifying for Jesus. And yet every Christian should carry some mark that he or she belongs to the Savior. There is a drastic one. Jesus said, "And if your hand or your foot causes you to sin, cut it off and throw it from you . . ." (Matt. 18:8). But I have both of my hands and feet, and they are in good shape. But Christ's law of self-denial is ever before us. There are many things that must be avoided, as the letter has indicated in referring to "the works of the flesh" (5:19), and there is "the fruit of the Spirit" which should mark us (5:22–23). If there is in our hearts a deep, indwelling possession of the grace of Christ, it will show upon our faces. Stand on a street corner some day and watch the men and women go by. How do their faces read? Every Christian should have upon his brow the visible mark that he dwells with Christ.

We are deeply marked when we are engaged in sacrificial service for Christ. The brands are burned in by the trials with sin and the world. Too many people have no marks. Their entire notion of religion and religious duties is confined to form and ceremony, to singing hymns and listening to sermons. The brands of a Christian become real when we become bond servants to our neighbors in the service of love. It is then that "the love of Christ controls us" (2 Cor. 5:14). This is true Christian freedom.

Triumph in the Scars

As has been said, the marks were for Paul like a trophy. The scars were not merely borne with a patient endurance nor with resignation, for he did not feel that he was carrying an unusual load. Instead these were marks of triumph. Paul gloried in the fact that Christ had won the victory, and that he could follow the chariot of the Conqueror. The highest honor of our lives comes to us when we kneel before Christ and have implanted upon our foreheads the mark of ownership. By it we become the masters of ourselves and of the world.

The "marks of Christ" are of all decorations the most honorable. The world in the main still does not think so. Of Jesus, they said, "Away with him, crucify him." Of Paul, they said, "Away with such a fellow from the earth! For he ought not to live" (Acts 22: 22). Of all those who bears the marks, the Lord said, ". . .you will be hated by all for my name's sake" (Matt. 10:22). But as men made free in the cross of Christ, we glory in nothing else.

A FINAL REVIEW

1. What are the "marks" of a true Christian?

2. What ideas in this course have meant most to you?

3. In the light of this study, how would you now define Christian freedom?

4. In the light of this course, just what would you say a true Christian has that a true Jew may be missing? Do you have it?

5. In what way, if any, has your life been changed by this course?

EXODUS: A Drama of Redemption

PROGRAM NOTES
1. E. E. Flack, "The Book of Exodus," *Interpretation* (January, 1949), III, 1, 78.
2. James MacGregor, *Exodus* (Edinburg: T. & T. Clark, 1909), I, 16.
3. J. R. Dummelow, *A Commentary on the Holy Bible* (New York: The MacMillan Company, 1963), p. 48. By permission.
4. E. E. Flack, *Interpretation*, III, 1, 81.
5. Edward Mack, *The Preacher's Old Testament* (Westwood, N.J.: Fleming H. Revell Company, 1923), p. 26. By permission.
6. Joseph M. Gettys, *Surveying the Pentateuch* (Richmond: John Knox Press, 1962), pp. 18–19.

PROLOGUE
1. Frederic Kenyon, *The Bible and Archaeology* (New York: Harper & Row, Publishers, Incorporated, 1940), pp. 69–70. By permission.

ACT ONE
1. Winston S. Churchill, *Amid These Storms* (New York: Charles Scribner's Sons, 1932), p. 289.

ACT TWO
1. Jack Finegan, *Let My People Go* (New York: Harper & Row, Publishers, Incorporated, 1963), p. 48.
2. George Livingstone Robinson, *The Bearing of Archaeology on the Old Testament* (New York: American Tract Society, 1941), p. 40.

ACT THREE
1. John Bright, *A History of Israel* (Philadelphia: The Westminster Press, 1959), pp. 120–121.
2. John D. Davis and Henry S. Gehman, *The Westminster Dictionary of the Bible* (Philadelphia: The Westminster Press, 1944), p. 510.

ACKNOWLEDGMENTS

ISAIAH 40—66: The Freedom of Servanthood

CHAPTER 1
1. Paul Scherer, *Event in Eternity* (New York: Harper & Row, Publishers, Incorporated, 1945), pp. 1–2. By permission.

CHAPTER 3
1. From *God's Trombones* by James Weldon Johnson. Copyright 1927 by The Viking Press, Inc., 1954 by Grace Nails Johnson. Reprinted by permission of The Viking Press, Inc.
2. Ernest Gordon, *Through the Valley of the Kwai* (New York: Harper & Row, Publishers, Incorporated, 1962), pp. 215–216. By permission.
3. Anthony T. Hanson, *The Church of the Servant* (London: SCM Press, Ltd., 1962), pp. 13–14. By permission.

CHAPTER 4
1. Paul Scherer, *Event in Eternity*, pp. 200–201.

CHAPTER 7
1. Barnard of Cluny, Twelfth Century, Trans. John Mason Neale.

3. Harry Emerson Fosdick, "God of Grace and God of Glory." By permission.

ACT FOUR

1. M. Ryerson Turnbull, *Studying the Book of Exodus* (Richmond: John Knox Press, 1925), p. 39.

ACT FIVE

1. Alfred Edersheim, *The Exodus and the Wanderings in the Wilderness* (London: The Religious Tract Society, 1876), p. 120.

ACT SIX

1. William B. Ward, *God's Rule of Life* (Sermons on the Ten Commandments published by the First Presbyterian Church of Spartanburg, S. C.), p. 11. By permission.
2. C. Ellis Nelson, *Love and the Law* (Richmond: John Knox Press, 1963), p. 13.
3. Joy Davidman, *Smoke on the Mountain* (Philadelphia: The Westminster Press, 1954), p. 48.
4. G. Campbell Morgan, *The Ten Commandments* (Westwood, N.J.: Fleming H. Revell Company, 1901), p. 39.
5. *Ibid.,* p. 41.
6. *The Heidelberg Catechism,* 400th Anniversary Edition. United Church Press, 1962.

ACT SEVEN

1. Walter W. Moore, *Supplementary Notes on Exodus* (Printed for the use of students at Union Theological Seminary in Virginia), p. 34.
2. Charles R. Erdman, *The Book of Exodus* (Westwood, N.J.: Fleming H. Revell Company, 1949), pp. 105–106. By permission.

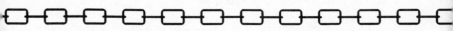

2. Ernest Gordon, *Through the Valley of the Kwai,* pp. 145–146.

CHAPTER 8

1. Daniel ben Judah, the Yigdal (Fourteenth Century). Trans. Max Landsbeng and Newton Mann.
2. William L. Sullivan, *Under Orders* (Peterborough, N.H.: The Richard R. Smith Co., Inc., 1944), pp. 36–37. By permission.

CHAPTER 9

1. From *The Meaning of Christ,* by Robert Clyde Johnson. © 1958, by W. L. Jenkins. The Westminster Press. Used by permission.
2. G. A. Studdart-Kennedy, *The Unutterable Beauty* (London: Hodder and Stoughton Limited, n.d.), pp. 127–128. By permission.

CHAPTER 13

1. By Henry Sloan Coffin in *The Interpreter's Bible,* Abingdon Press.
2. From *The Kingdom of God* by John Bright. Copyright 1953 by Pierce and Washabaugh (Abingdon Press).

JOHN: The Way to Life

CHAPTER 1
1. John Bunyan, *The Pilgrim's Progress* (Philadelphia: John C. Winston Company, n.d.), pp. 7–10.
2. Floyd V. Filson, *The Gospel According to John,* The Layman's Bible Commentary (Richmond: John Knox Press, 1963), Vol. 19, pp. 8ff.
3. Alan Richardson, *The Gospel According to Saint John* (London: SCM Press, Ltd., 1959), pp. 26–28.
4. John Baillie, *Invitation to Pilgrimage* (New York: Charles Scribner's Sons, 1942), p. 49. By permission.

CHAPTER 2
1. Helen Kromer, *For Heaven's Sake* (Boston: Baker's Plays, 1963), pp. 18–19. By permission.

CHAPTER 3
1. According to tradition, the rabbis conducted theological studies under a tree. It may be that Nathanael was zealously searching the sacred writings in line with such studies when Philip summoned him. See Wilbert F. Howard, "The Gospel According to St. John," *The Interpreter's Bible* (New York & Nashville: Abingdon-Cokesbury Press, 1952), VIII, 488–489.
2. From *New Worship and Song.* The Pilgrim Press.

CHAPTER 4
1. *The Heidelberg Catechism,* 400th Anniversary Edition. United Church Press, 1962.
2. E. C. Blackman, "Faith, Faithfulness," *The Interpreter's Dictionary of the Bible* (New York & Nashville: Abingdon-Cokesbury Press, 1962), II, 222–236.
3. Paul Tillich, *Dynamics of Faith* (New York: Harper & Row, Publishers, Incorporated, 1957), p. 1.

GALATIANS: The Life of Freedom

CHAPTER 3
1. *The New English Bible* © The Delegates of the Oxford University Press and the Syndics of The Cambridge University Press, 1961.
2. This and all further references to Luther are from: Martin Luther, *A Commentary on St. Paul's Epistle to the Galatians,* trans. Theodore Graebner (Grand Rapids: Zondervan Publishing House, n.d.).
3. R. C. H. Lenski, *The Interpretation of St. Paul's Epistles to the Galatians, to the Ephesians, and to the Philippians* (Columbus, Ohio: Lutheran Book Concern, 1937).

CHAPTER 4
1. J. B. Lightfoot, *Saint Paul's Epistle to the Galatians* (New York: The Macmillan Company, 1900), p. 84.
2. Emil G. Kraeling, *I Have Kept the Faith* (Chicago: Rand McNally & Company, 1965), p. 71. By permission.
3. This and all further references to Calvin are from John Calvin, *Commentaries on the Epistles of the Galatians and Ephesians,* trans. William Pringle (Grand Rapids: Wm. B. Eerdmans Publishing Company, 1948).

CHAPTER 5
1. Alfred Noyes, "Victory," *Collected Poems* (Philadelphia: J. B. Lippincott, 1920), III, 147. By permission.

CHAPTER 7
1. Words and Music Copyright, 1954 Renewal, Rodheaver Co., Owner. Used by permission.
2. Olov Harman, *Holy Masquerade,* trans. Karl A. Olsson (Grand Rapids: Wm. B. Eerdmans Publishing Co., 1963), pp. 20–21. By permission.
CHAPTER 8
1. Reprinted from *Days of My Years* by Pierre van Paassen. Copyright 1940 by Pierre van Paassen and used with the permission of the publisher, The Dial Press, Inc.
CHAPTER 9
1. *The New English Bible* © The Delegates of the Oxford University Press and The Syndics of The Cambridge University Press, 1961.
2. From *The New Testament in Modern English* © J. B. Phillips, 1958. Used by permission of The Macmillan Company.
CHAPTER 10
1. *Oxford Dictionary of Quotations* (London: Oxford University Press, 1955), p. 143.
2. Johann Heermann, "Ah, Holy Jesus, How Hast Thou Offended," *The Yattendon Hymnal,* ed. and trans. Robert Bridges and H. Ellis Wooldridge. Used by permission of the Clarendon Press, Oxford.
CHAPTER 11
1. C. K. Barrett, *The New Testament Background: Selected Documents* (New York: Harper & Row, Publishers, Incorporated, 1961), pp. 19–20.
CHAPTER 12
1. John Knox, *The Early Church and the Coming Great Church* (New York & Nashville: Abingdon-Cokesbury Press, 1955), pp. 153–154.

2. *The Bible a New Translation* by James Moffatt. Used by permission of Harper & Row, Publishers, Incorporated. Copyright by James Moffatt 1954.
CHAPTER 7
1. *The Heidelberg Catechism,* 400th Anniversary Edition. United Church Press, 1962.
CHAPTER 10
1. Orson Bean, *TV Guide.* By permission.
2. Daniel Crawford, *Thinking Black* (New York: George H. Doran Company, 1912), p. 195.
3. J. Paul Getty, "The World Is Mean to Millionaires," *The Saturday Evening Post* (May 22, 1965), No. 10, p. 10. By permission.
4. Dietrich Bonhoeffer, *The Cost of Discipleship* (New York: The Macmillan Company, 1959), pp. 45–46.
CHAPTER 12
1. Some say that Telemachus was a legendary character. I heard the story first from a guide in the Colosseum itself, and later from Leslie Weatherhead, the famous London preacher.
2. Dietrich Bonhoeffer, *The Cost of Discipleship,* pp. 46–47.
CHAPTER 13
1. J. B. Lightfoot, *Saint Paul's Epistle to the Galatians,* p. 225.

EXODUS: A Drama of Redemption

James Sprunt grew up in South Carolina and graduated from Davidson College and Union Theological Seminary in Richmond, Va. He holds the Th.M. degree from Princeton Theological Seminary.

After three pastorates in Virginia, he served the Lookout Mountain Presbyterian Church in Chattanooga, Tenn., and then the First Presbyterian Church, Raleigh, N. C. He is now pastor of the Bethel Presbyterian Church near Staunton, Va.

Dr. Sprunt has written two Bible study books, *These Are Written,* on the Gospel of John, and *Messages for Homemakers,* on Deuteronomy. He has also published two books of sermons, *I Believe* and *Windows on the Word.*

THE AUTHORS

JOHN: The Way to Life

Vernon H. Kooy has been since 1953 Professor of New Testament at New Brunswick Theological Seminary, New Brunswick, N. J. He came to that position after serving three pastorates in the Reformed Church in America, at Clover Hill, N. J., Far Rockaway, Long Island, N. Y., and Lodi, N. J.

A graduate of Central College and of Western Theological Seminary, he holds his Th.M. degree from Princeton Theological Seminary and his Th.D. degree from Union Theological Seminary in New York. He has also done research study at Heidelberg University, Heidelberg, Germany.

Dr. Kooy is author of a briefer study on John, *That You May Believe . . . And Have Life,* and was a contributor to the *Interpreter's Dictionary of the Bible.* He has served for six years on, and has been chairman of, the Theological Commission of the Reformed Church in America.

ISAIAH: The Freedom of Servanthood

Robert Hayden Bullock, a native Texan, is a graduate of Austin College and holds his B.D., Th.M., and Th.D. degrees from Union Theological Seminary, Richmond, Va.

He has served in Texas as the pastor of the Bellaire Presbyterian Church, as the Minister of Christian Education of the St. Andrew's Presbyterian Church of Houston, and as the Associate Minister of the First Presbyterian Church, San Antonio. He is currently the pastor of the Northwood Presbyterian Church, also in San Antonio.

From 1946 to 1954 Dr. Bullock served as Professor of Bible and Greek at Austin College, Sherman, Texas.

He is author of *Hammer on the Rock,* a study of Jeremiah.

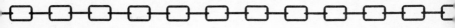

GALATIANS: The Life of Freedom

Bernard J. Mulder graduated from Hope College and Western Theological Seminary and for fifteen years served as pastor in Reformed churches in Michigan and Iowa. He was for nine years editor and manager of *The Church Herald,* the official weekly journal of the Reformed Church in America. In 1965 he retired after being for twenty years Executive Secretary of the Board of Education of the Reformed Church in America.

During these years he also served for nine years as editor of the monthly *Religious Digest,* and for five years he edited the quarterly journal, *Christian Education,* and served as president of the National Protestant Council of Higher Education.

He and Mrs. Mulder served as consultants to the Near East Curriculum Council in the preparation of a syllabus for a three year series for the Arab Christian Sunday School.

Dr. Mulder is author of two books, *The Kingdom of God* and *The King Came Riding.*

51-8020-ANJ